CHRIS

About Island Press

Island Press, a nonprofit organization, publishes, markets, and distributes the most advanced thinking on the conservation of our natural resources—books about soil, land, water, forests, wildlife, and hazardous and toxic wastes. These books are practical tools used by public officials, business and industry leaders, natural resource managers, and concerned citizens working to solve both local and global resource problems.

Founded in 1978, Island Press reorganized in 1984 to meet the increasing demand for substantive books on all resource-related issues. Island Press publishes and distributes under its own imprint and offers these services to other nonprofit organizations.

Support for Island Press is provided by The Geraldine R. Dodge Foundation, The Energy Foundation, The Charles Engelhard Foundation, The Ford Foundation, Glen Eagles Foundation, The George Gund Foundation, William and Flora Hewlett Foundation, The James Irvine Foundation, The John D. and Catherine T. MacArthur Foundation, The Andrew W. Mellon Foundation, The Joyce Mertz-Gilmore Foundation, The New-Land Foundation, The Pew Charitable Trusts, The Rockefeller Brothers Fund, The Tides Foundation, and individual donors.

About The Conservation Fund

The Conservation Fund is a national nonprofit land and water conservation organization that protects land through partnerships with corporations, nonprofit organizations, and public agencies. The Conservation Fund encourages entrepreneurial solutions and new approaches to land and water conservation. In addition to land conservation activities, the Fund has established an American Greenways Program to help establish a national network of linked open space coridors, a Civil War Battlefield Campaign to safeguard America's Civil Water battlefield sites, a Freshwater Institute to develop economically feasible and environmentally sound approaches to use of the nation's freshwater resources, and a Land Advisory Service to provide land use planning, ecological assessment, and technical assistance on all aspects of land conservation and development. Since 1986, The Conservation Fund has acquired and protected more than 320,000 acres of land valued at nearly $127 million for only $63 million. The Conservation Fund land conservation projects include wetlands, wildlife refuges, abandoned railroad corridors, Civil War battlefield sites, scenic areas, greenways, and other areas of natural or cultural significance.

Greenways

Greenways

A Guide to Planning, Design, and Development

The Conservation Fund

Loring LaB. Schwarz
Editor

Charles A. Flink
Robert M. Searns
Authors

ISLAND PRESS

Washington, D.C. • *Covelo, California*

This publication was made possible through the generous support of

Dupont

with additional funding provided by

The Curtis and Edith Munson Foundation
The Wallace Genetic Foundation
The Town Creek Foundation

Library of Congress Cataloging-in-Publication Data
Flink, Charles A.
   Greenways : a guide to planning, design, and development / Loring LaB.
Schwarz, editor : Charles A. Flink, Robert M. Searns, authors.
      p. cm.
   ISBN 1-55963-137-6 (cloth). — ISBN 1-55963-136-8 (paper)
   1. Greenways—United States. I. Searns, Robert M. II. Schwarz,
Loring LaB. III. Title.
HT167.F59 1993
307.3—dc20   93-16835
                                                              CIP

Printed on recycled, acid-free paper

Manufactured in the United States of America

10 9 8 7 6 5 4 3 2 1

Contents

Foreword

Aldo Leopold once said "Everything is connected to everything else." *Greenways* is a book about connections: connections between people and the land, between public parks, natural areas, historic sites, and other open spaces, between conservation and economic development, and between environmental protection and our quality of life.

The Alabama in which I grew up as a boy was a green place. The landscape was defined by gentle mountains, stretches of hardwood and pineland forest, and in the south, broad expanses of wetlands laced with rivers and streams. A mosaic of natural communities covered the state's landscape. In the summers I hiked in the foothills of the Appalachians and chased deer in the endless woods south of Birmingham. Today, rampant, haphazard growth is consuming the landscape I treasured as a child, leaving isolated parcels of open space with limited recreational or biological value. Wetlands and wildlife are disappearing. Wild and free flowing rivers are being dammed, while residential and commercial development is cutting off public access to rivers and wild lands in urban areas. Today people in all parts of the country are having a harder time experiencing the outdoors.

What's more, unplanned growth is severing our connections with a place, our essential orientations, our sense of roots. As Wallace Stegner once said "If you don't know where you are, you don't know who you are." Yet today a person suddenly dropped along a road outside of almost any American city wouldn't know where he or she was because it all looks the same. Is it Albany or Allentown, Providence or Pittsburgh? Who can tell?

Don't get me wrong. Over the past twenty years conservationists have made great strides. We've passed new laws to clean up air pollution, water pollution, and toxic waste, to protect wetlands, sand dunes, and other critical environmental areas. We've set aside millions of acres of land for parks and nature preserves and added thousands of buildings to the National Register of Historic Places. But, despite the gains, the special character of America's cities and countryside is disappearing faster than ever. The truth is, the American landscape is becoming more fragmented and blighted by the day.

Many people feel a growing dissatisfaction with the quality of new development. For all the improvements in environmental quality, people still ask, "Is this all there is? Can't we do better? Can't our communities be more distinctive? More liveable? More beautiful? Can't we have more connection with nature and the outdoors?" There is a reservoir of feeling about land in America, and that feeling must be translated into an awareness of the steps it takes to protect it. There is more at stake, of course, than the loss of farms or wetlands or scenic woodlands. If the character of the land is changed, what about the people?

We obviously need to continue to emphasize ecology and the health of natural systems. We need a whole ecosystem approach to restoring

America's great water bodies like the Gulf of Mexico, the Great Lakes, and the Chesapeake Bay. We also need a more holistic vision for the land. This brings us to greenways. Less expensive, more expansive and flexible than traditional parks, greenways provide a kind of community trail system for the everyday outdoor activities that Americans are pursuing close to home: jogging, biking, boating, horseback riding, cross country skiing, or just plain strolling.

Greenways are of course not new. Fredrick Olmsted coined the term *parkway* in 1865, and Benton MacKaye proposed perhaps America's greatest greenway, the Appalachian Trail, in 1921. Greenways typically follow water courses, ridgelines, hiking trails, country roads, abandoned railroads, urban waterfronts, and other linear corridors. They give shape and definition to open space. They improve our quality of life by providing a kind of green infrastructure for our communities.

In his book *God's Own Junkyard*, Peter Blake once said "Parks do to the landscape what museums do to painting and sculpture. They embalm it. They tend to elevate us on weekends and holidays rather than enriching our everyday life." On the other hand, greenways can enrich our everyday lives by providing recreation and access to nature within a few minutes of almost every household in America. What's more, greenways are not limited to recreation. They can help promote tourism by enhancing an area's unique natural and cultural attractions and by creating more places for outdoor recreation. They can also provide pathways for people commuting to and from work by providing an alternative to the automobile.

Today few Americans walk or ride to work, primarily because the transportation network is so hostile to walking and cycling. If people could walk or bike to work on a greenway, the demand for auto travel could be reduced, thereby helping urban communities meet air quality standards while easing congestion and improving the quality of life. A 1992 Louis Harris Poll found that 53 percent of Americans would bicycle to work, at least occasionally, if there were more safe, separate, designated bike paths in their community. The tools and techniques in this book will help communities develop those safe, separate, designated bike paths.

Greenways can also serve as movement corridors for wildlife and can be established on private land, with an understanding that they are limited to protecting a scenic vista or historic site. They can provide a buffer against harsh views and a filter against nonpoint source pollution, sediment, and runoff into our rivers and streams. Greenways are really links in a chain of opportunities that begin in our own backyards. These opportunities begin by our recognizing the potential in each and every piece of open land. Greenways allow us to treat land and water as a system, as interlocking pieces in a puzzle, not as isolated entities. This book will help us to develop that system. It will do that by providing new awareness of the economic and social value of open spaces. It will also do it by drawing upon the years of experience in greenway planning, design, and development by the authors and editors of this book.

The goal of The Conservation Fund's American Greenways Program is to create a nationwide network of greenways. We work to compliment and coordinate the work of other public and private organizations. Our earlier publication *Greenways for America*, by Charles E. Little, set out the origins, history, and philosophy of the greenway movement while describing some of the nation's most outstanding greenways. *Greenways: A Guide to Planning, Design, and Development* deals with more practical concerns: land acquisition, trail design, flood control, liability, insurance, maintenance, and so on.

Greenways: A Guide to Planning, Design, and Development has been prepared in response to the growing demand for practical information and advice on planning, designing, and building greenways and linear parks.

This guide does not attempt to prescribe a single strategy or set of techniques for greenway creation. Rather it introduces a variety of techniques, provides illustrated examples of how these techniques have been applied, and pulls together an enormous amount of hard-to-find information on the nuts and bolts of greenway creation. The three writers bring more than thirty years of combined greenway experience to the table, and each chapter has been reviewed by upwards of twenty other national greenway experts.

Whereas the editor and authors have attempted to provide the most authoritative, accurate, and up-to-date information possible, there will undoubtedly be some areas where new ideas, new information, and new technology will further illuminate the material presented. For this reason, reader comments and suggestions are encouraged.

My own general interest in conservation and greenways in particular grew out of the sense of loss I felt at seeing the destruction of those treasured natural places that I cherished as a youngster growing up in a small southern town. But this book is borne out of a sense of opportunity and the firm belief that we can reclaim and restore even the most derelict landscapes, providing a resource for both people and wildlife. It provides a new way of looking at land and community—a new "green" way.

The Conservation Fund is indebted to the DuPont Corporation, whose generous support made this book possible. We are grateful for the vision provided by the President's Commission on Americans Outdoors and the thousands of local greenway activists who are making greenways a reality across the country.

Edward T. McMahon, Director
American Greenways Program
The Conservation Fund
Arlington, Virginia

Preface

What Is a Greenway?

Ask ten different people to describe a greenway and you will likely get as many answers. The word *greenway* connotes two separate images: *green* suggests natural amenities—forests riverbanks, wildlife; *way* implies a route or path. Put them together and they describe a vision of natural corridors crisscrossing a landscape that has been otherwise transformed by development.

Within the developed landscape, greenways serve a dual function: they provide open space for human access and recreational use, and they serve to protect and enhance remaining natural and cultural resources. In a broader sense, the word *greenway* is a generic term for a wide variety of linear open spaces that provide connections and thereby foster movement of some sort, from neighborhood bicycle routes to pristine wildland corridors that guide migrating wildlife in their seasonal travels; from revitalized urban waterfronts to tree-shaded footpaths along a stream, far from the city.

Creating a greenway can cost millions of dollars, or it can require little more than convincing landowners to protect a band of healthy vegetation along a local stream. An understanding of community goals, resource constraints, and recreational needs, spiced with local talent and imagination, can shape a greenway and its purpose into just about any form.

Because the realm of possibility seems endless, to define the word *greenway* would indeed limit the vision. Greenways then become only what we have said they can be, and then the flexibility that ensures us political and public acceptance for each unique project is gone. On the contrary, the greenway idea is, and should remain, elastic. We can, nonetheless, define the clear core of the greenway concept as Charles Little has done in his classic work, *Greenways for America*:

> A greenway is a linear open space established along either a natural corridor, such as a riverfront, stream valley, or ridgeline, or overland along a railroad right-of-way converted to recreational use, a canal, scenic road, or other route. It is any natural or landscaped course for pedestrian or bicycle passage. An open-space connector linking parks, nature reserves, cultural features, or historic sites with each other and with populated areas. Locally, certain strip or linear parks designated as parkway or greenbelt.

Little goes on to describe five general types of greenways:

1. Urban riverside (or other waterbody) greenways, usually created as part of (or instead of) a redevelopment program along neglected, often run-down city waterfronts.

2. Recreational greenways, featuring paths and trails of various kinds, often of relatively long distance, based on natural corridors as well as canals, abandoned railbeds, and public rights-of-way.

3. Ecologically significant natural corridors, usually along rivers and streams and less often ridgelines, to provide for wildlife migration and species interchange, nature study, and hiking.

4. Scenic and historic routes, usually along a road, highway or waterway, the most representative of them making an effort to provide pedestrian access along the route or at least places to alight from the car.

5. Comprehensive greenway systems or networks, usually based on natural landforms such as valleys and ridges but sometimes simply an opportunistic assemblage of greenways and open spaces of various kinds to create an alternative municipal or regional green infrastructure.

While categorizing greenways helps us to understand the different forms they may take, in reality, types blend and overlap. How you categorize your greenway may depend on your favorite aspect of it. Take, for example, the C&O Canal, located along the Potomac River in Maryland and the District of Columbia. One of our oldest greenways, the canal provides a riverside path heavily used by D.C. commuters and day recreationists. Its trail terminates at a popular urban waterfront promenade in Georgetown. Along the route streamside vegetation protects the Potomac's water quality and provides wildlife habitat for terrestrial and aquatic species. On almost any day, the river is studded with canoes and kayaks within magnificent view of the Capital skyline and the lush green shores of Virginia and Maryland. The canal itself and its associated historic structures provide the curious with a glimpse into our past, as well as spectacular panoramas of a nationally significant river. The C&O Canal is an important component of Maryland's recognized state greenway "infrastructure"; furthermore, bridges spanning the Potomac connect the canal to bicycle paths on the Virginia shore and, at Harpers Ferry, into West Virginia.

Likewise, any one greenway can hold many and varied values to those who use it or live nearby: It can be a nonpolluting commuter route, a horse or bicycle trail, a means to promote stream-water quality or to preserve wildlife habitat, a method of buffering land uses such as residential development or agricultural activity, or a way to safeguard a viewshed or the historic character of an area.

The strength of the greenway movement, and the attraction of the concept itself, lies in its diversity of form and function. The greenway concept is flexible enough to adapt to many combinations of local needs, values, and conditions.

What Makes Greenways Different?

While the greenway concept is hardly new, the growing attention greenways have been receiving within the planning, conservation, and recreation communities is a recent phenomenon. Why this renewed interest in an idea that has been around for some time? How do greenways differ from other open-space initiatives? The use of trails for transportation is, literally, as old as the hills. Greenbelts as buffers between towns and as transition zones between conflicting land uses is also established practice in many areas. Why are nonprofit organizations, business interests, and public sector planners focusing on the protection of linear open spaces, and why are communities dedicating time and money to put greenways in place?

Let me offer a few reasons for the increasing popularity of greenways: Research and surveys of the American public conducted by the President's Commission on Americans Outdoors (PCAO) indicated an increasing interest in linear forms of recreation—walking, jogging, bicycling—as well as a sincere desire to protect our natural heritage. The Commission also found that while most Americans appreciate the natural splendor protected within our national parks, few can visit them regularly. More open space and recreational opportunities are needed near cities, where most of us live. In its 1987 report, the Commission responded to the basic recreational needs of modern Americans by recommending a nationwide system of greenways.

In fiscally tight times, when public funding for open space is greatly reduced, greenways can address a panoply of needs with minimal outlays of cash. Because potential greenways often consist of relatively narrow corridors of land—often within low-cost bottomlands, floodplains, abandoned railbeds, and other undevelopable locations—they may not cost much. Rather, these linear strips that cross ownerships and jurisdictions challenge greenways activists to protect land creatively through zoning, voluntary registration, and easements, in concert with traditional acquisition techniques. By creating greenways, local governments can make a true contribution to the quality of life within their communities at a relatively low cost.

Because most greenways are community resources, the lifeblood of most greenway initiatives is volunteer energy and landowner support. Even federal agencies involved in creating greenways concede that a top-down approach doesn't work. Citizens themselves must take control, mold their greenways to reflect the needs of their community, and develop a sense that the greenway's success is a vital part of the community's future. These citizen volunteers epitomize the prairie fire of enthusiasm the PCAO calls upon to build a nation of greenways, segment by local segment.

Greenways offer a wide variety of benefits and strike a harmonious chord with diverse groups. Unusual partnerships are forged for their protection—an added advantage in times of limited funding. In fact, the synergism among groups that have traditionally competed with one another for use of the land may be a greenway's most lauded characteristic. Most greenways support several uses, and joint ventures between unlikely partners are becoming more common: between conservation activists and recreationists, between both these groups and developers, and between all of the above and public agency planners. A greenway project can preserve critical resources while encouraging dialogue among partners, setting common ground on which to focus further cooperation and coordination. Greenways also can foster "vertical coordination" from the local grassroots level up through the administrative hierarchies of public organizations and corporations.

Finally, recent landscape design trends and ecological research support the wisdom of open-space planning that compliments the shape and flow of the land. Landscape features, such as streams, rivers, ridgetops, and beaches, are often linear. These natural features often provide a backbone for a greenway project or network.

About This Book

The idea for this book evolved with hundreds of inquiries we received after *Greenways for America*, by Charles Little, was published in 1990. Local greenway activists, inspired by Little's tales of successful greenways, now wanted specific information on exactly how to make *their* greenway visions become real. Of course every greenway project poses a different set of variables to work with. Clearly, individualized guidelines are not possible. Through this book we hope to offer readers the confidence they need to approach the overall process of greenway creation, while providing as much detail as possible for each step along the way.

One critical aspect of greenway work is recognizing your limitations. Where possible, without advocating substandard practices, the authors provide specific instruction. However, depending on the complexity of the greenway and the expertise of members in the group, greenway leaders will, at times, need the help of a landscape architect, engineer, hydrologist, or other professional. Whether or not you feel competent to proceed entirely on your own, this book will familiarize you with the necessary terminology and present the options available to you so that you can make more informed decisions.

When Less Is More

Highly developed recreational and urban greenways require more planning, design, construction, and management—and consequently more space devoted to them in this book. Although we feel obligated to provide as much detailed information on greenway construction as possible, the American Greenways Program of The Conservation Fund has consistently championed the view that the primary function of a greenway can be to protect natural, cultural, and historic resources. Ecological greenways have shown themselves to be immensely valuable as movement corridors for species, vegetative filters of sediment and nonpoint pollution from runoff along streams, and moderators of air pollution and temperature extremes in cities. All greenways need not provide recreational benefits, and some may require only a footpath, some remedial environmental work, and minimal maintenance. We ask you to recognize that intensively developed greenways can conflict with the natural value of a greenway. We suggest that you select and use only those development techniques that suit local community needs and are in harmony with the natural environment. Seek the help of a land-use professional if you have doubts.

A Note to the Reader

Any organizing scheme for an undertaking as complex and individualized as greenway creation is necessarily arbitrary. The chapters in this book roughly correspond to the chronological stages in the process. Recurrent and overlapping tasks, however, such as meeting with local landowners and revising design plans, dispel any notion of an absolute sequence of events. Certain special topics such as fund-raising or land stewardship have been treated thematically in their own chapters.

Keep in mind that the way you approach a task may differ over time. Also be aware that major greenway responsibilities either never end or require periodic review. You will continue to seek funds for different aspects of greenway work, to market your greenway, to develop better maintenance techniques, to protect natural and cultural resources, and to adjust the design of your project. We encourage readers first to skim the book to become familiar with the entire greenway planning process—and then zero in on the most appropriate chapters. Good luck to you!

Loring LaB. Schwarz
May 1993

Acknowledgments

Many people have left their mark on this book. A debt of gratitude is due those who have shared the long haul.

Most special thanks go to Patrick F. Noonan, President of The Conservation Fund, for his leading role in promoting the greenway concept nationwide, his vision in recognizing the need for this book, and his solid support in helping us to get it into the hands of those who need it.

Virginia Read, manuscript editor, had the ability to take a rough draft and visualize what it would take to turn it into a book. Her sense of humor and her dedication to The Conservation Fund and to quality has made all the difference.

Few people are as efficient, resourceful, and cheerful as Lisa Gutierrez, Projects Coordinator for the American Greenways Program and photo editor for this book. Her ongoing support in all stages of the book's development and knack for coming through in a pinch are duly noted.

This book could not have happened without the hard work and generous sharing of knowledge and skills that Chuck Flink and Bob Searns have acquired over the many years they have spent developing greenways.

Ed McMahon, Director of the American Greenways Program, was our stabilizing force. His objectivity, editing skills, and dedication to the greenway concept have kept us all on an even keel during the many months it took to finalize the manuscript.

Jack Lynn's ready expertise in the publishing field has been invaluable since the formative stages of this book.

Jonathan Labaree, of the Atlantic Center for the Environment, generously provided us with camera-ready copies of National Park Service illustrations (prepared by himself and Jane Shoplick) for Chapter 7.

Friends Tom Flanagan and Brenda Barnes, as well as Andy Schwarz, volunteered their time with manuscript preparation, usually at a moment's notice.

Scores of individuals responded to requests for information or review of manuscript segments. Their help is deeply appreciated; they are listed on the following pages.

A note of personal gratitude goes to my own mentors over the years—Joseph and Gloria LaBarbara, Pat Noonan, Norton Nickerson, and Bob Jenkins.

Finally, my most heartfelt appreciation to Andy, Devin, and Teddy, whose support and ready sense of humor have made my contribution possible.

Loring LaB. Schwarz

We would like to thank Charles E. Little for his inspiration and guidance. It is our hope that this work will inspire Americans to create greenways with the enthusiasm and community spirit embodied in *Greenways for America*. We also owe special thanks to Keith Hay for his hard work in the formative stages of this book.

Quite frankly, without a strong editorial hand, this book might have been without purpose. To this end we owe a great deal of thanks to Loring Schwarz and Ginny Read. Special thanks are also due Patrick Noonan of The Conservation Fund for producing this book. Ed McMahon, Jack Lynn, and Lisa Gutierrez, of the Fund, also played vital roles. Terri Musser, of Greenways Incorporated, shaped and produced most of the graphics for this book. We are appreciative of her hard work and clear and concise illustrations.

We are especially grateful to all of our reviewers, who graciously shared their knowledge and expertise. We particularly appreciate the assistance provided by Elizabeth Watson for Chapter 9, "Preserving Our Cultural Heritage," Robbin Sotir for the section on soil bioengineering in Chapter 8, and Hugh Duffy for the funding information in Chapter 6.

We would like to thank the staff of Greenways Incorporated and Urban Edges: Beverly Tant, Jennifer Toole, Glenn Morris, Rick Wilson, Andy Baur, Tracy Esslinger, and Diana Maglischo—many thanks for your assistance and for keeping the ship afloat and productive.

Finally, without the full support of our family and friends, this book would not have been possible. Mr. Flink extends his love and appreciation to Richard, Jane, and Marjorie Flink for their moral support. Mr. Searns extends his love and appreciation to his wife Sally Preston, his children, Bryn and Noah, who put up with the demands of the book and backed him all the way, and to James and Bernice for their guidance and support.

Charles A. Flink and Robert M. Searns

The following individuals gave freely of their time and considerable knowledge in reviewing drafts of the manuscript: Mark C. Ackelson, Associate Director, Iowa Natural Heritage Foundation; John L. Barnett, ASLA, Landscape Architect/Planner; Mark Benedict, Florida Greenways Coordinator, The Conservation Fund; Nancy Brittain, AICP Community Planner, Blackstone River Valley National Heritage Corridor Commission; Page Crutcher, Southeast Region Greenways Representative, The Conservation Fund; Jim Cummins, Associate Director of Living Resources, Interstate Commission of the Potomac River Basin; John S. DeKemper, Greenway Planner, Mecklenburg County Park and Recreation Department; Alfred Edelman, A.I.A. Architect; Karen Firehock, Save Our Streams Program Director, The Izaak Walton League of America; Joan Florsheim, Associate, Philip Williams and Associates, Ltd., Consultants in Hydrology; William L. Flournoy, Jr., Chief, Environmental Assessment Section, The North Carolina Division of Planning and Assessment; Mary Hampton Carter, Chairman, South Suburban Park Foundation; Kiku Hanes, Vice President, Director of Development, The Conservation Fund; Keith Hay, Western Director, American Greenways Program, The Conservation Fund; Susan L. Henry, Preservation Planner, Preservation Planning Branch, Interagency Resources Division,

The National Park Service; David C. Hobson, Capital Programs Director, Northern Virginia Regional Park Authority; Jean Hocker, President, Land Trust Alliance; Jonathan E. Jones, Vice President, Wright Water Engineers, Inc.; Jill Keimach, Project Manager, San Francisco Bay Trail Project; Loren Kellogg, Save Our Streams, Izaak Walton League of America; Peter Lagerway, Bicycle Coordinator, City of Seattle, Traffic Engineering; Charles E. Little, Author, *Greenways for America*; Ann Lusk, Chair, Vermont Trails and Greenway Council; Jack Lynn, Public Relations Director, The Conservation Fund; James Mackay, City and County of Denver Department of Public Works; Shelly Mastran, Director of Rural Programs, National Trust for Historic Preservation; Erik Olgeirson, Consulting Ecologist; Betsy Otto, Greenways Director, Openlands Project; Elizabeth Porter, Manager of Metropolitian Greenway Planning Projects, National Park Service; Jim D. Priddy, Manager of Parks, South Suburban Park and Recreation District, Littleton, Colorado; Bob Proudman, Trail Management Coordinator, Appalachian Trail Conference; Christopher J. Rigby, Maryland Lands Coordinator, Chesapeake Bay Foundation; David S. Sampson, Executive Director, Hudson River Valley Greenway Council; Anne C. Sloan, Greenways and Resource Planning, Maryland Department of Natural Resources; Daniel Somers Smith, Editor, *The Ecology of Greenways*; Timothy W. Smith, Scott Consulting Engineer; Bob Smith, Principal, DHM, Inc.; Leslie B. Snyder, Assistant Professor, The University of Connecticut; Robbin B. Sotir, President, Robbin B. Sotir and Associates; Samuel N. Stokes, National Park Service, Recreation Resources Assistance Division; Cheryl Teague, Landscape Architect, D. R. Horne and Company; Edith R. Thompson, Urban Wildlife Biologist, Maryland Department of Natural Resources; A. Elizabeth Watson, Principal, Mary Means & Associates, Alexandria, Virginia; Suzi Wilkins, Director of State Programs and Acting Director of Conservation, American Rivers, Inc.; and H. William Woodcock, ASLA, Manager of Planning and Construction, South Suburban Park and Recreation District.

The following respondents to a 1991 questionnaire shared experience and advice, which have been incorporated throughout the book: Anne McClellan, Neighborhood Open Space Coalition (New York City); Susan Sedgwick, Meramec River Greenway (Missouri); Lorah Hopkins, Schuylkill River Greenway Association (Pennsylvania); David R. Callum, Mettawee River Interstate Greenbelt Project (Vermont/New York); Rod Larson, Cedar Valley Nature Trail (Iowa); Clois Ensor, Redding Land Trust (Connecticut); David Froehlich, Wissahickon Green Ribbon Preserve (Pennsylvania); Jill Kiemach, Greg Froese, San Francisco Bay Trail Project; Barbara Rice, Bay Area Ridge Trail, San Francisco; Bob Myhr, San Juan Islands Ferry Corridor Greenway (Washington); Valarie Spale, Salt Creek Greenway Association (Illinois); Staff of the Heritage Trail (Iowa); Laurel Parker, Pima County Flood Control District (Arizona); Brian Steen, Big Sur Land Trust (California); Anne Lusk, Stowe Recreation Path (Vermont); David Sampson, Hudson River Valley Greenway Council (New York); Kyle Gulbronson, Delaware Nature Society; Tim Brown, Town of Cary (North Carolina); Staff of Orono

Land Trust (Maine); Dennis LaBarg, Falling Spring Greenway (Pennsylvania); John Varvaryanis, Westchester Greenway (New York); Nancy Jones, Delaware River Greenway (New Jersey/Pennsylvania).

The following individuals provided information at later stages of manuscript development: Kathy Ducket, DuPage River Greenway, Illinois; Jennifer Ealy, Chittenden Greenway, Vermont; David Getchell, Maine Small Boating Waterway; Sally Grove and Robert Chipley, Science Division, The Nature Conservancy; John Hobner, Director of Environmental Impact, Baltimore County, Maryland; George Johnson, Rhode Island Department of Environmental Management; William C. Krebs, Maryland Greenways Program; Jonathan Labaree, Atlantic Center for the Environment; Keith Lang, Rhode Island Field Office, The Nature Conservancy; Jonathan McKnight, Maryland Department of Natural Resources; Reuben Rajala, Appalachian Mountain Club; Thomas Schueler, Metropolitan Washington Council of Governments; and Roxanne Zaghab, Baltimore Harbor Endowment.

1

Envisioning Your Greenway

"To make a greenway is to make a community."
—Charles Little, author of *Greenways for America*

Greenways almost always begin with two key elements: an outstanding natural or cultural feature and committed visionary leadership. The initial divine moment of inspiration is important, but the subsequent process of endeavor—research, organization, design, promotion, troubleshooting, negotiation, fund-raising, and plain hard work—transforms the initial vision into a permanent public amenity that many generations will enjoy. Taking the first step from idea to plan of action can be daunting. Fortunately, others have taken this step before, and we can profit from their experiences.

Why Create a Greenway?

First, you need to ask yourself, "Why do I want to do this? Why create a greenway?" There are many kinds of greenways and many reasons for creating them. Being able to articulate your reasons will help you fix your primary greenway vision and determine which approach best suits your project. Several general areas of concern have led to greenways in communities across the country. First, greenways offer a way to preserve vital habitat corridors and to promote plant and animal species diversity. A greenway can also serve as a critical filtering zone: its wetlands can absorb contaminants in surface runoff, and trees, shrubs, and cover vegetation along the corridor cleanse and replenish the air.

In an increasingly urban nation, greenways provide much-needed space for outdoor recreation and offer accessible alternatives to those who don't live near traditional parks. A greenway is ideally suited to such popular outdoor activities as jogging, walking, biking, fishing, and canoeing. Greenways provide safe, alternative, nonmotorized transportation routes for commuters going to work and children traveling to and from school. Greenways link us to our communities and, by lessening our dependence on the automobile, can improve air quality and reduce road congestion.

Greenways offer a way to protect our nation's cultural heritage. They give us access to buildings of historic and architectural significance in the community. Greenways allow us to look back at our past and our traditions—to revisit remnants of settlements and the industrial centers that defined our history.

Greenways offer ideal possibilities for joint-use partnerships along corridors with sewer, utility, and fiber-optic lines and railroad interests.

In some communities, they can also serve as emergency vehicle and evacuation routes.

Greenways can help preserve the rural character of a community or safeguard areas of visual interest by protecting ridge lines, river corridors, and scenic resources. In rapidly urbanizing areas, a greenway offers visual relief; its wooded breaks can frame and distinguish neighborhoods in an otherwise undifferentiated urban sprawl. In the countryside, greenways can work with programs that preserve farmland and expanses of scenic open space.

Greenways are community amenities with an economic value. They enhance the quality of life and can increase the value of surrounding properties. Greenways have been shown to draw tourists and have been the catalyst behind new commercial development and the revitalization of former town centers. Greenways planned as elements of subdivisions can benefit home buyers and developers alike.

Different Circumstances, Different Styles, Different Strategies

You know why you want to create a greenway, and you may even have a corridor in mind. The question is how to proceed. Because greenways can wind through myriad rural and urban settings, complex issues are involved, including resource protection, land ownership, flooding, wildlife, road crossings, recreation, maintenance, economic development, safety, liability, and development costs. Creating a successful greenway system, therefore, means addressing and overcoming a host of potential challenges. Needless to say, without a road map, it is easy to get bogged down early in the process.

If we look at some examples of successful greenway projects, we see that each presented a different set of opportunities and obstacles. The greenway groups in each of the following four models focused on their primary objectives—their greenway vision—and developed a strategy that built on their strengths and fit their individual circumstances, as you will need to do.

The Platte River Greenway: Shooting from the Hip

Denver's South Platte River had once been the highway of settlement for pioneers and fortune seekers heading west. Its waters were—and still are—the lifeblood to cities and farms from Denver to Omaha. By the mid-1960s, however, the river had become a polluted dumping ground, lined with rubble, stockyards, and marginal industries. The people of Denver had written it off until a devastating flood in May 1965 killed twelve people and caused millions of dollars in damage.

The city of Denver undertook a major study, at a cost of hundreds of thousands of dollars, which detailed ambitious plans for parkways, commercial development, and apartment buildings along the riverfront. The estimated price tag for the project was a staggering $630 million. Not surprisingly, given the cost, not much happened.

Another damaging flood occurred in 1973. A heightened awareness of the real danger of a future flood, combined with upcoming city elections and the demands of a powerful citizens' group for a riverfront park on railroad-owned land, all pushed the future of the Platte into the spotlight. The Democratic mayor, Bill McNichols, appointed Joe Shoemaker, the Republican head of the powerful State Senate Joint Budget Committee, to chair a bipartisan task force to address the issue of the river. Shoemaker turned to influential businesspeople, leaders of Denver's minority communities, a progressive downtown developer who had recently saved a blighted historic district, a historian, and two rising politicians with clout in the northwest Denver wards, whose citizens were clamoring for the park. At McNichols's urging, the city council appropriated $1.5 million for the task force—the railroad property was valued in excess of $300 million. The mayor also offered Shoemaker the services of two city planners.

Less than seven years later, Denver had in place a ten-mile-long $10 million greenway along the South Platte River, running from city limit to city limit. The suburbs were soon linked in, and today the people of metropolitan Denver enjoy a multicounty greenway system—one of the most extensive urban greenway networks in the nation (see Figure 1-1).

In the San Francisco Bay Area, State Senator Bill Lockyer noticed people using a shoreline trail while he was having lunch at a bayside restaurant in Hayward. The City of Hayward had built the trail for local use, but the Senator conceived the idea of connecting that trail to similar trails throughout the region. He then wrote legislation that resulted in state funding for the planning and design of a four-hundred-mile system serving the entire Bay Area.
—Jill Keimach, Association of Bay Area Governments

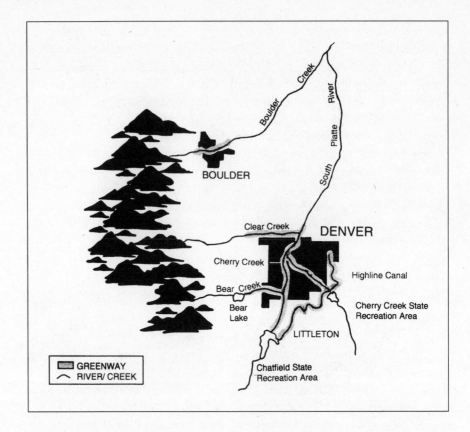

Figure 1-1 The Platte River forms the backbone of the Denver Greenway system; its numerous tributaries and trails make up one of the largest urban greenway networks in the nation.

How did Denver do it? How did it turn around a sorry urban river? No formal master plan existed. Shoemaker preferred to move directly ahead with building greenway improvements. Simply put, Denver had the key ingredients in place: a shared vision, an influential organization, a strong leader to champion the project, capable support staff, seed money, and perhaps most important, the political impetus to make it happen. Although there was no formal plan, there was a well-developed strategy. Joe Shoemaker knew how to make the most of what he had at hand: he involved the people who could get the job done, and together they built the greenway piece by piece, sparking community support for additional segments as they went along.

Capital Area Greenway: Starting with a Plan

Unlike many American cities, Raleigh, North Carolina, was originally laid out according to a city plan that included five public squares, one the site of the state capitol. Large-scale growth in the 1950s and '60s began to overpower the landscape, and proposed road developments threatened the remaining public parks and wetlands. This, combined with increasing yearly flood damage from streams feeding the Neuse River, contributed to the growth of a new public environmental awareness.

A 1969 parks and recreation master plan made reference to the term *greenway* as a system of "green fingers" that would reach throughout the city. Two years later, William Flournoy, then a graduate student at North Carolina State University's School of Design, proposed to study the greenway concept in more detail and was awarded a grant through an annual city program that funded student recreation-related projects for North Carolina State University. Flournoy produced a 100-page document, *Capital City Greenway*, which laid out the range of possible recreational, economic, and ecological benefits of greenways and recommended a system of linear open spaces that would link Raleigh's more traditional parks, schools, shopping centers, and other locations. Flournoy outlined the way floodplain zoning, easements, stream bank buffer zones, and erosion control measures could preserve stream environments and reduce sediment loads that had muddied once-clear waterways. The report also suggested a system of footpaths and bikeways and canoe trails.

Although Raleigh's city council accepted the plan, there was no consensus among city agencies as to how to proceed. Coincidentally, as in Denver, events in 1973 again got things underway: first, a series of destructive floods brought the issues of floodplain development and sediment control into the public arena, and regulatory ordinances were enacted. At about the same time, public disfavor with the city council led to a referendum that lent more political power to Raleigh's neighborhoods. With neighborhood support, the new council appointed an eighteen-member greenway advisory commission, which, though given administrative assistance by the planning department and construction and operational support by the parks department, was independent of either.

Because the greenway concept was relatively new at the time, the commission launched a concerted community education effort. Commission members and citizen advocates made hundreds of presentations to groups all over town, extolling the various benefits of greenways. A local environmental group was tapped for commission members and expertise; the local chapter of the Sierra Club funded a multiprojector slide show; and the League of Women Voters made greenways part of its environmental agenda.

Construction began in 1975, and over the next seventeen years, with the help of garden clubs, homeowner groups, and other neighborhood advocates, more than twenty-seven miles of multiuse paths were built along preserved floodplain corridors (see Figure 1-2).

Like the Platte River Greenway, Raleigh's greenway effort grew in large part from an increasing awareness of the need for limited development in the floodplain area. Raleigh's impetus was William Flournoy's plan, which cost the city only $1500.

With Raleigh's success, other communities in the area took up the cause. There are now greenway programs in place throughout the six-county region surrounding Raleigh. The Capital Area Greenway has served as the inspiration for greenway projects in more than thirty-five cities in North Carolina alone.

In 1974, in response to a perceived demand for expanded open space and recreation opportunities, the Mecklenburg County (North Carolina) Park and Recreation Commission appointed a thirteen-member committee to study the feasibility of a greenway system. The Commission worked with two major criteria: projected population growth within the community and linkages of open space within the existing park system. The final report called for a greenway network and designated twenty creeks as potential sites. In 1978, the citizens of Mecklenburg County voted a park bond package that included $4,000,000 for land acquisition and development of several of the proposed greenways.
—John S. DeKemper, Mecklenberg County Parks and Recreation Department

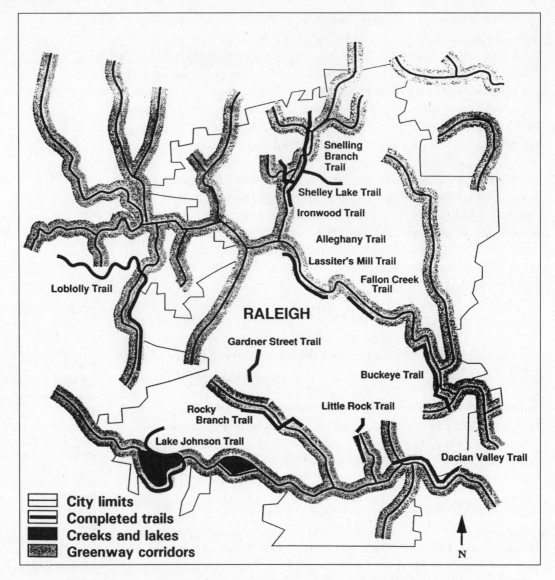

Figure 1-2 The Capital Area Greenway system in Raleigh, North Carolina, currently contains more than one thousand acres of protected floodplain land and approximately thirty miles of multipurpose trails. (Courtesy of Charles E. Little.)

Willamette: Greenway Through Due Process

The pride of Portland, Oregon, the Willamette riverfront is part of the larger Willamette Greenway, which extends from the river's headwaters above Eugene to its confluence with the Columbia River just below Portland. Along the way, the greenway corridor passes through cities, towns, forest, and farmlands. Like the Platte, the Willamette river valley was, and still is, home to industry and commerce and serves as a major corridor for shipping and logging. By the early 1960s, the Willamette was shamefully polluted, and its adjacent lands were succumbing to less-than-sensitive development.

In downtown Portland, a planned freeway was converted into a riverside greenway as part of the Willamette River Greenway System. (Charles Flink)

Unlike the Platte and Raleigh systems, the Willamette greenway concept began at the state government level. Thanks to the initiative of two forward-thinking governors—Tom McCall and Robert Straub—the Oregon State Legislature declared the Willamette corridor a greenway in 1967. Probably the first legal designation of a corridor as a greenway in the nation, this pioneering step called for local and state action aimed at protecting the river as a resource corridor, while still expanding recreational opportunities. During the next several years, the state park and transportation agencies began to acquire lands and develop riverfront recreation and access sites. The state also enacted strict development review over both public- and private-sector improvements along the Willamette corridor. The intent was to keep the majority of land along the corridor in private hands while protecting the public's right to its enjoyment.

Under this legislation, each jurisdiction must submit for review by the Oregon Land Conservation and Development Commission any plans for riverfront development or greenway improvements. A setback was established to keep development 150 feet away from either bank of the river. Although not totally effective because of existing development, the setback has encouraged the creation of public parks and open spaces along the corridor (see Figure 1-3).

Spearheaded by Linda Dobson, principal coordinator of the Willamette project, several miles of trail have been installed through the developer dedication requirement. Fifteen riverfront parks, including several nature preserves, are linked to the trail. Through an ambitious acquisition program, the city of Eugene also secured significant public ownership along this segment of the Willamette.

Stowe Recreation Path: Community Action

The Stowe Recreation Path in Stowe, Vermont, was originally conceived as a walking path along the shoulder of a seven-mile road that runs from the village up Mount Mansfield. The Better Business Association voted in favor of the path in 1964, but nothing happened until 1977, when local resident Claire Lintilhac commissioned the state's highway department to design a safe bike route alongside Mountain Road. Because of heavy road traffic, numerous driveways, and, in winter, the presence of snow banks along the shoulders, the highway department's plan followed the same general route but moved the path to the river valley. In 1981, the town's Chamber of Commerce formed a planning committee, which requested that a bike path coordinator be hired. That coordinator was Anne Lusk.

With no land and no money for construction, Lusk knew the key to her project was community support. She began writing greenway articles for the *Stowe Reporter* and talking to local residents. After more than a year had passed and the proposed route had been more clearly defined, Anne met face-to-face with each of the landowners through whose property the greenway would pass. Because some property owners worried about the path's location on their land, the project engineer walked each area with Anne and the property owner, discussing design considerations and owner preferences. From a design perspective, this was certainly not the most practical method, but Lusk's approach—and her persistence—-paid off. By 1984, 2.7 miles of path had been built on twenty-seven donated easements (requiring a total of sixty signatures), with $300,000 in construction costs to cover the installation of benches, completion of an eight-foot-wide paved trail, and purchase of signage. Funds were secured from a variety of sources, from foundation grants to the proceeds of a Valentine's Dance to the $186,000 raised by "selling" pieces of the path. Practically every community organization participated by helping to raise funds and donating money, benches, flower bulbs, and administrative assistance. Three years later the townspeople voted to approve funding for a path extension, and the five affected property owners donated their land. By 1989, the completed path totaled 5.3 miles and had cost $680,000.

Stowe's greenway is smaller in scale and includes a higher percentage of privately owned land than the Platte River Greenway, the Capital Area Greenway, or Willamette. The path allows public access to the river and provides a safe and convenient passageway for walkers, runners,

"Listen to the people who live, work, and recreate in the proposed greenway area. We have found vast differences between needs and goals in just an eighty-mile bi-state corridor."
—Delaware River Greenway

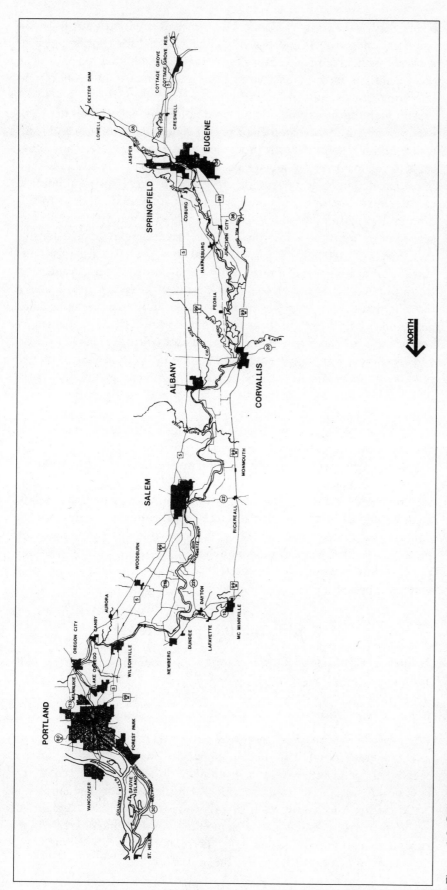

Figure 1-3 Orientation map of the Willamette River Greenway, one of the longest continuous greenways in the United States. (Courtesy of Oregon Department of Transportation.)

bikers, and cross-country skiers. The Stowe Recreation Path has won many national awards and has served as a model for countless greenways across the country. Because the community adopted the path as its own, residents have taken charge of its maintenance and continue to raise funds for its upkeep.

Although these examples demonstrate different approaches to greenway planning and development, they all share visionary, forceful leadership and a resource worth protecting. Clearly, there are many other ways to create successful greenways. Which approach works best? That, of course, depends on the specific greenway resource, the local political climate, available funds, community support, and many other factors. If a natural or cultural resource is threatened—for example, rural open space put up for sale—you probably won't have time to do an extensive inventory and detailed plan. You'd want to see what regulatory measures exist to limit development, rally public support, raise funds, and try to purchase the land or secure an easement as soon as possible. On the other hand, a regional system that seeks to link existing public lands and protect wildlife might focus first on a thorough natural resource inventory to see where sensitive ecological and cultural areas lie. An urban recreational greenway might first come up with a general overall plan, working in concert with the public and with city planning or parks department staff. No one process is sacred and no recipe for success guaranteed.

The chapters that follow discuss the basics of greenway creation: assessing resources, planning, organizing a greenway advocacy group and forming partnerships, building public support for the project, raising funds, securing and protecting the land, designing and implementing the greenway, and managing the corridor. You won't necessarily follow a chronological line from plan through organization through construction or management. You'll need to decide what is appropriate for your project and what needs to be done when. We will lay out the possibilities and show how others have done it so that you can begin to arrive at your own best strategy.

"Get Started!"
—San Francisco Bay Trail

Getting Started: First Steps

To help get you started, let's examine the first issues you'll need to address.

Resource Corridor

What special feature offers greenway potential? It might be a river of local, statewide, or national interest, a historic canal or a creek, a rail line scheduled for abandonment, a prominent ridge line on the edge of a city, or a historic road, trail, or critical wildlife corridor. The landscape could be predominantly rural or urban or it could have elements of both. The corridor might also be something you imagine or create in response to community needs, thus necessitating a careful map and ground examination to determine the best route.

The first step in describing your greenway, therefore, is to understand the resource corridor. What does it have to offer? Are there unique land forms, exceptional flora and fauna, or historic or cultural values to be considered? Where does the corridor begin and where does it end? Is it continuous, or are there gaps? Is the corridor only of interest locally, or could there be state or national involvement? How much of the land is in private hands and how much is publicly owned?

Usually, a single key element like a river or stream is the impetus for a greenway, but sometimes a community may have in mind a network of trails or open space that will connect several types of resource corridors into a single system. Denver's Platte River Greenway, for example, is merely the central spine of a larger network that includes the tributary streams, canals, trails along highway rights-of-way, and other links in an area-wide hiking and biking trail system. When planning your greenway, be sure to consider the larger regional context or system into which it might fit.

Greenways are by definition linear. They link together places, people, and things. Ideally, the corridor should be continuous, although interruptions are sometimes unavoidable. In Santa Rosa, California, a proposed greenway corridor temporarily vanishes in the center of town, where the creek it runs alongside disappears into a tunnel, to emerge several blocks downstream.

Theme

What will be the corridor's primary function: recreation, preservation, economic development, or some combination thereof? Who will use it? If the future use of the greenway is not already obvious from its physical features, you will need to come up with a *theme*, or primary vision. Later, you will refine the theme as you assess the resource corridor and solicit the input of the community.

A common greenway objective or theme is the creation of a continuous nonmotorized trail for recreational use, as a commuter route, or as a safe walkway for children going to school. Economic development is another popular theme. Some greenways attract tourists or promote redevelopment. Chattanooga, Tennessee, is creating "Riverway," a twenty-mile multiuse greenway along the Tennessee River. The riverway concept includes a park and trail system, a new hotel, a major freshwater aquarium, shops, restaurants, industrial development, and office and apartment buildings. Ultimately, as much as $750 million will be invested in public- and private-sector projects along the corridor.

More and more, greenways are focusing on wildlife and resource corridor preservation themes. This approach usually includes protection or enhancement of aquatic life. In West Windsor Township, New Jersey, a local environmental commission created a nonrecreational greenbelt system to protect stream corridors and wetlands, provide habitat and migration corridors for wildlife, and buffer developed areas of the township.

Other greenway themes include historic and cultural preservation, protection of significant geological features, environmental education, and water recreation. In many cases, the corridor will determine the theme. There may already be strong community sentiment about the use of the corridor. A good way to identify a theme is to write down a list of potential uses and benefits. The list might include biking, hiking, nature study, canoeing, picnicking, and fishing. As you make the list, talk to citizens and community leaders to gauge their views. There may be conflicting goals that need to be reconciled.

Vision Statement

A vision statement can take the form of a video. The Maryland Greenways Commission produced "Greenways: A Vision for Maryland," a fifteen-minute video that highlights important connections between Maryland's people and their natural and cultural resources, particularly the Chesapeake Bay. The film, underwritten by the state coastal zone management agency, introduces citizens and officials to the greenway concept and benefits of a statewide system of greenways at meetings, workshops, and via public television.

Once you have defined your greenway resource and you have an idea of how and if it will function, it's a good idea to put your thoughts down on paper. The initial description of your project might consist of a rough sketch map, a few photos or slides, and a brief one- or two-page narrative that defines the basic corridor, what it has to offer, and the vision of the corridor as a future greenway. Be careful about addressing land acquisition. Unless affected property owners have been apprised and involved, the vision statement should show general areas of use rather than actual parcels of land. The last thing you want is for a tenant or property owner to see a published map that shows the greenway routed across his or her land.

A private citizens' group in New York State published *A Greenway for the Hudson River Valley: A New Strategy for Preserving an American Treasure*, an unofficial report that sets forth reasons why the Hudson River Valley Greenway is so important and suggests ways to proceed with its creation. This document is a fairly elaborate example of a vision statement, in keeping with the scale of the project and number of jurisdictions involved. Most vision statements are informal and unpublished.

Feasibility

Once you have a concept in mind, you must ask if the project can be accomplished as envisioned. At this stage, we are really talking about a common sense evaluation, not the thorough analysis outlined in Chapter 2. You should consider the following:

- *Cost.* The cost of proposed improvements—and what it will take to maintain them—should be considered relative to community resources

- *Political support.* Different communities have different values and aspirations when it comes to spending money and imposing regulations. Will your community support the funding and possible regulatory measures you have in mind, or do you need to modify your approach?

- *Ownership.* When ownership is overlooked it can be disastrous. Greenway trails have been forcibly closed or removed when it was discovered they were built on private property or even placed on a conceptual map without owner approval. Chapter 2 will discuss researching ownership in more detail. For now, note that owner-ship can take many forms. The bottom of the river or stream running along your greenway may be entirely privately owned, but someone else may own the water rights and may have the power to reduce or even stop flows in the stream. Know who all the owners are and what their needs and rights are.

- *Scale.* You should ask yourself how big a project you are ready to take on. The resource corridor may extend through several communities. It might even cross county or state lines. Project scale will depend in part on the nature of the corridor, availability of right of way, and your goals, support, and resources. . In most instances, for better or worse, project scale will be determined, at least initially, by the human resources available and the political will to pursue greenway objectives. The early planning process, however, should always keep in mind the bigger picture. What started as a bike path along a mile or two of local riverbank might one day evolve into a major greenway system of regional or even national significance.

- *Operations and maintenance.* Is there an entity in place to take care of the greenway or can one be created? Can funds or volunteer services be secured to meet anticipated operations and maintenance needs?

By *ownership* we mean those who ultimately take possession of the greenway amenities, be they land or improvements. Someone must be responsible for the long-term stewardship of the greenway. Liability questions may arise during the design, construction, and use stages. Few private entities have the resources to take on this kind of burden. This is why finding a public agency partner such as a parks agency or water district early on is important, both to lend credibility to the endeavor and to assure the level of support needed.

The Community

Understanding your community is critical. You should research its transportation, recreation, environmental, utility, and open-space needs. You should be aware of local land-use laws and ordinances. You should have a idea of local economic development goals and how a greenway might fit in—by promoting tourism, for example. Visits to your local planning department, the chamber of commerce, and the convention and visitors' bureau are a good way to begin. At this stage, you should also talk with community leaders and local recreation groups or conservation organizations. You might also contact people involved with neighboring efforts to see what their experiences have been.

How do you build a base of public support for your greenway? A well-structured public participation process will almost always help your greenway effort. In Raleigh, for example, support from the neighborhoods was considered the key ingredient to moving from plan to action. You want public input for ideas and suggestions and to counter

"It was Joe Kupek who first thought of the idea of creating a long-distance hiking/biking trail on this abandoned railroad, extending through the Youghougheny Trail at either end. Joe wrote a ten-page proposal and sent copies to various state and federal agencies. I began doing the same, until nearly every agency that might have any remote connection to the project was very familiar with it.

"The first real break came when Congressman Murtha included the trail in the America's Industrial Heritage Project, which covers a nine-county area in southwest Pennsylvania. The primary focus of the project is on the development, enhancement, and interpretation of the iron/steel, coal, transportation, and agricultural themes within the nine counties. The project hopes to assist the improvement of the area's economy by incorporating the industrial heritage themes into a regional tourist promotion effort."
—Hank Park, Allegheny Highlands Trail, speaking at the Maryland Greenways Conference, November 1990

any possible opposition. Citizen workshops, hearings, and public meetings are important.

Keep in mind that there are several different types of *publics*, for example, the general citizenry, special interest groups, public agencies, organized user groups, and adjacent property owners. How you work with each of these groups will vary. In some instances, one-on-one meetings and discussions are best. Be sure to delegate the right person to work with each key stakeholder. For example, a respected landowner along the corridor who supports the greenway might be the best emissary to adjacent property owners.

Leadership

Who will get the word out? Who will open the necessary doors? Who will get the project moving? Early leadership may come from a person, a citizens' group, a government agency, or a combination of all three working together.

Whatever its makeup, the greenway advocacy group may evolve into a nonprofit corporation or join with an existing one. Begin to think about who will be part of this group. What talents and expertise are available in your community?

It is also essential that the group stay focused. While other causes may be worthy or vital to the community, implementing the greenway is a full-time job. Nothing can be more damaging to the cause than diverting attention to other pet projects or interests of particular members.

Pilot Project

Based on your answers to the feasibility checklist, you may want to narrow your focus to a discreet section of the corridor that can build long-term support for the rest of your greenway. Most successful greenway efforts start out with a pilot project, usually an initial segment such as a length of trail that demonstrates your greenway vision. The pilot project should be a segment of work that can be funded and built within one year. It should also be highly visible and accessible to the public.

Seed Money

At this stage, your key financial objective is to find seed money to get your greenway effort off the ground. Seed money could come from several sources. The best source may be a commitment of funds from the city council, county commission, or other public agency. In some instances, it may be possible to piggyback your greenway planning funding onto a larger public works project, such as a flood control study or a parks and recreation master plan.

You can also turn to private-sector sources, including foundations, corporations, service clubs, and individual donations. Casper, Wyoming, for example, working through a private local land trust, secured an initial grant of land and money from the Amoco Corporation. Service clubs have played a role in getting many greenway projects off the ground.

Possibly, state and federal sources can augment your seed money fund. Check with your local planning department, your state parks and recreation department, or the state coastal zone management agency for leads on state and federal funding programs.

Staff and Consulting Services

Who will carry out the day-to-day work of planning, developing, and maintaining the greenway? When you're just getting started, volunteers may be able to provide a number of the needed organizational skills. Consultants can provide such technical services as planning and design. At some point, however, particularly in complex urban recreational greenways that involve environmental assessment, land-use planning, landscape design, and engineering, professional staff services will be required. Someone needs to oversee planning, manage consultants, raise money, and carry out the day-to-day tasks of a major capital endeavor.

There are several ways to go about staffing. The cities of Denver and Raleigh provided city planners and office space to the greenway effort. Other greenway organizations have hired staff themselves or have contracted with an outside consultant or consulting firm for staff and office services on a retainer basis. In most cases, having competent, committed staff is essential to greenway implementation. Local, state, and federal officials can be a good source of free technical advice. You should also consider local business executives who may have expertise in required fields, as well as university, college, and high school teachers, graduate students, and other academics.

Most consulting professionals, from landscape architects to biologists, will be happy to meet with you initially at no charge to discuss your interests and objectives. Some larger law firms, accountants, and other professional firms provide a certain amount of pro-bono, or donated, services for civic causes like greenways. Some of the members of your greenway group may be able to offer these services. In all cases, be sure that the professional's agenda matches your own.

Phasing

What will get done when? How do you set project priorities? How long should it take?

Building a greenway is an ambitious endeavor. The project may take many years. In the beginning, the important thing is to assure continuity and to concentrate on a pilot project you know you can complete. The key is to plan logical segments that can stand alone and inspire the public while subsequent segments are in the works. When starting your greenway effort, think about how the project will play out over the next decade or longer.

The greenway process can be long, taxing, and at times frustrating. It is important to begin the process with enthusiasm and a strong commitment for the long haul. Don't expect quick results. For most greenway advocates, half the fun is the challenge of overcoming problems and seeing progress each step of the way. The key is to accomplish something meaningful each year and to persevere until the greenway is complete.

2

Developing a Plan

"Do what you can with what you have, where you are."
—Theodore Roosevelt

There is no single way to plan and implement a successful greenway. Different communities use different methods, but most begin with a plan. There are advantages to beginning with a plan. Planning makes you consider various options and choices; it can focus your efforts and save money and time. A plan can serve as a blueprint for future work, which can be modified to adapt to changing circumstances. The planning documents themselves are valuable communications tools to use not only to secure funding and support for your greenway, but also to solicit feedback from government officials and public works, planning, recreation, and transportation departments. The very process of developing a plan becomes a tool for increasing political support. In addition, because greenway advocates think regionally, having a plan aids in coordinating the many jurisdictions involved.

A plan specifies actions that must be carried out to successfully complete the greenway vision. No matter what its form, a good plan provides you, your community, and others with a comprehensive understanding of all the issues, recommendations, and strategies involved. The plan can help build public support for the greenway and for any future extensions or enhancements.

The plan must also be defensible. Keep in mind that even though you feel that a greenway is a great idea, other residents of your community may not agree. In order to ensure that you have thoroughly evaluated the greenway concept from every conceivable angle, your greenway plan should provide accurate and supportable evidence of need, compatibility, and soundness.

The level of detail in a greenway plan will vary from project to project, depending upon available resources, the scale and complexity of the project, the time available for plan preparation, the threat to the natural resource, and the degree of public involvement. A greenway plan may require only a few well-written pages of text along with a simple graphic illustrating the location, route, and key links in the greenway (for example, schools and parks). Or the plan may be a lengthy written document containing maps, drawings, and colorful promotional materials. In either case, the process used to prepare the plan is essentially the same.

The preparation of almost all greenway plans involves two key ingredients: a thorough investigation of the greenway project area and the involvement of the public. This chapter presents the ideal scenario a professional planner would follow. If you have a comparatively simple greenway project, and your group plans to conduct the inventory without professional assistance, you should consult the references listed at the back of the book and seek the assistance of local officials who are familiar with your local plan approval process.

The greenway planning process is generally composed of three major stages: *inventory and analysis*, preparation of the *concept plan* (also called a draft master plan), and preparation of the *final master plan*. The inventory and analysis is an assessment of the natural and cultural resources of the corridor. The concept plan defines goals and objectives and sets a recommended program of actions that will be further refined at the master plan stage. The greenway master plan will most likely be a professionally prepared document that includes a layout of improvements, the specific parcels for acquisition, standards and specifications for such facilities as trails, and detailed cost estimates.

Depending on the complexity of your project and the type of planning assistance you receive, these stages can be further broken down. For our purposes, we will focus on these three stages. Keep in mind that no planning approach is written in stone. The results of the inventory and analysis will largely determine your strategy and how detailed and formal the actual plans will be. Some greenways proceed directly from vision statement to final plan; others, such as the Platte River Greenway, were planned one segment at a time; and some, like the Stowe Recreation Path, were developed without a formal plan.

The entire planning process is illustrated in Figure 2-1; please refer to this chart as you proceed through the process. Because public involvement plays such a key role in greenway development, the first half of this chapter outlines some guiding principles about how best to involve the community in the planning process.

Involving the Public in Greenway Planning

In most successful greenways, local residents assisted in the planning and decision-making process. In some cases, they completed the plan from start to finish. In professional jargon this is called *participatory planning* and is an essential part of greenway development.

Involving local residents in greenway planning gives you the opportunity to build a solid base of support for your project. Through continuous involvement, the public has an opportunity to become invested in the plan and to work for its success. Generally, once people learn the merits of greenways, they become supporters.

As you begin to work with the public, you need to resolve three fundamental issues: (1) Who needs to be involved in the planning process? (2) How should they be involved? (3) At what point should they become involved? Note also that the level of public participation will depend on the project. For example, trails across public land will require less input than those that may involve easements on or through private land.

"Public participation was the driving force behind the creation of the Hudson River Greenway Plan. Over the course of two years, seventeen public hearings were held. In 1990 alone, staff spoke to over 100 groups, ranging from local elementary schools to chambers of commerce. A written report was modified further after public review. The Report to the Governor ttruly represented the input of the residents of the valley."
—David Sampson, Executive Director, Hudson River Valley Greenway Commission.

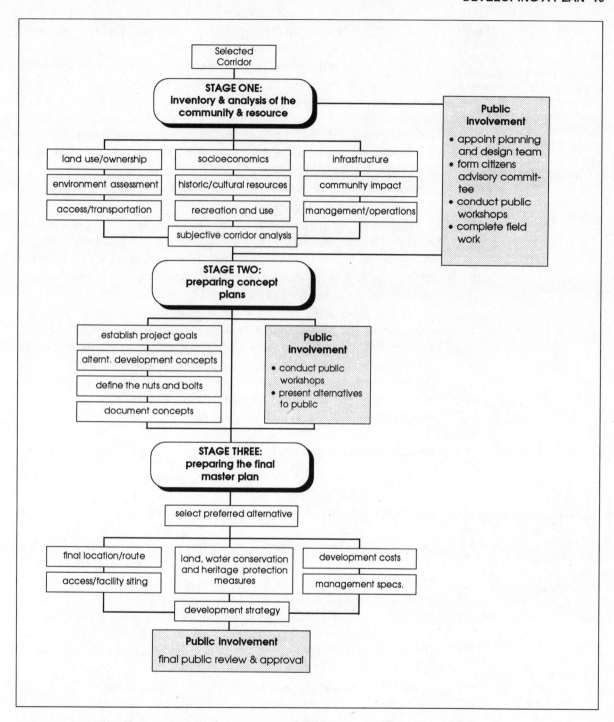

Figure 2-1 The greenway planning process.

Determining Who Should Be Involved

Even if a group of local citizens and agency personnel developed the plan, the time comes when more diverse input is needed. Who are the people who need to be involved? Why? What do you need from them? What are you prepared to offer them? How long should they remain

"Early on, the Stowe Recreation Path Coordinator listed all necessary permits and systematically acquired them. Permits were needed for crossing a road and installing bridges. In applying for permits, expect a 'domino effect'—once you've been approved for one permit, you're clear to apply for another."
—Anne Lusk in Parks and Recreation, January 1989

involved? The answers to these questions will vary from community to community, but some guidelines can be offered.

Always involve those individuals or organizations that are directly affected by the proposed greenway, especially local landowners and businesses. It is important to get the support of neighborhood associations, which tend to carry much weight at the local level. Invite all interested persons to join the planning process, and make sure that they are always notified of meetings at which critical decisions will be made about the route of the greenway.

Others to involve include conservationists, recreationists, and outdoor enthusiasts; staff from local, state, and federal agencies who might be responsible for approving, funding, or managing the proposed greenway; police, fire, and emergency medical officials; representatives from local schools, colleges, and universities; utility companies; private interest groups and nonprofit organizations; and local civic organizations, service clubs, and scouting groups.

Within your community there are people skilled in law, architecture, engineering, the physical sciences, land-use planning, design, construction, medicine, education, conservation, and art. Seek out those who can contribute to the planning process and future development of your greenway. Also involve potential funders; getting them involved at the beginning of the process not only makes them aware of your efforts but could earn their respect and future support.

How to Involve the Public

There are several ways to involve local residents. First, ask them to serve as a member of the *greenway planning and design team*: a working committee that researches and collects relevant information, conducts field work, writes the planning text, draws up necessary maps, sends out meeting notices, and sets up meeting rooms. Committee members need to complete an accurate assessment of existing resources, determine accurate planning and design recommendations, and make intelligent and easy-to-understand presentations about the proposed greenway project. To do so requires a working knowledge of real property and public access and use laws and a familiarity with the basic principles of land-use planning, engineering, conservation, and public policy.

"One important note about these meetings. In every town there is a room where town business is conducted, where the table faces a lot of chairs, where angry voices have been heard. I did not have the meetings in that room. We met in a pleasant setting, sometimes in a home; we sat anywhere that was comfortable, drank coffee and tea, and at home-baked cookies."
—Anne Lusk, "Greenway in Vermont," Parks and Recreation, June 1989

Another effective method for getting the public involved is to form a *greenway planning advisory committee*. Members may not necessarily have the technical expertise required for planning and design, but they can advise you on social, political, and economic issues. The committee should reflect the larger community and include elected officials, representatives from civic, minority, and special interest groups (for example, outdoor enthusiasts, the physically challenged), members of the business and education communities, real-estate agents, and members of philanthropic, arts, and science organizations.

Most importantly, include potential opponents. These people often have legitimate concerns and, if willing to devote the time and effort, can be a valuable asset. Avoid opponents who are not capable of offering constructive criticism or who are ideologically opposed to any public ownership of property.

When recruiting members for the advisory committee, make clear that this is a "working," not a "judge and jury," committee. In other words, members should not expect to simply voice approval or disapproval of what is being proposed. Instead, their role is to:

1. review the recommendations of the planning and design team on such issues as routing, location, and design details (such as the style of fencing, the color of benches, and the type of trail surface) and evaluate recommendations, concerns, and criticisms about the greenway;

2. define funding, implementation, and management strategies;

3. discuss land-acquisition strategies that might involve local landowners, businesses, government agencies, and land trusts;

4. formulate marketing and promotion ideas for the greenway;

5. promote land stewardship activities to protect and preserve sensitive habitats, unique landscapes, and historic resources.

This level of involvement will help your overall greenway planning effort and should also convince opponents that they *do* have a voice in how the greenway will be created. Most importantly, committees involve a range of different types of people and help build a broad base of knowledge and support for the greenway.

Both the greenway planning and design team and the greenway planning advisory committee should be limited to about twelve people. For planning purposes, larger committees grow unwieldy and have difficulty achieving consensus. (If you want to include more people, form smaller subcommittees).

Committees should be organized early in the planning process and meet as often as necessary. Try to complete the planning process in six to twelve months. Maintaining focus longer than a year is difficult. At times, a committee's life span is limited to the planning process. In other cases, an advisory committee will continue to meet through the development stage and may be involved in managing the greenway.

Decision Making. Invariably with participatory planning, someone will join the process in the middle or final stages and request that a topic that was resolved in stage one be discussed again. Accurately recording group decisions can help to avoid rehashing subjects that have already been resolved.

Providing closure to an issue is the most difficult aspect of participatory planning. We recommend that you either (a) vote on specific issues, or (b) achieve group consensus. Voting can take place openly or through secret ballot. Although it does reach a decision, voting can cause hard feelings or discomfort for local citizens who are trying to work through unchartered waters. Also, it is difficult to reverse a bad vote. With

In Vermont, the Chittenden County Greenway plan emerged from a four-week planning charrette in 1990. During the first two weeks, ten local workshops were held to identify routes and connections. After consolidation and review, the plan was presented at a public meeting and enthusiastically approved. The plan calls for a three-hundred-mile network of bike paths and foot trails and "conservation corridors" interconnecting neighborhoods, schools, parks, and workplaces in that region.

Participatory Planning Techniques

Listening

Listening promotes understanding. Understanding another person's point of view can be the most difficult aspect of participatory planning. This relates equally to face-to-face meetings with landowners, talking to corporate donors, and evaluating concerns raised at a public hearing. It's essential that you allow people enough time to respond, give them your full attention, and show that you can understand their perspective—even if you don't agree with it.

Brainstorming

Brainstorming usually occurs within small groups of up to fifteen persons. Participants offer whatever ideas come to mind, without subjecting each to analysis. This stream-of-consciousness method can produce some ground-breaking approaches that might have been dismissed under critical scrutiny.

Research Assignments

Research assignments give participants time to thoroughly think through an issue, problem, or recommendation, conduct research, and provide an informed response. These assignments are especially useful early in the planning stage, when people need time to familiarize themselves with complex new topics or to catch up to more experienced members.

Role Playing

Role playing is often useful when opponents need to better understand and appreciate other points of view. With role playing, participants become, in effect, actors and trade sides. They can state opinions and express difficulties they might not otherwise have recognized. A skilled facilitator is needed to orchestrate the process and keep the dialogue on track.

Charrettes

A charrette is an intensive two-, three-, or four-day work session in which individuals, usually qualified professionals, quickly assemble and assimilate essential data, conduct a brief overview of site conditions, define development scenarios, and develop a plan of action for greenway development. Charrettes are effective when time is limited and a quick but professional resolution to a problem is needed.

"Develop a concept. Test it with friends. Refine it. Get a core support grtoup. Present the idea to the public. Fundraise. Go for it. The work will never end."
—San Juan Island Greenway

consensus, by agreeing to a set of fundamental principles rather than a right or wrong policy, both sides achieve a bit of victory. Fence riders are likely to feel comfortable with the results. You can build consensus by stating the extreme viewpoints and then working back to a middle ground until all parties agree that an acceptable position has been achieved.

Public Meetings. An ongoing series of public meetings and one-on-one discussions with community leaders is a must. Public meetings should be structured with an agenda and a capable meeting leader, but they should also be open so that all participants feel that they can make their comments heard and help shape the process.

Be sure people are informed about meetings. Many city, county, and regional planning agencies keep mailing lists of government agencies, homeowners' associations, conservation groups, bicycle clubs, and others. Use these lists to contact interested people, and be sure your greenway organization is on the mailing list as well. It is important to be working with these various interest groups before, during, and after the planning phase.

Whenever you have a meeting on the greenway, bring drawings, reports, photos, or slides that easily describe your greenway. Be careful not to identify individual parcels of land unless you have already secured an easement or purchased it.

Public Workshops. Another method of involvement is the public workshop. In workshop settings, members of the public are invited to learn about the greenway through a formal presentation made by greenway advocates and then are asked to provide their opinions and recommendations about the proposal. Workshops are different from public hearings or public meetings in that the audience is asked to actively participate in decision making (see Figure 2-2).

Workshops should be open to everyone, regardless of greenway persuasion. Workshops usually should be held after you and your committees have put together substantial information about the project. You don't want to conduct a workshop with too little information; on the other hand, you don't want to overwhelm the public with too much technical information. The best time to hold a workshop depends on the circumstances of your greenway. Many groups find it helpful to

- Determine the most convenient time for your meeting. Try to avoid important dates like holidays, elections, or other public agency meetings.
- Arrange to hold meetings at a centrally located facility. School auditorium, town and church halls, and libraries are all possible sites.
- Prepare materials such as agendas, outlines, surveys, or worksheets to be distributed before the meeting begins.
- Provide refreshments and breaks, especially if you are conducting a longer workshop or seminar.
- Arrive early for your meeting. This will allow you to arrange the room and set up. This is also a good time to meet and talk with people as they arrive, which can help both you and the audience to relax.
- Rearrange the seating to accommodate your meeting format. For example, a semicircular arrangement can help involve people in a discussion.

Acceptable Arrangement of Tables and Chairs for Public Meetings - Small Groups

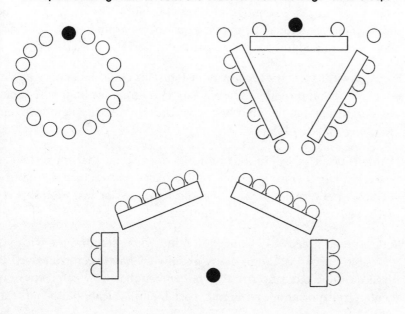

Figure 2-2 How to set up a public meeting room.

conduct workshops to review the completed resource inventory, the draft concept plan, and the draft final master plan.

Field Work. A final way to involve the public is through field work. Field work consists of data collection, inventory of natural and cultural resources, soil analysis, on-site evaluation of route alternatives, tours of successful greenways in other communities, presentations, investigation of land ownership, and similar activities. Several additional techniques can be used to actively engage the public in the greenway planning process (see the box on page 22 on participatory planning techniques).

Defining a Study Corridor for the Greenway

For most greenways, the resource corridor is a river, a community- or region-wide system of waterways, an abandoned railroad corridor or canal, a utility right-of-way, a mountain ridge line, or an ecologically sensitive landscape. The land may be publicly or privately owned. How do you begin to gauge the full value of the land in its present condition and define its potential for use as a greenway? What is a reasonable length of corridor to consider?

Defining the length and width of your greenway corridor is the first major hurdle to clear. We recommend that you define a broad area of land as a *corridor of study* for the greenway. For local communities, these study areas can be as wide as a thousand feet or more. For regional and statewide greenways, such as the Hudson River Valley Greenway, the study area can be several miles wide and many miles long (see Figure 2-3). For interstate greenways this corridor might be as wide as fifty miles. There are no exact, scientific specifications to apply, but you should use the following criteria:

1. Select a corridor large enough to allow flexibility. The route should be only generally defined to allow adjustments from public feedback and to accommodate any possible donation of land or easement.

2. Focus on your primary greenway vision. This could be to save an endangered plant, provide a place where people can walk, link regional parks to residential neighborhoods, or prevent development from encroaching into floodplains.

3. Define a point of origin and point of destination that make logical sense. Usually this involves selecting a major natural or built feature, such as a park, major stream or river, roadway, or historic property that is known to most of your community.

4. Keep a broad greenways concept in mind when defining the width of your study area. Although many greenways have been conceived to serve outdoor recreation needs, remember that they offer environmental, transportation, economic, social, and educational benefits as well.

In Guilford County, North Carolina, the Bicentennial Greenway begins at the historic Guilford Courthouse National Military Park and traverses urban and rural landscapes to the High Point City Lake Park, sixteen miles south. Since most of the land was in private ownership, local greenway advocates defined a broad study corridor along the length. The corridor is being refined, designed, and developed in small manageable segments.

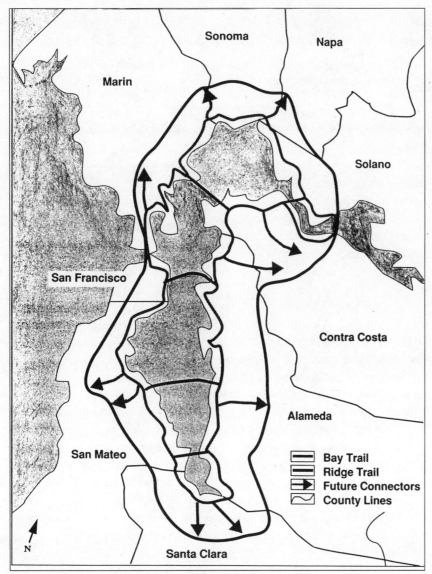

Figure 2-3 San Francisco's Bay and Ridge Trail System, an example of a multiple origin and destination, circular greenway system. (Map courtesy of Charles E. Little.)

Bay Trail
Ridge Trail
Future Connectors
County Lines

"[Here is an example of] the early process for the Greenway to the Pacific (200 linear miles; half by land and half by water). The first step is to overlay maps showing all opportunities for acquisitions or easements:
•Utility ownerships and easements
•Railroad abandonments and existing rights-of-way
•State Forest ownership
•Wildlife sanctuaries and other points of interest
•Water corridors and land owned and managed by ports (e.g., Port of Portland, Longview, and Astoria) for camping and support for designated canoe corridor
•Dikes and dike management areas
•Large landownerships (timber companies)
•Little-used and abandoned roads in timber areas (both private and public)
•Any already designated land as nonbuildable for any reason
•Whatever else we think of along the way."
—Al Edelman, Board Member, Greenway to the Pacific

5. Base the corridor length and width on what you honestly believe you, your organization, and the community can realistically evaluate. This chapter will help you gauge what your group is capable of doing.

Preparing a Base Map of the Study Corridor

To illustrate the size and scope of your project, you will need to produce a base map. The most economical way to do this is to contact the nearest office of the U. S. Geologic Survey (USGS) and describe the length and width of your study area. The USGS can then supply you with the necessary topographic maps. These maps may also be available through a local, regional, or state planning agency, a professional blueprinter, or a

---

How to Contact the U. S. Geologic Survey

The U.S. Geologic Survey is normally listed in metropolitan telephone directories under Department of the Interior. By mail, write to:

U. S. Geologic Survey
Reston, Virginia 22092
or Denver, Colorado 80225

---

college or university. USGS maps are prepared at different scales; the one most applicable to your needs is the 1 inch to 24,000 inches, referred to as the 7.5 Minute Series Topographic. In addition to topographic information, these maps illustrate streams, rivers, lakes, major wetlands, roads, buildings, vegetative cover, and the location of major utility lines, railroad corridors, towns, cemeteries, and major historic, cultural, and recreational properties.

To make permanent and long-term use of the maps, spend a little extra money and ask a blueprinter to transfer the greenway study area onto a sheet of Mylar (transparent plastic material). The blueprinter can also enlarge or reduce the scale of the map. The Mylar map provides you with a high quality, durable original, which can be reproduced hundreds of times onto blueline print paper.

It may have been some time since your area was mapped by the USGS, so the information on your map may be slightly out of date. Survey as much of the study area as you can without trespassing on private property, and update the map. Once you are sure of the location of all additions or alterations, you can update the Mylar original.

Use your base map to work with your advisory committee, to share ideas with other organizations, and to discuss options with landowners whose property you would like to include in the greenway.

Inventory and Analysis

After you have completed the base map and defined the study area, you enter the first major stage of planning: the evaluation of physical, cultural, political, and socioeconomic characteristics of the corridor. This *inventory and analysis* will provide you with the information you need to set the parameters of your greenway. The information you collect should be based on available facts, not hearsay or supposition. For example, instead of assuming that everyone will welcome a greenway, conduct an informal opinion survey of key property owners, local officials, and important organizations to determine the degree of support or opposition present in your community.

After completing the evaluation, you should know the major physical features of the corridor, which government regulations apply, who owns the land, and whether or not the properties are of historic or natural significance. You also will have examined available financial resources, long-term management obligations, and potential alliances with other organizations. This information will help you determine how best to secure or protect the land, design trails and other facilities, and market and manage the greenway. It will also serve as an educational tool for the community.

Inventory and analysis is a critical first step in greenway planning: it lays the foundation for your plan. A qualified consultant can conduct the entire assessment, but a full-scale inventory may be quite expensive if done by professionals. Your group can save money by doing some of the groundwork. To encourage you to complete as much of the inventory and analysis as possible, we have provided a thorough list of what should be assessed and some recommendations for whom to contact for assistance, if needed. Generally, on low-budget projects (for example, a simple foot trail), you probably won't need as detailed an inventory assessment as on more complex, highly developed projects. Do keep in mind that you are trying to build a defensible argument for your greenway.

How to Conduct an Inventory and Analysis

Ideally, your inventory should be conducted during different seasons of the year (if appropriate) and under various weather conditions. For example, in the winter and late fall, you can usually view the topography, geological formations, soils, adjacent buildings, and the overall character of the landscape without obstruction. You should do the same once trees and shrubs have fully leafed out; you may be amazed at how different the landscape appears. One of the best times to evaluate drainage patterns is just after—or during—a heavy rain.

To help you keep track of all the necessary inventory and analysis elements, use the Greenway Data Checklist shown in Figure 2-4. Make sure that you carefully record the information that you collect. Use a tape recorder for personal dictation and group discussions, a notebook with clipboard, and a camera that uses 35-mm film. Working in pairs is generally safer and more efficient. If your field survey is conducted in a rural area, take local hunting seasons into consideration and always obtain the landowner's permission before stepping on private property and alert officials in advance of your visit.

Land Use and Ownership. The first question to ask in evaluating a proposed greenway corridor is: Who owns the land? Is it publicly or privately owned? Use your base map to highlight those parcels of land already in public ownership, and look for a pattern that suggests the best route for the greenway. Although it's best to begin with public land, do not assume that it is automatically ideal for the greenway. The public agency that owns the land may have different ideas about further use of the land.

Land ownership information is usually available from your local property tax assessor's office. The county recorder's office maintains records of deeds, easements, mortgages, and other title encumbrances referenced by name of grantors and grantees. The county assessor's office can provide tax maps that show the approximate ownership of parcels

The Rhode Island Department of Planning's "greenspace" spatial analysis identifies and maps open space areas where many important landscape features overlap. This Geographic Information System technology overlays thirteen "datasets" corresponding to six open space themes: water resources, hazard lands, forest resources, agricultural resources, rare species and wildlife, and recreational and cultural resources. Additional data on local greenways, nineteenth-century urban parkways, scenic highways, and proposed hiking or bicycling facilities further identify the state's potential greenway network. Rhode Island's resulting greenways concept plan will be revised, based on local review.

Greenway Inventory Checklist

Project Name: Date:

Description:

Land Ownership:
- [ ] Current use of land
- [ ] Zoning/types of use permitted
- [ ] Location of property lines
- [ ] Impact of greenway - current land use, ownership, activity
- [ ] Contact made with property owner

Environmental Assessment:
- [ ] Vegetation - species variety, size, growth habit, age, health
- [ ] Geology - landform type, composition, suitability
- [ ] Soils - type, composition, suitability
- [ ] Hydrology - drainage, water table, streams, tributaries, ponds, wells, springs, urban influence, wetlands
- [ ] Topography - steepness or flatness, longitudinal slope vs. cross-sectional slope
- [ ] Significant natural features - rare/endangered, unique, landmark
- [ ] Wildlife - species, nesting grounds, migratory routes, food sources
- [ ] Climate - wind, sun angle, exposure, rainfall

Access and Transportation:
- [ ] Existing access - motorized, nonmotorized, water-based
- [ ] Desired access - location, type
- [ ] Existing transportation within site - type, purpose, size
- [ ] Existing transportation available to & from site - types, purposes, sizes, relationships to each other
- [ ] Intersections - types, level of safety/danger, crossing type needed
- [ ] Relationship of greenway to existing transportation corridors - physical dimensions, traffic volume, noise, views

Figure 2-4 Greenway inventory checklist. This form is used to ensure that all critical elements have been examined when conducting the evaluation, inventory, and analysis of a greenway corridor.

and who owns them. These maps will usually do for planning purposes, but they are not precise. (This research can easily be done by volunteers.)

After you have learned the name of the public or private property owner, answer the following questions:

1. What is the current land use for the parcels you are evaluating? Is it agricultural, residential, industrial, or is it used for some other activity?

☐ Future transportation plans - expansions, modifications, additions
☐ Mass transit - linkage, mutual benefits

Socioeconomic Analysis:
☐ Political subdivision/jurisdictions regulating greenway
☐ Governing laws/regulations
☐ Organization of support - primary support, supplemental support
☐ Organizations in opposition - concerns, critical problems, & issues
☐ Fiscal resources/constraints - who, how much, additional resources
☐ Community events - types, times, additional desired events

Historic & Cultural Resources:
☐ Historic - National Register listings, components of historic districts
☐ Cultural - local, regional, national

Community Recreation:
☐ Inventory of community recreation activities and programs
☐ Providers - local government, private for-profit, nonprofit groups
☐ Facilities - types, location, capacity, usage
☐ Recreation needs assessment - critical needs greenway can satisfy
☐ Facility needs - develop greenway in conjunction w/ other facilities

Public/Private Infrastructure:
☐ Existing utilities - both within & around greenway: water, sanitary
    sewer, electricity, cable TV, fiber optic, telephone, natural gas,
    storm sewer
☐ Future utility plans - expansions, additions, possibility for installment
    or right-of-access fees
☐ Utility providers & operators - supporters or opponents in terms of
    maintenance, financial support, access
☐ The greenway as a utility - easement widths, ability for joint use

Community Impact:
☐ Physical impact - type, location, affect on community
☐ Cultural/social impact - opportunities, problems
☐ Economic opportunities - types, dollars, timeframe, who will benefit

Figure 2-4 (*continued*)

2. What land uses are permitted on the parcel or parcels of land that you are evaluating?

3. Is the land zoned for a particular use?

4. In your opinion, what impact would the greenway have on the land's current use or owner? How does the landowner feel about your assessment of the impact? You should make every effort to meet with the landowner to describe the greenway vision. This meeting should not be scheduled, however, until you have obtained enough

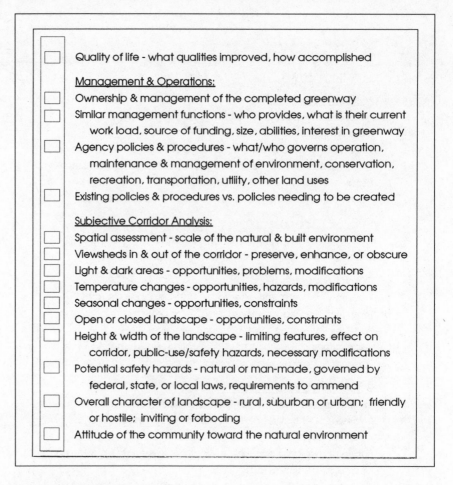

Figure 2-4 (*continued*)

information to engage in a productive discussion and to address the landowner's concerns; for example, be prepared to answer questions about maintenance, crime, and liability.

5. How will current land use affect natural resources found on or near the targeted property?

You can find the answers to most of these questions from your local planning agency. It has information on local land use and zoning and can help you assess the impact of the greenway on the parcel of land in question. Talking to a successful greenway or conservation group in your area can also provide valuable information. Real-estate appraisers can help you determine the market value of the property.

Environmental Assessment. An environmental assessment involves a careful examination of the physical features of the landscape, including the soil, geology, vegetation, water, climate, and animal life. Many types of environmental assessment exist for greenway planning and development. The level of environmental assessment we recommend meets the basic requirements of local, state, and federal agencies. (If your greenway receives state or federal funding, you may have to conduct a more thorough environmental assessment.) Environmental assessments fulfill three major objectives:

1. to conduct a descriptive on-site inventory that defines the natural features and attributes of the landscape within and immediately adjacent to the greenway;

2. to speak with experts to determine if the ecological systems within and surrounding the greenway are capable of supporting the activities you propose; and

3. to determine what environmental or development permits are required to alter the land use or character of the greenway corridor.

Environmental assessments should always list and describe the natural features within the greenway. Collecting and properly interpreting this information is critical to determining whether the environment can support public access and use. Issues typically addressed include:

1. *Vegetation.* Identify plant species, including evidence of disease and the location and number of species and plant communities. Aerial photographs are a good method for defining the limits of vegetative growth (for example, conifers versus deciduous trees; wetlands versus dry lands; open space versus agricultural land), but field work is required to identify dominant species. A botanist, horticulturalist, forester, or landscape architect can identify native vegetation found within the greenway. Endangered species units, native plant societies, and state natural heritage programs can help identify sensitive biological features.

2. *Geology.* Geology includes the identification of rock and landform type, its age and formation, and an analysis of the capacity of the land to support prolonged public use. You should also identify areas of special geographic interest. A professional geologist can correctly assess and interpret these characteristics, although you may be able to use local or state geological surveys or geology maps prepared by the USGS. You can also enlist the help of staff in the local U. S. Soil Conservation Service office or a local geological society.

3. *Soils.* The issue of soils includes the identification of the soil layer by type, development potential, and engineering properties. Your local Soil Conservation Service office usually has a soil survey for your community, as well as charts rating the soils according to their suitability for agricultural use, wildlife habitat, and development. The charts also detail such soil limitations as permeability, shrink-swell capacity, and composition.

4. *Hydrology.* Hydrology addresses the identification, for example, of drainage patterns and capacity, watersheds, wetlands, water quality, stream-bank erosion, and signs of urban stress. You must evaluate both on-site and off-site drainage patterns; one of the major issues is the potential for flooding within the corridor. The USDA's Soil

Conservation Service or Cooperative Extension Service can help, or you can work with a hydrologist or hydraulic engineer. The Federal Emergency Management Agency also provides detailed maps illustrating the floodplain of most major streams and rivers in the country. The USGS can also provide a hydrologic atlas that includes mapping of groundwater and surface water for certain regions of the country. State agencies may have prepared wetlands maps or have available maps prepared by federal agencies such as the U.S. Fish and Wildlife Service's National Wetlands Inventory. The public health department or a local chapter of Save Our Streams, organized by the Izaak Walton League of America, may be able to help you assess water quality.

5. *Topography.* Topography is the determination of the slope or fall of the land within the corridor. There are two primary types of slopes to be concerned with: the cross slope, from one side of the corridor to the other, and the longitudinal slope, from one end of the corridor to the other. Slopes of 5 percent or less are considered to be flat; slopes between 5 and 15 percent are considered rolling terrain or moderate; and slopes of 15 percent and greater are hilly, mountainous, and severe. The USGS maps or the Cooperative Extension Service can help you identify the slopes present within your greenway, or you can work with a professional land surveyor or landscape architect.

6. *Wildlife.* The issue of wildlife is concerned with the identification of the different types of wildlife present within the corridor, the location of nesting and breeding grounds, and the existence and location of animal trails or migratory and movement routes. Does the corridor landscape function as an essential migratory stop for certain species? Is the corridor the only available route? Are endangered or threatened species present? The U. S. Fish and Wildlife Service, your state wildlife office or natural heritage program, or a local wildlife biologist or nature center are best qualified to assist you in this regard. You may also be able to enlist the help of local naturalists, birdwatchers, and hunters.

7. *Microclimate.* The identification of wind patterns, sun exposure, the amount of rainfall, and local temperature within the greenway corridor falls within the area of microclimate. These factors influence the natural features within the corridor. If greenway development significantly alters these conditions, the resource you seek to protect could be lost. Contact a qualified climatologist at the nearest college or university or through your Cooperative Extension Service for relevant statistics.

Access and Transportation. The extent of public access is an important variable that must be defined for each greenway project. It will depend on (a) the degree of accessibility you desire, (b) the capacity of the corridor landscape to absorb the impact of human use, and (c) the accessibility of the corridor to a variety of potential users.

Accessibility involves both access to the greenway and transportation through the greenway. If you are applying for public funding, there may be certain access requirements you must comply with. The best resource for information on community-wide access and transportation will be your local department of transportation. For information on a specific property, check the deed restrictions on the property title at the office of the clerk and recorder (also called the register of deeds). Public rights-of-way, easements, and other public access information should be thoroughly described in the deed.

Access. You need to know what type of access currently exists within the corridor. This will determine how and where you will legally be able to access the property with trails and maintenance vehicles. Access can be divided into four types: pedestrian (including disabled); vehicular (motorized and nonmotorized); water-based (nonmotorized water craft and motor boats); and other (for example, equestrians, roller-bladers, cross-country skiers, and balloonists).

Transportation. Defining the way people and vehicles will move around and through the proposed greenway is also important. You will want to determine the type of transportation, if any, that currently exists: Whom do these transportation corridors serve? How might the greenway enhance the existing transportation system? What type of transportation system can and should the greenway support? If, for example, the greenway will be accessed by cars, tour buses, or other motorized vehicles, parking and the impact of paving on the area will need to be considered. In order to answer these and other questions, complete the following steps:

1. Locate existing or proposed bicycle paths, sidewalks, or trail systems in your community and see if these systems can be linked with your greenway project.

2. Determine any potential intersection with existing transportation or utility corridors and the level of danger present between existing or proposed uses. Note the sight distance, regulated design speed, length of crossing, and so on. Together, these factors will determine the type of crossing that you will need to design.

3. Determine future transportation plans. Are new roads planned within the study area? If so, can underpasses or overpasses be secured? Are any other expansions or modifications to existing roadways planned?

4. Determine whether any of the transportation corridors provide for mass transit. How does this relate to your proposed greenway? Can you secure funding from the transportation department for the improvements?

Socioeconomics. The success of a greenway depends on the way in which political, legal, and financial issues in a community are addressed. The following factors should be thoroughly evaluated.

Political Subdivision/Jurisdiction. Determine who the governing jurisdictions are in your community and how the elected officials of these

Hixson, Tennessee, near Chattanooga, is one of the fastest growing areas in the state. North Chickamauga Creek, a prized local asset with clean water and many recreation possibilities, winds through the community before joining the Tennessee River. The North Chickamauga Creek greenway plan focuses on eight miles of the creek. Conservation easements will provide access for trail-based recreation or will be implemented purely for the protection of riparian lands. Tennessee Valley Authority land serves as the southern terminus of the greenway and transition to a proposed twenty-mile River Park.

jurisdictions have reacted in the past to environmental, conservation, transportation, recreation, and utility issues. Which jurisdiction governs land-use decisions for the greenway property? Are there community associations, homeowners' organizations, or citizens' groups that have influence in the community and should therefore be included in the planning process? Most of this information can be obtained from the local municipal clerk, alderman, or mayor's office. Back issues of the local newspaper can also provide valuable insight into the community's political climate. Find out whether a similar effort or proposal has been made in the past. If so, what was the reaction?

Increasingly, greenways are being developed across political boundaries. If your study area encompasses more than one political jurisdiction, you will need to identify all applicable governing agencies.

Governing Laws/Regulations. Numerous laws regulate wetlands, air quality, water quality, land use, soil erosion, and waste disposal, all of which affect greenway planning and development. You will need to identify local laws that apply to your project. Your local planning agency, municipal clerk, or municipal attorney can provide you with copies of applicable laws and regulations. Determining appropriate state and federal laws may prove more difficult; ask local officials for information or contacts.

Also consider how laws might help or hinder your proposed greenway. For example, new storm-water discharge laws mandate buffers between the discharge point, such as a storm sewer outlet, and a natural stream channel. Greenways can provide the required vegetated buffer and can be promoted as an effective way to satisfy this federal requirement. Vegetated greenway buffers can also help reduce pollution of local streams, and by functioning as an alternative commuter route for pedestrians and bicyclists, greenways can reduce automobile travel and improve air quality.

Organizations in Support. Determine who the likely greenway supporters are. Are community leaders involved? How strong is their support? Are supporters members of a public agency, a corporation, or a nonprofit organization? Can they enlist other support? Are there other greenways within your community, neighboring community, or state that you can approach? Likely supporters include local environmental and conservation groups, land trusts, and such recreation groups as bicycling and fishing clubs or running organizations.

Organizations or Individuals in Opposition. You should always determine who is, or might be, opposed to the greenway. Are they local citizens? What are their concerns? Are they idealogues connected with some group that has written laws or policies against greenways? Are they speculators with a hidden agenda? Is the opposition interested in resolving differences? Are their concerns valid?

As with individual landowners, you should meet with those opposed to the greenway early in the planning process to explain the purpose, function, and long-term objectives of your project. Again, however, it is best to wait until you have properly prepared an accurate and thorough analysis of all relevant information so that you can explain and defend the greenway.

Fiscal Resources/Constraints. Define the financial resources that are available for the project. What are the financial constraints? Whom can you count on to financially support the greenway—a public agency, a for-profit group, or a nonprofit organization? Can you leverage these funds to obtain other financial support? For example, if you obtain seed money from your local municipality, can you use this to secure other funds from private donors, state agencies, or federal programs?

Community Events. Familiarize yourself with any local events that might generate support for your greenway. Are there events at the regional, state, or national level that might be adopted by your community to support the greenway? For example, in High Point, North Carolina, the local greenways committee began sponsoring a "Greenway Day" a year before the ground-breaking ceremony for its pilot project. The committee also set up a community-wide High Point Greenway Trust Fund. Attending Greenway Day and investing in the greenway system have now become community traditions.

Historic and Cultural Resources. America's waterways, rail corridors, and trails are rich in history. Greenways provide an opportunity to protect not only these corridors, but also historic settlements, transportation routes and artifacts, and other remnants of an earlier age. If you are fortunate enough to locate historic and cultural resources on the land you are evaluating, you should check to see if these are currently listed or eligible for inclusion in the National Register of Historic Places. Are they part of a historic district within your community? Are they of historic significance to the local community but not officially registered? Might these resources be of national significance? If so, they could be considered for congressional designation as a Heritage Corridor.

To answer these questions, consult local sources such as the library, community newspaper, historic preservation organization or agency, or the town historian. Other sources of information include elderly residents of your community, former owners of the properties involved, the U. S. Department of the Interior, the National Trust for Historic Preservation, and local colleges or universities.

Recreation Resources. Greenways are often associated with outdoor recreation. Unless you are planning an ecological greenway with limited human access, you should conduct an inventory of recreation activities and programs within your community, to determine the following:

1. Who are the local recreation providers: government agencies, private for-profit groups, and/or nonprofit organizations?

2. What recreation facilities exist in or near the proposed greenway? What is their capacity and usage?

3. Has the local parks and recreation department, or other organization, completed a recreation needs assessment, and if so, what are the critical recreation needs of the community? Other studies, such as trail

linkage plans or bicycle trail plans may already exist. Can the greenway satisfy some of these needs?

The best source of information on recreation programming and activities is your local parks and recreation department. If you need information on standards for recreation planning, design, or implementation, refer to your State Comprehensive Outdoor Recreation Plan, which is available through the local parks department or state parks agency. The National Recreation and Park Association in Washington, D.C., is also a good source of information for standards and trends.

Public–Private Infrastructure. You should also evaluate your greenway in terms of its ability to satisfy infrastructure needs. Infrastructure—electric, oil, and gas utilities; telephone service; water systems; and waste disposal—can make efficient joint use of land identified for a greenway.

The following list itemizes common infrastructures and their suitability to serve a dual greenway purpose:

1. *Sanitary sewer lines.* Sanitary sewer lines offer excellent joint-use potential; most sanitary sewer easements contain enough land area to accommodate greenway use.

2. *Water lines.* Standard commercial and residential service line easements are too narrow for greenways; however, major trunk service lines, from intake areas to treatment plants, are ideal for joint use.

3. *Electrical lines.* Although there is some concern about the health effects of electromagnetic fields on humans, cross-country transmission lines can be ideal for joint use.

4. *Cable TV.* Cable television easements are generally too small and not well located for greenways.

5. *Fiber optic cable.* Joint-use is possible if the easement is wide enough.

6. *Telephone.* Standard residential or commercial service easements can be too narrow or poorly located for joint use. An exception: AT&T and the state of Washington recently cooperated to create a greenway along an old railroad line right-of-way that crosses the Cascade Mountains and accommodates a cross-country telecommunications line.

7. *Oil and Natural Gas.* Oil and natural gas easements are ideal for joint use. Because they are highly flammable and high-pressure products, however, you must exercise extreme caution when working near the transmission lines. Any disturbance of the right-of-way surface must be approved by the company and the surface landowner.

8. *Storm sewers.* Storm sewers offer an excellent joint-use opportunity, especially given the new National Pollutant Discharge Elimination System (NPDES) permits required by the Environmental Protection

Agency. NPDES requires communities of a certain size to deal with nonpoint contamination and provides funding.

You need to ask the following questions when inventorying for infrastructure resources:

- What type of infrastructure exists within or around the proposed greenway corridor?

- Who provides and operates this infrastructure? How do they feel about the proposed greenway? Can they use the greenway to complete required maintenance activities? Would they support its development financially?

- Are there plans to expand utility lines in your area?

- Can you charge an installment or right-of-access fee to a utility that wants access to the greenway corridor?

- Who owns the land on which the utility is located? Does the utility company own title, or was it granted an easement? (95 percent of rights-of-way easements for utilities are for subsurface use only. All access to and use of the surface is usually retained by the landowner.) If by easement, does the utility have the right of public access? If utility owned, has the utility granted easements already for other types of land use? Who would be liable in the event of public access and joint use of the easement?

The best source for this information would be the utility companies. You could start by approaching their public relations offices. You can also check with your local planning agency or the public works, engineering, and transportation departments for maps that show the routing and location of major utility lines within your community.

Impact of the Greenway on the Community. To understand the impact of a greenway on your community, you should begin by examining possible effects on the landscape.

1. What are the planned changes and where would they occur? How will these affect the character of the community?

2. Consider whether the greenway will resolve or create cultural and social problems. For example, can it reunite neighborhoods torn apart by highway projects and urban development?

3. Will the greenway create economic opportunities? What do you anticipate these might be, and who would benefit? Roughly how much money would be generated and what would be the time frame?

4. Will the greenway improve the quality of life for residents of the community? How? Will it provide educational opportunities?

The best way to predict the greenways's impact on your community is to talk it over with local residents, especially those who might be directly affected by it. Better yet, study a similar project in a surrounding community. Always look for ways in which the greenway can be linked with other community concerns and projects.

Additional Considerations. The greenway corridor must also be evaluated on the basis of the following considerations:

1. *Views within and ouside of the corridor.* Is the view appealing and, if so, will a greenway preserve and enhance it? If the view is unappealing, can the greenway obscure it? What views should be restricted or opened?

2. *Light and dark areas of the corridor.* Are there well-lit areas and dark spots within the corridor? Are these advantages, or do they pose problems for use and management of the corridor?

3. *Temperature changes within the corridor.* Are some areas warmer or cooler than others? Do they offer any advantages or do they pose safety concerns?

4. *Open or closed landscape.* Are there areas within the corridor where a person might feel closed in, or is the landscape open and expansive? Do these areas represent opportunities or problems?

5. *Height and width of the landscape.* What features limit the height and width of the corridor, for example, bridges or slopes? Can these features be modified? Do they pose safety hazards?

6. *Odor and noise.* Try to identify the odors and noises that emanate from adjacent lands. Are these offensive or pleasant? Do they pose a health hazard? Can they be eliminated?

7. *Sense of security.* Is the corridor a safe place for a wide range of greenway users? If not, can it be made more secure? Are the sight lines within the corridor unobstructed? Are there multiple entry and exit points between the corridor and adjacent public lands?

Long-Term Responsibilities. One of the most perplexing issues in creating a greenway is management of the completed project. You should find out who currently provides similar management services within your community. In most cases, management services are provided by your local parks and recreation or public works departments. Find out their current work load, source of funding, size (manpower, equipment), and abilities and whether or not they are interested in assuming management responsibilities for the greenway or if new policies and programs are needed.

Recording Your Inventory and Analysis

Accurately recording all of the information that you collect during the inventory and analysis can be daunting. Three basic methods can make this task more manageable: overlay mapping, recording field notes, and photographing the landscape.

Overlay mapping is a process that was made famous by landscape architect Ian McHarg in the 1960s. The underlying principle is to separate the environment into component parts, such as hydrology, vegetation, soils, and slope, and map the fundamental properties of each. In this manner, each resource can be evaluated independently or in combination with some or all other resources to more accurately define its relative importance.

The use of translucent plastic allows the maps to be overlaid to see the combined effects of the different resources. Most often, constraints to traditional forms of urban development are mapped on each individual resource map. When the maps are combined, the dark areas illustrate the most constrained or highly sensitive areas for development, the lighter areas indicate the least sensitive (see Figure 2-5).

Specially developed computer-aided drafting (CAD) systems enable you to generate overlay maps in two dimensions. Some communities have access to geographic information systems (GIS) that contain resource information that you may request. For example, Hudson River Valley communities will be able to tie into GIS capability provided by the Hudson River Greenway Council to enable better municipal greenway planning. If you are able to make use of CAD or GIS, it can save time and labor *if* the information entered into the computer is accurate and verifiable. GIS analysis is a useful way to identify possible regional greenway networks.

Field notes can be compiled in a number of different, sometimes sophisticated, ways. Although handwritten notes and laptop computers are useful, a voice recorder might be the easiest and most efficient way to record in the field. To begin, note the day, time of analysis, weather conditions, names of those accompanying you, work task to be performed, and other essential data. Cite where you are when making the notation. Your descriptions should correspond to points on the map.

Photographs of the landscape provide essential information in a permanent visual form. You can use either black-and-white or color film, but color photographs and slides are more appealing and more closely resemble actual conditions. Keep in mind, however, that many newspapers accept only black-and-white prints.

Following are some guiding principles on photographing greenways.

- Always use a person as a scale of reference when photographing a landscape element. When photographing a close-up of a small object, place an item of known length and size (such as a pencil or ruler) in the photo to serve as a frame of reference.

- It's often best to shoot on partly cloudy to overcast days; this will eliminate glare, minimize some shadows, and offer a less distorted representation of the landscape.

- Include a mix of close-ups, mid-range shots, and distant views of the resource; avoid too many photos that show the broad expanse of the landscape.

We recommend that you take both slides and prints. Use the slides in making presentations to large groups and the prints as working documents. If your group owns or has access to a video camera, videotapes offer perspective that still photos do not.

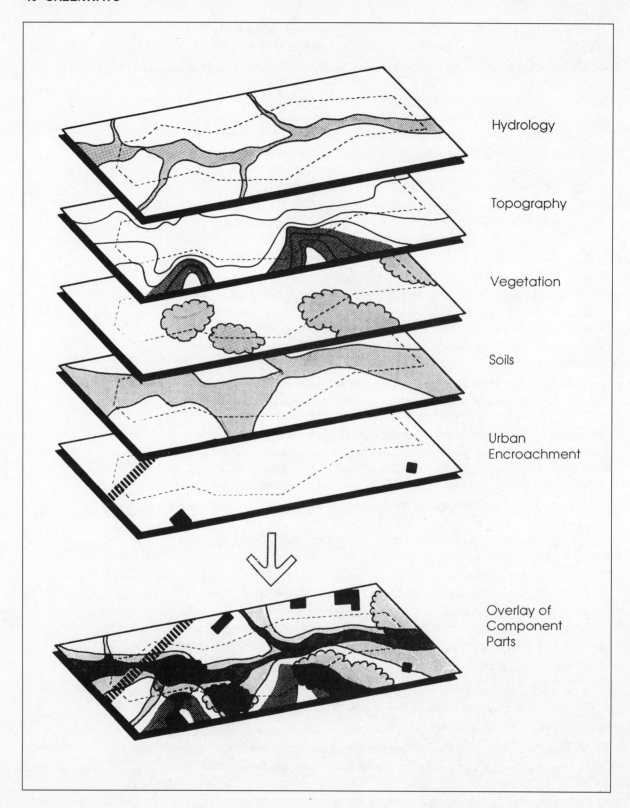

Hydrology

Topography

Vegetation

Soils

Urban Encroachment

Overlay of Component Parts

Figure 2-5 The overlay mapping technique.

Preparing the Concept Plan

When you have finished your inventory and analysis, you are ready to move on to the next critical stage of the planning process— the concept plan. Preparing the concept plan allows you to dream, make ambitious plans, and explore ideas before you work toward a final master plan.

There are two primary tasks that you and your group must complete in preparing a concept plan. The first is to establish a clear set of goals for your project; the second is to explore options or alternatives for the location, route, and development of the greenway. Both tasks should involve the larger community in the decision-making process.

The concept plan can be produced in several ways. You may have within your organization all of the necessary tools. Teaming up with a local government agency is another option. Agency staff from the parks, planning, engineering, transportation, and public works departments may be able to provide labor, materials, and ideas. Consultants with experience in greenway planning can provide objective, focused, and professional attention.

One of the most important elements of your concept plan will be a program that defines a course of action for greenways development. A *program* can be thought of as a series of tasks that your group and supporting organizations will complete to develop a greenway. For example, a program item might be to obtain a $30,000 grant from a prominent local philanthropic foundation to fund the purchase of a valuable piece of land, or to determine where and what type of public access will be allowed in the study area. A program usually takes two forms: (1) a graphic illustrating the way you would like to develop the corridor (see Figure 2-6), and (2) a written description of management and administrative policies that will direct your development strategies.

Determining Goals

Involve as many people as reasonably possible in the goal-setting stage, and brainstorm for ideas. This is the first opportunity that you will have to begin building consensus for your greenway.

A minimum of five goals should be considered in examining the possibilities for the proposed greenway corridor:

1. *Human goals*. Who should use the greenway and for what purposes? Who will be affected? How should the greenway be developed to accommodate stated needs?

2. *Environmental goals*. How should the greenway protect and enhance water, vegetation, wildlife, air, and other natural resources and ecological systems?

3. *Implementation goals*. Who should implement the greenway? A public agency or private organization? Will implementation require action and cooperation among multiple agencies? Will it require special joint powers or other agreements that would create a new special-

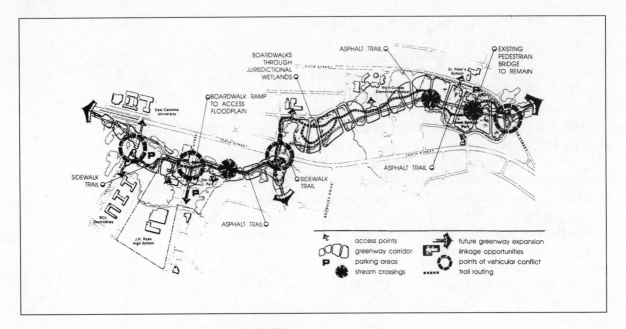

Figure 2-6 Greenway concept master plan. (Courtesy of Greenways Incorporated)

interest entity? This may all depend on who owns or has jurisdiction over the land the greenway traverses.

4. *Long-term management goals.* Who will manage the greenway after it has been developed? What level of management will be required?

5. *Economic goals.* How much money will be needed to develop and maintain the greenway? What type of financial resources are likely to be available from federal, state, local, and private resources? What economic benefits will the completed greenway bring and to whom?

Most of these questions will have been answered in the inventory and analysis phase. Also, the more questions you ask during the goal-setting stage, the more complete your greenway master plan will be.

Exploring Alternatives

After defining a broad range of goals, your next step is to prepare alternative development scenarios. The term *development* is used in a broad sense here to include any physical modification of the existing land use and landscape, policies and management strategies.

Each alternative development scenario poses the question "what if?" and invites reasonable solutions. They can be prepared for the entire study area or for individual aspects of the greenway. Examining alternatives will reveal the interrelationships among components; for example, is public access compatible with protection of the landscape? You should explore at least three alternative development scenarios; each should creatively respond to actual conditions of the site, the socioeconomic status of the community, the needs of the public, and the established goals for the project. Alternatives should be distinctly different

How to Set Goals for Your Greenway

Step 1: Individuals are asked to think of their personal ideas, interests and pursuits for the greenway, write these down and submit them to a group leader, committee chair, or facilitator. This can be done anonymously if desired.

Step 2: Each written statement is publicly transferred and recorded on a large sheet of paper, blackboard, or white board, in full view of all others. Goals should be grouped under the five major headings and subsequent divisions.

Step 3: After all individual statements are itemized, the group discusses, clarifies, and simplifies the ideas into specific action-oriented goals for the

project. This should be accomplished by major headings. Complete one heading and move on to the next. Keep the discussion focused.

Step 4: The group determines which goals are most appropriate to the project by voting or reaching a consensus. This can be accomplished by a show of hands or by ballot, listing the top five picks in each category.

Step 5: The group further clarifies and refines goals to accurately reflect the full intent of the statement.

Source: Authors and adaption of *Riverwork Book*, National Park Service, 1988.

from one another, in order to explore the broadest possible range of ideas.

For example, you may have two goals that need to be reconciled. One of your goals might be "providing access to all people throughout the entire greenway corridor." Another might be "protecting the land and water resources for future generations." Your earlier analysis of topography indicates that you have steep slopes within the study area—some exceeding 15 percent—and the flat slopes are floodplain lands that contain several jurisdictional wetlands and streams. You are presented with *at least* two alternatives: (1) you could provide access to all users by planning for the installation of boardwalks to span the jurisdictional wetlands, a bridge to cross over the stream, and an environmentally sound method for traversing the steep slopes; or (2) you could deny access to all of these areas, maintaining environmentally sensitive lands in their natural state, and consider alternative limited access routes. The preferred alternative development scenario might be a plan that limits access in sensitive resources areas.

As you develop alternative scenarios, keep in mind a few guiding principles:

1. Respect the rights of private property owners.

2. Maximize the use of public landholdings.

3. Propose development only to the extent you really need to; avoid major alterations to the natural environment if possible; improve and protect the natural functions of the environment where possible.

4. Limit the number of intersections with existing vehicular travelways and streams.

5. Promote cost-effective solutions for facility development.

6. Seek solutions that are not management intensive.

7. Pursue connections between your corridor and other ecological and man-made systems.

8. Encourage safe, enjoyable, and environmentally compatible use of the natural environment.

Defining the Nuts and Bolts of Your Scenarios

When you have finished exploring uses for the greenway and have planned various development scenarios, you will need to add a dose of reality. Objectively assess the advantages and disadvantages of each greenway scenario based on:

1. Environmental impact

2. Development costs

3. Management requests

4. Safety and security

5. Regulatory compliance (What permits are required for facility development and landscape improvements? Does the greenway plan meet minimum local, state, and federal laws and ordinances?)

6. Quality of life (How will the greenway affect the quality of life, tourism, business, and industry of the community and region?)

7. Aesthetics (Does the greenway enhance the natural or man-made beauty of the landscape and community?)

It is a good idea to talk to knowledgeable people in your community about these topics to provide corroborating evidence when you present your concepts to the public. Further, we recommend that at this stage you limit yourself to broad conclusions. For example, provide lump sums rather than itemized estimates of costs so that the public doesn't become overwhelmed by details. Don't underemphasize or mislead the public regarding the impact of the greenway on the community, but at this stage, try to focus on the bigger picture.

Documenting Your Alternative Development Scenarios

Document your scenarios using illustrations and text. Drawings, graphs, perspectives, and diagrams are a powerful way to convey your ideas and goals to others. Use blueline or blackline copies of the base map to illustrate your scenarios. Color can add interest and help to differentiate individual elements.

Text complements illustrations, detailing your project in ways that pictures alone cannot. Accompanying text can further clarify each alternative. The text must be well organized, accurate, and easy to understand. Short paragraphs and bulleted summaries should be sufficient to convey the completed design concept.

Presenting Your Alternative Scenarios to the Public

Once you have documented the alternative scenarios, you will want to review them with local residents, local government staff, maintenance personnel, police, fire, and emergency medical officials, politicians, potential users, and conservation and recreation organizations that might assist with the implementation and management of the greenway and whose approval is important. The purpose of these reviews is to obtain an *objective* evaluation of the scenarios, so be prepared to receive constructive and perhaps not-so-constructive criticism. Before you present your alternatives, you should have all the necessary facts at hand. These are critical meetings with the public and a valuable time for review; you want them to be productive and progressive. Be prepared! Get people involved in the decision-making process, and accurately record their responses.

As you present the scenarios, reinforce the fact that you are interested in how people feel about the proposals. Do they like a particular scenario because it benefits them in some way? Which parts do they find difficult to support? Can they specify which parts they feel might work? It is critical that you keep the discussion focused on the idea of the greenway. If you can get people excited about the idea, solutions to specific problems may follow.

Preparing the Final Master Plan

Preparing the Preferred Development Scenario

An important purpose of greenway planning is to *build on your strength* and not spend a lot of valuable energy attempting to change into a strength what the larger community perceives to be a weakness. If, for example, you learn from the alternative scenarios that the community favors early development of a greenway segment on publicly held land, you should focus energies in that direction, rather than pursue development on private lands that could take years to acquire and would require a substantial capital investment and possibly community disapproval.

This is not to suggest that you restrict your vision or that you automatically discard unacceptable components of initial proposals. Your final master plan need not exclude troublesome issues; however, it should be structured around elements that are more easily accomplished and offer early tangible results. The following three-step process is one way to define a preferred alternative:

Step 1. For each scenario, write each of the seven items listed under "Defining the Nuts and Bolts of Your Scenarios" (p. 44) as headings at the top of a sheet of paper. Under the appropriate heading, list all of the reviewer comments. Then, look for constraints and opportunities. For example, under "Safety and Security," several reviewers may have commented that most of the land in your study area is too steep to

The greenway planner for Cary, North Carolina, focuses on refining this rapidly growing town's greenway network. Each segment of the greenway fits into the town's overall master plan. The plan incorporates the use of utility easements, and an open-space ordinance requires that developers dedicate open space or make a payment into a town open-space fund. The thirty-two-mile Cary greenway system is a combination of town-built and privately built trails.

safelysupport the type of access you have illustrated. Or, under "Quality of Life," a majority of reviewers agree that having the greenway connected to the high school will provide a needed opportunity for outdoor science education.

Step 2: Next, list *only* the opportunities. Compare these against the five principles of greenway planning described under "Determining Goals" (p. 41). This should reveal some of the most obvious strengths of your alternatives. The scenario, or components of all scenarios that accomplish this objective and which have survived earlier public scrutiny, become the building blocks for your final master plan.

Step 3: Go back to the original goals for your project and determine which of the remaining attributes satisfy these. For example, your goal may have been to "provide access to the greenway in a safe, cost-effective manner." Limiting access to certain areas of the greenway and eliminating stream crossings allows you to achieve the goal, satisfy planning principles, and respect public opinion.

Through the participatory planning process, you reach compromises based on the concerns of the community, local landowner, or managing agency and regulatory requirements. Once you have arrived at a set of specific project goals, you should add these to your base map and describe them in accompanying text.

The Master Plan

The final master plan should emphasize the primary objectives that emerged from the planning process, as well as other elements of your vision that might be subject to further review. This can be accomplished through varying amounts of detail on a final drawing, a clear ordering of descriptive text within a summary report, graphic techniques, or a proposed phased development approach.

The final master plan should include revised drawings and text. In fact, it is a good idea to assemble all of your work to date and prepare concise statements that define major conclusions and recommendations. The final master plan now represents the single document that instructs future development of the greenway. As such, it should at a minimum define the following:

Final Location and Route of the Greenway. Give the exact location of all real property that might be part of the greenway and all points of origin and destination that will be served by the greenway. This does not mean that you need to conduct a physical land survey of the property. Make use, however, of existing municipal tax maps or orthographic maps that contain property lines and define the final size, boundaries, and position in the landscape of properties that are within the overall corridor (though be careful not to identify actual parcels at this point if they are not publicly owned). Keep in mind that the corridor may need to be adjusted in response to landowners' concerns. Boldly illustrate this final routing on your greenway base maps, define all major land features along the route, and list major public properties included in the greenway.

Land, Water, and Heritage Conservation and Protection Measures. Set out recommendations for protecting the landscape, historic and cultural resources, animal habitat, and ecologically sensitive landscapes (for example, a boardwalk crossing a wetland or a proposed building setback ordinance). Illustrate the location of these on your final drawings. Prepare detailed drawings and author specifications that describe how resources will be protected.

Access and Facility Siting. Determine where and to whom access will be provided. Define the user groups that will be accommodated. Illustrate all potential for linkage between points of origin and destination and connections with other systems. Point out facilities to support this use. Most recreational greenways should include, at a minimum, trail benches, trash receptacles, and a comprehensive signage system. Other facilities will depend on the goals of your greenway.

Management Specifications. In cooperation with a designated management organization or agency, clearly spell out and assign appropriate responsibilities for maintenance, safety and security, programming, and operation of the greenway. Discuss possible legal or political actions. For example, if the local parks and recreation department is willing to build, maintain, and police the proposed greenway, it is possible that additional staff will need to be hired by the department. This in turn means that the local governing body will need to approve an increase in the operating budget for this department.

Estimated Development Costs. You will need to outline fiscal strategies and anticipated costs for the protection of the environment, trail and facility development, operation and maintenance, and other expenses. You should also mention likely public and private funding sources for greenway development. Development costs can be separately defined as follows:

- Land protection costs

- Planning and design fees

- Construction costs

- Administrative costs

- Operation and maintenance costs

- Public relations and events costs

Development Strategy. Greenway projects take time to fully implement. An appropriate implementation strategy would take into account existing local factors such as land currently in public possession and available for greenway development, funding that can be committed to the greenway, and community support for the greenway and the community's ability to successfully manage it once completed.

Obtaining Public Approval of the Final Master Plan

After you have completed your final master plan, illustrated it on appropriate maps, and described it in clear text, you will want to make a final presentation to your community. Make sure that you know who

Federal legislation deauthorizing the Cross-Florida Barge Canal required that the land be turned into a greenway. A management plan adopted by the governor and cabinet, and up for consideration by the state legislature in Spring 1993 identifies important biological and recreational resources in the 110-mile-long corridor. The plan will:
• preserve a continuous cross-state greenway;
• require local governments along the greenway to plan for protecting and conserving greenway lands;
• restore the lower Oklawaha River to its natural state;
• create a new state division to manage the greenway. The Cross-Florida Greenway will be the cornerstone of the state's greenway network.

your audience will be and the amount of time you will have to make your presentation. Be sure also to define clear objectives.

You should keep your presentation short and to the point—no longer than 15 to 25 minutes in total length. Have on hand as many resource people as possible, including relevant consultants, supporters, and individuals or agencies who have accepted responsibilities for the greenway. Recognize those who have contributed to planning and the final plan, but keep it short and sweet. If possible, include speaking time for a user of a nearby greenway or someone initially opposed to the greenway who has become convinced of its value to the community. There is nothing like a convert to make a convincing argument for the greenway.

3

Partnerships: Organizing Your Greenway Effort

"Never doubt that a small group of thoughtful, committed citizens can change the world: indeed, it's the only thing that ever has."
—Margaret Mead

Planning is a vital and exciting part of greenway creation, but once you have a plan, you need to take action. The hurdles may seem insurmountable, and without the driving force of a committed group, paralysis can set in. Don't let this happen to your greenway vision.

There are many ways to mobilize community resources to create a greenway. A parks or community development agency can finance staff and carry out the plan. Chambers of commerce and local land trusts have done the same. In a number of instances, an entirely new nonprofit organization has been set up to carry out the greenway vision. Some greenways, like the Anne Springs Close Greenway in Fort Mill, South Carolina, have been developed through the efforts and resources of a single family.

"From the very beginning, work with groups you expect to oppose the project."
—San Francisco Bay Trail

In most cases, however, getting the greenway project underway calls for partnerships involving both the public and private sectors and such diverse interests as farmers, developers, conservationists, and outdoor recreation groups.

The material in this chapter is an overview of a complex topic and does not constitute legal advice, nor should it be relied upon as such. We recommend that you consult an attorney if necessary and refer also to the suggested readings at the end of the chapter.

Greenway Organizations

Greenways often begin with a well-organized advocacy group—people who will champion the greenway. Ideally, the group should be in place at the beginning of the process. It might form in several ways. The following are examples of general organizations types that have proved to be successful.

Citizens' Advisory Committee. A citizens' advisory committee is a group of citizens and community leaders appointed to assist a public agency in reviewing and helping to develop and implement a greenway master plan. This committee might evolve into a greenway advocacy group. For example, in Winston-Salem, North Carolina, the planning

The DuPage River Greenway Task Force, formed in December 1988, includes a wide range of public agencies representing Will and DuPage counties, as well as state and regional interests. The task force is the forum for defining and assessing the greenway area, providing recreational opportunities and management for the greenway, publicizing the greenway, resolving jurisdictional conflicts and responsibilities, and coordinating protection along the greenway.

department appointed a group of citizens to guide master planning of the Bethabara Trail Greenway.

Advocacy Group. An advocacy group is an organized and committed group of citizens, community leaders, and public officials assembled specifically to pursue a greenway project. The group promotes the greenway, secures funding, and is likely to have an active, if not leading, role in resource assessment, planning, phasing, coordination, and even construction management. An advocacy group may also be incorporated as a greenway nonprofit organization. For example, the Potomac River Greenway Coalition promotes the establishment of greenways along the Potomac River and its tributaries.

Greenway Nonprofit Organization. A greenway nonprofit organization is essentially an advocacy group that has incorporated under the U.S. Internal Revenue Code. One example, the South Suburban Park Foundation, formed in Littleton, Colorado, is developing a greenway in partnership with the South Suburban Parks and Recreation District, a public parks entity.

Land Trust. A land trust is a nonprofit organization formed to preserve such land and water features as forests, streams, and rivers. Usually, this type of organization is incorporated as a nonprofit organization and can acquire and hold land. In most cases, the mission of a land trust encompasses more than greenway creation, although the trust may choose to focus on a greenway project. The Land Trust Alliance is a national association of the many land trusts now in place in communities and regions across the country.

Environmental or Conservation Commission. An environmental or conservation commission is a special commission, known by various names, appointed by municipalities to pursue environmental objectives, including research, planning, fund-raising, and land acquisition. Such a group can also pursue a greenway program. In New Jersey, the West Windsor Township Environmental Commission created a greenbelt system during the late 1970s and 1980s to preserve forests and drainage corridors.

Public Agency Project. A public agency (for instance, a parks department) plans, funds, and implements a greenway. The Johnson County Park and Recreation District in Shawnee Mission, Kansas, is working to create and maintain the Mill Creek Streamway Park, a greenway system along eight county streams.

No matter how your group comes into existence, it needs a plan of action and, more importantly, committed, articulate members who will persevere no matter what the setbacks to see the greenway through to completion. You want as varied a group as possible to draw on available expertise and to represent varied community interests—public officials, landowners, legislators, agency staff, potential opponents, and utility and corporate executives, as well as those persons representing agricultural, cultural, environmental, and historic conservation communities.

Forging a Public–Private Partnership

The Greenway as Orphan Child

One of the most successful arrangements for seeing greenways to completion is the public–private partnership. By public–private partnership, we mean the joint effort of a private advocacy group and a governmental agency. Whereas the interest in greenways is growing nationwide, in most communities greenway advocates do not have the political clout of some other groups. In an era of budget cuts and scarce resources, greenway advocates must still scrounge to acquire backing. When you consider the broader range of community needs, from schools to sewer projects, finding political support for a greenway can be a formidable task.

What does it take to compete? First, you need a vision; and second you need to build alliances—among conservation groups, trail advocates, cycling and alternative transportation groups, business associations, farmers, the chamber of commerce, and others if mutual objectives so dictate. You will also need to describe how greenways will benefit *them*. Many successful greenways have parlayed these coalitions into political clout in the form of a public–private partnership.

Perhaps someday government will directly fund and develop greenways the way it does traditional parks and ball fields. Perhaps creative arrangements will evolve through which private-sector interests such as developers, homeowners' associations, and the tourism industry will bear the major cost of greenway development and maintenance. For now, a strong, well-organized advocacy group usually works best in concert with a supportive public agency (see Figure 3-1).

The Iowa Natural Heritage Foundation offers an example of greenway development within a larger umbrella organization interested in a broad conservation agenda. While pursuing several objectives aimed at preserving Iowa's open-space corridors, wetlands, woodlands, and rural heritage, the foundation has teamed up with local greenway and trail groups to create rail-trail and river greenways across the state. The foundation provides planning services and technical assistance in setting up local advocacy organizations, writing grant applications, raising funds, and acquiring land and also serves as a tax-exempt conduit for grants to local organizations. The foundation has developed its own greenway and trail projects, including the sixty-three-mile Wabash Trace Nature Trail.

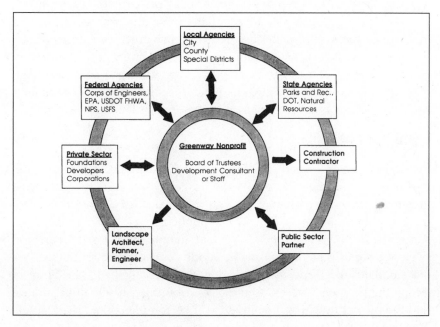

Figure 3-1 How a greenway nonprofit organization interacts with other entities. (©1992 The Greenway Collaborative. All rights reserved.)

"Form public–private part-nerships. Without these partnerships, your effort will be an uphill battle through the process."
—Delaware Nature Society

An interesting chapter in the history of the Gunpowder River Greenway in Maryland is the cooperative venture that has developed between Maryland's Department of Natural Resources and Genstar Stone Product Cor-poration. Genstar, in close coordination with the state, developed and transferred land to the state after mining operations. The corporation reclaimed the area to the Department of Natural Re-sources' recreation specifi-cations along a portion of the greenway.

The Role of an Advocacy Group

An advocacy group can become a consolidated voice for the diverse array of greenway users and promoters—working to build alliances and to represent community interests. In many cases the group will need to raise funds, market the greenway, prepare plans, and work with the public sector to develop the greenway.

Joe Shoemaker, Chairman of the Platte River Greenway Foundation, inspired the wisdom "no power is all power." Because advocacy groups, are nongovernmental, they have no official authority. Their ef-fectiveness springs from good will, a cooperative spirit, diplomacy, and the political clout of their individual members. Because the advocacy group has no official authority, it also has no official limitations. For ex-ample, jurisdictional boundaries don't matter; the private advocacy group can cross these boundaries just as greenways often do. The group can form partnerships with separate public agencies in any number of cities, townships, or counties along the greenway corridor. Whereas public entities sometimes do this through "joint powers agreements," an advocacy group can generally form such partnerships faster and more easily. These partnerships can lay the groundwork for a more perma-nent joint-powers arrangement down the road.

The private advocacy group can be bipartisan or nonpartisan, and it can work around political and bureaucratic obstacles that can constrain a government agency. Because it has no official authority, the private group will generally be better received by landowners, businesspeople, and others who might resist a government agency. This is true as long as the advocacy group is not identified with an unpopular special inter-est group (for example, development interests in a "no-growth" town or a group that wants to stop development in a "pro-growth" community). The advocacy group is free to negotiate, innovate, arrange deals, and otherwise maneuver as necessary to accomplish greenway objectives.

Another practical consideration is that the advocacy group can accept private donations for the greenway if incorporated as a nonprofit orga-nization. Governmental entities may have legal restrictions or cumber-some requirements concerning grants of money or land.

The Role of the Public Sector

The public sector—whether a local parks department, a planning de-partment, a state agency, or a federal agency—is equally vital. Most greenway projects, particularly those in urban areas, rely on govern-ment funding, and in many cases, a public agency will ultimately as-sume responsibility for operations and maintenance on the corridor. Even if a significant portion of the funds comes from private sources, most philanthropic and corporate donors will want to see evidence of strong public-agency support before contributing. They want assurance that the project in which they invest will be completed and maintained. This usually requires firm public-sector commitment.

Table 3-2

Public-Private Partnerships: Respective Roles, Benefits, and Limitations

Private Advocacy Group	Public Agency
1. No authority	1. Official authority
2. Must raise money	2. Taxing power and can float bonds
3. Flexible	3. Established policies and procedures
4. Entrepreneurial	4. May be bureaucratic
5. Perceived as private sector	5. Perceived as government
6. Small staff or no staff	6. Professional employees
7. Vision	7. Practical experience
8. Limited life cycle	8. Permanent entity
9. Limited resources	9. Significant resources
10. Greenways focus	10. Broad range of obligations

Partnerships

Public–private partnerships can provide the best of both worlds. Advocacy groups offer community spirit, entrepreneurial drive, volunteerism, and good corporate citizenship. The public sector partner brings financial resources and professional experience to such areas as construction and maintenance, as well as long-term commitment to the endeavor.

The success of these partnerships depends on how well organized the advocacy group is and how much good will it builds with the public and with its governmental allies. Never underestimate the clout your advocacy group can have. Be sure the members of the advocacy group understand and protect their ability to bring about change outside of a government bureaucracy. Maintain the integrity and reputation of the group through proper conduct and careful selection of board members.

A good working relationship between public agency staff and advocacy group members is critical. Each side should understand the other's aspirations and obligations (see Table 3-2). For example, a public agency must answer to the community as a whole and may have to weigh priorities and decisions differently than a greenway advocacy group focused on one mission. This will call for special cooperation on both sides to make the partnership work. Learn to share the credit and the sense of ownership. Above all, remember, you are partners.

The Northern Indiana Public Service Company (NIPSCO) leases land it owns to the State of Indiana for the Calumet Trail. The eighty-foot-wide transmission corridors are maintained to NIPSCO's specification; daily maintenance is performed by Indiana's Department of Natural Resources and the National Park Service.

Private Partnerships

Private–Private Partnerships

There are many productive ways individuals, organizations, and businesses can work together to create a greenway. Because they often manage linear strips, utilities, railroads, and agricultural interests deserve special attention.

On Block Island, Rhode Island, the escalating cost of land in this popular vacation spot has made the purchase of a home by many native islanders and year-round residents virtually impossible. A unique partnership between an affordable housing group, the Block Island Economic Development Corporation, and the Block Island Land Trust led to acquisition of a 27.5-acre site for joint use as affordable housing and greenway connection. The Block Island Chamber of Commerce supported the greenway, since conservation is the island's greatest economic asset. The Rhode Island Foundation and the Champlin Foundation provided major funding.

Agriculture

Many states have programs to buy development rights from farmers. This allows farmers to continue working their land at a lower, more favorable tax rate. These and other programs that preserve agricultural land can foster the creation of greenbelts or improve the scenic or open-space values of an adjacent greenway. For example, conservation easements can provide a greenspace buffer between conflicting land uses, provide a vegetated filter strip along streams to protect surface water from runoff, or protect a scenic view. Agreements to provide wildlife habitat (perhaps via subsidized planting of wildlife food crops) or bridle path greenways are other possibilities for bringing agriculture into the greenway movement. In all cases, it is important to be sensitive to farmers' concerns—for example, their need for fencing and vegetation control practices, threats to livestock, and liability. The New Jersey Open Lands Management Law is a useful model for bringing private landowners into the trail network. It provides technical assistance and funding for the development and maintenance of privately owned land for recreational purposes. Eligible projects include fencing, installation of water bars, styles, berms, parking areas, roads, trails, screening, and repair and restoration of vandalized crops.

Utilities

An inventory of existing and planned infrastructure (see Chapter 2) will show you where utility lines could possibly be used for recreational trails or future joint use projects. Successful joint use with utilities can provide greenways with an ongoing source of acquisition, development, and management funds.

For twenty years, Illinois' Prairie Path (a nonprofit trail group) leased a section of trail from the county, which had purchased the right-of-way from Commonwealth Edison. When liability coverage became too costly for the group, DuPage County assumed responsibility for liability and management of the trail, and the nonprofit group assumed a lesser role.

When seeking access to an *existing* utility corridor, realize that utility companies often have only an easement on the land. The corridor surface is usually owned by someone else. Negotiations may be further complicated by lease arrangements between the landowner and other commercial or agricultural users. It may take time to work out an acceptable agreement. Utility companies are often concerned about liability, damage to their facilities, access for management and repair, and adequate policing of the corridor. State commissions or local zoning boards may also restrict how the corridor may be used. Be sure to work closely with utility owners in developing greenway facilities. You don't want to hit a gas pipe, sewer line, or a fiber optic cable. Remember that

Since utility companies can provide important trail components in your overall greenway system, it is important to address their concerns in your plan. (Lisa Gutierrez)

some utilities actively manage their corridors for wildlife values, manipulating food and cover plantings as part of their vegetation management program.

By *joint venturing*, greenway groups have formed partnerships with utilities to reduce acquisition, development, and management costs. For example, the W&OD Trail in Northern Virginia receives $500,000 per year for leasing its right-of-way to a fiber optics company; overall the park nets $250,000 above expenses each year.

Joint ventures between utility companies and greenway groups may be attractive since trails provide easy access for maintenance activities and excellent public relations. Utilities can save considerable amounts of money when working with greenway groups in the early stages on a railbanked rail corridor, since the transportation purpose of the corridor (utility transport and trail use) is upheld and there may be no acquisition costs. Keep in mind that gas companies normally spend an average of $1 million per mile for new facilities. By working together to *acquire* an abandoned railroad, any funds spent by the utility can be used to match federal Intermodal Surface Transportation Efficiency Act of 1991 (ISTEA) funds to develop the trail.

There are also advantages to working with utilities that are seeking new corridors. Permits may be easier to obtain if there is a public interest partner. Also, utilities are susceptible to public opinion in the *early* planning stages—and public support by a greenway group helps. Also, if access is sought by your group, the utility may need to satisfy an access requirement in the permit stage.

To explore joint partnerships, contact the public relations representative at the utility or the appropriate state regulatory agency.

The Burke-Gilman Trail (Seattle), Glacial Drumlin Trail (Wisconsin), and Cedar Valley Nature Trail (Iowa) have negotiated fiber-optics installations with communications companies to help pay for capital and maintenance costs of the greenways. Companies find that locating cables along trails has its advantages: no major digging will take place, and installation is easier than in active railroad beds or along other routes.

Railroads

Abandoned railroad corridors have tremendous potential for use as trails and greenways. At its peak, the U.S. railroad system had almost 300,000 miles of track. Today half of these tracks are no longer used, and about 4000 miles of track are abandoned each year. Abandoned rail corridors, with their gentle grades, make ideal multipurpose trails. As of January 1993 there were more than 500 rail-trails, totaling more than 6000 miles across the United States.

The process of converting a rail corridor to a trail can be difficult and complex, depending on the type of railroad ownership and the willingness of adjacent landowners to relinquish claims to the rights-of-way. In 1983, the National Trails Act was amended to allow for "rail-banking." This is a process by which railroads do not have to abandon rights-of-way but may hold them for future transportation use. In these cases, railroads may transfer rail corridors to state or local governments or nonprofit organizations for use as a trail.

The Rails-To-Trails Conservancy (see Appendix A) works with local communities and groups to acquire abandoned rail lines and convert them for use as recreational trails. The National Park Service also provides technical assistance to communities in rails-to-trails efforts through their River, Trails and Conservation program (see Appendix A).

Organizing an Effective Nonprofit Organization

A nonprofit organization is a legal entity under both state and federal law; it is usually a corporation registered in the state in which it principally operates. Why incorporate? First, because incorporation gives your group legal standing, allowing it to accept grants, enter into contracts, hire employees, and if need be, incur debt. Incorporating allows your group to accept tax deductible donations and limits the liability exposure of individual directors, officers, and employers. Unlike for-profit corporations, however, nonprofit organizations have quite stringent limitations on benefits that might accrue to directors and officers. Be sure you understand those limitations.

Depending on your objectives and the other organizations in your community, you might choose to affiliate with an established nonprofit organization rather than create a new group. Perhaps there is already a land trust, parks advocacy group, or some other existing nonprofit entity willing to take on the greenway effort. This would save the time, cost (usually less than $400, depending on the cost of legal services and state registration fees), and paperwork involved in setting up a new organization, and the greenway could benefit from the resources, reputation, and connections the existing group already has in place. Land trusts are ideal, as their mission is land conservation. Cooperative agreements are good vehicles for structuring a relationship.

The main disadvantage of affiliating with an established nonprofit entity is that the group may not fully support the greenway, especially if it competes with the nonprofit organization's other objectives. Affiliation may also mean loss of direct control over funds and possibly lack of liability protection for the greenway advocacy group. In some instances, it may be appropriate to team up temporarily with a nonprofit organization. This could be a big help if donors approach before you have your own organization set up. The nonprofit partner can accept and hold grants for the greenway under its tax-exempt status while you put your own nonprofit organization in place.

Many greenway groups have successfully affiliated with other organizations that had kindred goals. In Pueblo, Colorado, greenway advocates joined with an existing nonprofit organization called the Nature Center of Pueblo, which operated an interpretive center on the Arkansas River adjacent to the greenway trail. The Nature Center and the proposed citywide greenway were highly complementary. The two organizations eventually merged and now share an executive director, staff, office space (at the Nature Center), and other resources. This team has been successful both in implementing the greenway and in expanding the Nature Center.

Forming a Nonprofit Organization

If you cannot or prefer not to team with another group, you will need to establish a new nonprofit organization (see Figure 3-2). How do you do it? Simply put, you form a corporation under the laws of your state. To incorporate, a group of people organize and adopt articles of incorporation and bylaws. The articles of incorporation list the names of the incorporators, the address of the nonprofit organization, the first board of directors, the purpose of the nonprofit organization, and other information about its role. The bylaws describe how the nonprofit organization will function, addressing such issues as board structure, the selection and rotation of officers, committee formation, membership structure

The Bay Circuit Corridor, a 160-mile network of trails, waterways, parks, and other open spaces encircling metropolitan Boston, was first envisioned in 1929 by Boston landscape architect Charles Elliot. During the 1980s, state funding for planning and acquisition solidified the Bay Circuit vision. With loss of state dollars, the National Park Service is now helping the Bay Circuit Alliance, a new nonprofit organization, develop and implement a community planning process that has involved more than twelve local organizations and fifteen active communities. Fifteen miles of trail were added in 1991, bringing the total length of trail formally dedicated to thirty miles.

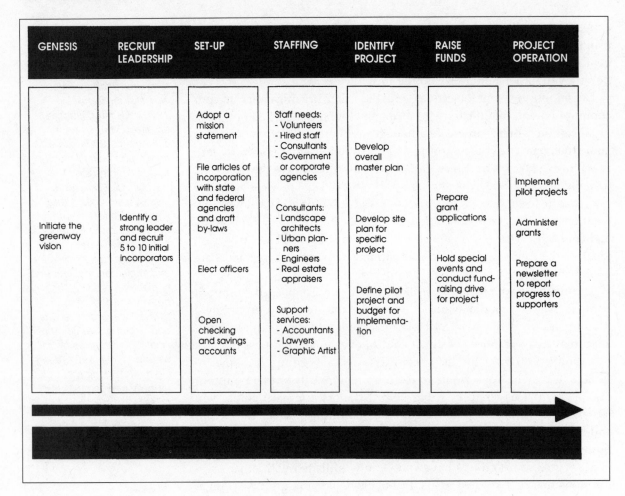

GENESIS	RECRUIT LEADERSHIP	SET-UP	STAFFING	IDENTIFY PROJECT	RAISE FUNDS	PROJECT OPERATION
Initiate the greenway vision	Identify a strong leader and recruit 5 to 10 initial incorporators	Adopt a mission statement File articles of incorporation with state and federal agencies and draft by-laws Elect officers Open checking and savings accounts	Staff needs: - Volunteers - Hired staff - Consultants - Government or corporate agencies Consultants: - Landscape architects - Urban planners - Engineers - Real estate appraisers Support services: - Accountants - Lawyers - Graphic Artist	Develop overall master plan Develop site plan for specific project Define pilot project and budget for implementation	Prepare grant applications Hold special events and conduct fund-raising drive for project	Implement pilot projects Administer grants Prepare a newsletter to report progress to supporters

Figure 3-2 Evolution of a greenway nonprofit organization.

and voting rights, meeting schedules, indemnification, and record keeping and the handling of funds.

We recommend retaining a lawyer to draft your articles and bylaws. You can sometimes borrow sample articles and bylaws from other local nonprofit groups with similar objectives, such as a nature center or land trust. Even so, always have a lawyer review them to ensure that they are appropriately modified to meet your specific needs and to conform with applicable federal, state, and local law. Note that some states require several other documents. Check with your secretary of state's office. In some states, several filings are necessary, but once you have the papers drawn up, have them registered with the secretary of state, and pay a registration fee, you're in business.

Relationship to Public Sector

Before filing articles of incorporation, any relationship between your nonprofit organization and a public-sector agency should be spelled out in a memorandum of understanding or cooperative agreement. This is a nonbinding expression of intent to work cooperatively in all areas relating to greenway funding, development, and maintenance.

Try to avoid detailed assignments of responsibility. Early on, you might issue a joint statement of mission for the greenway. Or it may be more complex: an agreement by the public sector agency to accept funds and lands for greenway improvements as long as it preapproves such gifts and can certify that these improvements will be properly overseen. Put another way, if the public sector will ultimately bear responsibility for the use and maintenance of any greenway improvements on public land, then the public sector must preapprove what happens on these lands.

Obtaining Tax-Exempt Status

Before you collect any money or receive any donated land, you need to consider a number of additional details. First and foremost, you should apply for tax-exempt status from the U. S. Internal Revenue Service. Tax exemption means that donors have the added incentive of deducting their gifts from their federal and state income taxes. Contact your state and local revenue departments for details about tax-exempt provisions in your area.

Securing tax-exempt status customarily begins by filing under Sections 170(h) and 510(c)(3) of the Internal Revenue Code. To receive tax-exempt status, earnings must not accrue to the nonprofit's directors, officers, members, or anyone else. Certain types of lobbying and political activities are also regulated. To file, you should request Forms 1023 and 1024 as well as Publication 557 from the IRS. Publication 557 will guide you through the necessary forms. Beware of using the word *foundation* in your application or as part of your organization name. Foundations do not enjoy all the tax benefits that public charities do.

The IRS awards tax-exempt status retroactively to the date of filing. You should be able to start accepting deductible donations as of this date, but confirm this with your lawyer or the IRS.

Housekeeping

Once your nonprofit organization has been set up, you need to consider some basic housekeeping items. Foremost is insurance. Ideally, from day one, the nonprofit organization should carry an adequate liability policy that protects its board of trustees and employees. An attorney and an insurance specialist should be contacted at the start (see also Chapter 14).

Accurate bookkeeping is also essential. This need not be complex, perhaps just a well-managed checkbook that contributes to annual tax reporting. Most groups require the signatures of both the chairman or executive director and the treasurer on all disbursements. A budget should also be set up for projects underway. A budget should be able to manage board appropriations, earmarked grants, funds encumbered by financial commitments to a consultant or contractor, and other cash flow items. An annual independent audit and financial statement is a must if you are going to solicit funds. You may be able to persuade an

"It takes time to establish a reputation and standing in the community. Keep at it... You can accomplish a great deal as a citizen group."
—Schuylkill River Greenway Association

Land Trusts

Land trusts are uniquely positioned to lead the way in the creation of a greenway system. Land trusts are truly community based; their members know the land, the people, and the culture. They know which land resources are critical in their area. They can be advocates for government action when that will work better. They can build bridges between the private and public players and gain the confidence of uncertain landowners in a way that government sometimes cannot. Trusts can move quickly when time is short and can combine real-estate skills with philanthropy and volunteerism to reduce the costs of land protection.

Most important, people affiliated with land trusts know how to do the creative transactions that protect land. A trust is in a unique position to provide a range of services: identifying appropriate properties; building coalitions of public and private interests to gain greenway support (moral, financial, and political); attracting government participation by doing some of the planning, negotiating, fund-raising, and landholding and management; protecting land independently where government involvement is either inappropriate or unattainable; and teaching others how to protect land, perhaps by encouraging the formation of a land trust in a neighboring community or providing technical assistance to a less experienced body.

Source: Jean Hocker, President, Land Trust Alliance, in "Greenways and Land Trusts–A Natural Partnership," *Exchange*, Summer 1987.

accounting firm or a qualified retired accountant to donate services or reduce the fee.

Don't overlook state or local legal requirements relating to charitable solicitation. You may need certification and fund-raising permits. Check with the office of the secretary of state where corporations are registered. Your city's excise and license bureau should be able to tell you if local fund-raising registrations or permits are required. Remember also to file an annual federal tax report on Form 990, Return of Organizations Exempt from Income Tax, available from the IRS. You may also need to file state and local tax reports.

The Mission Statement

To succeed, your nonprofit organization *must* stay focused on greenway development. One way to ensure that everyone understands this is a brief mission statement. The statement should be flexible enough to allow you to maneuver when you need to. For example, you may not want to restrict your area of activity to one city or township, but may be thinking instead in terms of a regional greenway system. A limited geographic area may prevent you from getting 501(c)(3) (tax-exempt) status and dampen your ability to raise funds. A typical hypothetical greenway mission statement might read: "to foster and encourage the acquisition, retention, development, and use of park, open space, and greenway amenities in the greater (name of your community) area."

The Life Cycle of a Greenway Nonprofit Organization

A greenway nonprofit organization is likely to have three phases in its life cycle: (1) setup, (2) implementation, and (3) stewardship. Understanding these phases may help you to select board members, set policy, and define a mission.

The setup phase may last one to three years and is probably the most challenging. This phase involves presenting a new idea to the public and winning over potential donors and supporters. During this phase, the nonprofit organization establishes credibility, secures seed money, and oversees completion of a pilot project. Nothing establishes credibility like a ribbon-cutting ceremony on a successful first-phase project. Visible results are essential to early success.

The implementation phase usually continues another five to ten years but can, in fact, last an indefinite period of time. During this phase, more and more segments are completed until the basic greenway vision has been realized. You should periodically remind the public of your achievements with ongoing dedication ceremonies and other events as each new segment is completed. During this stage, the board and staff gain valuable experience.

Stewardship involves preserving and protecting the greenway you have built. Stewardship efforts may include oversight of maintenance, review of land-use decisions affecting the greenway, educational programs, and volunteer care-taking projects such as cleanups and tree plantings. Whether the same nonprofit organization takes on this role or whether a nonprofit entity is needed at all at this point will depend on the managerial arrangements. For example, a recreational greenway might be completely managed by a parks agency. An ecological greenway primarily owned by a land trust might more appropriately be managed by that nonprofit organization.

The Board of Trustees

"People give money to people." Remember this adage when selecting a board of trustees. No matter how noble your cause, it's the people who champion it that count. Who are the movers and shakers in your community? Who is willing to commit time and energy? Who is on a first-name basis with the key decision-makers in business and government? Who are the community activists behind the greenway? These are the people you want out campaigning for your project. Also consider those who have concerns about your project. These people can be a valuable asset if you can win them over.

All board members should:

- know what their organization is up to and perform their duties with good faith and diligence;

- avoid financial conflicts of interest in the outcome of board decisions;

- attend board meetings. Monthly or even biweekly meetings may be necessary during the initial stages of the project. Later, bimonthly or quarterly meetings may suffice, especially if there is an executive committee that meets more frequently.

- bring at least one of the three W's to the board—wealth, wisdom, and work. By wealth, we don't just mean personal contributions. Members can also give by helping to secure funding from other

"Get one person who makes it his or her business to spend time to succeed to the point of obsession. This is a must."
—*Falling Springs Greenway*

sources or offering in-kind services. Wisdom and work are self-explanatory. You want people with good judgment, open minds, and diplomatic skills willing to commit their time.[1]

Begin with a chairperson who can provide the leadership to see the project through. The chairperson should be well connected, well respected, and committed to the greenway. Ideally, this first chairperson can help select the other board members. Avoid selecting board members who have a different or hidden agenda, those with partisan political objectives, people concerned with "backyard" issues who tend to disappear once their own interests have been resolved, and whiners and hand-wringers. You want dedicated, hard working, and diplomatic team players who can get the job done.

How large a board do you want? This depends on a number of factors, including local politics and the nature of the project. A small board might have seven to nine members. The advantages of this size are easier decision making and more efficient communications. In addition, each member will likely have a greater sense of personal involvement. A large board might consist of twenty to twenty-five members. This offers a larger pool of ideas and expertise, more contacts, and more bodies to volunteer time. The main disadvantages of a large board are more cumbersome decision making and the need for more staff time. A larger board can meet this challenge by appointing an executive committee to handle day-to-day operations, thus offering the best of both worlds.

Volunteers

Volunteers are often the backbone of a successful community effort. Their unpaid commitment and enthusiasm is often noticed by potential funders, politicians, and other citizens. There are countless opportunities to recruit local talent. Volunteers can research land ownership, make slide presentations, and take care of administrative duties. They can lead group tours of the greenway corridor and visit other successful projects for inspiration and advice. With professional supervision, volunteers can inventory plant and animal species. They can be effective fund-raisers and can help with tree planting, cleanup, wetland improvements, and even trail building. The Triangle Greenways Council in North Carolina is a good example. Volunteers built twenty miles of trails with tools and materials funded by small grants. Skilled volunteers may even be able to build such structures as small bridges, retaining walls, and erosion-control devices. Local carpenters can help build a deck across a wetland; a nearby farmer might do some grading work with his or her tractor. The key is to determine what volunteers can handle and what is better left to professional contractors. Be sure to work diplomatically with any local labor organizations to avoid possible conflicts.

---

[1]Adapted in part from Don Coppock *et al.*, *The Nonprofit Primer: A Guidebook for Land Trusts*, 2nd ed. (Oakland, Calif.: California Coastal Conservancy, 1989).

The key to a successful volunteer program lies in organization. Adequate tools, supplies, training, safety management, and a host of other considerations must be addressed. Good project planning is essential. Nothing is more discouraging than volunteering your time and then standing idly around because no one's in charge and you don't know what to do.

Several states now have nonprofit organizations that can recruit, train, and organize outdoor volunteers. A number of local parks agencies have volunteer program coordinators. In addition, some large corporations and military units offer volunteer-oriented community services with personnel from their ranks. You may want to check with some of the larger companies in town and the local military base or National Guard.

Staffing

In most cases, building a greenway will demand more time and expertise than an all-volunteer group can provide. Ideally, the project should have full-time or at least part-time staff. Obviously, you want capable, qualified people. This can be handled in several ways:

1. *The board hires its own executive director and support staff.* This is great if you can afford it. It also means you have employees, an office, and all of the associated expenses and headaches.

2. *The board contracts with a consultant.* Under this scenario, the board hires a professional fund-raiser or project coordinator who contracts for services on a consultant basis. The services might be limited to fund-raising or may include all aspects of planning and project administration. The consultant usually provides his or her own office and support services. This approach can be far less costly than hiring an executive director and staff and can be quite effective. The main drawback is that the consultant may have other clients and commitments that compete for his or her time.

3. *The project is staffed by the existing staff of a local land trust, nature center, or other kindred organization.* This shared staff arrangement can be quite cost-effective and productive, depending on demands already placed on the staff. The other organization must be strongly committed to the greenway if it is to provide staff.

4. *Staffing and possibly even office space are provided by the participating government agency.* This arrangement can also promote a good public–private partnership. On several greenway projects, staff has been provided by a city planning office.

Regardless of how you provide for staffing services, be sure that everyone involved understands what you expect. Have a written contract that spells out objectives to be achieved within specific time frames.

Clearly, there are many ways to organize a greenway effort. The approach you choose will depend on many factors, including the type of greenway you want, the availability of public and private funding, and the alliances you are able to build. It is important to build coalitions, draw on community resources, and learn from the experiences of other greenway efforts. In all cases, however, the key is having a committed core group of people—whether inside or outside government, whether small and informal or large and highly structured—who will tenaciously hold to the greenway vision and see the process through to completion.

In addition to the contact organizations listed in Appendix A, the National Center for Nonprofit Boards, 2000 L Street, N.W., Suite 411, Washington, DC 20036 (202-452-6262) is a source for information on nonprofit organizations.

4

Building Public Support for Your Greenway

"It's not how much it's worth; it's how much people think it's worth."
—Harvey Mackay (author of *Swim with the Sharks without Being Eaten Alive*, Random House, New York, 1988)

Marketing Your Greenway

Implementing a greenway plan requires a solid base of public support. You need to capture the imagination and support of the community as well as those who control financial and regulatory resources. This is where marketing comes in.

Marketing is essentially communications—both learning what people want and telling them what you have to offer. Because greenways tend to be public amenities that are, in most cases, supported by tax dollars, marketing also involves what parkland and recreation expert John Crompton calls *sanctioning*: winning the approval of those average citizens who may or may not use the facility but who will support it with their tax dollars. Winning public support is absolutely essential if your project is to receive its fair share of the community dollars needed to build and maintain it.

Who Are the Public and What Do They Want?

The Different Publics

Communities are made up of myriad factions. A good marketing program identifies them and tailors the message to each audience. Various interests ranging from bicycling organizations to adjacent landowners may have representative organizations or staff who can be contacted for advice and support. A few important types of public support to look for are the following.

Allies in Positions of Authority. Allies in positions of authority include elected officials, agency staff, and business executives. Winning these allies is key to a successful greenway effort. Meeting with them one-on-one to explain your project certainly helps. Working through mutual acquaintances is also effective. Keep elected officials apprised of community news; like landowners, elected officials don't want to find out about the greenway by reading a newspaper article.

The involvement and support of local officials is crucial; state and county agencies are not likely to proceed with a trail project in the face

In a recent study of Charlotte and Raleigh greenways, researchers showed that greenways have become an important element in the life-style of senior citizens, the most active and daily users of the greenway. They also found that the majority of greenway users live within five miles of the facility with usership decreasing with increasing distance from the greenway.
—Owen J. Furuseth and Robert E. Altman, Carolina Planning, Vol. 16, No. 2, Fall 1990

Eighty-eight percent of Americans walk and jog for recreation, and 82 percent enjoy a drive in the country, according to a new Recreation Roundtable/Peter Hart survey. The Recreation Roundtable (202-662-7420), consisting of leaders from the $300 billion per annum recreation industry, aims to improve understanding of recreation issues, especially in Washington and on Wall Street. Other favorite activities identified in the survey (and the percentage of Americans who enjoy it) are swimming (55 percent), biking (44 percent), fishing (37 percent), camping (29 percent), backpacking and hiking (18 percent), and skiing (15 percent).
—Common Ground, Vol. 2, No. 4 May/June 1991

of opposition from local officials. Take officials out on trail walks to develop an awareness of the greenway's potential. Provide a short description of the project and well thought-out, written responses to any questions they might raise. Make it sound so appealing that local officials will want credit for creating the greenway.

If your greenway crosses jurisdictional boundaries, make a presentation to the governing bodies of each jurisdiction. You may be asked to meet with the local planning commission or other community leaders and officials. You may also offer to hold public meetings and assure them that you would be willing to meet with any local group.

Grassroots Support. Grassroots support allies are usually politically astute and responsive to public interest and opinion. One of the best ways to win them over is to build a strong base of grassroots support in each jurisdiction along your greenway corridor. If your project becomes popular with their constituencies, it will be hard to ignore.

Sometimes this power base will grow out of the action of a vocal community group, as in the example of Denver's Platte River Greenway. In other cases, an aggressive public awareness and promotion program builds the support. For example, after diligent promotion by grassroots greenway proponents, Farmington, New Mexico, passed a gross receipts tax, allocating $1.9 million to the creation of a greenway.

Some communities have simply moved ahead with a pilot project. Seattle's Burke-Gilman Trail is a good example of this approach. When the first segment of this rails-to-trails conversion was opened, people used it, liked it, and called for more. Public demand caught the ear of Seattle's decision makers, and they rallied to the cause.

Allies on the Outside. Outside allies include people and organizations with different objectives who might nonetheless benefit from the greenway effort. For example, a soccer association might be interested in the joint use of a park site you have slated for acquisition and might support the greenway if it includes a soccer field. In Boulder, social service advocates joined with open-space proponents to support a bond issue that proposed to fund both an open-space land acquisition program and such social programs as a battered women's shelter. The potential for such alliances and partnerships should be considered when reaching out to the community with your greenway plan.

User Groups. User groups are probably a greenway's strongest supporters. They don't always agree, however, about what the greenway should be. User groups are bicyclists, walkers, joggers, equestrians, educators, bird-watchers, canoeists, anglers, boaters, wheelchair recreationalists, and all others who will visit and use the greenway. They are often organized in clubs or associations that can provide advice and technical assistance, review your plans, and help with building community support. These groups often have start-up money, and they can also fill the city council chambers when appropriations or other greenway-related actions are being considered. It's important to try to unite these constituencies in support of your greenway.

Nonuser Advocates. Nonuser advocates are people who may never visit the greenway but who will support it for other reasons, such as civic pride, economic development, or environmental protection. Nonuser support shows broad-based, solid grassroots backing for your greenway.

The Unorganized (Silent) Public. The unorganized public are the quiet people who don't show up at public meetings or write letters to the editor, but they *do* vote. Remember the sanctioning taxpayer mentioned earlier? Communicating with this group may be your toughest challenge, especially if you are proposing any tax increases or regulations that will affect their property. Reaching the general public can be vital if a bond issue or other politically sensitive action is part of your strategy. Favorable media coverage can help, as can tailoring your message to the local political climate; for example, you might not want to propose funding the greenway through a property tax if the community has just voted down a property tax increase. (See the box on page 68 for economic arguments supporting greenways.)

Adjacent Landowners, Tenants, Businesspeople. People who have a direct interest in what happens to land along the corridor constitute an important group. You want their support. They can be quite powerful allies when you approach politicians and private-sector donors. It is always a good idea to meet with each property owner or individual who might be affected in any way by the proposed greenway, particularly if any of his or her property is near or adjacent to or overlaps the proposed route or if any regulations may affect that person's land. Talk to these people one-on-one. Find out what their concerns are. Don't limit your contacts to people directly on the greenway route, but include those who live or operate businesses within a reasonable distance of the corridor.

Government Agency Decision Makers. Government agency decision makers include government entities responsible for flood control, water and sewer systems, transportation, environmental protection, water quality, wildlife, archeology, and other issues that may affect or be affected by your greenway.

Talk with staff and department heads. Find out what their needs are and look for ways you can help each other. You may be surprised by the number of areas of potential mutual benefit. Be sure you also identify those who might stand in the way, and try to find ways to win them over.

Utility Companies. Utility companies are gas and electric, telephone, and other service companies. Areas of concern include trespass and liability, but many areas of mutual benefit exist, such as shared trail and road maintenance. Utilities can derive good public relations benefits from and cut their costs by joint venturing.

Determining What the Public Wants

Determining what the public wants can be a little tricky if this is the first greenway in your area. Determining what the public wants is like

Scenic Hudson, a private nonprofit organization at the forefront of the movement to create a greenway along the Hudson River, sponsored a survey of 403 valley residents from an eight-county region. Three-quarters of the respondents supported the linking of parks and historic landmarks with other open space in the Hudson River Valley. The positive responses transcended education, income, race, age, and political and gender differences.
—Marist Institute for Public Opinion, "A Survey of Public Attitudes in the Hudson River Valley," Poughkeepsie, N.Y., 1987

"Patience and good public education are important assets in dealing with any public acquisition program. Respect landowner positions, negotiate fairly, with one spokesman from the group making all the landowner contacts."
—Iowa Heritage Trail

Economic Benefits of Greenways

Real-property values
: Many studies demonstrate that parks, greenways, and trails increase nearby property values. In turn, increased property values can increase local tax revenues and help offset greenway acquisition costs.

Expenditures by residents
: Spending by local residents on greenway-related activities helps support recreation-oriented businesses and employment, as well as other businesses that are patronized by greenway and trail users.

Commercial uses
: Greenways often provide business opportunities, locations, and resources for commercial activities such as recreation equipment rentals and sales, lessons, and other related businesses.

Tourism
: Greenways are often major tourist attractions, which generate expenditures on lodging, food, and recreation-oriented services. Greenways also help improve the overall appeal of a community to prospective tourists and new residents.

Agency expenditures
: The agency responsible for managing a river, trail, or greenway can help support local businesses by purchasing supplies and services. Jobs created by the managing agency may also help increase local employment opportunities.

Corporate relocation
: Evidence shows that the quality of life of a community is an increasingly important factor in corporate relocation decisions. Greenways are often cited as important contributors to quality of life.

Public cost reduction
: The conservation of rivers, trails, and greenways can help local governments and other public agencies reduce costs resulting from flooding and other natural hazards.

Intrinsic values
: While greenways have many economic benefits, it is important to remember the intrinsic environmental and recreation value of preserving rivers, trails, and other open space corridors.

Adapted from *Economic Impacts of Protecting Rivers, Trails, and Greenway Corridors*, National Park Service, 1990. For further information contact The Conservation Fund, 1800 North Kent Street, Arlington, VA 22209 (703-525-6300).

"The Impacts of Rail-Trails: A Study of Users and Nearby Property Owners From Three Trails" provides comprehensive documentation of a wide array of economic and other benefits accruing to users, neighboring landowners, and local communities along three rail-trails.

shooting at a moving target; values and interests vary among different demographic groups and can change over time. For example, new kinds of recreational equipment will come on the market and alter public activity patterns. Mountain bikes and roller blades have introduced a whole new set of trail needs. The traditional wheelchair has evolved into racing and sport varieties, and roller blades are replacing skates.

Demographics also change constantly. The so-called baby boomers are now reaching middle age. This in itself will alter greenway-related needs and demands. As large segments of the population age, will increased leisure time and the desire to remain fit increase the need for greenway trails? Will this segment of the population want to jog and bike long distances, or will they prefer a shorter stroll? Consider all age groups, life-styles, and trends. Try also to imagine the situation ten or fifteen years hence. In what ways will the situation be different?

There are several ways to determine public demand. First, find out what the public has already said it wants. One commonly used technique is the public opinion survey. This can be done inexpensively by telephone poll, mail-out questionnaire, or other technique. Today, polls can even be taken by computer. Missoula, Montana, has a call-in

Property Owner and Tenant Concerns

When approaching landowners, try to anticipate their concerns so that you can answer their questions and calm any fears. Try to determine whether their concerns are real or the result of misinformation, hostility toward government, or simple territorial instincts. Always listen carefully and make sure landowners know you take these matters seriously. Landowner opposition can sink a greenway project or color public attitudes so that funding is difficult to secure. Remember, the greenway will affect them as much as anyone, so explain how the greenway will benefit them. Common landowner concerns are:

• *Liability.* Always be prepared to discuss liability issues. What happens if someone is injured on the landowner's property? Is the landowner covered by adequate insurance, either his or her own or as provided by the land trust or state or local government liability legislation?

• *Crime.* Even though there has been no documented increase in criminal activity on greenways, crime is almost always a concern (see the box on page 76). In *Greenways for America* (pp. 186, 187), Charles Little cites the example of Seattle's Burke-Gilman Trail. Police officers who patrolled the trail were interviewed about problems with crime and vandalism. Their response was that "there is not a greater incidence of burglaries and vandalism of homes along the trail." The police noted that problems in parks are generally confined to areas of easy motor vehicle access. Despite fears that greenways will be used by "outsiders," it's usually the local citizens who use the path. Merely opening a greenway to public use may in fact discourage unsavory activities in derelict areas. Safety issues will be different in a small, rural trailway than in a large recreational greenway in a big city.

• *Property Taxes and Property Values.* Some people favor developing open space to expand the tax base. Expansion of the tax base, however, does not necessarily mean increased revenue to the local government. Development almost always means an increase in infrastructure and public service requirements, and the cost of providing these services often outweighs the additional tax revenue.

The other property tax issue you will probably face is a concern that the local government will increase taxes to pay for the greenway. In fact, increased tax revenues are usually generated by an increase in property values on land near the greenway. The exceptions would be jurisdictions where property assessments lag behind market values and states that have passed legislation limiting real-estate tax increases. Some communities have levied additional taxes to pay for greenways, but these taxes usually take the form of special assessments. Landowners who donate easements can actually *reduce* their own property tax assessments. In addition, easements reduce the cost of full acquisition for the town.

• *Private Property Rights.* Some landowners are opposed to putting land into public ownership for any reason. You simply may not be able to change their minds, but we advocate that you stress the benefits to the community—*their* community.

• *Maintenance.* Be prepared to answer a landowner's concern that the government can't maintain what it already manages, let alone new property.

• *Privacy.* Landowners may be concerned about trespassing and privacy or about the trail interfering with agricultural or business activities on their property. To address this concern, some greenways use fences and landscaping to buffer private property; others, like the Stowe Recreation Path, literally give the landowners a blank map and let them site the path across their property.

• *Land Use.* Be prepared to explain the concept of conservation easements. Organizations like the Land Trust Alliance and the Trust for Public Land can offer you assistance and provide you with information about easements and how other groups have used them.

computer forum where citizens and public agency staff can discuss greenway planning.

You might talk with your parks and recreation agency to see if they have done a recreation needs assessment or projections for future use. You might also approach park managers or sporting goods and bicycle shop operators. They should have a sense of current trends and

Some Guidelines for Dealing with Landowners

• Meet with landowners one-on-one in friendly surroundings at a time that's convenient for them. If you know someone who knows a particular landowner, have that person arrange the meeting or come along. You may want the same person to meet with *all* the landowners to assure consistency.

• Be honest and forthcoming, courteous, and persistent. Never give the impression that you are making secret deals behind anyone's back.

• Know the property and its value to the greenway system. Know exactly what you want to protect. (Your resource assessment and goal setting process will help you determine this.) A landowner may, for example, object to a trail but not to the protection of a historic building or wildlife habitat on the property.

• Anticipate the landowner's concerns. These concerns include loss of privacy, wildlife impacts, liability, fear of crime, possible increase in local taxes for management, or removal of lands from the tax base.

• Learn everything you can about the affected landowners. What is their financial situation? Their attitude toward the greenway? Their current stewardship of their property? Volunteers and research can help here. Volunteers may know some of the landowners and what they think.

• Know your facts. Have some national and state greenway statistics on hand. Be familiar with a similar successful greenway nearby. If the landowner requests information, get back to him or her promptly.

• Have a conceptual plan with good supporting data, maps, and so on. (This should be a preliminary plan with the general outline of the area, not individual parcels of privately owned land. You don't want to put the property owner on the defensive.)

• Have legal counsel available to answer questions about liability, tax benefits, and other matters.

• Involve landowners in the planning process from the beginning.

In a survey of adjacent landowners along the Luce Line rail-trail in Minnesota, the majority of adjacent landowners (87 percent) believed the trail increased or had no effect on the value of their property. Sixty-one percent of the suburban residential owners noted an increase in their property value as a result of the trail. New owners felt the trail had a more positive effect on adjacent property values than did continuing owners. Appraisers and real-estate agents claimed that trails were a positive selling point for suburban residential property, hobby farms, farmland proposed for development, and some types of small town commercial property.
—Leonard P. Mazour, 1988, cited in Economic Impacts of Protecting Rivers, Trails, and Greenway Corridors (National Park Service, 1990)

recreation equipment. Check with national manufacturers of bikes, canoes, cross country skis, and other products.

Sometimes you can determine trends from national opinion polls. Colorado Springs accomplished a fairly low-cost assessment of the trail-user market by looking at national survey data and then extrapolating a likely local pattern by identifying the same age and income groups living in Colorado Springs. The National Parks and Recreation Association can provide information on recreational trends.

Pitfalls to Avoid

Here are some common mistakes you can avoid when trying to build community support:

• Never publicly suggest a special tax, regulation, or assessment without checking with community leaders and other knowledgeable individuals to determine the likely level of support for or opposition to the proposal.

• Don't make your greenway project a cause or vendetta against some polluter, dam builder, or other entity threatening the corridor. Avoid confrontational politics. Even if your greenway group was originally conceived in response to a direct threat from a developer or utility, focus now on the greenway.

• Avoid affiliation with a political candidate or political party. Make the greenway effort nonpartisan.

• Never underbudget the project. It is better to overestimate at the beginning than to have to go back and ask for supplemental funds.

Thirteen Pointers for Handling Flak

Criticism can be flattering.

The criticism conservationists receive these days acknowledges the movement's maturity and clout. While facing criticism is never pleasant, some approaches are better than others. Here are thirteen suggestions that may make the task easier.

1. In actuality and appearance, make sure everything is done ethically at every state of every project. The "Statement of Land Trust Standards and Practices" published by the Land Trust Alliance (202-785-1410) provides helpful guidance.

2. Anticipate problems. Analyze how your project benefits the community. Prepare factual responses in advance.

3. Involve other organizations and community leaders in support.

4. Advise political leaders in advance of a public announcement.

5. When you announce your project, distribute a well-thought-out statement (or news release, testimony, etc.) that disarms potential criticism in advance. Telling the story the way you want it told from the beginning, combined with a solid, worthwhile project, can do much to stem criticism before it happens.

6. When criticism comes, determine its source. Does it come from legitimate citizen concern or from one of the national "anti-conservation" groups? Spot the latter by looking for scare phrases like "locking up the land," "attack on property rights," or "radical preservationists." Community criticism lacks vitrioloc rhetoric and sincerely seeks answers.

7. Consider what's at stake compared to the time it will take to respond.

8. If responding, be positive. Don't be defensive. Stress benefits. Act quickly.

9. Don't refute specific allegations. Use facts to tell your side without adding credibility to your critics' charges.

10. Don't be clever or sarcastic. Don't attack the attackers. Sell your position on its merit. Be reasonable.

11. When responding to community concern, state your case clearly in a public forum. Make sure your supporters are there. Answer questions, but don't argue. Have a written statement for the press.

12. Logic doesn't help with the people who are ideologically opposed to conservation. Respond with a written, positive statement that doesn't take a lot of time.

13. When talking to reporters, don't trust "off the record" statements. Remember, journalists are paid to report news.

—*Jack Lynn*

Jack Lynn, executive director of Conservation Communications (703-683-2996), has worked in land conservation public relations at the national level since 1969.

Once you publicize your costs, stay consistent or your credibility will suffer.

- Never exclude or appear to exclude an individual or interest group from the planning dialogue.

- At a meeting, never engage participants in a debate or shouting match. Listen, write down what they say, and calmly lay out the advantages and options for them. Select committee members with open minds, cool tempers, and diplomatic skills as spokespersons for your greenway at public meetings (see the box above).

The Ideal Marketing Tool—A Pilot Project

The best way to build a greenway constituency is to actually develop a piece of it and invite people to come out and use it. Ideally, your pilot project should benefit a broad cross section of users, from walkers to bicyclists to equestrians. A good pilot project will demonstrate what the greenway is and what it has to offer. It shows the public that the project

A completed pilot project on Denver's Platte River Greenway includes a trail segment, a landscaped mini-park, and a trailhead. The pilot project demonstrated what a greenway can be and set a standard of quality for improvements to come. (Robert Searns)

"Our strongest asset is our voice. We have been able to coordinate activities and make things happen."
—Schuylkill River Greenway

is real and can also jump the hurdle of a laborious planning and analysis process.

If the city council or others are reluctant to commit to a pilot project, it may be helpful to invite speakers in from other communities that have successful greenway projects. A few slides of a successful project elsewhere can be quite convincing. This is especially true if greenways have been constructed in neighboring communities.

Here are some additional tips for a successful pilot project:

- Be sure you own the land or have secured the right of way.

- Be sure that your pilot project makes sense. An inaccessible riverfront park or a trail that goes nowhere would not serve your ultimate objectives.

- Capture the community's imagination; start where the most public support is likely to be. Ideally, the pilot project should help gain community and government backing for your greenway and attract new sources of funding for the more difficult segments.

- Be sure the pilot project is substantial enough to make an impression. It should showcase as many of the greenway's benefits as possible and should be in a visible and accessible location.

- Think ahead to likely future segments. They should build at regular intervals on the pilot project.

The Communications Challenge: Getting the Word Out

"What greenway? Never heard of it. No one ever goes down by the river except the drug dealers and bums. Do you mean that 'sidewalk' along the river? What is a greenway anyway?"

These are the kinds of remarks heard during the early stages of a greenway project. Building support for your greenway includes getting the word out. People need to know how your project will benefit them and the community. In the early days of greenway development, this is no small task. Fortunately, there are an increasing number of successful greenways nationwide to cite as examples.

Charles Little's *Greenways for America* and the June 1990 issue of *National Geographic* are two excellent sources of information about successful greenway projects. Several national organizations can provide information on successful greenways. Still, *greenway* is not yet a household word. How do you get the word out? People today are deluged with information. To communicate successfully, you must identify and target the various segments of the community. A director of public works needs different kinds of information than does a cycling enthusiast.

After you've identified your audience and decided how to tailor your message, you need to select the best way to reach them. Most likely, you won't have a huge public relations budget. Spreading the word, then, will be a challenge. One way to get attention is with a pilot project. If you build it and people use it, they will tell their friends.

There are, a number of other low-cost steps you can take to publicize your project while you're building it.

The Master Plan Report

If you have prepared a greenway master plan, there will no doubt be a published report. This report and the planning process that led up to it are among the first formal instruments of communication. Ideally, the news media have been invited to and have participated in the various public meetings and workshops held during the development of the plan, and they have primed the public with progress reports. The communications value of the master plan report, however, is limited to a fairly narrow, though important audience, which includes key agency staff and decision makers, elected officials, certain community leaders, local planning and design professionals, and possibly the news media.

As we have seen, the report should be presented in an attractive, graphic format, it should lay out specific goals, and it should address technical questions and budget and phasing strategies. The report is a guide for future planning and decision making along the greenway corridor. To assure broad readership and reduce printing costs, the report should be no more than seventy or eighty pages for a substantial

The Monadnoch-Sunapee Greenway, administered by the Society for the Protection of New Hampshire Forests, has produced a greenway guide and annual newsletter called "Ramblings." The Concord, Sudbury, and Assabet Rivers includes information on access points, natural history, and suggested routes. A local land trust, the Sudbury Valley Trustees, distributes the guide, which was written by Ron McAdow.

"Celebrate Greenways," an all-day event in Chittenden County, Vermont, invited all county residents to bike, jog, walk, rollerblade, use baby joggers, canoe, kayak, or row their favorite segment of the greenway system and rendezvous at a celebration party later in the day. The Chittendon Greenway Board, a group of citizens and local officials who assist greenway work in communities and promote a regional network of paths and trails, promoted the event.

The Bay Cycle Classic and Fun Ride, an annual event in San Francisco, sparks community support for the completion of the Bay Trail, a hiking and biking path along the shorelines of the San Francisco and San Pablo Bays. The first day features a bike race. The second day is devoted to "fun rides," including the World's Shortest Political Race, in which thirty elected officials bicycle one lap of the greenway. As a result of this event, several officials have joined the Bay Trail Board. The Bay Cycle Classic always draws local television, radio, and print coverage, which in turn helps publicize the trail system.

project. On smaller projects, the report might be only ten pages or so. Detailed research and background information can be included in a technical appendix or project file. Distribution of the Master Plan Report may be limited; some communities place copies in libraries for public use.

The Executive Summary

The Executive Summary is a four- to ten-page synopsis of the master plan. It is a great, inexpensive public relations tool, and in these days of desktop publishing, it needn't be expensive. The summary gets the main points across to busy community leaders and agency decision makers and all other constituents who may not have time to read the more detailed plan. This document should be concise, attractive, and persuasive. It should summarize costs and highlight such key elements as project goals and phasing. A map of the corridor should be included.

Project Brochures

Use brochures to explain the greenway in brief text accompanied by a map, some photographs, and artwork. Present it in an attractive layout. This is the ideal written communication tool for a greenway. The brochure can be a sophisticated four-color booklet or a simple sheet printed in one color and folded. The key is to make it clear, attractive, and inspirational.

The brochure should focus on local needs and benefits of the greenway and should include an address and phone number for more information, as well as a tear-out panel or envelope that can be sent in with a contribution or completed volunteer checklist. You may also want additional brochures for specific pilot projects. Also consider the life of the brochure. One designed to sell the project won't do later on when you are trying to educate greenway users.

Several thousand copies of this kind of brochure can be printed for less than $500. A good project brochure can, in many cases, substitute for the longer and more costly executive summary.

Slides, Lectures, Videos

Thanks to the carousel projector, almost anyone, even someone with minimal artistic skills, can present an idea through a slide presentation. Producing a simple yet effective slide show early in the greenway process is essential. Slides are versatile and attractive: presentations can be easily updated and tailored to the interests of a particular viewing audience.

Keep it simple. Generally, a ten- to fifteen-minute slide show with forty to eighty slides will do fine. This is a good length for both city council meetings and service club breakfasts. (For presentations limited to ten to fifteen minutes including questions, it helps to have a ten- to twenty-slide version on hand.)

Fact Sheet for Presenters and Facilitators: Potomac River Greenway Forums

This fact sheet, designed for a series of public workshops, conveys basic information about greenways and provides a common base from which discussions can lead.

• The Report of the President's Commission on American Outdoors in 1987 proposed a nationwide greenways network to link together the urban and rural spaces in the American landscape and to provide people with access to open spaces close to home. Although there were greenways in existence and the concept was not a new one, the report (along with concerns about rapid development and disappearing open space) spurred many additional greenway projects around the country. Adjacent communities are finding ways to link greenways across boundaries. The Potomac River region should bcome a part of this nationwide effort.

• Representatives of many agencies and organizations in the region have come together to form a "Potomac River Greenways Coalition" in order to encourage and support greenway planning and implementation. Their mission is "to preserve and enhance the Potomac River and its environs as a greenway system protecting the natural, recreational, historical and cultural features of the river valley for present and future generations."

• What are greenways? Greenways are natural areas set aside for conservation and, in many cases, for recreation. They are primarily linear corridors—fingers of green of many shapes and sizes, extending across the landscape. Greenways link people with outdoor resources and provide wildlife migration routes. They can provide off-road transportation alternatives for walkers and bikers. Greenways can be any length, and ideally will link communities across America into a vast and varied network of open spaces.

• Greenways are not necessarily "parks" or public land. A greenway may or may not include a trail or public access in a particular location. Some parts of a greenway may be simply a scenic resource or a protected wildlife habitat. A greenway can be protected in many ways, including a voluntary action by a private landowner such as donating a conservation easement along a small strip of land, or simply agreeing to maintain a buffer strip of vegetation close to a waterway.

• Benefits of greenways. Greenways have significant environmental, conservation, and economic benefits. They can reduce flood damage, protect wildlife habitat, protect water quality and help recharge the water table, improve landscape aesthetics, build community pride, enhance awareness and appreciation of wildlands and provide tourism opportunities. Recent studies show that greenways increase the value of nearby properties and are beneficial to the economy of a community.

• Private landowners' rights must be respected in all cases; greenway creation should not involve a government taking of land. Privately owned lands are included in a network of greenways only with the cooperation and agreement of the owner. Landowners who agree to allow a trail to pass through their land are generally protected from liability through state laws; and those who donate conservation easements—even without allowing public access—enjoy significant tax benefits.

• How is a greenway established? Any public or private site which is managed for conservation or recreation can become part of a greenway. Communities should examine their resources and decide which areas can and should become part of a greenway system. Greenway planning and implementation must be a *cooperative* effort, through a public/private partnership of citizens, organizations, business and government agencies at all levels.

Also prepare a project fact sheet that anticipates some of the questions people will ask (see the box above). The fact sheet should outline the benefits of the greenway project and address such points as estimated acquisition and development costs and maintenance costs, as well as include information about any current concerns such as water quality, flood control, or crime. Handing out project brochures at the presentations also helps.

Organize your presentation like a short essay. It's helpful to put together a brief written outline to use as a guide. Start with the vision.

American Greenways Fact Sheet: Crime and Vandalism

Issue: Do recreational trails and other types of greenways cause crime, vandalism, and other disturbances? What evidence is there to support or to alleviate the concerns of adjacent landowners?

Facts: There is little evidence to support the fear that greenway trails will produce disturbance to private landowners. In fact the evidence is to the contrary.

• A 1980 study by the Minnesota Department of Natural Resources compared landowners' attitudes on a pair of proposed trails with landowner attitudes along a pair of similar trails already established. On the proposed trails 75% of landowners thought that if a trail was constructed it would mean more vandalism and other crimes. By contrast, virtually no landowners along the two constructed trails (0% and 6%, respectively) agreed with the statement "trail users steal." (Minnesota Department of Natural Resources, 1980)

• A 1987 study of Seattle's Burke-Gilman Trail found little or no crime or vandalism experienced by adjacent property owners. The study surveyed property owners, realtors, and police officers. According to the realtors, property "near" the trail is significantly easier to market and sells for an average of 6% more than similar properties located elsewhere. Nearly two-thirds of adjacent landowners believed that the trail "increased the quality of life in the neighborhood"; not a single resident thought the trail should be closed. (Evaluation of the Burke-Gilman Trail's Effect on Property Values and Crime, Seattle, Washington, Engineering Department, 1987)

• A former opponent of the Burke-Gilman trail (whose home is on the trail) stated that the "trail is much more positive than I expected. I was involved in citizens' groups opposed to the trail. I now feel that the trail is very positive; [there are] fewer problems than before the trail was built; [there were] more litter and beer cans and vagrants [before it was built]." Not a single resident surveyed said that present conditions were worse than prior to construction of the trail.

• A 1992 study by the National Park Service of the impacts of rail-trails on nearby property owners found that "a majority of landowners reported no increase in problems since the trails opened. That living near trails was better than they had expected it to be, and that living near the trails was better than living near unused railroad lines before the trails were opened." (*Impact of Rail-Trails*, National Park Service, 1992).

• Comments from adjacent landowners interviewed for the NPS study included the following:

"Vandalism, robbery, and safety concerns I originally had were unfounded." (Landowner on California's Lafayette/Moraga Trail)

"I was very opposed to the idea at first, fearing that it would be used by motorcyclists, but I am very pleased with the trail—it provides a safe alternative to using the highway for joggers and bicyclists, and it gives me a safe and comfortable place for my walks." (Adjacent landowner on Florida's St. Mark's Trail)

"We are a small town and most everyone uses the trail at one time or another. The city of Durango has no bad comments to make on the trail; they all like it very much." (Public official on Iowa's Heritage Trail)

• A 1988 survery of greenways in several states has found that "such parks typically have not experienced serious problems regarding . . . vandalism, crime, trespass, [or] invasion of privacy . . . Prior to developing the park facilities, these concerns were strongly voiced in opposition to proposed trails. After park development, however, it was found that fears did not materialize . . . concerns expressed by the neighbors opposed . . . have not proven to be a postdevelopment problem in any of the parks surveyed." ("A Feasibility Study for Proposed Linear Park," Oregon Department of Transportation, Parks and Recreation Division, May 1988)

• A 1990 study by the Appalachian Trail Conference of crimes on the Appalachian Trail found that despite use by 3–4 million persons per year, there were only 0.05 crimes per 100,000, or 1 in 2 million. This means you are more likely to be struck by lightning or victimized in your home than as a hiker on the Appalachian Trail. (Source: Appalachian Trail Conference, Harpers Ferry, West Virginia)

For additional information contact the American Greenways Program, The Conservation Fund, 1800 North Kent Street, Suite 1120, Arlington, VA 22209 (Phone: 703-525-6300; fax: 703-525-4610).

Discuss key issues and challenges, followed by a brief tour of the corridor that takes the viewer step-by-step along the route. You might close with examples of what has been done elsewhere, including before and after shots of successful greenways in other communities. The Conservation Fund, state parks departments, the National Park Service Rivers, Trails and Conservation Assistance Program, and communities that have completed greenways all have slides of successful projects available for loan or purchase.

Once you have developed a presentation, where do you show it? Start with presentations to elected officials such as city councils and county commissioners. Try to make at least an annual presentation to these groups in the form of a progress report. The slide presentation can also be shown to service clubs, recreation groups, school classes, garden clubs, and any organization with a potential interest in the greenway.

Consider putting together a speakers' bureau consisting of agency staff, advocacy group members, and other community supporters who can present the slides. After all, nothing is more convincing than a speaker's own enthusiasm. Schedule a series of speaking engagements to various organizations. In Leesburg, Virginia, for example, a group of fifteen greenway advocates made more than two hundred presentations to launch its project.

For one-on-one presentations, a small book of photographs that your prospect can leaf through while you talk is much more effective.

What about videos and film? These can be spectacular and certainly have their place. Whether you make a video will depend on the scope of your project, the resources of your group, the life span of the material in the video, and the need for such a production to get your points across. Professional video and film production can be quite expensive, running anywhere from $10,000 to $60,000 or more. You may be able to recover some of your expenses by selling copies of the video to interested individuals and greenway groups. Another option is to have your slide show transferred onto video by a production company that specializes in slide-to-tape transfer. This method allows you to simulate movement, but you will sacrifice the ability to modify and update your presentation. Setting up equipment is cumbersome, even with the newer video projectors.

Remember, impressive greenways have been created with the enthusiasm of the advocates, some nicely done drawings, and a handful of slides. Some people may wonder about your priorities or your finances if you spend a small fortune on promotional materials.

Displays

An inexpensive project display is easily assembled from several drawings and photographs, especially those of people using completed segments of your greenway. Think about where and how often your display will be used, for example, in schools and shopping centers. Someone will have to set up the display and stay with it. You may also

"We started sponsoring activities that would bring people back to the stream and let them know what it could be. Just a couple of weeks ago we sponsored the fifth annual trout derby. We stocked the stream with trout. We brought people down—all sizes, shapes, ages—and everyone fished and won prizes for their catches. There are catfish in the lake and trout in the stream. Last year over seven hundred people came out to enjoy the event."
—Barbara Taylor of Maryland Save Our Streams, speaking at the Maryland Greenways Conference, November 1990

want to consider a greenway poster, bumper sticker, decal, or calendar as a fund-raising and public relations vehicle.

Newsletters

With desktop publishing it is easy to produce an effective newsletter, and local businesses will often pay for printing in return for a plug. Like slide shows, newsletters need not be slick. A one- or two-color flyer on a folded eleven- by seventeen-inch sheet of recycled paper will do. Remember that a few good photos can do much more than pages of text. Work with the postal service to obtain bulk mailing permits and special nonprofit rates. Be aware that the postal service is quite strict about the size and format of bulk mail, so be sure you understand and adhere to its requirements.

If you include a donation coupon and return envelope in the packet, your newsletter can bring in some revenue, often enough to pay production and mailing costs. The money, however, is not as important as the fact that the newsletter keeps your constituency informed.

The key to successful newsletter mailings is a good list. A mailing list takes time and effort to assemble. The list should include elected officials, user-group members, homeowners' associations, neighborhood groups, public agency staff, environmental groups, service clubs, owners of area businesses, contributors, potential foundation and corporate donors, and newspaper and television reporters. (Recreational and user groups tend to have good mailing lists from club memberships and special events.) Finally, consider sending your newsletter to out-of-town organizations and national groups that may share your interests. It's a great way to exchange information and network ideas.

One creative alternative or perhaps a supplement to your own newsletter is to place an article in another organization's newsletter This could be a local conservation group or even a local utility company. Often, the water or electric company includes a small newsletter with the monthly bill. Perhaps you can persuade them to allow you to include an article in their mailer. You would certainly be reaching a broad segment of the community.

There are different schools of thought as to how frequently to issue newsletters. Some successful greenway organizations do so only once a year (in which case it may really be an annual report), others send quarterly or monthly mailings. The frequency will depend on cost, available resources, and the stage of your development process. A newly formed group might want to issue newsletters less frequently than a well-established effort with a significantly developed greenway and a great deal more to report. (If cost is a problem, but you want to report more frequently, consider piggybacking onto another organization's newsletter with a greenway page or insert.)

Tours, Ground Breakings, Ribbon-Cutting Ceremonies

One of the best ways to make people aware of your project is to bring them to it. You can do this at the beginning of the project and again after

In 1985, a major event, the Roaring Twenties Festival, was organized to promote the Meramec Greenway in St. Louis, Missouri. Corporate sponsors provided funds for the two-day, five-stage, carnival, restaurant, and exhibit extravaganza. A key group of volunteers on six subcommittees organized the festival and managed the four hundred volunteers necessary for the event. Marketing and public relations were critical skills for the event.

Youngsters learn about local wildlife at the Merkle Wildlife Sanctuary and Visitor Center on the Patuxent River Greenway, Maryland. (Loring Schwarz)

different phases of the effort have been completed. Tours by bus, car, bicycle, foot, or even boat can accomplish a lot. Tours can be a group event (for example, the whole city council) or one-on-one affairs. Leading elected officials, potential private sector donors, and media people on individual tours should be considered, since you want to give each of these important persons all of your attention on the site.

Ribbon cutting and ground breaking ceremonies, on the other hand, *should* be major group events. Get lots of people out there, especially the news media. Be sure the elected officials and agency heads who supported you are in front of the crowd and the cameras. Give them credit. Thank them. Honor them. Give them an award. Make sure the voters know how they helped make the project possible. Plan these events carefully so that no one feels left out or underappreciated.

Special Events

Many kinds of events can dramatize the value of your greenway. Volunteer projects and public service events are two of the most effective ways to draw favorable attention. It is difficult for a politician not to support a stream that was just cleaned by a thousand Girl Scouts or Boy Scouts. In Denver, volunteers planted thousands of trees along the banks of the Platte River in a single day. This mega-landscaping event, held each April for three consecutive years, brought tremendous media attention as well as major corporate sponsorship.

Races, bicycle and horse trail rides, group walks, and festivals are also great ways to draw attention to what your corridor has to offer. These kinds of events can also serve as fund-raisers. A number of communities developing river-oriented greenways organize raft or canoe races that follow the greenway corridor.

The Yakima River Greenway Foundation in Washington state sponsors a popular annual Gap to Gap Relay Race, which includes bicycling, canoeing, and running and helps people appreciate the river as a recreational resource. Denver's Great Relay Race offers a forty-mile course along the South Platte River, where a baton is passed among equestrians, wheelchair racers, walkers, skaters, cyclists, runners, and, before the trail was complete, even "bushwhackers" who made their way along undeveloped segments of the corridor through junkyards and urban underbrush. The bushwhacking segments offered a dramatic illustration of what was still needed to be accomplished along the greenway. Special events, such as a Halloween spook trail or fishing derby, attract many first time visits from families, who tend to return to the greenway.

All in all, events can pay off, but they do take significant planning and organization. You want everyone to have a good time and no one to get hurt. Plan your events carefully and remember that they are just a means to an end—the creation of your greenway.

Interpretive Programs

Understanding the natural, historical, and cultural character of the corridor can do much to further the greenway cause. Contact local historians, schools, conservation groups, and even adjacent property owners for information. Public knowledge of the greenway's role, both in the natural world and in the community, can be a great source of civic pride.

Start with guided tours, pamphlets, nature walks, and other special programs. Invite conservation groups and educators to use your greenway for their programs. Later, depending on the goals and theme of your greenway, consider locating nature centers, museums, living history programs, and other interpretive attractions along the corridor.

The Brooklyn-Queens Greenway ran a logo contest to create a symbol for the route. Newspapers and a television station funded the competition, which ran in local junior and senior high schools.

Pueblo's Nature Center on the banks of the Arkansas River is an integral part of the Pueblo greenway system. The Center provides tours, exhibits, and a volunteer program to explain river valley ecology to greenway visitors.

Awards

Awards are another way to get the word out. Soon after the first trail segment along Denver's Platte River Greenway was completed, an adjacent property owner was spotted dumping rubble down the side of the river bank. The local authorities were called, and the property owner was "persuaded" to clean up the mess. Not only did he clean it up, but once educated about the value of the greenway, he enhanced the area with landscaping. This inspired the idea of giving cooperative property owners an award. Thus was born the Friend of the River Award. Each year several people who help enhance the greenway are given a special plaque signed by the governor and the chairman of the greenway foundation. The list of award candidates has been expanded to include elected officials, reporters, agency heads, and corporate donors who have supported the greenway effort. Plaques along the greenway can give supporters credit for easements or donations.

There is another side to awards—those your project receives. Winning awards helps build the project's image in the eyes of the community, brings favorable media exposure, and boosts the pride of those who have backed the effort. If you have a special project, consider applying for awards given by any number of organizations, including the American Society of Landscape Architects, the American Planning Association, the American Institute of Architects, the National Park and Recreation Association, Keep America Beautiful, American Greenway Program, and the Take Pride in America Program.

Terra Communications, the nonprofit arm of Altered Image, an advertising agency in Princeton, New Jersey, donates its marketing services to charities. Moved by the message of the Delaware River Greenway staff, Terra Communications agreed to produce and underwrite a ten-minute, three-projector slide show transposed to video for general distribution, including network TV. Staff of the Delaware River Greenway suggest that similar nonprofit branches of ad firms exist elsewhere.

Working with the News Media

The news media offer one of the most effective ways to make the public aware of your greenway. Good news coverage also gives your project credibility and increased political significance. Media attention can bring problems, however. If not presented sensitively, news media coverage during the planning process may create misunderstandings with landowners or other interested parties who have not yet been won over. You need to plan a media strategy ahead of time so you won't be caught off guard.

To plan a good media program, you need to think about the segments of the public you most want to reach and how to do so. You also need to consider the journalists in your area and how to capture their interest. Get to know the reporters who regularly cover environmental or community issues. Send them information. Take them on tours and show them how the greenway will benefit the community. From time to time, you may want to grant an exclusive story to a particular reporter.

Know your facts. When you talk with the media, especially at the beginning of a greenway effort, have some supportive facts and figures about national greenways on hand. You may also want to encourage them to write about similar successful projects in other communities. If the media press you for specific information before you have fully evaluated the pros and cons of an issue or completed your plan, don't

Boulder, Colorado, built a fish observatory along its greenway on the banks of Boulder Creek. Trail users can stop at the observatory and view fish from beneath the surface of the water using specially engineered viewing ports set below water level. Visitors can buy fish food from a dispenser; proceeds benefit the greenway.

Checklist for Community Involvement

☐ Meetings
☐ Citizen advisory committee(s)
☐ Surveys
☐ Interviews
☐ Media coverage
☐ Public service announcements
☐ Letters to the editor
☐ Brochures
☐ Slide shows
☐ Workshops

☐ Newsletters
☐ Posters and flyers
☐ Stationery with logo
☐ Events and festivals
☐ Volunteer projects
☐ Speaker's bureau
☐ School programs
☐ Videos
☐ Question and answer sessions

Adapted from Eugster *et al.*, *The Riverwork Book*, National Park Service.

---

go out on a limb and suggest ideas you can't back up. Provide only that information that your planning team or advocacy group has agreed upon. If you don't know, say so and offer to find out. Respect the reporter's deadline, and make sure you get back with the information in time, or explain why you can't.

Discuss costs in terms of benefits and provide examples of how a greenway can attract tourism, increase property values, and improve the quality of life. A million-dollar project might sound more palatable, for example, if expressed in terms of cost-per-user or cost-per-citizen. In a large metropolitan area with a million likely users, the cost would be only a dollar per person. Communicate the value of the project and how the community can become involved.

Don't assume that the media understand the greenway concept just because they came to your presentation or meeting. Supply them with premeeting information packets and take the time to point out helpful details.

In the event you are attacked, don't be defensive or combative. Stick to the facts and stress your greenway's benefits to the community. Be careful of quotes that can be taken out of context and avoid talking "off the record." Finally, be aware that news coverage is quirky. A late-breaking political scandal can easily pre-empt your story.

Newspapers

Newspapers are probably the most important media outlet. News articles offer more detail than television reports and provide a printed record of the coverage that you can later cite or reproduce for inclusion in a grant application. There are several kinds of newspaper exposure, including general-interest news stories, feature articles in weekend supplements, editorials, and letters to the editor. If possible, get to know the newspaper publishers and owners.

A News Release Checklist

☐ Include the name, address, and phone number of a contact person in the upper left-hand corner.

☐ Include the date that you would like the story published in the upper right near the title. (If you say "for immediate release," the story can be published at any time.)

☐ Include a brief title followed by a concise, interesting, and objective account. Type double spaced with side margins. Keep the release less than two pages—one is better.

☐ Include several direct quotes if appropriate.

☐ Be sure the names of people and organizations as well as other facts are double checked for accuracy.

☐ If appropriate, include an eight- by ten-inch glossy black-and-white photograph with descriptive information labeled on the back, as well as the date taken and name of the photographer. Try to have an action photo, such as one showing people *doing something* on the greenway site.

☐ If possible, put the release on attractive letterhead with a catchy logo to capture the reporter's attention. Be sure to list the name and telephone number of a contact person for further information.

☐ Send background information with the release, such as a fact sheet, a brochure, a map of the project site, and other information that can help the reporter without overwhelming.

Adapted from Samuel N. Stokes *et al.*, *Saving America's Countryside: A Guide to Rural Conservation* (Baltimore: Johns Hopkins University Press, 1988) and J. Glenn Eugster *et al.*, *Riverwork Book* (Philadelphia: National Park Service, 1988).

Radio and Television

Both radio and television are excellent means to announce events and to get coverage on daily news programs. Talk shows can also be useful forums, radio shows in particular because they have a broader listening audience than television talk shows, which often air at low-volume times like Sunday mornings. Contact the station's public affairs manager or news department.

Television coverage can be quite effective in two areas. The first is news stories, such as a report on the placement of a large pedestrian span or a ribbon cutting ceremony. Remember that the more action and visual appeal, the better the chances for television coverage (for example, a volunteer tree planting is more attractive than a legislative session). The other area is the special assignment report in which the greenway is the topic of a special feature report, usually spanning several days' programming. For television coverage, you need to get on the station's "day book," or they may not show up. Be persistent.

Most cable television services offer one or more public access channels. These may be of value both to draw public input during the planning process and later to build public awareness. You may want to ask the cable company for viewership numbers, if available, before deciding to invest the time.

News Releases

A news release is a written statement about your project or a special event relating to your project such as a ground breaking. It is usually issued to a list of media outlets in the community and even, if appropriate, to national wire services. News releases should be concise, focused, and interesting. Try to hit on no more than one or two main themes or points. Perhaps you can think of a catchy headline for the story, such as "Greenway Trail to Connect Two Cities." Compile a good list of media outlets, including TV stations, major newspapers, and community papers. If possible, include an exciting photo or other "hook" in the release to attract attention.

Timing on news releases depends on the media outlet, the size of the community and readership, and the frequency of publication. Generally, a news release can be sent out a week or two before an event such as a ground breaking or ribbon cutting ceremony. Releases for feature stories such as those in the Sunday supplement may need to go out well in advance. Similarly, if you want your event posted in a community events calendar, you may have to notify the publishers a month or more in advance. For all media outlets it is a good idea to send a follow-up reminder to arrive a day or two before the event, just in case the release got overlooked in the flurry of other news stories.

News releases intended for coverage in the daily paper or television report should be sent to the assignment editor or assignment desk. You should also send copies to reporters you know personally or who cover a special beat that might relate directly to your greenway.

Public Service Spots and Donated Advertisements

Many radio and television stations air a certain number of public service announcements. In some instances, broadcasters will donate studio time and professional services to help prepare advertisements and announcements. In addition to public service spots, some broadcasters will contribute financial support and lend the services of broadcast personalities for special events. Another way to use donated media coverage is through contributed advertisement space, such as a free announcement in the newspaper. Possibly, an advertising agency can be persuaded to contribute services in preparing ad copy. Such ads can be used to promote the project and to thank contributors.

A final note on working with the news media: consider designating an official spokesperson for your project who thoroughly understands the details of your effort and is skilled at working with the news media. Appointing an official liaison helps avoid misinformation, contradictory statements, and the premature release of details about a sensitive issue like a land acquisition. The staff should know to refer all questions to this person.

Building grassroots support for your greenway is essential. People become familiar with your effort, and that builds political support. Your organization gains credibility and clout. Good communications on your part also give people a chance to send feedback in the form of ideas, suggestions, and even constructive criticism. By being open and keeping the community informed, you avoid surprises and can head off opposition. Favorable publicity also helps draw support from corporations that want to be associated with a positive community undertaking. In short, getting the word out is essential to greenway success.

5

Funding Your Greenway

"Can anybody remember when the times were not hard and money was not scarce?"
—Ralph Waldo Emerson

Even the best greenway plan means little if there are no funds to carry it out. How do you garner these resources and let them work for you? Apart from an exciting greenway vision, an effective organization, and a marketing program, you need to know what your project will cost, who is likely to fund it, and how to obtain that funding.

Organizing a Fund-raising Campaign

A successful fund-raising campaign, like any business venture, requires a plan of action. Begin with your marketing program and consider the pilot project and phasing scheme. Temper your pilot project budget by estimating what you think you can raise from various funding sources in one year. In setting a target, be ambitious but realistic. Don't promise what you don't think you can deliver.

Public versus Private Funds

A number of projects, like the Yakima River Greenway, have eschewed public funds and raised almost all of their money from private sources. Many greenway projects, however, especially those with significant constructed improvements like paved trails, must depend upon a combination of public and private funds.

In public–private partnerships there must be a substantial contribution from both sides. For large urban projects, donors may want to see evidence of public-sector commitment. If you are relying on private funds to pay more than half the cost of such projects, you may be overestimating. In many cases, raising 20 to 50 percent of the cost of a major greenway from private sources is doing very well.

A first major question to answer, therefore, is what combination of public and private funds will be used. Finding the answer might begin with a visit to the local parks and recreation department, the state parks department, the local water management district, the planning department, or other agencies likely to be involved in a greenway partnership. Explain the critical role of the public sector—both political support and funding—to these decision makers, and find out how they are prepared to help.

What if you approach funders and find that money is tight? This is where creativity comes in. You may have to learn to be a *bottom feeder*, a scavenger who finds small grants here and there. Many successful greenways have been financed this way. With luck, while you are looking for funding sources, you'll manage to secure a major grant.

Public Sector Sources

Direct Local Agency Funding

The sponsoring public agency (for example, the parks department or the public works or engineering departments) can often come up with a substantial contribution and may commit to funding the project in subsequent years. To secure this funding, you will need to sell the project to the public, elected officials, agency staffers, and other stakeholders and decision makers. In many communities it may be necessary to have the greenway formally incorporated into the comprehensive plan or the parks and recreation plan. Be sure the key public contributor is at the top of the credit roster when ribbons are cut and kudos given. Such a person is your partner and, in many cases, the ultimate owner and manager of the project.

State and Federal Grant Programs

In the current economy, straightforward state and federal grants for greenways are smaller and harder to win. Money still is available, but finding it takes some ingenuity.

Contact your state parks, natural resources, transportation, wildlife, flood management, planning, and water quality departments and your state's environmental protection or coastal zone management agency. Ask about programs that might fit your greenway.

Many federal programs are routed through state agencies, so it's best to start at the state level and check out all leads. Perhaps you can create new funding programs through your state legislature that will benefit your project and other greenways. Is this the tail wagging the dog? Maybe so, but this approach has been successful in several states. The creation of the Willamette Greenway in Oregon is a good example. Accordingly, it is always a good idea to work closely with your local delegation of state legislators so that they know about your project and its popularity.

Be equally resourceful at the federal level. The Corps of Engineers can contribute up to 10 percent of the cost of flood control projects to recreation and mitigation improvements associated with the flood control effort. Look through the *Catalogue of Federal Domestic Assistance* for funding programs. Appendix B provides a synopsis of federal funds for greenways-related projects. Contact the National Park Service's Rivers, Trails and Conservation program for ideas and technical support. Work closely with your congressional delegation.

The boxed information offers some funding leads at the local, state, and federal levels. Remember, this list is only a starting point. New programs are created each year, and existing ones change. Funding levels also change year to year. Many sources may require a match of local

The Vermont Trails and Greenway Council works with the Vermont Department of Transportation to inspire greenway activity across the state. The council knew there was interest in greenways when it offered $2500 to any community willing to develop a model plan and received 60 requests. The council went to the Department of Transportation to ask for funds so communities could create bicycle and pedestrian facilities. The Department of Transportation offered $500,000 for local greenway efforts and received more than $5 million in applications. The next year Governor Dean offered $5.5 million to meet the demand from communities.

The Recreation Division of the U. S. Forest Service is committed to recreation and partnership building. Its Challenge Grant Program promotes projects providing wildlife or recreation in or near national forests. Funds have been used for fishing projects, maintenance, wildlife enhancement, handicapped access, and trail connections to urban areas. The program also offers technical assistance and design help. Gaining the support of local forests and forest districts is key.

Potential Public Funding Sources

Local Funding

City Council or County Commissioners. Direct funding, local matching dollars for a state or federal grant if appropriate, regulatory measures such as greenway setback or requirement to provide open space and trail easements

City or County Parks/Recreation Agency. Direct funding; technical support; future maintenance

City or County Planning Agency. Funding of plans, staff, and office support

Mayor's Office. Direct funding; staff and political support

Public Works Department or Flood Control Agency. Direct funding of planning, land acquisition, and built improvements where there is a flood control benefit; technical advice

Wastewater Agency. Trail right-of-way along sewer easement; improvements and acquisition of wetland where water quality benefit is possible; technical advice

Environmental Services Agency. Direct funding of habitat and wetland projects; water-quality projects; technical advice

Local Department of Transportation or Bike Program. Funding of bike and pedestrian trails along greenway; technical assistance; help with intersections

Economic Development/Tourism Agency. Funding of plans and brochures; technical data on users and economic benefits

Municipal Water Department. Joint use of properties and canal rights-of-ways; direct funding if water conservation is demonstrated

School District. Direct funding of land if joint use of lands or educational programs along greenway; student and teacher volunteer research and labor

Local Environmental Commission (if applicable). Land acquisition; research and planning services

Local Public Arts Program. Direct funding of arts and cultural elements on greenway

Other Special Local Programs. For example, direct funding or other joint venture with a museum or nature center with compatible interests

State Funding

State Parks Agency. Direct funding; state trails and rivers programs; greenways that include, connect with, or are near state parklands; technical advice; administer federal Land and Water Conservation Funds (can match state or local funds—check with state liaison officer); state park agency-led greenways

State Fish and Game Agency. Direct funding for wildlife and fishing programs; stocking of rivers, streams, and lakes; wildlife viewing facilities and interpretive programs; land acquisition for wildlife programs; technical assistance; administer federal wildlife programs; may assist greenway as access to existing wildlife refuge

State Transportation Agency. Funding of bike and pedestrian trails along greenway; technical assistance; provide trail and wildlife circulation facilities as part of new highway or mass transit construction; administer federal bike and trail funding under Intermodal Surface Transportation Efficiency Act of 1991 (ISTEA); reforestation; wetland mitigation; wildflower plantings; adopt-a-highway programs; erosion control; water quality protection

State Rivers Programs. Direct funding; land planning and protection regulations; technical assistance; restoration; funding for protective buffers along rivers

State Corrections Agency. Prison labor for projects; produce greenway components like picnic tables and signs in prison shops

State Environmental and/or Health Agency. Water quality protection; wetland acquisition and development

State Lottery. Some programs include funding of parks, recreation, and conservation

State Mine Reclamation Agency. Help with possible use of reclaimed mine lands as greenway habitat or recreation land (for example, lakes left by gravel mining); help restore wetlands to remove mine contaminants from streams

State Coastal Zone Programs. Regulation of development in coastal zone; technical assistance and funding for projects fostering access and water quality

Agricultural Land Programs. Tax incentives and other tools to protect agricultural lands

Federal Funding

Department of the Interior

National Park Service. Inclusion of National Park Service land in greenway; funding via state liaison officer (usually in parks and recreation or planning department) from Land and Water Conservation Fund grants program (requires local match); small

(continued on page 88)

(*continued from page 87*)
grants, technical assistance to national, state, and local entities through Rivers, Trails and Conservation Assistance Program; historic preservation programs; the urban park and recreation recovery program; protection of certain river corridors under the Wild and Scenic Rivers Act of 1968; national landmarks program

U.S. Fish and Wildlife Service (FWS). Inclusion of FWS land in greenway; direct funding and technical project grants under Dingle-Johnson Wildlife habitat funding or Wallop-Breaux sport fish restoration program; wildlife habitat program of endangered species act; challenge grants

Bureau of Land Management. Project grants for forest restoration, wildlife habitat studies, riparian habitat restoration, and other programs benefiting the public land; prospect for rail-trail projects in western United States

Department of Transportation

Funding for greenways via the Intermodal Surface Transportation Efficiency Act of 1991 (ISTEA), which includes grants for transportation enhancements, trails, scenic and historic highways, walkways, and bicycle facilities, and for local and statewide transportation planning, including bike and pedestrian travel.

Environmental Protection Agency

Technical advice; water quality protection; direct funding of planning, public information, and wetland projects related to greenways

Department of Defense

U.S. Army Corps of Engineers. Direct funding of recreation and conservation improvements in conjunction with flood control improvements; technical advice; possible flood control/greenway joint ventures, such as recreational use of flood storage facilities; regulation projects affecting streams and wetlands under Section 404 of the Clean Water Act

Military Lands. Possible joint use of bases and other military lands as greenway open space or wildlife habitat; also surplus property potentially available

Department of Housing and Urban Development

Community Development Block Grants. Project grants to benefit cities, counties, and states. Emphasis on projects that benefit low- and moderate-income people.

Department of Agriculture

U.S. Forest Service. Inclusion of Forest Service lands and trails; help with tree plantings; project grants for trails, equipment, and expenses; technical advice; challenge grants

Soil Conservation Service. Direct funding of rural erosion control projects; soils mapping; technical assistance; provision of certain specialized plant species for revegetation programs

Cooperative Extension. Technical advice

Farmers Home Administration

Write-down on loans to farmers for conservation easements to protect wetland and wildlife habitat

Department of Commerce

Office of Coastal Zone Management. Section 306 grants available to states with approved plan for acquisition, planning, recreation, access in coastal zone

Economic Development Administration. Project grants to states, cities that promote long-term economic development and private sector job creation in areas suffering severe economic distress

Small Business Administration. Project grants for tree planting programs

Federal Emergency Management Agency

Local flood insurance programs, flood mapping

Department of Energy

Cleanup of contaminated sites

National Endowment for the Arts and Humanities

Grants for planning, funding art on greenways, and other greenway improvements

funds and state or local sponsorship. Contacts at these agencies may be able to suggest other leads.

Public Agency Joint Ventures

Which agencies stand to benefit from your greenway project? We've mentioned how a bike path can also serve as a floodway maintenance path, allowing the water management agency access for debris removal and stream bank repair. Might they fund all or part of your trail? Highway and utility projects offer the same opportunities. Can the new sewer line along the creek offer a trail right-of-way?

The flip side to this is that all flood control, highway, and sewer projects should undergo review for greenway compatibility. Does the highway crossing the stream leave enough room for wildlife circulation or a trail underpass? What impact will a stream channelization project have on the greenway? With persuasion and strong enough political backing you can be sure greenway benefits are incorporated into other public works plans.

Joint Development Techniques

Joint development involves the use of funds for private real-estate development in conjunction with new public facilities. The goal is to generate new sources of tax revenue and other benefits through public–private cooperative agreements. For example, incentive zoning allows developers to build at a higher density in return for providing park land, plazas, landscaping, or trails. Another approach involves lease-back of land: the public entity owns the land and provides a private developer with a long-term ground lease in return for lease income and certain public improvements, for example, greenway amenities.

Public Finance

Public finance can take several forms. Voters can approve a special tax to fund a specific greenway project. Jefferson County, Colorado, for example passed a one-half cent sales tax, which annually brings in more than $12,000,000 to fund the acquisition and preservation of open space. Colorado Springs levies a 5 percent tax on the sale of bicycles and bicycle equipment, which brings in more than $60,000 each year to support trails and bikeway projects. The towns along the Hudson Valley in upstate New York assess a ¼ percent tax on hotel stays, which helps support the Hudson River Valley Greenway effort. Hamilton County, Tennessee, earmarks a portion of its hotel/motel tax for the North Chickamauga Creek greenways. Block Island, Rhode Island, supports its open space acquisition with a ½ percent tax on real-estate transactions. Interestingly, there are efforts afoot in many states to allow public funds to be shared with nonprofit groups for local conservation projects.

Improvement districts are another way to raise revenue for a greenway. A special taxing district is established, and an assessment, usually a property tax, is levied in that district. Revenues are earmarked for funding improvements that benefit people in a specific geographic area.

Special assessment districts are commonly used for street improvements, a special public amenity such as an outdoor plaza or street landscaping, and in certain instances, park improvements. Since the early part of century, the city of Minneapolis has funded parkland acquisition using a method whereby the rate of taxation declines with distance from the park.

Selling bonds is another common public-finance approach; essentially it means that the public sector borrows money. Because most communities have statutory limits on the amount of debt they can incur, the first

The National Oceanic and Atmospheric Administration provides block grants on a matching basis for states to implement their Coastal Zone Management Plans. As of early 1993, twenty-nine states (including several in the Great Lakes region) have approved plans. Within Maryland, Coastal Zone Management funds have been used to start local land trusts, to produce a video on greenways, and to fund planning and design of coastal greenways. Local officials should contact the state's coastal agency for more information.

Although funding was cut back severely in the 1980s, the Federal Land and Water Conservation Fund may provide matching grants for open space and recreation. States must have an approved State Comprehensive Outdoor Recreation Plan (SCORP) to qualify for the funds, available on a matching basis. Projects are reviewed by state personnel, usually in the Parks and Recreation or Planning Department. Applications for funds should be submitted by your local government.

Intermodal Surface Transportation Efficiency Act of 1991 (ISTEA): Funding for Bicycle Paths and Greenways

The Intermodal Surface Transportation Efficiency Act (ISTEA) passed by Congress in 1991 includes several sections that can be used for the creation of trails and greenways. Here is a summary of the greenway funding provisions.

Transportation Enhancements

The biggest *new* source of funding for greenways comes from the transportation enhancement provision that *requires* that 10 percent of all surface transportation monies (about $3.3 billion over six years) be spent on transportation enhancements. Eligible projects must match federal monies with a 20 percent local or state match. Eligible projects include:

1. provision of facilities for pedestrians and bicycles
2. acquisition of scenic easements and scenic or historic sites
3. scenic or historic highway programs
4. landscaping and other scenic beautification
5. historic preservation
6. rehabilitation and operation of historic transportation buildings, structures or facilities including historic railroad facilities and canals
7. preservation of abandoned railway corridors including the conversion and use thereof for pedestrian and bicycle trails
8. control and removal of outdoor advertising
9. archaeological planning and research
10. mitigation of water pollution due to highway runoff

National Recreational Trails Fund Act (Symms Act)

ISTEA authorizes a new trust fund of up to $30 million per year for six years to help pay for recreation trails. No local match is required for the first three years. Grants can be made to private individuals, organizations, or government entities. Permissible uses of the funds are:

1. state administrative costs

2. environmental and safety education programs
3. development of urban trail linkages
4. maintenance of existing trails
5. restoration of areas damaged by trail use
6. trail facilities development
7. provision of access for people with disabilities
8. acquisition of easements
9. fee simple title for property and construction of new trails

Projects must be included in or referenced in the State Comprehensive Outdoor Recreation Plan (SCORP). Decisions are made under the guidance of a state-appointed recreational trails advisory board, and states have the flexibility to decide priorities.

Scenic Byways Program

ISTEA authorizes the use of federal funds to identify and designate federal, state, and local scenic byways. Funds may be spent on the construction of facilities for pedestrians and bicyclists along these designated highways.

Pedestrian and Bicycle Issues

1. A state may spend surface transportation funds (STP) for pedestrian walkways and bicycle facilities, including rail-trails *not adjacent to federal aid highways*.
2. A state may spend a portion of its National Highway System funding for bicycle transportation facilities on land *adjacent to* any highway in the system (except interstates).
3. A portion of Federal Land Highway Funds can be used for pedestrian and bicycle facilities on federal lands.

There are additional funds for air quality improvements and for metropolitan and statewide planning for walkways and bicycle facilities. With the exception of the Symms Recreational Trails Fund, greenway projects must compete with other highway projects for funding.

question to ask when contemplating a bond issue is how much bonding capacity the community has. How the money will be repaid also has a lot to do with the political success of a bond issue. Let's briefly look at a few methods.

General obligation bonds are repaid from the general revenue income of the community, primarily tax revenues. Politically, these are quite challenging. Mecklenburg County, North Carolina (population 530,000) raised more than $8.4 million in funds for a major greenway from a series of bond referendums for park and recreation facilities between 1978 and 1991. The funds have helped acquire more than two thousand acres of land and built miles of trails. Well-led citizen participation programs were key to passing the bond issues. Volunteers formed committees and raised money to campaign for passage. Committee members spoke to local PTAs and civic groups and distributed promotional materials at special events around the county. Letters were sent to thousands of voters, and recreational outings were organized. The Mecklenburg greenway represents one of the nation's premier examples of community commitment to greenways.

Revenue bonds are paid from revenues generated by financed projects. For example, a portion of receipts from ticket sales would pay off revenue bonds on a concert hall. Revenue bonds would best apply to special greenway amenities like an aquarium or other fee-for-use facility.

Tax increment financing pays off bonds from the increment of increased revenue generated on the property adjacent to the new public improvement. For example, you build a greenway next to some vacant run-down buildings, and as a result, the buildings are renovated, tourists flock to the area, and sales and property values increase, which in turn brings increased tax revenues. The increased tax revenues would be used to pay off the greenway bonds.

A good place to begin research on bonds would be to consult a bonding or urban finance expert. Sometimes financial houses that underwrite municipal bonds will provide free advice. Be aware, however, that they are in the business of selling bonds, so the possibility of bias, conscious or unconscious, is certainly there.

Private Sector Sources

Foundation Grants

Under federal and state tax laws, companies or individuals can set aside some of their wealth for charitable purposes. This is commonly done through the establishment of a special semi-independent entity called a foundation. The foundation has a board of trustees and often a paid staff, which reviews potential projects and funding requests. Projects that meet the foundation's grant guidelines and are approved by the board of trustees receive funding.

Foundations generally fall into two categories: private and community foundations. Private foundations include independent and company-sponsored foundations. The assets of most independent foundations usually come from gifts of an individual or family and can be good prospects. Company foundations are self-explanatory. Just because a

"Partners for Wildlife," sponsored by the U.S. Fish and Wildlife Service, offers challenge grants and technical assistance for projects that further fish and wildlife conservation on private lands. Projects could address habitat restoration, wetlands conservation, waterfowl management, or other areas. Contact your regional office for further information.

Delaware's "Suburban Street Fund" apportions $250,000 per year to state legislators for road enhancement projects in their districts. Since Governor Castle's urging to use a portion of these funds for greenways, legislators across the state have earmarked nearly $1 million for local greenway projects. In June 1990, the Delaware Legislature and Governor Castle approved the Land Protection Act. This Act included a $70 million bond issue for protection of nineteen state areas having natural, cultural, and recreation resource values, including greenways. Out of the first bond funds $2 million in seed money was earmarked to do a statewide greenway plan, to promote model greenway plans in communities, and to begin implementation of these models.

company has a foundation does not mean that the company won't also make grants.

Community foundations generally act as a "community chest," representing a number of local donor sources.

"Never underbudget your project. It is better to over-estimate at the beginning than to have to go back and ask for supplemental funds."
—Iowa Natural Heritage Foundation

Company Grants

Nationwide, businesses contribute more than $3 billion annually to a host of causes. Companies may donate money, land, equipment, and sometimes the services of their employees, both paid personnel on loan and employees who volunteer their spare time. One important difference between foundation giving and company giving is that companies are obligated to show their stockholders a return on investment. When approaching a company for money, consider what's in it for them. The most obvious returns are publicity, community good will, and company morale. An investment in a greenway can also improve the local quality of life, which may help attract more qualified employees and executives to the area.

Timing can be quite important when approaching companies for funds. Their budgets for the following fiscal year are decided on in the fall. Call on a company donor before the company's budget is made up. Remember that funding decisions are often made at local plants. Community giving funds are committed quickly.

Many corporate donors love volunteer community service projects, especially those in which their employees can participate. Companies will often fund these projects and supply volunteers, equipment, supplies, and even refreshments. In return, business donors receive promotional exposure and score points with their employees—and the community.

The forty-four-mile Washington & Old Dominion Trail from Arlington to Purcell-ville, Virginia, is solely owned and managed by the Northern Virginia Regional Park Authority. When the W&OD railroad was abandoned in 1968, public support led to purchase of the right-of-way for $3.5 million by the six jurisdictions involved. Easements for power lines and other utilities bring a profit to the authority. The park supports thirteen seasonal staff members, a trail manager, and a park ranger.

Individual Donors and Memberships

According to the *Nonprofit Primer*[1] fully 90 percent of all charitable contributions nationwide come from individual contributors. Methods of gaining these contributions take several forms, including membership drives and individual fund-raising campaigns.

Many nonprofit organizations solicit members as a way to raise money and build support. Membership in a nonprofit organization can mean legal status, including the right to vote on the election of officers and other matters. Nonvoting memberships are usually more appropriate for a greenway nonprofit group because of smaller operating costs. A list of prospective members can be built from the personal contacts of the board of trustees, group mailing lists (for example, bicycle clubs and conservation groups), and, perhaps, people who sign a trail registry or leave a donation in a contribution box on the greenway trail.

The best initial contact is a letter of introduction along with a brochure, an enrollment coupon, and a return envelope (ideally postage paid). In return for contributions, members receive a newsletter, a

[1] Don Coppock *et al.*, *The Nonprofit Primer: A Guidebook for Land Trusts*, 2nd ed. (Oakland, Calif.: The California Coastal Conservancy, 1989).

Innovative Funding Techniques

• Stowe residents devised some creative ways to raise money for their greenway. Pieces of the path were sold, $2 per inch and $45 per yard. The Greenways Gala Black Tie Dinner Dance and Auction raised $40,000 in one night.

• The San Francisco Bay Trail's brochure lists a variety of ways supporters can contribute to the trail's completion: loans of equipment, donations of expertise, funding, volunteer projects for corporate employees, donations of construction materials or improvements (benches, garbage cans, restroom facilities), and "adopting a segment" to keep clean and maintain.

• The Northern Virginia Regional Park Authority leases garden plots to adjacent landowners and has also leased land for storage and parking facilities. Along with income from lease of the right-of-way to utilities, these sources enable the Washington & Old Dominion Trail to net a profit and provide excellent service along its forty-four-mile length.

• In Pennsylvania, the Schuylkill River Greenway annual bikeathon raises funds for the design, construction, and management of the hiking/biking trail. Membership is offered to supporters.

• The Meramac Valley Greenway in St. Louis, Missouri, offers an "Executive Feast and Picnic" to garner corporate support. The Great Meramac Raft Float is popular with local greenway users.

Remember, your first concern is to build a greenway, not to make money. Don't participate in anything that could compromise the image of your project. Check tax considerations carefully to be sure your money-making activity does not endanger your tax-exempt status.

---

certificate of membership, and other benefits such as a discount card for purchases from supporting merchants.

Building a membership is a great way to build grassroots support and political clout for your greenway, but because of the time demands in cultivating and managing membership rosters, it may not be appropriate for smaller efforts. Questionnaires or petitions with a donation coupon attached offer a less costly alternative.

Large gifts ($500 and up) from individual donors usually result from a combination of personal contacts, enthusiastic selling, and luck. The best way to start the process is to have your board members provide lists of people they know personally who might be willing to give. Board members should be willing to sign request letters and follow up with calls or visits.

Planned Giving, Life-Income Gifts, and Bequests

Planned giving or bequests and life-income gifts offer an alternative for some donors. They take many forms ranging from a simple bequest of money in a will to complex life-estates in land and securities. *Planned giving* refers to a strategy worked out between donor and grantee for giving that addresses gifts while the donor is alive and after he or she dies. Planned giving can be mutually beneficial when tax and investment considerations are taken into account.

One useful approach is to use these techniques to help protect important privately held land. For example, a property owner grants a future interest in his or her property to a greenway nonprofit organization or land trust. The donor keeps a life estate (also referred to as a life tenancy), or the right to use and occupy the land during his or her lifetime, subject to agreements to not further develop the property or otherwise

Amoco contributed the first big segment of the Platte River Greenway in Casper, Wyoming. The project continued despite the effect of the oil glut on this energy center, during which the town lost one-third of its population. The greenway is eligible for funding through a 1 percent sales tax collected by the city.

In 1990 the Issaquah Trail Club of Puget Sound, Washington, dramatized the problem of pressure on open space resources with a five-day "Mountains to the Sound" March, from which a coalition of public agencies and nonprofit organizations emerged with plans for a Mountains to the Sound Greenway. The Bullitt Foundation in Seattle supported the effort through a $1 million grant to the Trust for Public Land (TPL) for land protection around Puget Sound. TPL will match the gift with $2 million more. —Common Ground, Vol.3, No. 1, Nov./Dec. 1991

compromise its open-space value. When the donor dies, the property passes to the land trust.

Other assets can be handled in a similar manner. For example, a donor might grant a greenway nonprofit organization or land trust ownership in a stock. Under the grant, the earnings on the stock would go to the grantor for the rest of his or her life. In other words, a life income is retained by the donor. After death, the principal and earnings go to the nonprofit organization. In this instance, the donor gets a tax write-off for donating the principal and continues to receive the earnings from that principal. Generally, this type of giving applies to well-established organizations. Except for protecting land, it is usually not useful in the start-up period or for initial capital projects. It is, however, a good way to build an endowment for long-term projects, land acquisition, and maintenance. This is a complex area; any nonprofit organization receiving bequests needs to employ legal and financial expertise.

Small donations, like memberships, can be pursued through direct mail appeals. Other approaches include the creation of a gift catalogue from which donors "buy" certain items for the greenway, such as trail footage, picnic tables, or trees (see Figure 5-1). Local newspapers or radio and TV stations will sometimes run special campaigns. The *Denver Post*, for example, ran a "Trees for Tomorrow" campaign, with daily articles and donation appeals that raised $40,000 to $50,000 for tree planting.

Service Clubs

Never underestimate what a service or city club can do for your project. Service clubs may be willing to sponsor special fund-raising events and can provide volunteers and publicity. In Grand Junction, Colorado, the local Lions Club raised more than $90,000 to kick off a greenway project along the Colorado River. Yakima Greenway received $5,000 from the local Kiwanis. The Rotary Club in Stowe, Vermont, supports the trail in many ways, including the hiring of a summer maintenance intern.

Special Events and Fund-raisers

Recently, in Chicago, the Open Lands Project raised more than $200,000 to kick off a metropolitan area greenways program by holding a benefit dinner. The dinner featured EPA director William Reilly as speaker and honored two local conservationists. Special events like these can be quite successful, not only in raising funds but in building exposure and credibility for the greenway. Special events may require up to a year of planning, however, and may not provide a significant return for several years. Such events can have a limited life span and may bring diminishing returns over time as a fickle public turns to other interests.

Other fund-raising events include foot races, bicycle tours, and even "rubber duckie" races in which contestants purchase a rubber duck at the event. Each "duckie" has a number on it. The duck that crosses the finish line first wins a prize for its contestant.

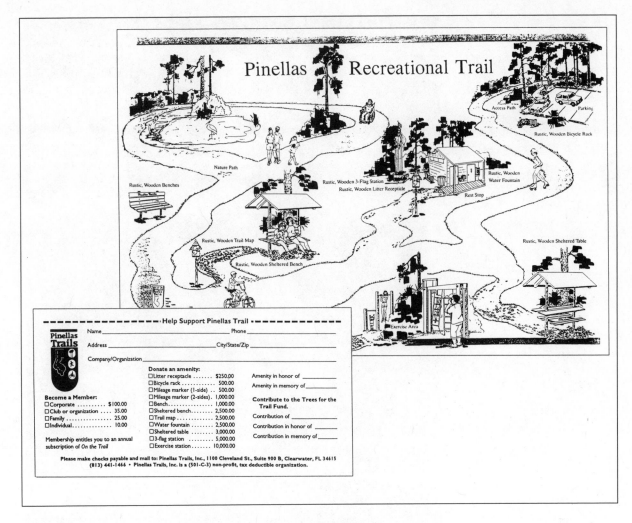

Figure 5-1 Sponsorship opportunities—the Pinellas Trail, Florida.

Getting Grants

Assuming you've now lined up your prospects and put together a fund-raising strategy, how do you ask for money?

Know Your Prospects

Think of fund-raising as selling. Get to know the people who make decisions about dispersing money and what it is they are looking for. In your strategy for each potential donor, be it a foundation, company, or individual, consider the mission of the organization. Government grantors usually have a specific mission spelled out in the legislation establishing the program. Private foundations often provide a mission statement and guidelines in their prospectus or grant application forms. You can also look at past giving patterns. If all past grants have been awarded to animal shelters, that foundation is probably not a first priority prospect for a greenway. The goals of a company or individual may be more difficult to ascertain.

Some greenway groups "sell" pavement bricks to greenway supporters to fund the development of the greenway.

Read the grant program description carefully. Are the requirements strict or is there some flexibility? Are there opportunities for creative piggybacking of objectives? For example, grants set aside for fishing programs might partially fund trails and trailheads if they allow better access to fishing sites. Be honest with your potential funder, but think creatively.

Always determine whether the grant requires matching funds—most government grants do. Foundations will also issue challenge or matching grants that require a significant percentage of matching funds from others. Challenge grants have a hidden benefit: whereas you may not have gotten 100 percent of the funding, the challenge itself can be a great psychological inducement to other contributors.

What do the people who award the grants want? Individuals make the decisions. Try to meet and talk with them one-on-one to get a reading of what their interests are. Read their annual reports and

Greenway Grant Programs

Recreational Equipment Incorporated (REI) awards seed grants of $200 to $2000 to state and local conservation groups for projects that enhance river protection. Distributed by the National Rivers Coalition, American Rivers, Inc., 801 Pennsylvania, Ave., SE, Washington, DC 20003.

Fish America Foundation provides funding to public and private organizations for projects that enhance or conserve water and fisheries resources, including community efforts. The grant award is approximately $10,000. Write the Fish America Foundation, 1010 Massachusetts Ave., NW., Suite 320, Washington, DC 20007.

California Greenways Creative Grants Program provides grants from $500 to $2000 to benefit greenway programs throughout California. Awards recognize creative strategies or problem solving by local groups. Contact the California Greenways Board, 633 Los Palos Drive, Lafayette, CA 94549.

World Wildlife Fund's Innovation Grant Program (formally Successful Communities Grants) provides grants of $5000 to $7500 to local and regional nonprofit organizations or their public agency partners to help communities implement innovative solutions to problems caused by unmanaged growth. Recent guidelines include projects focused specifically on wildlife, wetlands, and habitat protection. Contact the World Wildlife Fund/Innovation Grants, c/o Sonoran Institute, Suite D, 6842 E. Tanque Verde, Tucson, AZ 85715.

American Greenways DuPont Awards Program, administered by the Conservation Fund, provides grants of $500 to $2500 to local greenways projects. Grants could be used for almost any activity that serves as a catalyst for local greenway planning and development. Contact the American Greenways Program at the Conservation Fund, 1800 North Kent Street, Arlington, VA 22209.

The Global Relief Heritage Forest Program, American Forestry Association, provides funding for planting tree seedlings on public lands. Emphasis is placed on diversifying species, regenerating the optimal ecosystem for the site, and implementing the best forest management practices. Write the American Forestry Association, P.O. Box 2000, Washington, DC 20013.

The Design Arts Program of the National Endowment for the Arts funds projects that promote excellence in urban design, historic preservation, planning, architecture, and landscape planning. Contact the staff at Room 625, Nancy Hanks Center, 1100 Pennsylvania Ave., NW, Washington, DC 20506.

The National Recreation Trail Trust will provide state grants for trail construction and management beginning in 1993. The Fund will be administered by the Federal Highway Administration and grants disbursed through the state transportation departments.

consider how your greenway might mesh with their own agenda. Be careful not to offend anyone by appearing to go over someone's head. This takes skill and diplomacy. Remember the old adage "people give money to people," meaning personal contacts are the key to success.

Package Your Product

Be precise and to the point when you describe your project. Have a specific strategy in mind and describe it clearly. Whether you call it "a mile of greenway from X Street to Y street" or, more specifically, "the trail head at Y Street" will depend on the size of the request and the orientation of the donor. Avoid superfluous information.

The way you describe your project can make a difference. The term *trailhead/access area* certainly sounds more intriguing than *parking lot*. Show that the community needs the project. Highlight what makes your project unique.

Always ask for a specific amount of money. Sometimes it helps to meet with the donor ahead of time to establish a ballpark figure.

Targeting your request to what the donor is likely to have available is important.

Funding requests often begin with an introductory letter signed by a mutual acquaintance or friend of your project who knows the donors. You may then be asked to submit an initial letter of request. The letter briefly describes your project, the amount you are requesting, and supporting information. You should enclose a brief project brochure, if you have one. If further interest is indicated, you will than be asked to submit a formal application.

Your funding application should include a project budget, a schedule for completion of the improvements, and sources of matching funds if applicable. It should outline who will benefit from the greenway and who will develop and maintain the project. If requested, include location maps, sketches, photographs, and letters of endorsement. Finally, your application should clearly describe your organization, list the board of directors and the responsible staff, and include tax-exempt certification and an operating budget. Generally, grantors will provide application forms spelling out the required information.

Try to package your proposal in an easy-to-follow and easy-to-read format. You want to appear professional. A neatly designed one- or two-color single-fold brochure can almost always get your point across.

Long-Term Funding

The funding stream from most large sources tends to have a maximum life of three years. After that, donors will likely turn to other priorities. Thus, company and foundation grants should not be considered a reliable source of long-term income.

For reliable long-term funding you will need to develop more dependable sources of income. If you plan to build your greenway and disband, it may not matter. If you plan on an ongoing presence, it is quite important. You may want to turn to different sources, such as memberships, individual donors, special events, bequests, and workplace giving programs. Funding expert Richard Male suggests that, ultimately, 80 percent of your long-term operating budget should come from these sources.

One final word of advice: Never assume that you won't get funding. You should, of course, try the most likely sources first, but even the donor who only funds animal shelters might take an interest in your project if presented the right way.

The following organizations can provide information about fundraising and funding sources:

The Foundation Center
312 Sutter Street, 3rd floor
San Francisco, CA 94108
Publishes *The Foundation Directory* and *National Data Book*, which identifies reference collections in New York City, San Francisco,

Washington, D.C., and Cleveland, Ohio. You can contact Dialog (415-858-2700) for information on accessing the Center's database or On-Line Support (212-620-4230) for free materials to help search these files. Provides computer search printouts of listing of grants by foundations according to subject and geographic area. The Foundation grants index is an annual compilation of grants by recipient, key word, and subject.

American Association of Fundraising Councils (AAFRC)
25 West 43rd Street
New York, NY 10036
(212) 354-5799
Represents fund-raising consulting firms; does funding research.

The Federal Assistance Program Retrieval System (FAPRS)
Federal Domestic Assistance Catalogue Staff
General Service Administration
300 7th Street S.W.
Washington, DC 20407
202-708-5126 or 800-669-8331
Provides low cost on-line computer access to federal funding information.

The Grantsmanship Center (TGC)
P.O. Box 6210
Los Angeles, CA 90014
Provides reports, newsletters, and workshops on topics of interest to developing nonprofit organizations.

Environmental Grantmakers Association
1290 Avenue of the Americas, Suite 3450
New York, NY 10104
212-373-4260
For a nominal fee, will provide listings of foundations that offer environmental related grants.

6

Greenway Protection and Ownership

"Land—they ain't making it any more."
—Will Rogers

In the United States, decisions governing land use have historically been left to individual landowners, many of whom do not understand the ecological function of the land or the complexities involved in stewardship of its natural qualities. As a result, land use has often been at odds with healthy, functioning ecological systems.

Greenways, if properly planned and implemented, provide Americans with a new form of land use that respects the function of ecological systems. A well-planned greenway will use the natural features of the landscape, such as a floodplain or ridge top, while protecting both the rights of private property owners and the necessary functions of the natural environment.

Securing and protecting land for the greenway may be the most challenging task you'll face. All the issues you've read about thus far will come into play: funding, landowner concerns, marketing, and flexible planning. You may need to change your route because a landowner will not grant an easement or sell title. More happily, someone may unexpectedly donate property or an easement that was not considered in the original plan.

Securing Land for Greenways

Land ownership in the United States is based on real property law, which classifies the surface of the land, minerals beneath the surface or imbedded in the surface, buildings, and other features of the land as physical possessions of the landowner. When an individual buys a piece of real property, certain rights to that property come with the title. By law, each property right is considered separate from the right of ownership and can be sold, given, or traded as an "interest." All property rights are subject to local, state, or federal laws that seek to protect the public health, safety, and welfare. For instance, while you may subdivide your property and build houses, you may not build more houses per lot than allowed by local zoning regulations.

There are several ways in which rights to a parcel of property can be secured for greenways. We will focus on four primary methods: (1) management agreements, leases, permits, and licenses; (2) easements or partial rights to a specific piece of property; (3) purchase or donation of the title or all the rights to a parcel of land from a willing seller or donor; and (4) land regulation that prohibits or encourages certain uses. The method that works best will depend upon the type of land

"Be persistent and patient. Have good relationships with local government and the community."
—Wissahickon Greenway

New York State legislation (1991) for a Hudson Valley Greenway Compact establishes a permanent multijurisdictional Greenway Council. The Council encourages communities to become part of a regional greenway system through their open space plans, the use of a public benefit corporation to undertake specific greenway implementation projects including economic development, the creation of a Hudson River Trail along the length of the river which serves as the spine of the greenway, and the establishment of an agricultural advisory council to help deal with loss of farmland, agricultural tourism, and marketing.
—David Sampson, Executive Director, Hudson River Valley Greenway Council

ownership, your relationship with the landowner, your financial resources, your strategy for securing the land, regulatory tools, the degree of threat to the resource, and future greenway uses proposed for the land. Depending on your proposed greenway route and local enabling legislation, you may well use all of these methods. In Stowe, Vermont, because funds were lacking and because the route passed through privately owned property, the greenway was created by securing donated easements across private property.

The suggestions in this chapter are not a substitute for legal counsel. If you are negotiating for title or for an easement, contact a local attorney who can provide an up-to-date interpretation of local laws and advise you on the best course of action.

Temporary Binding Agreements

A temporary binding agreement is a short-term mechanism for securing a parcel of land. Within a limited amount of time the landowner can enter into other permanent binding agreements, such as a greenway easement, fee simple purchase, or new regulatory mechanism. A temporary binding agreement can take one of the following forms.

1. A *management agreement* between the landowner and greenway organization specifies who will manage the parcel of property during the life of the temporary agreement and how. These agreements work well if the landowner is a willing participant in the short-term and long-term management of the property for greenway purposes.

2. A *formal land lease* allows the greenway organization, as the lessee, to control access to the property and active land-use practices —such as forestry or mining—and to make minor improvements to the property to ensure the safety of the users. In some cases the organization pays the landowner rent during the term of the lease.

3. In some instances a landowner may grant a *long-term lease or permit* for greenway purposes. Such a lease or permit may run as long as 99 years or more. Often such leases or permits are granted for $1 and "consideration," such as liability protection and property tax relief on the portion of the land leased. In some cases, especially where the land of a government agency is involved, such as a highway department, a permit will be granted to have a trail or other greenway improvement cross the property. A revocable lease or permit may sometimes be granted, which allows the landowner to cancel the agreement if certain terms or conditions are not met, such as patrol or maintenance. This may be an option where wary landowners fear problems if a trail is opened across their property.

Greenway Easements

An *easement* is a mutually binding legal contract between a landowner and an individual or organization who has requested a special interest or right in the land. A landowner who grants or sells an easement essentially gives up some of the rights to his or her real property. The easement holder receives "less-than-fee interest" in the property. The easement usually defines specific boundaries, uses, and management obligations for the subject property and is a popular strategy for securing greenway land because it offers flexibility to both landowner and easement holder.

Two types of easements can be secured on real property: (1) an *affirmative easement* and (2) a *negative easement*. An affirmative easement allows the individual or organization that has acquired property rights to access and use the land at any time and to erect or place structures and improvements on the property. Examples of an affirmative easement would be one that allows a trail to be sited across a property and one that permits a utility company to install a natural gas pipeline within the subject property and allows the utility access at any time to inspect and make any necessary repairs or alterations to the pipeline and the landscape surrounding it.

A negative easement allows the individual or organization to restrict land use on the subject property but does *not* allow the easement holder to access or use the land or make improvements to or build on the land. An example would be a scenic easement that restricts the removal of vegetation, construction of a building, or alterations to the natural landform of the subject property.

Easements are usually created by grant, reservation, or dedication. An easement that is granted means that the landowner's rights are given to the recipient through a legal procedure. This is the most common way in which easements are created. Through reservation, a landowner agrees to attach specific language to his or her property deed providing for certain rights or interest in the property and at the same time reserves other rights for use at his or her discretion. Dedication of an easement occurs only when the landowner conveys property rights to a public agency, and the public agency agrees to accept responsibilities associated with the rights. Easements, whether sold or donated, usually reduce the owner's property tax.

Most easements are written up along with a drawing of the property and attached to a deed of the real property. Deeds are filed with the record of deeds office or the local government tax office in your community or both. Easements can be established in perpetuity or for a limited period and can be created to apply only to the current landowner or be legally binding for all succeeding owners.

Several specific types of easements can be used to secure greenway lands. A *right of public access easement* provides the general public with the legal right to access and use a specific parcel of land for defined purposes, such as walking, jogging, or bicycling. It restricts other activities, such as hunting, removal of vegetation, or access by motorized vehicles. It usually limits the ability of the grantee to manage natural resources within the easement. For example, the grantee may have the right of public access but not the right to protect vegetation in the greenway corridor. Therefore, the landowner could harvest the timber from the

The San Juan Island Ferryboat Corridor Greenway, a Washington state scenic roadway, runs to and around the San Juan Islands and north to British Columbia. The San Juan Preservation Trust seeks scenic easements from waterfront owners whose land can be seen from the ferryboat. Almost all greenway funds spent to date have been for negotiating easements with the private landowners. A combination of moral persuasion and building guidelines into local planning protects the greenway viewshed within the ferryboat routes.

"The land donated was sometimes the least desirable to the property owner. The path ran along the edge of a farm field, in the weeds and underbrush, or it traveled near the tree-lined edge of the property, out back and away from view. In other cases it was the land along the edge of the river, and rather than lose fifteen feet of property to erosion each year, the property owner retained his or her land with the assured path rip rap or rock stabilization that was to be installed along the river bank. I needed a total of seventy signatures for these deeds. I became a notary public and if necessary took along a witness when the property owner was comfortable about signing. The deed signing occurred in houses, offices, and even in cow barns. When the deeds were all recorded in the town clerk's office, everyone was publicly thanked for the contribution to the town...The tough part is getting the land."
—Anne Lusk

The Burke-Gilman Trail, formerly a Burlington Northern railroad route, is used by 750,000 people yearly. Encircling much of Seattle, it runs from the northern end of Lake Washington to and through the University of Washington to Lake Union. The city has negotiated a railroad abandonment/railbanking agreement with the railroad company (and other landowners) whereby the city will have the "right of first refusal" when and if the company surplusses additional rights-of-way.

greenway land without having to notify the grantee or greenway users, as long as right of access is not obstructed or denied.

A *conservation easement* defines physical limits on the use, treatment, and development of the land, to protect its natural resources while allowing the property owner to continue using the land. These easements are most often used to protect the physical elements, scenic character, ecological systems, or rare and endangered species found on a particular piece of land. For example, to protect a native rhododendron community on a north-facing slope, a conservation easement might be obtained from the landowner restricting any land use and development within so many feet of this habitat.

A *preservation easement* is an easement designed to protect the historical integrity of a structure or important elements of a landscape by defining guidelines that must be followed in making improvements to the property. For example, a preservation easement could be used to protect the ruins of a historic mill along a stream. The easement might specify that the mill be kept in its existing state or it might specify guidelines for its restoration.

A *joint-use easement*, another type of affirmative easement, defines the legal rights of the grantor and grantees for multiple use of a single parcel of land. It is one of the most popular kinds of easements because it provides a realistic method for making better use of limited land resources. For example, a joint-use easement might specify that within the boundaries of a specified corridor of land, a sewer line will be installed and maintained by a local water and sewer authority, and at the same time a multiuse trail will be installed and managed by the local parks and recreation department. It is important to clearly define stewardship responsibilities when setting up the easement.

An easement used for a greenway may be a composite of elements from the easements just described. Typically, greenway easements combine the best of conservation and access/use language to protect natural resources and their use.

Securing Title

Another method of securing land for greenways is through outright purchase or donation of the title. The owner of the property negotiates a contract to convey all rights to the property to the recipient in one of the following ways.

Fee Simple Acquisition. One of the most common methods of acquiring full rights and title to a parcel of land is fee simple acquisition, through which the landowner holds all rights to the property without restriction or reservation. Fee simple "determinable" is a subset of this method and means that the landowner holds all rights subject to a condition placed on the title, such as, "to Mr. and Mrs. Smith so long as the land is used for farming purposes, but when it is no longer used for farming it shall revert to the grantor and his heirs." If the Smiths subdivide the land for a housing development, the property automatically reverts to the seller.

When purchasing a piece of property fee simple, a lump sum fee for the title is negotiated between seller and buyer through a *standard contract* (buyer and seller agree on the conditions of sale and buyer pays seller in full upon the close of the sale); a *contingency contract* (buyer and seller agree on conditions of sale, but the sale is not binding until all contingencies are satisfied; otherwise, the buyer can back out of the contract); *installment contract* (buyer and seller agree on conditions of sale, but the seller retains title and use of property until the purchase price is paid in full).

Donations/Gifts. A landowner gives all or part of his or her property to an individual, organization, or agency. In many states the donor is eligible for property tax credits or estate and income tax deductions if the donation is for conservation or preservation. One example is a *life estate*, a unique subset of fee simple ownership. Upon the death of the landowner, the property is awarded to an estate-designated organization or agency. If the property is donated for conservation purposes, tax credits can be applied to the estate. This is becoming increasingly popular in the United States as property values continue to rise and dramatically affect taxes on large landholdings that have appreciated significantly since they were purchased.

Some land trusts will not accept donated land or easements unless money for their management has been identified. Many will ask the donor to fund an endowment for the property. Some local land trusts and nonprofit organizations will accept donated land for a short period of time and then give the land to a local, state, or federal government agency that is better able to manage the resource.

Purchase and Lease Back. An organization or agency can purchase a parcel of land and then lease it back to the seller for a specified period of time. The lease may contain restrictions regarding the use and development of the property. For example, a farmer who owns land bordering a stream may need to sell his land to obtain operating capital. After the transaction has occurred, the agency or organization would then lease the land back to the farmer, at a reasonable annual fee, for continued use as a farm.

Bargain Sale. A landowner agrees to sell land at less than its appraised market value and to treat the difference as a charitable income tax deduction. Bargain sales are attractive when the seller wants immediate cash for the property or initially paid a low price for the property and does not want to be liable for high capital-gains tax after the sale. Such a sale may also be attractive to a seller who currently has a fairly high income and could derive tax benefits from a below-cost sale.

Option, or Right of First Refusal. An option, or right of first refusal, is an agreement reached with a property owner to have the first chance to purchase a piece of property. For example, a local nonprofit greenway organization has reached an agreement with landowner Smith that he will notify them when he is prepared to sell his property. Several years later, Mr. Smith notifies the organization that he is prepared to sell. The organization is given a specified amount of time, usually ten to ninety days, to match any bona fide offer on the property and

Portland, Oregon's forty-mile Loop was originally proposed in the early 1900s by John Olmsted and Frederick Law Olmsted, Jr., landscape architect sons of the acclaimed designer of New York's Central Park. It was not acted upon until 1979, however, when citizens decided the project should be completed on an expanded basis—140 miles. A plan was prepared in 1983 and presented to city and county agencies, which incorporated the plan into each master zoning plan and the trail specifications in the parks plans. The trail connects thirty parks via railroad conversions and old and new paths along rivers and creeks. The forty-mile Loop Land Trust has raised and spent $2 million to plan and to buy land, which is owned and managed by local government agencies.

conditions of the sale. If a mutual agreement cannot be reached, Mr. Smith is free to pursue other buyers. An option gives the buyer time and, often, the crisis atmosphere needed to raise the funds to purchase the property.

Purchase of Development Rights. With purchase of development rights, the private property owner retains all ownership rights under current use but exchanges rights to future development for an up-front cash payment. This can be attractive if the landowner is in need of cash.

Condemnation. Condemnation is a mechanism for acquiring greenway properties mainly when complications with the deed make acquisition from a *willing* seller difficult. Generally, condemnation of property from *unwilling* landowners should be viewed as a last resort.

Regulating Land for Greenways

Regulation involves control of the use and development of land through legislative powers. Land-use controls can be used to protect land for greenway purposes. Land-use regulation varies greatly from locality to locality; to better understand your community's legal authority, you should consult a local municipal, county, or state attorney, state planning office, or town planning or zoning department. Most communities use comprehensive plans, zoning, and subdivision legislation to provide for the orderly and efficient growth of the community and to protect public health, safety, and welfare.

The Comprehensive Plan

Comprehensive plans (also called master plans) are developed by local, state, and federal governments to provide a framework for future growth and development. Comprehensive plans usually direct policy for a five-, ten-, or twenty-year period of time. They provide planning guidelines and are often interpreted literally by politicians, community planners, and state and federal officials as decisions are made regarding conservation, recreation, transportation, infrastructure, and urban development.

Community-wide comprehensive plans define land use for large areas, seeking an appropriate mix of agricultural, residential, office, commercial, institutional, industrial, and open space uses. They define the most suitable location for such public facilities as schools and parks. They also ensure that such public resources as roadways, water, and sanitary sewer facilities are properly sized and routed for efficient delivery of essential services to community residents. Although greenways are not specifically included in most comprehensive plans, older plans often contain the basic policy ingredients on which to build a greenway program: the preservation or protection of stream valleys, wetlands, forests, farmland, shorelines, marshes, swamps, beaches, and recreational areas. Communities in Raleigh and Winston-Salem, North Carolina, Montgomery County, Maryland, and Pima County, Arizona are just a

Nockamixon Cliffs, a geologically and botanically significant limestone formation, flanks a portion of the Delaware River. The Bucks County Conservancy purchased the cliffs and presented them to the state as part of the Delaware Canal Park System. This cooperative venture has cemented efforts to protect the Delaware River Greenway, which includes preservation of scenic hillsides bordering the riparian corridor, through the donation of development right easements, conservation easements, outright purchase, and voluntary protection by landowners.

State Comprehensive Outdoor Recreation Plans

State Comprehensive Outdoor Recreation Plans (SCORPs) are developed by the fifty states and five territories to address recreation, conservation, and open-space needs (do not confuse these with the "comprehensive plans"). These plans, prepared by state park and recreation programs, are usually updated every five years. The process used to prepare them is always open to public comment. As of this writing, Alabama, Arizona, California, Connecticut, Delaware, Georgia, Illinois, Maryland, Massachusetts, New Jersey, New York, Rhode Island, and the District of Columbia (thirteen of the fifty-five jurisdictions) have included open-space and greenway issues as part of their SCORP planning process. Other states are currently developing state-wide greenway plans outside the normal SCORP process. Contact your state liaison office in the parks department to find out if your state has a policy toward greenways. As a greenway supporter, you can influence the future growth and development of your community by participating in the SCORP planning process. Because local plan goals are often compared to SCORP guidelines when it comes to distributing state and federal recreation funds, lobby for a greenway component within the state plan. For example, in Maryland the state SCORP requires that all county recreation plans include a greenway component in order to be considered for the state's "Program Open Space" funds for recreation and conservation.

few that have successfully used comprehensive plans to buy or protect greenway land.

An important reason for making sure your project is included in local comprehensive plans is that it's a requirement for most government funding. For example, if your trail is not a part of the community's transportation plan, money from the local and state transportation department may not be available to you.

Note that in some states the comprehensive plan is merely advisory; it may note the importance of preserving open space and the rural character of a community but not dictate land use. In states where comprehensive plans do not have legal authority, it is important to reinforce the community vision with laws and regulations that have a clearly articulated preservation purpose.

Zoning Ordinances and Land Use Laws

Zoning is local legislation that regulates development by dividing land into separate land-use districts, or zones. Zoning was originally established to separate incompatible uses, for example, a junkyard from a residential neighborhood. The key to successful regulation lies in fair application and, most importantly, sound legal grounds. Generally, zoning must be justified in terms of protecting public health, safety, and welfare. It must also relate clearly to the community's comprehensive plan. Zoning is mostly administered at the local level, although in the 1980s a significant number of communities in rapidly urbanizing areas decided to combine municipal and county planning and zoning to better control development.

Historically, zoning has treated all land equally, without regard for natural features. It defines land according to lot size, setbacks, and development density. Little attention is paid to the carrying capacity of a particular parcel—its ability to accommodate human use and

The 1980 Mecklenburg County Greenway Master Plan called for sixty-five miles of "greenway necklace" through the county. Priority greenway segments are determined by the size of adjacent populations, environmental impacts of proposed greenways, and land use adjacent to greenways. Much of the protected land has been acquired through subdivision donations or rezoning of property. The goal of the plan is to provide greenway connectors to the most heavily populated areas, linking communities and neighborhoods. Most of the greenway segments are in the low-lying floodplains; they are joined together by connecting trails along roadways.

The plan for the Brooklyn-Queens Greenway connects preexisting open spaces with trails for walking and bicyclcing. County Commissions have fully supported designation of the greenway and have allocated more than $18 million for development. The greenway will link thirteen parks, two botanical gardens, the New York Aquarium, the Brooklyn Museum, the New York Hall of Science, the Queens Museum, Shea Stadium, the National Tennis Center, the 1939/1964 World's Fair site, three environmental education centers, four lakes, and a reservoir with a bicycle pedestrian path running from the Atlantic Ocean to Long Island Sound. There are many alternatives to acquisition that can create linear parks along major transportation properties and special greenways or bikeways to link residents.

The Wissahickon Greenway in Pennsylvania benefits from local cluster zoning provisions. Two-thirds of the more than thirty-five properties protected since 1980 were donations, acquired primarily through negotiations with developers. Another innovation involves trading of lands—the Greenway exchanged 1.5 miles of developable road frontage for fourteen acres of wooded stream corridor.

development. Properly developed zoning, however, can be used to protect environmental resources. There are several types of zoning that are of specific interest to greenway advocates, including overlay zones and zones identified for the transfer of development rights or cluster development.

Overlay Zone. An overlay zone is usually superimposed over existing zones or districts to add specific regulations to a particular landscape type within your community. For example, if you are interested in protecting the major river corridor within your community, you might ensure additional protection by applying a "River Corridor Overlay Zone" over existing zones and across many zoning districts. The overlay zone does not change the regulatory requirements of the underlying zones. Overlay zones create a new set of regulatory requirements that must be met before individual parcels of land can be developed. For example, development may be concentrated away from these overlay zones, special permits may be required for land uses in these areas, or an architectural review board may assess proposed new development to see that it is compatible with the landscape and the existing environment. Because greenways are long linear corridors that can span an entire community or region, an overlay zone is an effective method for achieving uniform control of land development and continuity in environmental protection practices.

Protective overlay districts can be used in concert with overlay zones. Depending on state and local laws, road corridors might be designated as scenic roads, and areas of special significance might be designated critical environmental areas or historic districts (Figure 6-1 shows the Willamette River Greenway Overlay Zone).

Transfer of Development Rights. The transfer of development rights (TDR) is gaining increasing attention as a method for protecting undeveloped land. By this means, the right to develop land at a certain density, specified by a particular zoning category, can be transferred to a specially designated parcel where higher density development is more appropriate. Usually, the landowner sells development rights while retaining ownership of his or her property.

For this transfer of rights to occur, a state or locality must have enabling legislation in place. The advantage of this regulatory technique for greenway purposes is that economic growth need not be sacrificed for the proposed greenway. With a transfer of development rights program in place, development density is transferred to an appropriate parcel in another part of the community, and the land required for greenway development is permanently secured.

Cluster Development. Cluster development involves grouping the same number of development units allowed under existing zoning more closely together, leaving more open space on the parcel. An answer to large-lot zoning, cluster development often protects vital open space where it is needed most—as a buffer between sensitive native lands and development. Because cluster buffers are most often found adjacent to natural landscape features, such as stream corridors, these buffers can theoretically be linked together to form a continuous greenway system.

River Natural Zone	River Recreation Zone	River General Zone	River Industrial Zone
Protects, conserves, and enhances land of scenic quality or of significant importance as wildlife habitat. Listed on official zoning maps, as the symbol "n."	Encourages river-dependent and river-related recreational uses, which provide a variety public access types to and along the river and which enhance the river's natural and scenic qualities. Listed on official zoning maps as the symbol "r."	Allows for uses and development that are consistent with the base zoning, which allow for public use and enjoyment of the waterfront and that enhance the river's natural and scenic qualities. Listed on official zoning maps as the symbol "g."	Encourages the development of river-dependent industries, which strengthen the economic viability of Portland as a an industrial harbor, while preserving riparian habitat and providing appropriate public access. Listed on official zoning maps as "i."

Figure 6-1 Willamette River Greenway Overlay Zone. The map illustrates the different zones that are present within downtown Portland, along the Willamette River Greenway. (Reprinted with permission of City of Portland, Bureau of Planning.)

Cluster development zoning must meet certain conditions to be of any real use in creating greenways. It must preserve environmentally sensitive areas by placing homes where they have the least impact on whatever resource the community deems worthy of protection; it must require the developer to set aside a sufficient amount of land as open space; and the open space must be contiguous.

Throughout the United States, greenways are being used as a marketing tool by real-estate developers. This subdivision in Apex, North Carolina, sells lots on the greenway at higher prices, and as evident by the sign, the lots were selling quickly. (Jennifer Toole)

"Persistence. If the project has great potential, setbacks should be viewed as learning opportunities to regroup and strengthen alliances for the next phase."
—Salt Creek Greenway

An ordinance developed by Lower Merion Township in Pennsylvania, just outside Philadelphia, requires open space preservation for at least 50 percent of tracts five acres and larger. Although some communities offer developers density incentives to use clusters, in fact, incentives for using this method over the conventional grid pattern already exist. By using cluster development, the developer saves on construction and infrastructure costs, and it has been shown that lots next to the open space area appreciate 9 to 23 percent more than those in the traditional grid.

Subdivision Regulations. Subdivision regulations are a set of community-wide standards that govern the way in which large parcels of land are divided into smaller units and define the development of urban facilities such as roadways, water and sewer systems, electrical systems, and the names of streets.

Subdivision regulations can contain performance standards that place the burden of proof on the landowner or developer to mitigate the impact of development on the landscape, especially in such areas as wetlands, steep slopes, parcels with rare vegetation, nesting grounds for wildlife, and stream corridors. Greenways can be used to satisfy environmental protection while at the same time offering the developer economically viable use of a landscape.

Although your jurisdiction may not have regulations specifically focused on greenway creation, many have the power to prevent the disturbance of sensitive environmental areas and to require the reservation or dedication of land as open space. For example, if a landowner wants to subdivide a parcel of land for residential purposes, local subdivision regulations might permit this action, provided a certain portion of the land, most importantly that area adjacent to a stream or river on the property, would be reserved or dedicated to the local municipality for greenway purposes. If the land is simply reserved as a part of the subdivision process, this would provide time for the local municipality or conservation organization to enter into negotiations with the landowner to secure a greenway easement or purchase the property. If the land is dedicated as a condition of the subdivision process, then upon approval of the subdivision plan the local government would have the designated parcel legally conveyed for public ownership.

Some communities require the provision of trail right-of-way and even trail construction as part of the subdivision process. Ideally, this requirement is tied to a community-wide comprehensive trails plan. If an area about to be subdivided does not lie on a planned trail or greenway route, the developer may be asked to make a "cash-in-lieu" payment toward a trails or greenway fund instead. The requirement may apply to commercial and industrial properties as well as residential.

Figure 6-2 is a summary of acquisition strategies.

Greenway Ownership

What is the best method for securing greenway land? You must first consider who will own the land. If the greenway is acquired to serve a public purpose, such as recreation or transportation, then a local government will most likely be the owner. If protecting a unique wildlife habitat is the primary goal, a local land trust might be the owner. Multiple ownership may be a possibility for regional systems, which offer a diversity of greenway types, or where maintenance costs are too high for one entity to bear. To help determine which acquisition tool is most appropriate, let's consider private ownership, public ownership, and mixed ownership (see Figure 6-3).

Private Ownership

Private ownership of greenways used primarily for recreation is not common. As existing public land resources become more heavily used and undeveloped land resources become more scarce, however, the most significant source of future land for parkland greenways may be existing private landholdings. Additionally, the trend toward fiscal restraint has caused local and state governments to rethink many traditional public services. The ownership of certain types of public land may become problematic for some local governments. Therefore, we are likely to see an emerging interest in private-sector ownership serving a public purpose. Three types of private ownership should be considered

Six jurisdictions and several land conservancies were recruited by a few key citizens to support the routing of the Westchester greenway through their lands. In connecting this existing open space, no new land trusts or additional land was needed. The few gaps in the system route were protected via easement. Members of the Appalachian Mountain Club maintain markings on the trail; jurisdictions maintain land if necessary. The spokesperson for the greenway, John Varvaryanis, says the greenway has cost the volunteers approximately $10 per year—the price of paint to mark the trail.

Acquisition Strategies for Greenways

	Explanation	Advantages	Disadvantages
Management agreements	Agreements between agency and landowner for a specific purpose.	Avoid purchase & other options, gain desired rights w/minimal hassle.	Only applicable with current landowner, and could be revoked at any time.
Land leases	Short- and/or long-term rental of land.	Low cost use of land. Landowner receives income and retains property control	Lease doesn't provide equity and affords limited control. Does not assure protection.
Permits and licenses	For fee agreements that specify specific uses - tied to a time frame.	An equitable arrangement that is specific to uses.	Is time and resource-base limited, not a long term method of protection.
Right of public access easements	Provides the public with the right to access and use a parcel of land for a specified purpose, limited to defined land area.	Can avoid need to purchase land from owner, provides right of public access and use. Excellent for greenways.	Can be time limited, usually restricts other uses, doesn't prevent owner from exercising other property rights.
Conservation easements	A partial interest in property generally or expressed purpose of protecting natural resources. Public access not always a component.	Inexpensive method for protecting natural resources. Landowner retains all other property rights, land remains on tax rolls.	Public access is usually restricted. Easement must be enforced. Easement may lower resale value.
Preservation easements	Same as conservation easement, most useful for historic landscapes.	Defines protection of historic elements of landscape.	Can restrict public access. Must be enforced.
Joint use easements	Accommodates multiple uses within one easement type: for example, sanitary sewer routing and public access. Should be one of the preferred methods for many greenways.	Provides opportunity to combine several public interests within one agreement. Easier for landowner to understand complete request - rather than several different requests.	Can be difficult for all landowners to agree to multiple uses along an entire greenway corridor. If one objects, the entire multiple use potential con be jeopardized.
Fee simple purchase	Outright purchase of full title to land and all rights associated with its use.	New landowner has full control of land. Allows for permanent protection and public access.	Cost of purchase may be outside local ability. Removes land from tax rolls.
Donations and gifts	A donation by landowner of all or partial interest in the property.	Provides permanent protection without public expenditures. Tax benefits to seller - charitable gift.	Receiving agency must be able to accept donation and capable of managing land.
Purchase and lease back	Purchase of full title, then lease back to previous owner. Subject to restrictions.	Essentially land banking. Income derived from lease payments. Owner is not displaced.	Lease may restrict public access. Land must be leased for appropriate uses.
	Explanation	**Advantages**	**Disadvantages**
Bargain sale	Part donation/part sale, property is sold at less than fair market value.	Tax benefits to seller, difference in sale price is considered charitable gift.	Seller must be agreeable to terms of sale. Bargain price may be inflated.
Option or first right of refusal	Owner agrees to provide first right of purchase to designated individual/agency.	Secures future right of purchase, provides time frame to negotiate terms with seller.	Does not ensure that owner will sell, or sell for a reasonable price.
Purchase of development rights	Local or state government purchases the rights of more intensive land use from current landowner.	Landowner derives financial benefit from selling rights. Lower property value reduces taxes.	Can be costly to purchase development rights.
Condemnation/eminent domain	The right of government to take private property for public purpose upon payment of just compensation. Can be exercised for recreational purposes in some states.	Provides tool for acquiring essential or endangered properties, if other techniques not acceptable.	Costly. Also creates a negative attitude about government and potentially the greenway concept. Only recommended as a last resort.
Installment sale	Allows buyer to pay for property over time.	If seller-financed, can lower taxes for seller. Buyer can negotiate better sale terms.	Long term financial commitment (30 years). Mortgage lien.
Land exchange	Swapping of developable land for property with high conservation value.	Relatively cost-free if trade parcel is donated. Reduces capital gains tax for original owner.	Owners must be willing to swap. Property must be of comparable value. Can be time consuming.
Exaction	As a condition of obtaining subdivision approval, local government requires developers to pay a fee or dedicate land to a municipal trust for open space.	New construction and development pays for its impact on open space. Good method during high growth periods.	Acquisition funds dependent on specific development. Difficult to calculate fair costs. Not effective during recessionary periods.
Transfer of development rights	Under legally established program, owner can transfer development rights from one property to another property designated to support increased density.	Cost of preservation absorbed by property owner who purchases rights. Allows local government to direct density and growth away from sensitive landscapes.	Difficult to implement. Very controversial. Often hard to identify areas where increased density is desirable. Must be established by legislation.
Cluster development	Permits high density development in parts of subdivision to protect sensitive lands.	Flexible and negotiable with landowner/developer. Can reduce construction and infrastructure costs.	Open space may not be linked. Processing time for development may be increased.
Performance zoning	A zone defined by permitted impacts as opposed to permitted uses.	Development occurs based on comprehensive, environmentally based strategy.	Criteria are hard to establish. Development plans more expensive to prepare.

Figure 6-2 Summary of acquisition strategies for greenways. (Adapted from *Tools and Strategies: Protecting the Landscape and Shaping Growth*, Regional Plan Association, April 1990.)

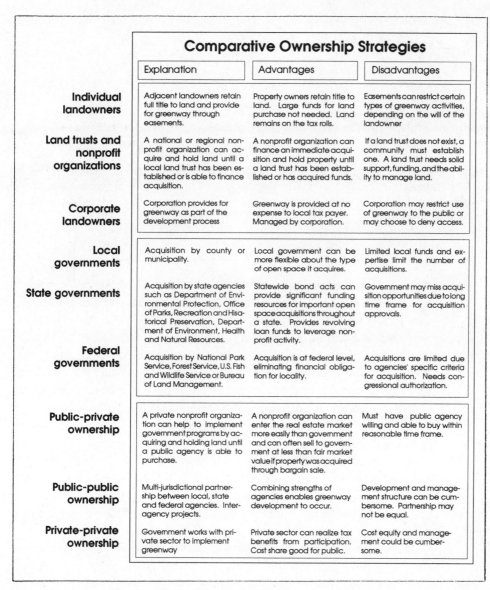

Figure 6-3 Summary of ownership strategies.

for greenways: land owned by individuals, land trusts and nonprofit groups, and corporations.

Individual Landowners. Many farmers and large estate landowners have ample land resources to maintain current uses, while providing opportunities for greenway development. One of the best examples of a greenway held in private ownership is the Anne Springs Close Greenway in Fort Mill, South Carolina (see Figures 6-4 and 6-5).

Land Trusts and Nonprofit Organizations. A land trust is a local, regional, or statewide organization directly involved with the protection of important land resources for public benefit. Land trusts can be found in rural, suburban, and urban communities or can be regional entities and are usually constituted as private, nonprofit, tax-exempt charitable corporations that use a variety of land-protection and ownership mechanisms to conserve natural resources. Direct land acquisition and

The Anne Springs Close Greenway

The Anne Springs Close Greenway, created through the vision of a single individual, Ms. Anne Springs Close, is a 2,600-acre private greenway surrounding two-thirds of Fort Mill, South Carolina. Situated less than twenty miles south of Charlotte, Fort Mill and its surrounding agricultural districts were in danger of being consumed by the suburban sprawl. Because the Close family controls a substantial amount of undeveloped land located in Fort Mill, it was in a unique position to ensure orderly, planned growth for a large portion of the community. To implement her greenway vision, Anne Close had the Conservation Fund complete a master plan for the family's 6,700-acre property. The plan identifies appropriate sites for a range of land uses and includes the greenway. The Close family officially dedicated land to the Anne Springs Close Greenway on Earth Day 1990. Through its gift, the family will preserve the natural and cultural resources of the area while maintaining the identity of the town of Fort Mill.

The Monadnoch—Sunapee Greenway is administered by the Society for the Protection of New Hampshire Forests. The original trail was established in the early 1920s by the society for (what were then called) "trampers" (hikers). The new trail follows higher country because the lower elevations are now taken in residential development. The path travels over highlands, through meadows, and along streams. The Society and the Appalachian Mountain Club are negotiating with owners for permanent protection agreements by easements, tailored to the needs of the individual landowners. Eighty private landowners host segments of trail; a few have generously provided campsites on their land.

easement are the traditional methods used by local land trusts to protect resources. Land trusts offer an opportunity not only to protect significant parcels of open space or greenway land, but also to provide short-term and long-term management solutions.

Whether or not a nonprofit organization will own and manage a greenway will depend on the type of greenway, the organization's resources, and its ability to manage the greenway. For example, unless the state provides adequate liability protection via a recreational use statute (see Chapter 14), recreational greenways are more appropriate in joint or full ownership by a public agency. In some cases, where the property is of regional or national significance, organizations like the Conservation Fund, the Nature Conservancy, and Trust for Public Land actually serve as real-estate brokers, helping local landowners make the necessary arrangements to transfer real property to public ownership for greenway purposes.

Corporate Landowners. Corporate landowners can offer the necessary legal and operating conditions for greenway purposes, such as permitting the right of public access on a part of their land. Numerous American corporations allow the public to attend and enjoy outdoor events on their property. Often these areas lie adjacent to streams, rivers, and lakes and would be a natural greenway setting. For example, in Cary, North Carolina, the Regency Park Corporation has allowed the North Carolina Symphony to use the shores of a man-made lake as the home for its summer concerts series. The lake, which also serves as a storm-water detention facility, is part of a larger private corporate greenway that contains rare hemlock trees, pedestrian trails, and public parking. The cost of public access, use, and liability are shared by both the corporation and the symphony. Municipal police and fire and medical services are provided at no cost to either party. After five years of operation, the Symphony remains a credible partner and has faithfully executed its responsibilities in the agreement.

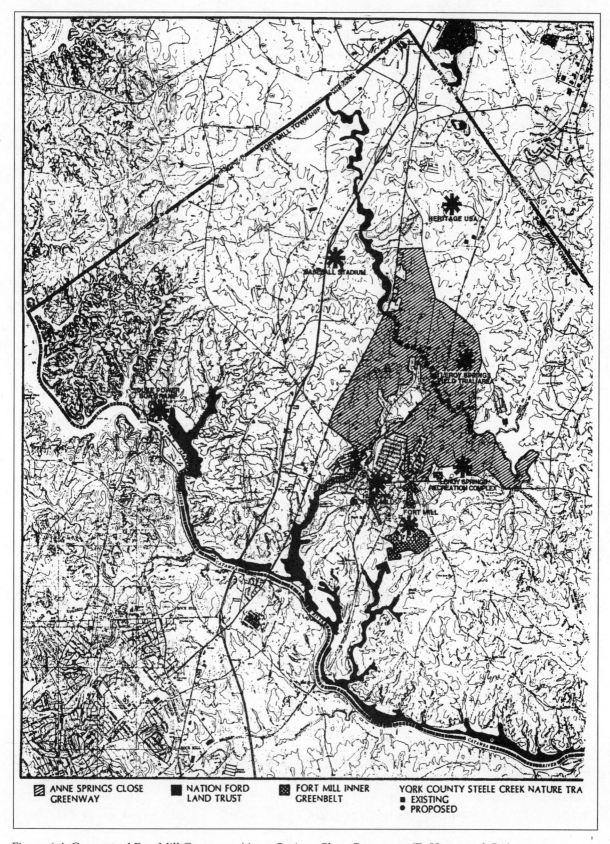

Figure 6-4 Conceptual Fort Mill Greenway/Anne Springs Close Greenway. (D. Horne and Co.)

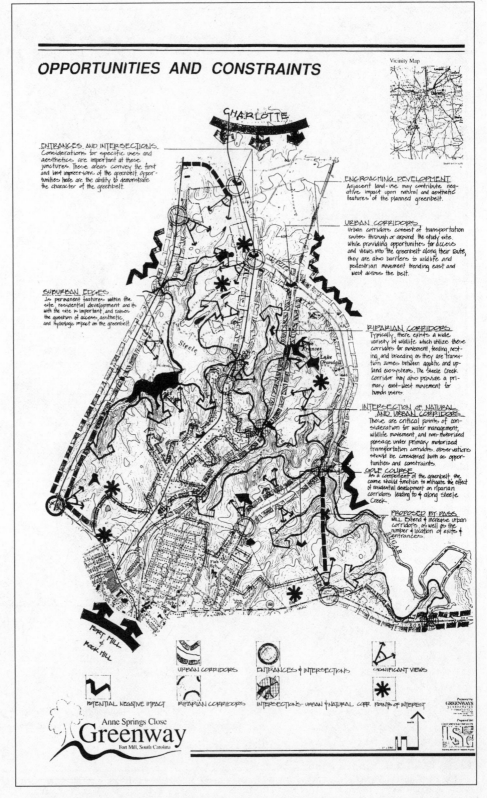

Figure 6-5 Greenway opportunities and constraints: Anne Springs Close Greenway. In 1992, Greenways Incorporated completed a hundred-year vision and a twenty-year master plan of the greenway property.

Public Ownership

Public ownership is currently the most common form of ownership for greenways, because most greenways encourage recreational access. It does have its pitfalls, however. For example, a community that holds fee simple title to several thousand acres of land collects no property tax revenues—the money that supports the operating funds for most communities—from these lands. A well-balanced program of public land ownership for greenways would include of a variety of ownership types, with emphasis placed on management agreements, easements, and regulatory authority. The City of Raleigh, North Carolina, has implemented a successful balanced approach regarding public land ownership for greenway purposes. Almost two-thirds of the more than one thousand acres of publicly accessible greenway lands have been secured through the use of a greenway easement, while the city continues to collect taxes on the land still held by the owner, and the owner may also qualify for various tax benefits.

Several different types of local, state, and federal agencies within the United States are empowered to own land. Deciding which agency would make the best owner of your proposed greenway will often depend on how responsive that agency is to the goals and objectives of your project.

Local Governments. Local governments are the most desirable public landowner for small single-jurisdictional and simple multijurisdictional greenways. Most successful greenways are a result of the participation of local citizens in the decision-making process that led to the creation of the greenway. Additionally, of all the public greenway owners, local governments are most responsive to the concerns and welfare of local residents and therefore best able to manage local greenways. Typically, the local parks and recreation or public works department is responsible for greenway stewardship, operation, and management. Public use and liability concerns are covered by local jurisdictional authority and capacity. Financial needs are most often met by appropriations from the general fund, from a capital improvement program, or through special financing.

State Governments. State governments can be a desirable public landowner for heavily used multijurisdictional, cross-state, and interstate greenways. Some states will assume all ownership requirements of a specific greenway. For example, the Missouri River Trail, a 200-mile greenway along the abandoned railroad rights-of-way of the Missouri Kansas Eastern Railroad, is now owned and managed by the State of Missouri. The state has acquired the abandoned rights-of-way to the corridor and is developing trails and installing trailheads at several locations along the route. Public access and liability are controlled and assumed by the state.

Some intrastate greenways require state government to coordinate ownership with local governments. Oregon's Willamette River Greenway is an example. In settings where no other prior public ownership of land exists, greenway lands are limited to state ownership of land

"Patience."
—Orono Land Trust

Since its founding in 1891, the Massachusetts group the Trustees of Reservations (TTOR), the nation's oldest regional land trust, has worked with local groups and state and federal agencies to protect land along the midstream portion of the eighty-mile Charles River, which empties into Boston Harbor. The Trustees, the Massachusetts Audubon Society, and several land trusts and municipalities now own and manage thousands of acres of open space in the Charles River basin and protect additional strategic areas with perpetual conservation restrictions. In addition, the natural valley storage program of the U. S. Army Corps of Engineers has protected thousands of acres of wetlands and floodplain bordering the river, thus avoiding the necessity for upstream flood control structures to protect metropolitan Boston. All of these efforts have extended the work of pioneering landscape architect (and TTOR's founder) Charles Eliot and his Metropolitan Park Commission in the downstream stretches of the Charles River basin. The result is a recreation and conservation corridor extending some sixty miles from the Esplanade through Boston's western suburbs.

submerged by the "ordinary low water" of the Willamette River. Submersible lands, those that lie between the ordinary low water and ordinary high water of the Willamette are *not* owned by the state. Neither, by greenway legislation, is any of the land above ordinary high water. Responsibility for the greenway is shared by three jurisdictions: the Oregon Land Conservation and Development Commission, the Oregon Department of Transportation, Parks and Recreation Branch, and local jurisdictions.

The Federal Government. Although largely viewed as a funding source, several federal agencies have shown interest in greenway development, and some are capable of owning greenway lands. Federal ownership is most likely in partnerships with local or state governments.

The National Park Service is the most likely federal landowner for greenways (National Parks, Heritage Corridors) and also pursues greenway initiatives at the national, state, and local level. The Forest Service's Challenge Cost-Share program encourages partnerships with citizens to promote greenways near and within national forests. A relatively new program within the Department of Defense, called the Legacy Resources Management Program, offers North American U.S. Military Bases financial support to protect significant natural resource lands and opens some of these lands for public use. The Federal Highway Administration is currently supporting a renewed interest in alternative transportation and protection of scenic and historic corridors.

Coordinating Greenway Ownership

Because of the legal, management, and operational requirements of greenways and the strained budgets of government agencies, many future greenways, especially greenways that cross jurisdictions, are likely to be owned by multiple public agencies or through specially created public–private partnerships.

Public–private ownership offers the best of both worlds: concern for public welfare and the creativity, tenacity, and spirit of private enterprise. A partnership of public agencies and private organizations offers a well-rounded, sound, and capable strategy for ownership and management of a greenway.

Public–public ownership is especially suitable when the greenway is located in more than one jurisdiction. The advantages of a public partnership include pooling of public resources, sharing of staff and management responsibilities, and in some cases, being more effective at raising revenues for land acquisition. Larger public agencies can assist smaller, less capable agencies, providing a proportionate cost share for project development.

Private–private ownership may be more common in future greenway development, as the burden of public services comes to rest more on the shoulders of local government.

The Research Triangle Park Pedestrian Trail system in North Carolina offers an example of private–private ownership. This greenway was created by a partnership among the park, the Research Triangle

Foundation of North Carolina, and corporate property owners within the park—IBM, Northern Telecom, and GTE. Property for the greenway was secured through a right-of-public-access easement, the use of existing public rights-of-way, and most importantly, in the development plans for the southern portion of the park by designating the land for use as a greenway.

Land development in the United States during the past thirty-five years has resulted in tremendous loss of farmland and open space, widespread urban sprawl, the degradation of air and water quality, and the destruction of sensitive ecological habitat. Greenways are a needed and practical use of our nation's land resources. To secure lands for greenways, greenway advocates must understand the basic underpinnings of real-property law and have a working knowledge of the various land protection tools.

Many of the strategies in this chapter contain tax implications for buyers and sellers of greenway lands. Consult a tax advisor or attorney to understand the full financial impacts of a land transaction before any formal negotiations take place.

7

Promoting the Natural Values of the Land

*"I am glad I shall never be young without wild country to be young in.
Of what avail are forty freedoms without a blank spot on a map."*
—Aldo Leopold

Over the past few decades global urbanization and population growth
have transformed the surface of the earth. Around the world, vast areas
that had been wild for millennia are being drastically altered by human
activities. Forests are being cleared at the rate of acres per second. Rivers and streams are being straightened, dammed, lined with concrete,
even dried up. Habitat vital to the survival of countless plant and animal species is being drained, filled, and developed. More than half the
wetlands in the United States have been lost since the founding of our
nation. Even with new laws designed to protect them, wetlands are still
disappearing at the rate of half a million acres annually. The open
spaces and wild areas that remain are becoming increasingly fragmented. Once flourishing species are confined to islands of wild space
in a landscape dominated by humans. We are only beginning to understand the extent of the damage global development has done to these
ecosystems.

In the wake of these impacts, greenways must become more than recreational amenities. Many see the rivers, streams, wetlands, and ridge
tops that greenways follow as vital open-space connections. Ideally, all
greenways should include conservation goals. This implies some new
and significant responsibilities for those who design, implement, and
manage greenway corridors.

This chapter won't provide all the answers, but it will raise some of
the questions you must ask when planning your greenway and give you
some general guidelines for designing a greenway that protects wildlife
and promotes ecological health. (We use the term *wildlife* to refer to all
plants and animals that inhabit the natural environment).

The Corridor Concept

Corridors take many forms and have varied functions. There are natural
corridors such as rivers, shorelines, and ridge tops, and there are man-made corridors that follow railroads, canals, roads, and utility lines.
Usually, a natural corridor is a swath of land, longer than it is wide. It
may exist as a distinct landscape feature, or it may link other natural
areas. Generally, a unifying element such as a stream or ridge line will
define a corridor, although the corridor itself may consist of many different vegetation or habitat types and perform many ecological functions. A corridor may even be a route—consider the migratory bird
flyways that depend on corresponding areas of protected land.

The Blackwater-Fishing Bay Wetlands Greenway encompasses a major section of the lower Eastern shore in Maryland and includes national wildlife refuge and state wildlife management area lands. Wildlife habitat and water quality values are primary here, and the area is an important link in the Atlantic flyway. Human use is limited to compatible activities such as hunting, fishing, crabbing, birding, and hiking loop trails. An environmental education center is planned by the Chesapeake Bay Foundation.

Many important movements of humans and nature occur along natural corridors. Drainage, travel, and commerce often follow corridors; wildlife in search of food, habitat, shelter, and breeding partners use corridors. Some corridors act as buffers for our water supplies, aiding in the recharge of underground aquifers and cleansing sediments and contaminants before runoff reaches our rivers and streams. Natural corridors come in many sizes and widths. A hedgerow may be only a few feet wide and run only a few hundred yards, yet serve as both a windbreak and as habitat, providing nesting places, food, and cover for animals within an area of cultivated fields. River and stream corridors might range in width from fifty feet to several miles, providing diverse habitats for a great variety of species.

Greenway planners may deal with corridors that are miles wide and hundreds of miles long. They might consist of an entire coastline or a wide swath of land known to be important wildlife habitat. For example, the U.S. Fish and Wildlife Service is attempting to preserve wildlife habitat along a 150-mile-long corridor on Texas's lower Rio Grande. A similar effort seeks to protect grizzly bear habitat along the Rockies from Yellowstone National Park in Wyoming to Glacier National Park in Montana. These "megacorridors" will no doubt become increasingly important as urbanization continues to encroach on wild areas.

Some corridors may be inconspicuous, yet of great biological, geologic, or historic significance. Florida's Lake Wales Ridge is one such corridor. Believed to be the remnant of an ancient shoreline, this archipelago of scrub habitat "islands" runs more than one hundred miles down the center of the state, varying in width from four to thirteen miles. The harsh growing conditions of its quick-draining sandy soils have caused the evolution of many unique and unusual plant species specially adapted to this setting. Whereas the ridge is not imposing—the average person would not spot it—it is like no other place on earth. Under the auspices of Florida's Conservation and Recreation Lands Program and The Nature Conservancy, efforts are underway to preserve this special corridor.

The Sears Greenway is a two-mile project linking major forest preserves in Cook County, Illinois. The greenway will be part of an eight-hundred-acre parcel to be developed as Sears' Corporate Marketing Headquarters. The Open Lands Project, Citizens for Conservation, Morton Arboretum, and other conservation groups developed a plan that calls for rehabilitation of wetland and prairie segments to the original natural character.

Corridors and Landscape Ecology

In the past few decades, natural and artificial corridors have become a topic of increasing interest and scientific study. In the 1960s, University of Wisconsin professor Phillip Lewis urged the preservation of a system of corridors that would crisscross the states of Wisconsin and Iowa. As a result of Lewis's efforts, the Southeastern Wisconsin Regional Planning Commission protected a corridor system traversing a seven-county area—a green infrastructure that is one of the most effective regional systems of environmental corridors in the nation. Ian McHarg contributed his overlay system, which delineates significant geologic and ecological elements and patterns in the environment. Both of these planners recognized that a high concentration of ecological features and processes occur along linear alignments, particularly waterways.

In 1986, Richard T. T. Forman and M. Godron published their landmark *Landscape Ecology*, which presents the environment as a complex web of landscape elements that change and evolve over time. This structure includes a dominant background *matrix* such as farmlands, suburbs, forest, and prairie. Corridors—be they rivers, streams, or even ditches—run through that matrix and may weave together several landscape elements and the system as a whole in a way that is vital to each element. In addition, there may be smaller landscape elements, called patches, such as a small remnant wetland along the edge of a suburban stream.

Landscape ecology has become an increasingly important part of greenway planning because it melds human and natural considerations and influences in real-world landscapes. It asks how human activities and the natural environment should interact. Given that recreational access along a corridor may be detrimental to certain natural values, how do we plan greenways responsibly? How do we reconcile conflicting needs? By combining scientific data with technical planning specifications, landscape ecology can help determine whether a corridor is sufficiently wide and natural to promote habitat integrity.

Conduits and Connectivity

Fragmentation of open space into increasingly small and isolated pockets is a result of urbanization, road construction, agriculture, and a variety of other causes. Biologically, fragmentation can lead to increasingly limited habitat and the extinction of local species. Many animals, particularly those that are wide-ranging, cannot meet their food requirements or successfully breed in the small areas to which they have been relegated. Without adequate range, these "area-sensitive" species suffer from interbreeding, roadside death, competition with other species, and starvation.

Natural corridors may help species escape danger, competition, fire, famine, or humans. They may be a conduit for colonizing new areas when existing conditions are harsh. They may aid wildlife in finding mates, food, habitat, and shelter. Seeds, pollen, nutrients, and other material may be transported by animals during their travels along the corridor or by water in river or wetland corridors.

A network of natural connections between suitable habitats is considered one way of stemming the disturbing trend toward declining natural diversity in small or isolated natural areas. For example, Pinhook Swamp, a thirty-thousand-acre preserve connection between North Florida's Osceola National Forest and Okeefenokee National Wildlife Refuge serves as a conduit connecting important habitat for wide-ranging black bear and panther.

Barriers

A barrier is an obstruction or constriction that may impede movement along a corridor, such as a stream narrowed by street crossings or routed through a culvert. Barriers affect both wildlife and human travel

The proposed "Greenway to the Pacific" will connect Portland, Oregon, to the Pacific coast. Originating at Portland's five-thousand-acre Forest Park, the greenway travels northwest through a transition landscape of increasing urbanization, fans out to enter a vast Douglas fir forest reserve, then crosses the Coast Range to the Pacific Coast and Columbia River estuary. The eastern return route will be a combination of land and water trails following the Columbia River, the Lewis and Clark Trail, and the Willamette River Greenway to Portland. A primary benefit of the corridor will be to ensure unbroken travel and dispersal for native wildlife.

(via trails) along corridors. A corridor itself may be a barrier to lateral movement from one side of the corridor to the other. For example, a wide stream, a steep ridge line, or a freeway each presents a barrier to certain types of movement. How do these and other kinds of barriers figure into your greenway planning? Note that while barriers might inhibit movement, they may also be vital to certain species because they keep predators at bay.

Habitat: Shelter, Food, a Place to Rest and to Breed

Corridors are not just paths of movement between habitats; they *are* habitat for a wide variety of species. Your greenway may provide refuge for common as well as rare species or community types.

When evaluating your corridor, you should ask:

- What species inhabit the corridor or could inhabit it given the right improvements or reintroduction of species?

- What kinds of native food and forage grow there or could grow there?

- Does the corridor provide places of escape from predators and cover for nesting and den building?

- Some animals require several types of habitat and need to travel between them. Does the corridor link similar or complementary habitat of target species? Is it composed of vegetative cover that will allow such movement?

- Can species migrate and disperse to avoid both overpopulation and inbreeding?

- Can a program of planting improve the habitat value of the corridor?

The Greenway Edge and Interior

The edge of a corridor is where it meets adjacent landscape or land-use zones. In nature, edges are dynamic places. There are a number of different kinds of edges to consider when evaluating a corridor. For example, there is the edge of a stream, and there is the edge where forest meets meadow. Each of these represents a transition zone, where soil conditions, vegetation types, light and shade conditions, as well as land use change. For example, at the edge of the forest, more sunlight reaches the ground, and a greater variety of grasses, shrubs, and other plants flourish here than in the interior. This provides more forage for animals that venture into the meadow to feed and then return to the cover of the forest. Edges or the areas close to them are the places where many species live.

Corridors also have edges where nature meets human activities. It might be the point where a farmer's fields meet a hedgerow or woodlot. It might be the back side of residences along a suburban stream valley or the boundaries of an oil refinery along an estuary or bayou. The impact of human activities along edges can be significant and in some

Be sure to order a copy of "How Greenways Work, a Handbook on Ecology" from the Recreation Resources Assistance Division of the National Park Service. A joint project with the Atlantic Center for the Environment, this handbook, written by Jonathan Labaree, serves as an introduction to basic ecological principles that apply to greenways. The Ecology of Greenways (Smith and Hellmund, editors), a more detailed and technical volume, will be published the University of Minnesota Press in 1993.

instances deleterious to wildlife. Farm fields can leach pesticides. Predators that venture from the corridor and threaten livestock may be poisoned, trapped, or shot. Land disturbed by development or agriculture can be a source of invasive species that thrive in transition zones—for example, raccoon, blue jay, deer, opossum, and weedy plants—and displace the native species in the forest.

The edge-to-interior ratio of a corridor is an important factor in considering the wildlife value of your corridor. According to some researchers, light, wind, and predators in a seemingly insignificant band of edge bordering a temperate forest may affect wildlife as deeply as a thousand to two thousand feet into the forest (see Figure 7-1). Because corridors usually have a high ratio of edge to interior, certain wildlife species (e.g., goshawk, martin, hooded warbler), which require extensive tracts of closed canopy forest, can be vulnerable to some of the edge effects just described.

Interior species are particularly vulnerable in greenways open to recreational use unless that use is carefully planned. Habitats need to be buffered, for example, from too much edge noise, visual distraction, and invasions of exotic species, parasites, predators, and disease. Heavily used trails and facilities should be kept away from sensitive habitat.

Whereas edges can be points of conflict, they can also act as buffer zones, screening out negative impacts. This buffering function will depend on the adjacent land uses as well as the width and character of the edge and the width of the corridor itself. How wide should a corridor be to provide these interior and buffering functions? Clearly, this varies with the type of corridor, although many experts believe that there should be at least a one-to-one ratio of interior habitat to edge habitat in a greenway that aims to protect native wildlife resources.

Ideally, before introducing trails or other disturbances, greenway corridors should be assessed by wildlife specialists. These specialists should be familiar with corridor issues, local species, local landscape conditions, and the specific corridor in question. Contact local wildlife clubs and state natural heritage programs, native plant societies, universities, state and federal wildlife agencies, and nature centers for help or for the name of experts you can contact.

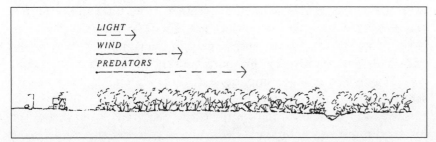

Figure 7-1 Gradual vs. abrupt edge transitions. Increased light, wind, and predators characterize the edge of a forest where it borders a field. Each effect penetrates differently into the forest, as indicated by the arrows. (Courtesy of the National Park Service and Quebec Labrador Foundation's Atlantic Center for the Environment.)

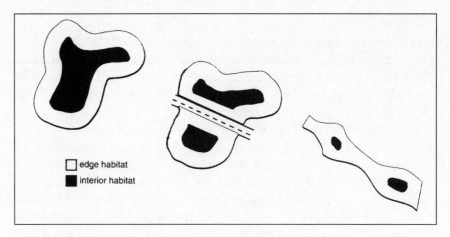

Figure 7-2 Effects of fragmentation and narrowness on interior habitat. The drawing at left shows a natural patch of land with edge effects penetrating around its perimeter. In the middle, a road has dissected the same patch, greatly reducing the amount of interior habitat. A greenway, right, will often have little interior habitat because it is too narrow to overcome the effects of edge. (Courtesy of the National Park Service and Quebec Labrador's Atlantic Center for the Environment.)

Finally, it is important to realize that many greenways (particularly narrow ones in urban and suburban areas) are virtually all edge and may do little to foster the survival of native wildlife species. (See Figure 7-2).

Vertical Structure

Corridors also have a vertical structure (see Figure 7-3), which may include, for example, a streambed with its bottom-dwelling organisms and hatching areas; the stream water, itself home to fish and other aquatic creatures; an understory of grasses, shrubs, logs, and rocks; a middle layer of large shrubs and small trees; and finally a canopy of large trees. Each of these levels has a specific function, and together they interact to form a system.

Stress, Disturbance, and Succession

It would be wonderful if corridors could be preserved like a snapshot: if we could define an ideal setting, delineate it, protect it, and keep it that way forever. Nature, however, does not work that way. Constant processes of stress, disturbance, and succession come into play. Forests and grasslands periodically dry out, burn, and then regenerate (see Figure 7-4). Flooding is another important disturbance phenomenon. In the semiarid high plains, the flood sequence sometimes comes in pairs: one washes away sediments and nutrients; the next redeposits them. Cottonwood forest regeneration is tied to these patterns of periodic scour and deposition.

Such processes invigorate and renew, creating a mosaic of habitat types and greater site diversity. What role does stress, disturbance, and succession play along your corridor? Can the corridor and adjacent land

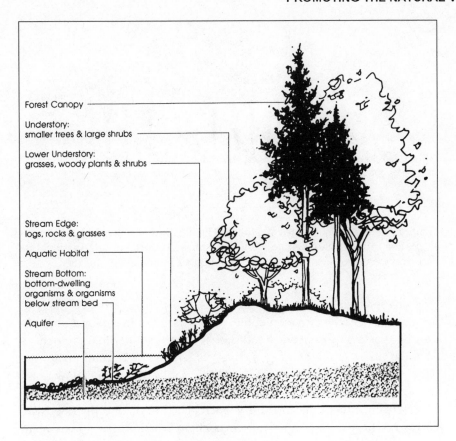

Figure 7-3 Vertical structure of a stream corridor.

uses tolerate natural changes (or lack thereof), or must artificial solutions such as controlled burning, fertilization, and irrigation be introduced to help mitigate the loss of certain natural functions?[1]

How Corridors Protect the Air, Land, and Water

Corridors are playing an increasingly significant role in the survival of wildlife. Their direct benefit to other resources and, ultimately, to people is sometimes less obvious. Usually decision makers, especially courts involved in land acquisition or zoning, want to see quantifiable (dollar and cents) benefits to the health, safety, and welfare of society when committing to a course of action that affects political and economic interests. What, therefore, are some direct tangible benefits of natural corridor protection?

Natural Floodplains: Flood Hazard Reduction

For humans, the most obvious but often overlooked benefit of corridor preservation is flood hazard reduction. Encroachment by buildings and

[1]Material in this section was adapted in part from Daniel Smith and Paul Hellmund, eds., *The Ecology of Greenways*, a draft handbook prepared by the National Park Service Rivers and Trails Conservation Assistance Program, Washington, D.C., 1991. The handbook will be published by the University of Minnesota Press in 1993.

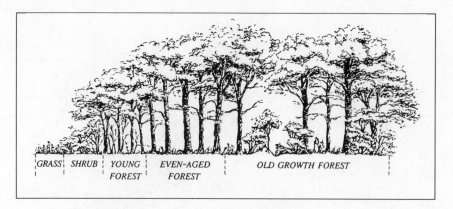

GRASS | SHRUB | YOUNG FOREST | EVEN-AGED FOREST | OLD GROWTH FOREST

Figure 7-4 Successional stages of a forest. The illustration shows basic stages of succession from an open field to old growth forest. (Courtesy of the National Park Service and Quebec Labrador Foundation's Atlantic Center for the Environment.)

In Tennessee the North Chickamauga Creek Greenway includes a quarter-mile asphalt trail that follows the creek and loops through hardwood and loblolly forests. On the east, the greenway is bordered by a 208-acre "Small Wild Area" (managed by the Tennessee Valley Authority), which supports a large population of Scutellaria montana, a federally listed endangered plant. The greenway master plan calls for an unsurfaced nature trail system for this sensitive area, which would link into the paved trail system.

other inappropriate uses in the floodplain of a river or stream is likely to have at least two negative outcomes: costly flood damage (and possibly loss of life) and extensive flood-damage mitigation projects such as channelization (straightening a river or stream and reinforcing the banks with grass, rock, or concrete). Wide, natural corridors allow flood waters to spread out and move more slowly, thus reducing damage downstream. Where the corridor is encroached upon and the floodway narrowed, flows speed up. Then, in a chain reaction, the downstream segments are hit by increased peak storm runoff, increased flow velocity, and erosion. The higher short-term cost of removing such structures as houses from the floodplain may be less over the long term than the expense of constant channel maintenance and flood damage repair. In many cases the least costly method is not to allow encroachment into the floodplain in the first place. Trails, parks, nature study areas, and other nonintrusive uses that can withstand flooding, however, may be appropriate.

Control of Erosion and Sedimentation

Natural corridor preservation can also reduce erosion. Setting aside corridors of green along waterways is an effective means of trapping pollution and eroded sediments in runoff water from nearby disturbed areas. This is true not only along streams but on hillsides and other unstable areas. Setting aside land with steep gradients, such as cliffs, shorelines, and dunes, as open space reduces the chance of erosion, mud slides, and other problems that are costly to remedy once areas are developed. Hedgerows, vegetated hillsides, and stream corridors help break the wind and keep valuable agricultural topsoil from blowing away. Figure 7-5 shows a greenway plan that respects the natural processes and capabilities of the San Miguel River.

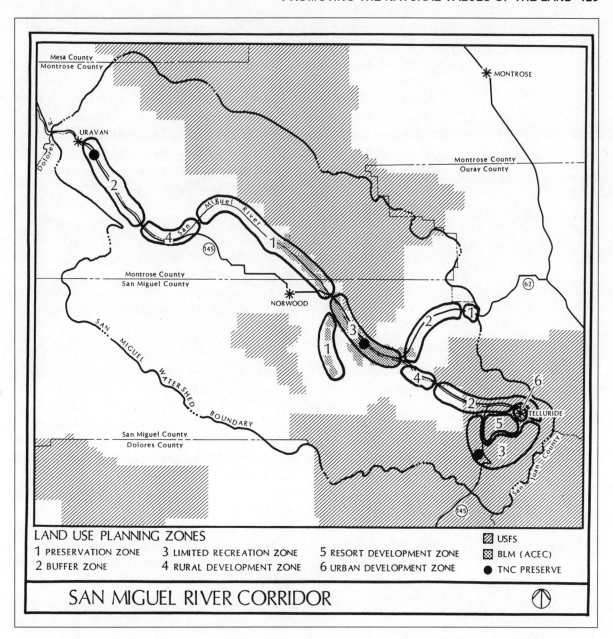

LAND USE PLANNING ZONES

1 PRESERVATION ZONE 3 LIMITED RECREATION ZONE 5 RESORT DEVELOPMENT ZONE
2 BUFFER ZONE 4 RURAL DEVELOPMENT ZONE 6 URBAN DEVELOPMENT ZONE

USFS
BLM (ACEC)
TNC PRESERVE

SAN MIGUEL RIVER CORRIDOR

Figure 7-5 San Miguel River Corridor. The Conservation Fund and the Nature Conservancy are working together to protect this ecologically rich river corridor, which is undergoing rapid change due to the pressure of ski area development. As one of the few rivers in the western United States without a mainstream dam, the San Miguel boasts healthy riparian communities and upland habitat, both threatened by the booming growth of Telluride. The deleterious effects of mining, timber, uncontrolled recreation activities, grazing, and water diversions are addressed in the greenway plan, which identifies six planning units based on natural values and settlement patterns. (D. Horne & Co.)

Clean Air and Water

Natural corridors can help cleanse air and water. Obviously, the wider and longer the corridor, the more effective the cleansing action. Trees and other plants remove carbon dioxide, carbon monoxide, and other toxic pollutants from the atmosphere, and they produce a net return of oxygen.

Rivers, streams, and other wetland corridors can both recharge the water table and clean contaminated water. Riparian vegetation can remove excess nutrients and sediments, either by causing them to settle out of the slowed stream flow or through metabolism of wetland plants. An increasing number of communities around the nation and the world are using either preserved natural wetlands or artificially created ones to treat sewage effluent. In many cases this method has proved less costly than more conventional mechanical and chemical means.

The Environmental Protection Agency under the Clean Water Act and amendments requires communities to manage the water quality of surface runoff, which often contains contaminants from lawn chemicals, agricultural fertilizers and pesticides, pet droppings, motor oil, and other harmful substances. Again, well-planned natural corridors with adequate buffer zones and natural wetlands offer municipalities a cost-effective way to replace or supplement costly treatment plants.

Climate Moderation

In her book, *The Granite Garden*, Anne Winston Spirn described how Stuttgart, Germany, benefits from a giant natural air-conditioning system. At night, cool, clean air flows down from wooded hillsides that surround the city, lowering summertime temperatures and removing air pollutants. The city's inhabitants save on air-conditioning costs and benefit from verdant wooded corridors. Recognizing the value of air flow corridors, the city has passed legislation that limits development in them. A hundred-meter minimum flow corridor width has been adopted in which trees and grasses are planted.

This concept is now in practice in the United States. The City of Dayton, Ohio, for example, encourages natural vegetation to grow along major highways that circle the city. These *vegetation corridors* now absorb pollutants and reduce wind velocities that have been an annoyance downtown.

Education

Natural corridors make great outdoor classrooms, particularly in urban areas. Many communities have nature centers and other interpretive programs located along greenways. These corridors offer first-hand opportunities to observe wildlife and plant species in their native element and to interpret human impact on the corridors' natural systems. Greenways are particularly effective in introducing and connecting urban residents to the natural world. They can instill a sense of outdoor stewardship through various volunteer programs, including tree plantings, cleanups, and other special projects.

Natural corridors also offer an opportunity to teach people about management practices that have been put in place to protect resources. For example, managers can demonstrate on site how a "no mowing" policy may enhance a greenway's overall natural values by promoting shrubby habitat for birds.

Signs can point out and explain the origin and functions of corridors within the urban environment. For example, a certain valley may have been the route of European explorers, later the railroads, and now the greenway. Interpretation can help a visitor to understand the role this once-natural landform played in the history of urbanization.

Species Protection

Disappearing habitat for rare and endangered species is possibly the most challenging problem facing the conservation community. Some greenway corridors address the needs of plant and animal species. They may be wide swaths of land that offer habitat or narrower conduits designed to promote movements of wide-ranging species. For example, the Florida panther is benefitting from underpasses and bridges that connect habitat in its home range. Corridors can also be a refuge for rare species. In the Midwest, unplowed prairie remnants along railroad rights-of-way have been managed as a store of rare prairie species.

Corridors also protect common but economically valuable species. Consider the value of breeding streams to the salmon fishing industry or healthy trout streams to a state's tourist trade. Certain game species need the edge habitat found in many corridors to breed and survive.

Potential Pitfalls

As far as native wildlife is concerned, the corridor approach is not without its faults. Corridors clearly are not a total panacea or substitute for large wilderness tracts or preidentified endangered species habitat. Following are several caveats to consider when pursuing and promoting the ecological values of your greenway.

Many Corridors Are Compromised

Most likely, the corridor you are considering for greenway status has already been narrowed or encroached upon by agriculture, roads, buildings, and other development. It may be subject to outside disturbance and stress that will preclude those species needing a larger and more pristine habitat.

Movement of Disease, Predators, and Fire

Whereas a corridor linking larger habitats might benefit wildlife by allowing more travel and potential breeding partners, the corridor can also permit the transmission of fires, predators, and infection. Identify the most sensitive species in your planning process, and be sure the corridor system can handle any potential diseases among the plant and animal species you want to protect. Consult with your wildlife department or other experts.

Impact on Native Species

Without careful management, the corridor might become a route for invasive, nonnative species. A good example of an undesirable species is the Russian Olive found along many rivers and streams in the West and Midwest. It is an attractive tree, but it displaces native vegetation and reduces habitat and forage. Not every tree and not every plant is appropriate for your greenway. Your corridor may become an unwitting accessory in spreading these undesirable species at the expense of the full range of native species you are trying to protect. Once established in your greenway, invasive species are difficult to remove.

Conflicting Uses

In some cases, a greenway corridor may invite human uses incompatible with plant and animal protection. Opening a corridor to recreational use with trails, boat landings, and other amenities may drive off some species. Even though some negative impacts might be mitigated through design and management solutions, difficult choices have to be made. Indeed, some greenways should not be open for human use.

Limited Knowledge

The Southeastern Wisconsin Regional Planning Commission promotes ecological corridors in its 2700-square-mile region. Geographic Information system (GIS) technology identifies significant corridors based on wildlife habitat, soil, hydrology, and land use. A scoring system that classifies segments by area, length, and width distinguishes between primary corridors of state and county concern and secondary corridors that are protected locally. Although many of the corridors occur on public land, local zoning and regulations protect corridors on private lands.

We can't always say for sure that a given corridor will function the way we plan; nor is there a magic formula for designing a greenway so that it can best support inherent natural values. Ensuring the health of wildlife and the environment requires a thorough look at the corridor by experts. Perhaps the habitat can be managed or rehabilitated to play an important role in local and regional natural systems.

Responsible Corridor Evaluation and Management

You want to create a greenway that respects the land and water resource values. You have an overview of landscape ecology and corridor preservation, but how do you integrate these considerations into greenway planning?

Evaluate the Resource

Nearly every greenway plan will promote natural values and aim to integrate these values with some recreational use. Some greenways have extraordinary natural assets, and the health of these assets should be an overriding concern in promoting the greenway. Drawing on the contribution of conservation biologists, water resource specialists, and landscape ecologists, we can refine the inventory guidelines in Chapter 2 with a checklist of items to help you better understand the natural assets of your greenway corridor.

You should also consult with state and local fish and wildlife agencies, state natural heritage programs, agricultural departments, universities, local birding and nature societies, and wildlife clubs for advice and information.

Corridor Evaluation Checklist

1. Define the corridor, including landscape characteristics, widths, limits, barriers, and the regions that directly affect it. Remember that greater width may provide adequate buffer from edge effects for interior species and habitat. Ideal width will depend upon local habitat type, the wildlife targeted for protection, and surrounding land uses. Evaluate whether the corridor is part of a larger network of corridors or ecological systems (such as a tributary stream) and, if so, what ecological role it plays in this larger network. Are there other natural areas in the region that would benefit from connection to this corridor?

2. Identify existing and potential habitat, including vegetation groupings and environments such as wetlands that provide food and cover. Remember that varied habitat is often the key to wildlife health and diversity. If possible, protect a variety of habitat types and other environmentally sensitive areas (groundwater recharge areas, intermittent streams, springs, and so on). Be aware that corridors composed of habitat similar to the natural areas they connect are probably best for promoting movement between the linked areas. For example, two forested areas linked by grass or open field are of less value to movement of forest wildlife than a corridor of forest land.

3. Identify key individual plant and animal species. Which are common? Are there rare or endangered species? Are species confined to small patches, or does the corridor support wide movement and distribution of these plants and animals? Are certain species likely to prosper or even dominate the corridor? Think about what management goals need to be set to protect these species. Be sure you consider a large enough planning region to assess the needs of these species.

4. Identify any applicable migration routes both along and across the corridor. Does the corridor include stopping points, such as rest spots or feeding areas on major transcontinental bird flyways? Does the corridor link presettlement habitat areas? Does it follow traditional wildlife migration routes?

5. Identify points of present and likely future human encroachment. How serious are the current impacts? Are there major development projects on the drawing boards—houses, roads, utilities, golf courses—that will adversely affect corridor values? Can buffer zones be created to prevent or reverse some of these impacts?

6. Check for invasive and undesirable species. Can measures be taken to reverse the spread of these species? Is there any evidence of disease or pest transmission along the corridor now or likely in the future as a result of greenway development?

Maryland Critical Areas legislation institutes a one-thousand-foot overlay buffer zone along the shores of the Chesapeake Bay and its tidal rivers. The Act states: "All development sites shall incorporate a wildlife corridor system that connects the largest undeveloped and most regular tracts of land within or adjacent to the sites in order to provide continuity of existing wildlife and plant habitat." This is usually done via easement or restrictive covenant. Counties determine the exact development through local planning.

Guidelines for Preventing Biotic Invasions

• Replant disturbed sites with native species.

• Avoid the temptation to plant exotic species because they have beneficial qualities such as erosion control or are a high-quality food source.

• Engage in active management schemes such as intentional burning where these conditions are favorable to native plant species.

• Always manage a greenway to benefit native species. This may require consultation with local botanists and zoologists who study local plant and animal species and their needs.

Source: Daniel S. Smith and Paul Hellmund, eds., *Ecology of Greenways*, University of Minnesota Press, Minneapolis, 1993.

---

7. Try to locate areas that are improving or degrading. This will give you a baseline management tool so that you can compare the future health of the greenway with present conditions.

8. How do you expect the corridor to change over time? What practical human intervention steps can be taken to help sustain the natural values of the corridor?

9. Are there geophysical changes occurring along the corridor, or do you anticipate such changes as alteration of the amount of stream flow, climate changes, aquifer depletion, slope erosion, or deforestation that will significantly change the character of the corridor and its ability to support the present plant and animal communities?

10. Are there especially delicate geological formations or features that need protection?

11. What are the ecological goals for the corridor, and what kinds of management programs can be put in place to sustain and enhance the corridor in accordance with those goals?

12. Does the corridor offer educational and interpretive opportunities?[1]

The Santa Fe Prairie is an important natural area that could be linked by the Centennial Trail to other points of ecological and cultural interest in the Chicago area. Located near a main Santa Fe interstate rail line, the Prairie is a rare, high-quality example of presettlement vegetation. The prairie has been restored and managed by local Nature Conservancy volunteers, who conduct controlled burns for natural regeneration of the prairie, collect seed, and propagate prairie plants. The site is protected by the Santa Fe Railroad and managed under a renewable short-term lease by Nature Conservancy volunteers.

Map Your Findings

It is helpful to present your analysis on a map showing the various components of your corridor, landscape elements, surrounding land uses, migration routes, and areas undergoing change. In addition to mapping, we recommend that you prepare a data file that includes your findings, comments, and the names of any people and publications you have relied on to complete your corridor evaluation.

---

[1]Adapted in part from Reed F. Noss, "Wildlife Corridors," in Daniel Smith and Paul Hellmund, eds., *Ecology of Greenways* (Minneapolis: University of Minnesota Press, 1993).

*Develop an Environmental Concept or Theme for
Your Corridor*

Critical to the success of corridor planning is to know your ecological objectives. This calls for an understanding of the species that currently inhabit the corridor and an identification of potential species if the habitat were to be improved. From this review, you can formulate a resource theme for your corridor. For example, you might be looking at an urban stream or ridge line corridor that is too narrow in many places to support large mammals or interior bird species but still could host other wildlife. An appropriate theme for such a corridor might be to manage for songbirds and small to medium mammals like rabbit, fox, and coyote. Additionally, the theme might stress migration between larger nonurban land tracts outside the city. The theme helps guide goals and shape policies for land preservation, recreational access, and stream and water quality improvements.

Integrating Ecological Values in Multiobjective Greenways

As we learn more about natural corridors and their role in an increasingly threatened landscape, we soon realize that planning multiple-use greenways is complex. One prime challenge is to bring technical engineering, the biological sciences, and greenway planning together in new and productive ways.

*Environment-Friendly Greenway Planning—Some
Guiding Principles*

- Minimize human—wildlife conflicts by siting recreation paths where there will be the least interference with natural values.
  - (a) Site trails and recreational facilities away from interior and sensitive habitats (see Figure 7-6).
  - (b) If traversing interior habitat, trails should be as narrow as possible to prevent disturbance of wildlife and the introduction of edge species. Maximize the use of lookouts, scenic overlooks, and other nonintrusive ways to enjoy and learn about the more sensitive areas.
  - (c) Know the species that need the most protection and try to accommodate them in your design.
  - (d) Use boardwalks, mulch, and natural materials to prevent damage to sensitive soils. Use permeable surfacing as much as possible.
- Parks along greenways should steer away from mowed turf grass and adopt more natural grooming techniques using native vegetation that is sustainable without chemical applications or excess watering.

The Florida Greenways Program has three local prototypes either under way or in the planning stage for 1993. The Loxahatchee Greenways Network based in southeast Florida is designed to link a number of natural areas in the Palm Beach/Martin county region. The Apalachee Greenways Network, scheduled to get under way in the spring of 1993, is a regional project focusing on lands in a six-county area of North Florida and South Georgia, surrounding Tallahassee. The Suncoast River Greenways Network will create a system of wildlife corridors and greenways for west central Florida.

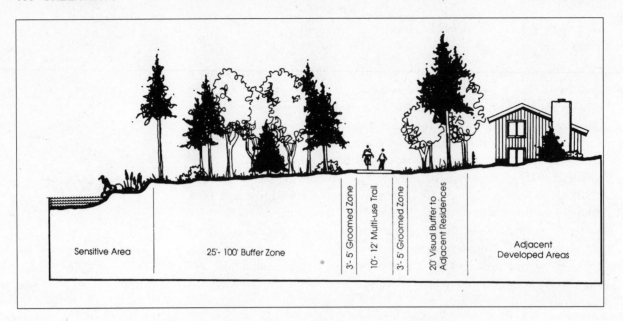

Figure 7-6 Typical cross section of a trail near sensitive areas.

- Existing vegetation, such as trees, should be preserved and all ground cover within the drip lines of trees protected. State or local tree planting programs may provide funding, planning, or technical assistance for revegetating areas.

- Limit access and activities near and within sensitive areas. Even nonsensitive areas are prone to compacted soil, trampled vegetation, disturbed wildlife, and soil erosion with overuse. If necessary, limit activities in these areas to bird watching, nature study, hiking, cross-country skiing, and nonmotorized boating.

- Be mindful that some species are disturbed to varying degrees at different life stages and seasons. Time and plan your activities with this in mind.

- Target species that may need a mosaic of different habitat types. Manipulation of vegetation within the greenway may be necessary to provide the right mix.

- Keep an eye on changes in habitat quality of adjacent lands. Institute dense vegetation buffers in problem areas to screen out undesirable effects if possible. Try to promote sound land conservation practices and best management practices by neighboring landowners and land managers. (Best management practices are conservation measures that control soil loss, reverse degraded water quality, and protect wetlands.)

- Have a plan for removing exotic or noxious species that invade the corridor. A noxious plant management program should begin with identification of harmful, exotic, undesirable, and illegal species in the area. Consult your state wildlife and agriculture departments. Control methods might include mechanical removal,

Volunteers plant thousands of trees, shrubs, and wetland plants as part of a corridor restoration effort. (Robert Searns)

cutting before plants go to seed, and planting species that shade or crowd out undesirable ones. There is also the option of chemical control with herbicides. This technique carries with it some user and environmental risks; it should be approached with caution and avoided if other solutions are available.

- Have a multiagency review process that sets standards and guidelines for any actions affecting the corridor. This includes both capital projects like bridge and highway construction and maintenance activities like mowing along a stream or managing vegetation under power lines.

- Try to restore and protect habitat along corridors where traditional animal migration routes have been identified.

- Address ongoing stewardship of the land, including revegetation and repair and placement of any man-made facilities such as nesting boxes or livestock encroachment controls. Maintain revegetation with native plants.

- Track the health of the corridor and how it functions over time. It is possible that in a sensitive yet healthy corridor the best

In the town of Falmouth, on Cape Cod, citizens are integrating deer and associated wildlife migration needs with future land development by mapping wildlife corridors that exist between already protected open-space preserves. Recommended three-hundred-foot-wide corridors of indigenous vegetation are protected through the subdivision process. Automobile speed limits have been reduced to lessen the incidence of wildlife road kills.

management may be the minimal amount necessary to keep it as it is.

Protecting a natural landscape while promoting use of the resource is quite a challenge. Landscape ecology and the science of corridors can be both complex and imprecise. Add the constraints of limited funds and a tight time frame and the task can be formidable. Regardless, it is important to build a convincing case. It may not always be practical to conduct a thorough analysis of the corridor when bulldozers are poised to obliterate it if you don't move quickly. On the other hand, over- simplification and a hasty solution might jeopardize a resource that took millions of years to evolve. This is where the science of corridor planning needs to team up with the political realities of greenway creation.

For further assistance in creating a greenway corridor, see Appendix A and the following organizations:

The U.S. Fish and Wildlife Service
Contact your regional office or the Department of Interior
Washington, DC 20240
202-343-5634

National Institute for Urban Wildlife
10921 Trotting Ridge Way
Columbia, MD 21044
The Urban Wildlife Program sponsors voluntary registration of private land as wildlife habitat. Individuals, associations, cities, and forums can be recognized for their efforts. The institute also offers excellent published material on urban wildlife.

State Natural Heritage Programs
The state natural heritage programs are a nationwide network of state and regional data bases initiated by the Nature Conservancy with state and federal governments to track rare species and habitats. They make up the most comprehensive natural history of plants, animals, and natural communities. Contact the Nature Conservancy or your state game and fish agency for the contact in your state.

American Forestry Association
1516 P Street, N.W.
Washington, DC 20005
202-667-3300
The American Forestry Association advocates intelligent management and use of forests, soil, water, wildlife, and all other natural resources. AFA's Global Releaf promotes tree planting efforts. The Heritage Forest Program provides funding for tree planting programs on public lands.

8

Caring for Rivers, Streams, and Wetlands

*"Each water course is a natural garden, self-sustaining and refreshing.
Landowners and municipalities would do well to protect their water courses as
prized community assets."*
—John Ormsbee Simonds, *Earthscape*

The centerpiece of most greenways is a water feature: a river, stream, canal, lake, or coastline. Greenways can link people with these natural features. On a state or regional scale, rivers and wetland systems provide the backbone for large greenways connecting parks, refuges, and population centers. More and more communities are rehabilitating local streams, or, in some cases, freeing them from man-made structures so that they become part of the fabric of local life and not merely a place for dumping refuse.

The Value of Stream Systems

A stream is a dynamic system of water, energy, soil, and rock, driven by solar energy, gravity, and water. Some streams are slow moving, some are fast. Some are wide and deep, and some are desert arroyos that have surface flow only during infrequent storms. A stream is much more than water flowing in a channel carving its way into the landscape. Like the tip of an iceberg, a stream is the visual manifestation of a much larger and more complex system. A stream corridor includes the floodplain through which it moves, the underlying water table and aquifer system, associated wetlands, and adjacent riparian zones that are rich in plant and animal life.

Drainage corridors and their associated wetlands play an extremely important role in supporting the earth's flora and fauna. A case study by Colorado wildlife expert David Weber estimated that, while riparian zones account for only 2 percent of the landscape, more than 60 percent of Colorado's wildlife lives along stream corridors. Rivers carry nutrients that sustain wetlands, estuaries, and coastal areas, which in turn support the rest of the food chain.

The role of spawning streams, marshes, and tidal estuaries is critical. According to *Wetlands*, a publication of the Urban Land Institute, it is estimated that on the southeastern coast of the United States more than 95 percent of the commercial fish and shellfish and 50 percent of recreational fish caught depend on coastal estuaries for their survival. The dollar value of the fish and shellfish catch in Louisiana alone is more than $170 million annually. In addition to supporting the fishing industry, rivers support agriculture by replenishing the fertility of farmland, depositing topsoil in the floodplain. They can be an index of watershed

The Delaware Nature Society is currently working to create four greenways along stream corridors in Northern New Castle County. The ecological greenway theme promotes passive recreation and environmental education; no construction will be required. Stream restoration and landowner stewardship are integral to the plan. Greenway Coordinator Kyle Gulbronson says, "Our worst pitfall to date has been distinguishing in the public's mind that our program is the creation of an environmental/land preservation greenway and not an open recreation greenway with improvements. However, the response by landowners has been very positive."

quality, warning us of environmental problems on land. Finally, rivers, streams, and associated aquifers provide drinking water.

How Natural Streams Function

Greenway planners should have a basic understanding of how stream corridors function. Not only does this knowledge help protect the resource, it can also help protect investments in greenways from flooding and erosion.

The Hydrologic Cycle

Deer Creek, Harford County, Maryland, joins the Susquehanna River just a few miles north of its confluence with the Chesapeake Bay. The creek, a state scenic river, is the home of the Maryland darter, possibly the world's most endangered fish. A partnership among the Department of Natural Resources, the Harford Land Trust, the Deer Creek Watershed Association, and Harford County will protect the creek and link three state parks along its shores into a regional greenway system.

The study of precipitation and how it affects a watershed is called *hydrology*, and the engineers who analyze precipitation and attempt to predict flooding patterns are called *hydrologists*. The hydrologic cycle is the driving force behind stream corridors. The process begins when solar heat causes water to evaporate. At some point, moist air is cooled and clouds form. With further cooling, small droplets or ice crystals form, and when these crystals become large enough they fall to earth as precipitation. Cooling is the result of frontal systems (the colliding of cold air masses with warm moist air), *convection* (the rising of air caused by surface heating), or *orographic cooling* (where moist air moves uphill, cools, and the moisture condenses).

The pattern, duration, and quality of rainfall vary from location to location as well as from season to season. In every drainage basin, however, rain falls, the water runs downhill, and, ultimately, it is reevaporated to begin the cycle again. In addition to precipitation, runoff is also produced by lawn watering, crop irrigation, and other human activities.

Watersheds, Water Tables, and Aquifers

Any study of a stream corridor must consider the watershed. The watershed is the area of land from which water drains to a given point, usually a body of water such as a stream. Several watersheds together make up a drainage basin, which may cover several counties or states. The size, geology, shape, gradient, climate, and vegetation of the watershed determine the character of the stream. What occurs in the watershed also affects water quality in the stream. This point should not be overlooked when planning a greenway corridor. Deforestation, construction, or agriculture in a watershed, for example, can result in excess eroded sediment, which can clog a stream and kill aquatic life miles away. Know your watershed, its history, the activities now occurring in it, and how those activities affect the quality of local streams. For example, landfills and other industries might add toxic pollution to watersheds, large paved areas may cause excess surface runoff, which can erode streams, and farms may leach pesticides, fertilizers, or sediment. A U. S. Geologic Survey topographic map can be used to determine the configuration of a watershed and which upland and upstream areas are affecting your stream.

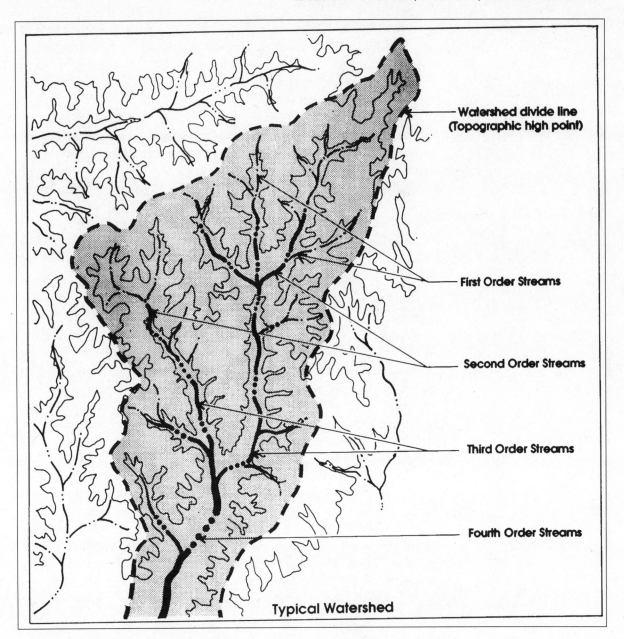

Figure 8-1 Flow patterns in a watershed.

In addition to surface runoff and flow patterns in a watershed (see Figure 8-1), there are larger, underground water systems called the *water table* and the *aquifer*. Aquifers consist of porous soils and rock that absorb, convey, and hold water underground. The water table is the level of water in the ground. Riparian aquifers and water tables that run under and adjacent to streams constantly interact with surface flow.

Aquifers perform many vital functions for both humans and nature. They support riparian vegetation by providing water to the roots. They store water for domestic and agricultural wells, providing both drinking and irrigation supplies. They supplement low stream flows during dry periods. During storms or floods they receive water but, depending on the relative water levels, may release it into streams during periods of low flow. In arid and semi-arid regions of the country, streams tend to replenish the aquifer, while in wetter areas like those in the eastern United States, aquifers tend to replenish streams. They also support wetlands, helping to sustain a rich plant life, which in turn nourishes numerous bird and mammal species. Ecologists studying certain rivers also have discovered vast subterranean ecosystems characterized by previously undiscovered species of worms, shrimp, insects, and micro-organisms. These underground worlds are vital parts of the food chain.

Aquifers are quite vulnerable to human activities and can easily suffer the effects of depletion from overuse or pollution from surface contaminants. They recharge (replenish their water) via porous zones in the soil called *aquifer recharge zones*. Building over these recharge areas also can adversely affect aquifers and the water table, as well as the stream and wetlands systems they support.

Floodplains

The floodplain is the area along the stream corridor subject to regular inundation. There are several classes of floodplain. One is the five-hundred-year floodplain, or the land area that has at least a 0.2 percent chance of being inundated in any given year. Another term you might encounter is the *maximum probable flood*, used as a basis for dam design. The more commonly used measure is the *hundred-year floodplain* (sometimes called the base floodplain), or the area that has at least a 1 percent chance of being inundated by flooding in any given year.

Most local floodplain regulations use the hundred-year floodplain as the principal demarcation, restricting certain types of structures and improvements within this area. In many communities, the Federal Emergency Management Agency (FEMA) has mapped the hundred-year floodplain and requires participating communities to have flood management plans that impose certain restrictions on development in return for federal flood hazard insurance in accordance with the National Flood Insurance Act of 1968. Note that the dimensions of a floodplain

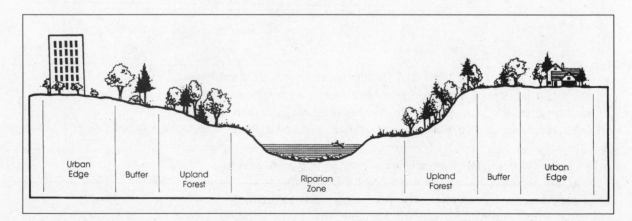

Figure 8-2 Corridor cross section.

can change over time, especially when urbanization reduces the amount of ground absorption. Increased overland flow may, in turn, increase the frequency of flooding. The regulatory floodway is another common point of demarcation. This is the path of flow that must remain unobstructed both horizontally (water width) and vertically (water depth) over one hundred years so that water levels in the hundred-year floodplain do not rise more than a designated amount. Numerous other measures of flooding range down to two-year and even one-year floodplains.

Properly functioning floodplains are vital to the survival of stream corridors and wetland species and, thus, play a major role in greenway planning. Because they are inappropriate building sites, floodplains offer ideal locations for parks. It is essential that greenway planning include an analysis of floodplains and associated wetland areas. Greenway planning should encourage policies to preserve, enhance, and protect these areas. Floodplain delineation can help identify areas where greenway improvements must be designed to withstand inundation. For example, a bike path may need to be anchored with rock or other reinforcement if it is subject to frequent flooding. Generally, floodplain delineations can be obtained from the city or county engineer or from flood hazard maps prepared by FEMA.

Wetlands

Wetlands are often associated with surface waters such as rivers, streams, and lakes. These vegetative communities, also called marsh, swamp, bog, wet meadow, floodplain, pond, and shallow lake, are affected by the local water table, temperature, rainfall, season, and water level of nearby streams and rivers. (Tidal wetlands are affected as well by tidal influences). Nontidal wetlands can be dominated by trees, shrubs, or herbaceous plants and are covered by or saturated with water part of the year.

Riparian forests and other wetland types together contribute to the health of the stream ecosystem if allowed to function properly. Greenway planners must strive to preserve wetlands, not only because the law requires it under Section 404 of the Clean Water Act, but also because these areas are extremely difficult to replace once lost.

Riparian Forests

Riparian forests are highly productive streamside vegetative communities, which offer important benefits to the stream ecosystem. As corridors, they connect habitats along streams and rivers from the mountains to the seas and provide migration routes, food, and shelter for a varied pool of life forms. Many types of plants grow in moist fertile riparian soils. Turtles, mink, river otters, eagles, and many other species may depend on this zone for food or habitat. Temporary pools form breeding areas for frogs, toads, and salamanders. Trees and shrubs shade the river channel; the resulting cooler temperatures are a critical ingredient for healthier populations of fish and other aquatic species that find food

Benefits of Healthy Riparian and Floodplain Plant Communities

• Provide temporary storage and gradually convey floodwater to stream and water table.

• Absorb the destructive energy of floods in meanders and marshes of the riverbank.

• Reduce the level of downstream flooding through storage and friction with vegetation upstream.

• Filter and store sediment from erosion in the watershed.

• Filter and trap excess nutrients and pollutants from the stream and from overland runoff (mainly nitrogen and phosphorus) from fertilizers, eroded soils, agricultural operations, and so on.

• Slow the velocity of storm runoff, thus reducing erosion of the stream channel.

• Create aesthetically pleasing settings for urban, suburban, and rural open space and recreation opportunities, which bring millions of people closer to nature.

Adapted from material by John Barnett and others in Boulder Creek Report, City of Boulder, Colorado.

and shelter in the vegetation. Humus and leaf litter retain rainwater as it falls and allow it to percolate into the soil, which gradually releases the water to the stream.

Riparian forests and floodplain vegetation can stabilize the riverbank, preventing erosion. Vegetation has been shown to be an effective means of reducing nonpoint pollution in the stream by filtering eroded sediments and contaminants in overland and subterranean flows. They also filter out excess nutrients in the stream, which cause algae to grow and reduce light and oxygen needed by aquatic life (see Figure 8-2).

How Streams Interact with the Landscape

The interplay of moving water with the landscape is complex. Experts who study the process are known as fluvial geomorphologists. Measures based on better understanding of this interplay can reduce flood damage and preserve vital stream habitat (see Figure 8-3).

Stream Channels

The stream channel is the portion of the drainage corridor that carries ordinary surface flow. Stream channels are dynamic; their water has tremendous power to erode and transform the land. Most natural streams, however, tend to reinforce their bottoms and banks with rocks, pebbles, and sediment. Others have sand as their dominant bed form or boulder-sized bed material forming step-pool sequences.

The Streambed

The variation in streambed material, along with slope, relative roughness, and width-to-depth ratio, are important determinants of how stream channels evolve. In general, streams deposit sediments in areas of relatively slow flow.

Sinuosity

Streams tend to set up meander patterns as they work their way through the landscape. This process is referred to as *sinuosity*. On the

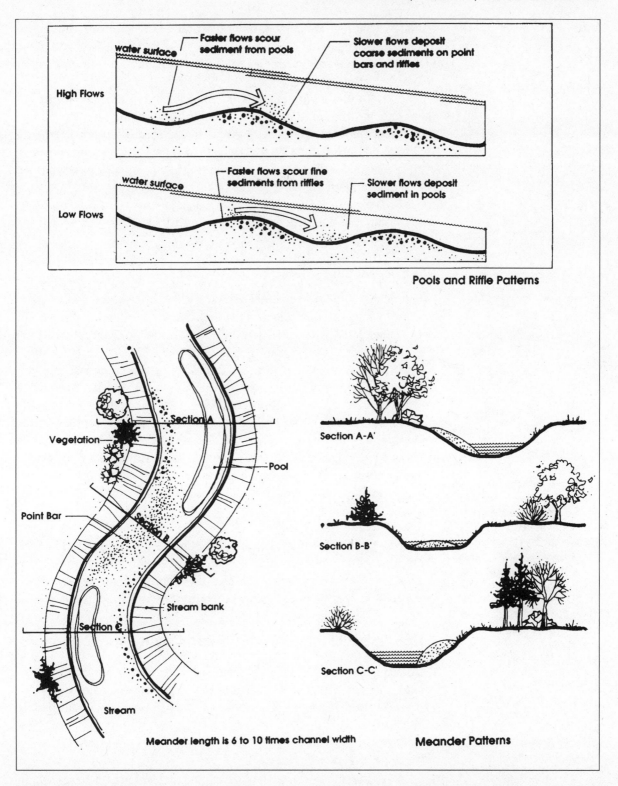

Pools and Riffle Patterns

Meander length is 6 to 10 times channel width

Meander Patterns

Figure 8-3 How streams behave. (Adapted from drawings by John Barnett in a publication called *Boulder's Greenways*, City of Boulder, 1991.)

outside of bends, the faster moving water tends to scour out pools. These provide aquatic life with quiet places to take cover and feed. Slower moving water inside bends deposits sediment-forming bars that also offer resting spots, especially for bird life.

The length of a meander can vary from six to ten times the width of the channel. Riffles tend to form between meanders and help to stabilize the stream bottom, serving as natural grade control structures. Being shallow and turbulent, riffles also help oxygenate the water, which is critical for species like trout and salmon. Many aquatic insect larvae, called microinvertebrates, that live in riffles are a principal food source for fish. The sequence of meanders, pools, and riffles absorbs and dissipates the tremendous energy of the water, reducing erosion and flood damage.

The Channel Edge

When talking about the channel edge it is also important to consider the concept of *roughness*. Whereas a smooth bank edge free of plants and debris may look attractive, it is not well suited for aquatic wildlife. Aquatic creatures need a rough bank with plenty of structure. By *structure* we mean root, logs, overhanging shrubs, boulders, and vegetation. Structure in creeks also includes scour pools formed by turbulence around bedrock or large boulders. These structural elements provide cover, shade, food, and homes for numerous amphibians, reptiles, birds, and mammals. A rough stream bank also slows down floodwaters, thus decreasing damage downstream. Concrete or channelized stream banks are not only poor wildlife habitat but actually help speed up flood waters, increasing the potential for downstream flooding, scouring, and erosion.

In relatively stable, humid settings, stream channels develop and evolve to the point where they can contain the 1.5- to 2-year flood, although this may not be true in semiarid areas or highly erosive landscapes. Clearly, many factors affect the configuration of a natural stream, including flows, gradient, vegetation, and geology.

How Urbanization Alters Stream Quality and Behavior

Altering natural stream flow patterns with dams, urban encroachments, and other intrusions disrupts the elegantly balanced ecosystem of a stream in many ways. The result can be devastating to both people and nature.

Altering the Watershed

Certain land uses, including deforestation, agriculture, and urban development, tend to increase impervious surfaces, speeding the flow of precipitation into the water course, causing soil erosion, flooding, and changes in temperature. Erosion, in turn, destabilizes the stream banks and deposits excess sediments into the stream. Sediment smothers habitat, diminishes feeding and breeding grounds for aquatic species, clogs

In Pima County, Arizona, a river park system preserves a network of rivers and marshes by turning degraded and eroded banks of the county's major water courses into recreational facilities, trails, and wildlife habitat. The park concept emerged as part of the major structural flood control program after severe flooding in 1983. The Army Corps of Engineers requires river park development as environmental mitigation for constructed bank protection. The Pima County Department of Transportation and Flood Control District design and build parks; the Parks and Recreation Department maintains them.

A "confined stream" refuses to remain confined and creates a serious erosion problem in an urban neighborhood. (Robert Searns)

the gills of fish, and cuts off light to underwater plants. If enough sediment is deposited, stream bottoms may become shallower, increasing downstream flooding.

Altering the watershed has other effects on water quality. Debris, agricultural chemicals, motor oil, sewage, and many other contaminants are flushed—sometimes directly—into the stream with deleterious effects. The decline of crabs and fish in the Chesapeake Bay, for example, has been linked directly to agricultural runoff and storm water drainage from urbanized areas in the bay watershed.

Finally, there is encroachment into the floodplain—filling it, building on it, lining it with concrete or rock, removing vegetation, and so on—a process that continues at a rampant rate today.

Altering the Stream Channel

One result of development in the floodplain has been faster and greater volumes of storm runoff, increasing both stream corridor flooding and property damage downstream. Without the absorptive and moderating

"It became very clear in the course of this poll and the interviews that followed in the communities that what had happened over a period of time was that the water quality declined in these neighborhood streams. They lost their worth. They were not places children were encouraged to go, to play, and learn about the wonder and beauty of the natural world; instead mothers told them, 'Don't go near the ditch, stay away from that place.' The stream was a place tires got dumped and sometime drug pushers plied their wares. What could have been a wonderful community asset became a neighborhood liability. Because the community felt that it didn't have a lot of control in fixing the situation, it was easier to remove it from consciousness.

So people just weren't aware anymore that they had a stream in their neighborhood. Only 14 percent of those polled even knew the stream was there."
—Barbara Taylor, Maryland Save Our Streams, Maryland Greenway Conference Proceedings, 1990

capacity of streamside forests and wetlands, a rainstorm can cause powerful flooding in the watershed. For example, a violent thunderstorm in Washington, D.C. in the late 1980s swelled creeks and streams beyond the capacity of its denuded banks, resulting in a flood that washed a parking lot full of cars into the Potomac River. Increased volume and velocity of water can also degrade the bottom of urban streams, causing them to cut and erode the landscape.

In many cases, the response to flood damage is to build dams, weirs (check dams), channels, and other flood control devices that may provide short-term local protection but will ultimately contribute to the instability and destructiveness of streams. So begins a vicious cycle that can lead to channelization—the straightening and sometimes hardening of a stream with uniform banks. Channelization can permanently transform an entire stream or river—witness the Los Angeles River, now little more than a concrete culvert.

If we consider that many urban floodplain areas have already been developed and that land taken out of the floodplain through flood control improvements is much more valuable to its owners, preserving large urban floodplains can be a difficult sell. This is a dilemma. The people of Littleton, Colorado, however, did just that in the 1960s, when they persuaded the Army Corps of Engineers, through an act of Congress, to apply money originally earmarked for channelization to the purchase of six hundred acres in the floodplain as a riparian preserve.

Finally, there is the issue of the flow capacity of urban streams. Because stream channel right-of-way is so confined in many urban areas, the remaining channel has little or no vertical and horizontal clearance, or *freeboard*. In other words, the channel is at or below the capacity needed to convey the flood. Vegetation creates *friction*, which impedes the flow of water and lessens the channel's capacity to convey floods. The result is that trees are banned, vegetation is either mowed or altogether removed, and in many cases a lifeless utilitarian drainage channel is all that remains. Consider, however, the position of the public officials who gut these channels: they are liable if existing houses and developments are flooded or, worse, if lives are lost. Often, the problem can be traced to the planning process that first allowed floodplain encroachment.

Clearly, in many areas concern for a river's health and measures to protect public safety might overlap. This is where the disciplines of greenway planning and flood control come together. Be sure to involve flood control officials and drainage engineers in your planning, and make sure they involve you in theirs.

In-Stream Flow

Yet another factor to consider in greenway planning is the impact human settlement has had on day-to-day in-stream flow, especially in the arid West. In-stream flow is the volume of surface water normally moving down the streambed or river. Western states have long valued water as a commodity more precious than oil or gold. Ranchers and farmers want water for their livestock and crops; municipalities and industry need to have water too.

Western water law is extremely complex. Water law, however, rests on two basic premises: "use it or lose it" and "first-in-time is first-in-use." First-in-time basically means that the first person to develop the water and claim ownership has senior rights over those who follow. These rights can be bought and sold but not at a small cost. A water rights holder, however, must put the water to a beneficial use. If the water is not used in a legally defined productive way, the right may be lost—hence, "use it or lose it."

Sadly, habitat and recreational use rank last in the water rights priority checklist. In fact, in several states, habitat and recreation are not even considered legitimate beneficial uses of in-stream flow. Several states have new laws that change that policy but have not acquired senior rights to protect habitat and recreational objectives. In theory and in practice, senior water rights holders can literally dry up a stream or river to meet agricultural or municipal needs. In Arizona, water diversion is largely responsible for the elimination of 95 percent of the state's riparian habitat.

Some western communities address the low-flow problem by purchasing water rights, encouraging or mandating water conservation, or modifying the channel to provide aquatic habitat at lower flow levels. There are now in-stream flow protection programs at both the federal and state level, and some nonprofit organizations like the Nature Conservancy have purchased water rights for in-stream flow. With increasing demand for scarce western water, however, as well as the increased value placed on water for nonconsumptive recreational uses, the issue of in-stream flow will continue to be critical in stream stewardship and greenway planning.

Some Options for Rehabilitating Altered Watercourses: Structural versus Nonstructural

Structural solutions deal directly with floodwaters and how they are *conveyed*. Nonstructural planning calls for minimum alteration of the stream channel and is usually less costly in the long run than a structural alternative. Nonstructural techniques include floodplain zoning, acquisition and protection of floodplain lands, removal of structures from the floodplain, flood proofing of existing buildings, flood warning systems, flood insurance, and planting vegetation in streamside buffers. Certainly from a resource standpoint, the nonstructural approach is preferable.

Although the nonstructural approach has gained increasing acceptance, it is still a challenge to convince resistant local governments. One of the main challenges of the nonstructural approach is the expense of acquiring land. As we mentioned earlier, there may be a strong political bias toward structural solutions because they redefine the floodplain (effectively taking lands out of it), thus increasing property values and presumably generating more tax revenue. The extra cost of road and

In Worthington, Illinois, the Salt Creek Greenway, part of the DuPage County Stormwater Management Plan, includes trail opportunities, restoration of native species within the floodplain, removal of flood prone properties, and stream rehabilitation projects. DuPage and Cook County Forest Preserve Districts can acquire land along the creeks for greenway purposes.

utility crossings through undeveloped floodplain land may be harder to justify since fewer properties are served. A solid public participation program may help overcome this resistance. Ideally, there are workable combinations of structural and nonstructural solutions.

Resource-Sensitive Solutions for Flood-Damage Reduction and Stream Rehabilitation

The following sections describe some of the "softer" solutions for handling floodwaters. Some of these mimic the natural processes of the river.

Establishing Streamside Buffer Zones

Conservation Reserve Programs, like the one in place in Maryland, protect soil and water resources by providing incentives in the form of rental payments to farmers for removing highly erodible lands from production. The program focuses on land along streams and wetlands where buffers between agricultural land and water sources can serve as vegetation strips, which filter nonpoint pollution.

The planting of streamside buffers, including forests and filter strips of grasses, shrubs, or trees, can successfully check runoff sediments and pollutants from cultivated fields and other nonpoint sources in much the same way as their natural riparian counterparts. Federal, state, and county programs promote the rehabilitation and regrowth of riparian vegetation for their ability to hold the soil in place and restore optimal water temperature and as an effective means of controlling nonpoint pollution.

A variety of factors determine whether a strip of vegetation along a stream will intercept threatening sediment and nutrients. The most important is width. Many have found that as the width of the buffer is increased, the percentage of sediment removed increases but at a smaller increment. Buffers of adequate width, which take into account surrounding land use, soil, vegetation, slope, and other factors, can remove nearly all of the sediment and nutrients that would otherwise end up in the stream. Recommended buffer widths range anywhere from twenty-five to more than a thousand feet, as in Maryland's Chesapeake Bay Critical Area. One expert, T. R. Scheuler, recommends one hundred to three hundred feet as a necessary width for removing smaller sized particles or urban runoff. A buffer of six hundred feet might be necessary to support a full diversity of songbirds. Two other experts, Raymond Palfrey and Earl Bradley suggest a 150-foot strip of 3 percent slope is needed to trap 90 percent of sediment load in planted grass. Cooper *et al.* (cited in Daniel Smith and Paul Hellmund, eds., *Ecology of Greenways*) suggest that eighty to one hundred meters is needed to trap a 50–75 percent sediment load in coastal North Carolina.

Some states and jurisdictions have established standard setbacks—which cover most pollution in a variety of circumstances. Other communities have formulas for determining the best buffer. Baltimore County, Maryland, for example, uses a formula for determining forest buffers needed for prospective developments along streams. Starting out with a seventy-five or one-hundred-foot stream buffer (depending on whether trout are in the stream), additional widths are factored in for degraded vegetation, steep slopes, or eroded soils. Buffers can be up to three hundred feet wide.

Based on existing research, Palfrey and Bradley recommend a minimum buffer of one hundred feet from the mean high waterline or edge of water bodies or the edge of tidal–nontidal wetlands. This buffer also would include the hundred-year floodplain, certain soils, and uplands adjacent to water bodies and wetlands. In areas with high nutrient loadings, buffers could be up to three hundred feet to protect water quality. Palfrey and Bradley recommend including the floodplain, riparian forest, and areas of groundwater recharge within and outside the floodplain.

In evaluating or establishing a buffer to protect your greenway, take into account the natural features of the land, such as soil permeability, wildlife potential, the extent and effectiveness of existing vegetation, the configuration of the greenway slopes (and whether they are vegetated), and surrounding land uses. You may be able to widen your buffer. Forest and shrub species with deep roots that aerate soil and provide habitat may be a better choice than planted grass. If grasses are used, they should be deep-rooted, have densely branching top growth, and be able to recover from floods.

Buffers are not a total panacea—if buffer width and configuration are inadequate for the task, they can become choked with sediment and lose their capacity to absorb nutrients. Contact your local office of the Soil Conservation Service, the Environmental Protection Agency (EPA), the U. S. Department of Agriculture, your local or state water quality agency, or your state university for specifics on recommended local buffer widths.

Retention/Detention Devices

Water can be stored in, among other things, small ponds or other depressions, constructed wetlands, large ponds, or lakes, soil, and a stream or floodplain. These storage devices may offer many advantages over stream channelization, not the least of which are the preservation of open space and recreational opportunities on retention ponds. Note that successful detention/retention programs require work on the channel to increase the capacity to convey floodwater.

The concept of *conveyance storage* is also intriguing. A portion of storm runoff is stored in the corridor that conveys it. One approach uses slow-velocity channels with large cross sections to contain floodwater—a great excuse for the preservation of more natural streams and wetlands.

The important thing to remember about man-made storage is that the system can be complex and must be carefully modeled and designed to fit storm patterns and the hydrology of the watershed. In some instances, the flood problem can actually be worsened downstream if detention facilitates discharge into the floodplain at the wrong time. Generally, regional detention is preferred because there are personnel to regulate the floodgates. In all cases, detention/retention systems must be planned on a systemwide basis, taking into account the entire

Soil Bioengineering

Soil bioengineering is an applied science that combines structural, biological, and ecological concepts to construct living structures for erosion, sediment, and flood control. Living plant materials are used as the main structural components to stabilize and naturalize stream banks. The systems are most successful when they are installed in the dormant season. Mainly woody vegetation, which roots readily from cuttings, is initially installed in specific configurations that offer immediate soil protection and reinforcement. In addition to providing a high measure of protection, the soil bioengineering systems develop roots that provide soil mantle reinforcement. The top growth provides an additional surface vegetative cover. Environmental benefits derived from the vegetation include more diverse and productive aquatic and riparian habitats. Such habitats may include shade, organic additions to the stream, cover for fish in the form of vegetation and deep pool development, and improved water quality. Aesthetically, these systems can enhance river corridors.

Most soil bioengineering installations require an interdisciplinary team of professionals working together. Typically, a team would consist of a biologist, a habitat specialist, a botanist, a fluvial geomorphologist, a hydrologist, a civil engineer, a soil scientist, and a soil bioengineer. All these participants, including the soil bioengineer, need to be well trained and experienced in the technology. Whereas the concept may appear simple, the execution of the site analysis, design, and construction installation is complex.

The following material is meant as general information to better understand the merits of soil bioengineering systems and to acquaint the reader with some of the specific tools and terms of the technology. All installations would require appropriate guidance from a knowledgeable soil bioengineering professional (see Figure 8-4).

Live Stake

Description. Live stakes are living, woody plant cuttings capable of rooting with relative ease. The cuttings are large enough and long enough to be tamped into the ground as stakes. They are intended to root and grow into mature shrubs that, over time, will serve to stabilize the soils, enrich the riparian zone for habitat restoration, and improve water quality. Typically, this is the simplest and least expensive system to organize and install.

Effectiveness. Although live stakes are of little value when initially installed, once the roots and vegetation have become established, live staking can be a successful stabilization method for simple or small problem sites on small stream systems. This technique is effective when construction time is limited and an inexpensive and simple solution will handle the problem. Live staking is also an effective way of securing natural geotextiles such as jute mesh, coir (coconut fiber fabric), or other blanket surface treatments.

Live Fascine

Description. Live fascine structures are sausage-like bundles of live cut branches. They are tied together securely and set into trenches on the stream bank. Normally, they are placed on contour in the slope face. They are shallowly installed and create little site disturbance compared with other systems, such as a live cribwall, which requires in-stream work. To be successful, these systems require careful assessment and installation.

(continued on next page)

drainage system, both up- and downstream, and making the most of natural wetlands and vegetated buffers.

Soil Bioengineering

Soil bioengineering offers promise where structural solutions are called for. This technique relies heavily on natural vegetation, natural channel shaping, and careful maintenance to stabilize stream corridors.

Soil bioengineering may initially appear to cost more than the traditional concrete channel or rip-rap approach. However, it requires less maintenance than the hard-channel approach and provides environmental benefits as well.

Again, the key to successful soil bioengineering is technical understanding of stream hydraulics (how water behaves in the channel). The

(continued from previous page)

Effectiveness. When properly used and installed, live fascines offer reasonably inexpensive and immediate protection from erosion. Regardless of their survival, fascines usually work well to reduce erosion on shallow gully sites. These systems are an effective stabilization technique, especially when rooting is established or when combined with live stakes. Live fascines are capable of holding soil on the face of the stream bank; this works particularly well when combined with a surface cover such as jute mesh or coir fabrics. Live fascines provide surface stability and connecting support for colonization by the surrounding plant community and thereby enhance the development of aquatic riparian and upland slope vegetation.

Live Cribwall

Description. A live cribwall installation is a rectangular framework of logs or timbers, rock, and woody cuttings that can protect an eroding stream bank on fast-flowing steep gradient streams. Live cribwalls require thorough assessment and a full understanding of stream hydraulics. Compared with other soil bioengineering systems, live cribwall installations are complicated and expensive to design and install. Live cribwalls require in-stream work and may not, therefore, be suitable in some situations because of fisheries concerns.

Effectiveness. Live cribwall systems are effective on the outside bends of main channels, where strong currents are present. They cause deposition to occur and therefore create a natural toe protection for the bank above. After they have been established, these installations maintain a natural stream bank appearance and provide excellent habitat for a variety of riparian corridor and aquatic and upland slope life. Live cribwalls are quite useful where space is limited on small, narrow stream corridors and in areas where bank cutting is not a viable solution. The log or timber framework provides immediate protection from erosion and bank failure, while the plants provide long-term durability. The live cribwall is also useful on streams that carry heavy bed load material.

Joint Planting

Description. The joint planting system involves installation of live stakes between previously placed rip rap rock. (The term *rip rap* refers to rock or other heavy material placed along a stream bank, a steep hillside, or shoreline to control erosion or washout.) It serves as an adjunctive backup, intended to increase the effectiveness of the conventional system by forming a living root mat in the material base upon which the rip rap has been placed. The rock needs to be loosely dumped or no thicker than two feet in depth. Joint depth is an excellent way to combine soil bioengineering with conventional systems.

Effectiveness. Typically used where a rip rap rock installation is already in place, a joint planting system will enable a stream bank to look and function more naturally over time. It provides additional protection for high torrent and steep gradient stream systems and assists in dissipating energy and causing deposition to occur along the stream banks.

Source: Robbin B. Sotir, Robbin B. Sotir and Associates.

designer must address the issues of stream flow velocity, freeboard (including clearance under bridges), channel roughness, and friction. The soil bioengineer and the conventional drainage engineer need to work together.

Soil bioengineering also involves proficiency in plant selection and placement. Plant selection can be particularly critical in arid and semiarid climates. Some experts recommend using cuttings from such plants as willow that have been harvested on site or nearby. Others recommend nursery-grown stock, although this may be riskier if the plants are not adapted to local soils and growing conditions. Species selection should also favor plants with deep and branching root systems because these plants do the best job of holding soil in place. Plants should be chosen with a consultant who understands local planting constraints and appropriate species selection. Save Our Streams, a program of the Izaak Walton League, provides bioengineering information for limited local stream rehabilitation projects that can use cuttings from local willow trees.

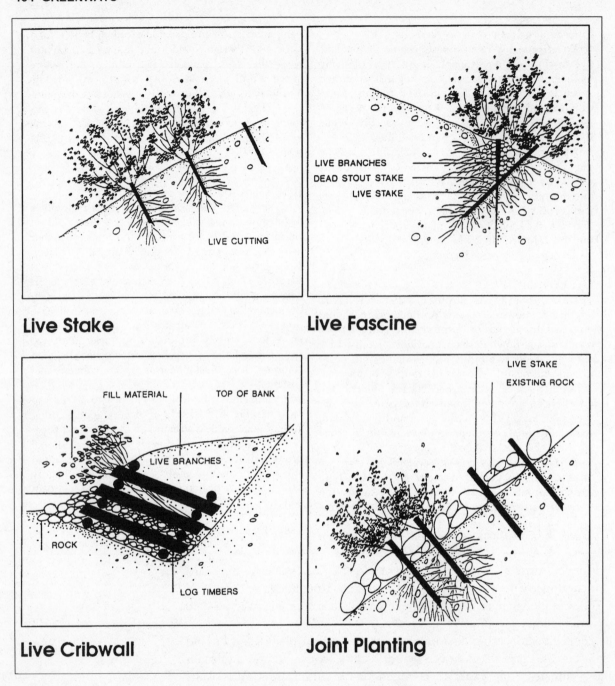

Live Stake

Live Fascine

LIVE BRANCHES
DEAD STOUT STAKE
LIVE STAKE

LIVE CUTTING

Live Cribwall

FILL MATERIAL
TOP OF BANK
LIVE BRANCHES
ROCK
LOG TIMBERS

Joint Planting

LIVE STAKE
EXISTING ROCK

Figure 8-4 Soil bioengineering. (Drawings and technical information provided by Robbin B. Sotir & Associates.)

Channel Restoration

In many instances, drainage master planning includes the restoration and revamping of previously channelized segments of a stream. This may offer an opportunity to introduce more effective multiobjective solutions.

One of the newer approaches calls for a *multistage channel*. The channel has a *low flow* or *trickle channel*, which carries day-to-day water. Ideally, this channel follows the natural *thalweg* (the centerline where the minimum flow of water would travel) as closely as possible. Above the trickle channel, terraces carry flood flows. Terraces are planted with native grasses, willow, and other stream-compatible vegetation. Rock and log deflectors may be used to help control bank erosion.

The multistage channel has several advantages. First, it has a more natural appearance. Second, the terraces support vegetation and wildlife. Vegetation helps control erosion and absorb pollutants. Third, the multistage channel tends to be self-cleaning and can convey more floodwater. The faster, constantly moving water in the low-flow channel can flush out sediment, leaving a cobble and gravel bottom, which better supports aquatic life. Sediments are more likely to deposit on the terraces where they support the growth of vegetation, rather than in the streams where they can clog fish gills and smother eggs.

This approach does not work on all streams. Streams with primarily sand bottoms, for instance, may not be stable enough to function this way. It is advisable to consult with drainage engineers, stream geomorphologists, aquatic biologists, wetland ecologists, and soil bioengineers when considering a terraced approach (see Figure 8-5).

Grade Control Structures

When a stream is altered, the water often speeds up and becomes more erosive. This causes, among other things, *downcutting*, or degradation of the channel bottom. A traditional way to deal with this is to line the channel bottom with concrete. Energy dissipators have also been used. Such devices may consist of concrete teeth set upright in the channel to absorb energy when the stream drops in grade.

Attractively designed grade control structures offer an alternative. These structures can consist of one or more small weirs (check dams) across the stream. They might be one to four feet high and could be built of concrete, steel sheet piling, or rock. Note that in some cases broken concrete may be used if it is in small enough chunks, properly placed, and covered with a veneer of natural rock or other aesthetically appropriate material. The grade control structures slow stream flow and cause sediment to deposit above them, which builds up the stream bottom. Properly designed, such structures can look like a small waterfall.

Key design considerations for grade control structures include using several low structures instead of one high one to allow fish migration and facilitate boating; using a meandering or curving shape rather than a straight line across the channel for better appearance and habitat creation along the curved edges of the structure; notching the structure to allow fish migration; avoiding a hydraulic keeper wave at the bottom of the structure, which could trap boaters or waders; and using large rocks and boulders to form the visible portion of the grade control (or drop) structure rather than dumped small rock or broken concrete. In all cases, the design of the grade control structure should consider the potential impact on stream habitat.

Some communities have taken the concept of grade control even further. With the advice of engineers, landscape architects, and aquatics

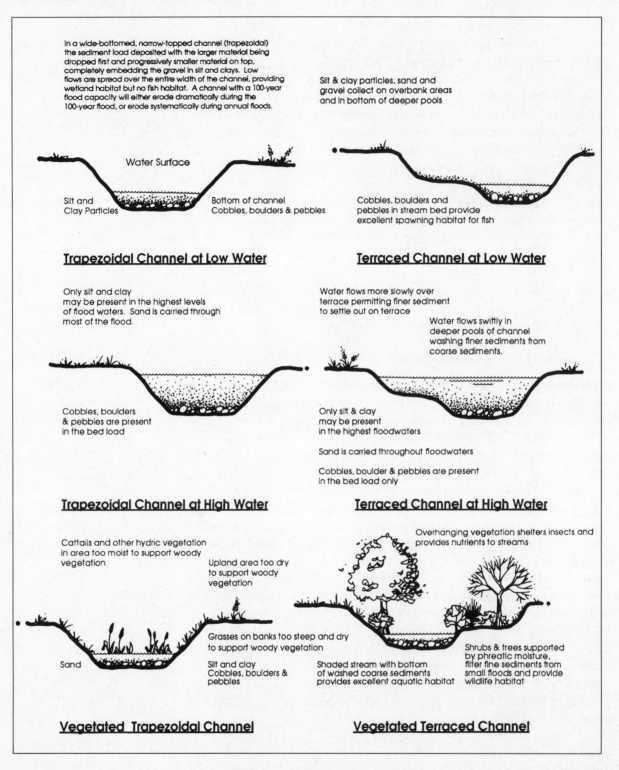

In a wide-bottomed, narrow-topped channel (trapezoidal) the sediment load deposited with the larger material being dropped first and progressively smaller material on top, completely embedding the gravel in silt and clays. Low flows are spread over the entire width of the channel, providing wetland habitat but no fish habitat. A channel with a 100-year flood capacity will either erode dramatically during the 100-year flood, or erode systematically during annual floods.

Silt & clay particles, sand and gravel collect on overbank areas and in bottom of deeper pools

Water Surface

Silt and Clay Particles

Bottom of channel Cobbles, boulders & pebbles

Cobbles, boulders and pebbles in stream bed provide excellent spawning habitat for fish

Trapezoidal Channel at Low Water

Terraced Channel at Low Water

Only silt and clay may be present in the highest levels of flood waters. Sand is carried through most of the flood.

Water flows more slowly over terrace permitting finer sediment to settle out on terrace

Water flows swiftly in deeper pools of channel washing finer sediments from coarse sediments.

Cobbles, boulders & pebbles are present in the bed load

Only silt & clay may be present in the highest floodwaters

Sand is carried throughout floodwaters

Cobbles, boulder & pebbles are present in the bed load only

Trapezoidal Channel at High Water

Terraced Channel at High Water

Cattails and other hydric vegetation in area too moist to support woody vegetation

Upland area too dry to support woody vegetation

Overhanging vegetation shelters insects and provides nutrients to streams

Sand

Grasses on banks too steep and dry to support woody vegetation

Silt and clay Cobbles, boulders & pebbles

Shaded stream with bottom of washed coarse sediments provides excellent aquatic habitat

Shrubs & trees supported by phreatic moisture, filter fine sediments from small floods and provide wildlife habitat

Vegetated Trapezoidal Channel

Vegetated Terraced Channel

Figure 8-5 Alternative stream channel treatments. (Adapted from drawings by John Barnett in a publication called *Boulder's Greenways*, City of Boulder, 1991).

Landscape architect and engineer team up to create an attractive yet functional energy dissipator. This Boulder Creek structure is designed to reduce stream-bottom scour during a storm, yet it appears as a playful sculptural component in a floodway park. (Robert Searns)

experts, the city of Boulder rebuilt the bottom of Boulder Creek using carefully placed rock drop structures to create pools. Similar projects have been carried out using small log weirs and rock to anchor the weirs.

Rip Rap

One common form of bank stabilization is known as rip rap. The term *rip rap* refers to rock or other heavy material placed along a stream bank, a steep hillside, or shoreline to control erosion or washout. Auto bodies, broken concrete, tires, and other trash are unacceptable, structurally, aesthetically, and environmentally. Rip rap should be a last resort if vegetative (bioengineered) solutions are not viable. Generally, rip rap should not be grouted (mortared with concrete). Rip rap works best in most applications if it is merely laid on a *filter bed* and thus can move and shift somewhat along with the stream. Ideally, rock should be carefully selected for natural-appearing size and color.

Partnerships for Multiobjective River Greenways

The Chain of Lakes project in Iowa will add fifty acres of newly constructed wetlands and oxbow lakes. The lakes are developed from reclaimed borrow pits resulting from sand and gravel operations along the Cedar River in Black Hawk County. The project, a partnership with the U.S. Army Corps of Engineers, aims for a recreational and aesthetic enhancement of the Black Hawk County urban riverfront, including a multiuse trail adjacent to the floodway. One of the objectives cited in the concept plan is the development of riverfront parks on flood control levees and along existing flood walls.

Urban Drainage Corridor Management

Greenway planners will, in many cases, find themselves as go-betweens for stream preservation advocates and the public works department, which, ideally, is trying both to preserve attractive streams and to protect lives and property from flooding. This fact creates both an opportunity and an obligation. The obligation is to understand the concept of urban flood management. The opportunity is to discover new and innovative solutions by bringing divergent interests together.

Storm Drainage Planning

Drainage engineering is a discipline in transition. The traditional approach had often been to get the water from point A to point B as quickly as possible using as little right-of-way as possible. In the 1960s the U.S. Army Corps of Engineers spent more than $30 million to straighten the ninety-eight-mile meandering Kissimmee River into a forty-eight-mile "efficient" canal draining into Lake Okeechobee. The damage to adjacent lands (some of Florida's richest wildlife habitat) was monumental—so bad in fact that the Corps is now returning portions of the river to its original meandering state at a cost double the original $30 million it took to straighten it.

The Kissimmee experience—and others like it—has led to new thinking about drainage engineering. Today, most drainage engineers are willing to work in partnership with greenway advocates in multiobjective planning, although in some areas old solutions are still applied. Whereas part of the problem is one of attitude, there are circumstances that still prompt hard-channel approaches. Often there is simply not enough room or right-of-way in heavily urbanized areas to revert completely to natural floodplain processes. Engineers are often called in to fix an earlier unwise zoning decision that allowed inappropriate use of the flood zone.

In Aurora, Colorado, Horseshoe Park on Tollgate Creek offers a good example of successful joint venture planning by greenway advocates and drainage officials. Initially, the creek was straightened to carry off excess floodwater. A local project drained existing wetlands and left a utilitarian ditch. A local landscape architect worked with hydrological engineers, the public works department, the parks department, and wetlands ecologists to create an alternative. A broad shallow bowl was created to hold floodwaters, and a series of small grade control structures were used to slow flows and break up the channel. This also created more meandering and braided flow patterns and helped to bring back the wetland. Native species were then planted, and sweeping turf grass swaths serve as a transition from the newly created natural areas to nearby residential yards.

Legal and Regulatory Tools

Watercourse and Legal Precedent

There is a long tradition of watercourse law in the United States. Watercourse law lays out the rights and duties of riparian (stream-front) property owners. One key tenet is that a riparian property owner has the right to protect his or her land from flood damage but not in such a way that it unnecessarily inflicts damage on another property owner. Public entities have also been held accountable under this principal. In some ways this is a double-edged sword. A public entity might be accountable not only for damage caused upstream by a dam or downstream by a culvert, but also for not extending a culvert or channelization project. Be assured your local public works officials are aware of their legal exposure in any stream management decision.

Another legal principal to consider in flood management is the right of a community to manage floodplain development through its police power, zoning, subdivision regulations, and other methods. Clearly, preventing development in the floodplain is the best way to prevent flood damage and preserve stream corridor resources. Generally, communities have the right to restrict development on private and public

Point and Nonpoint Sources of Pollution

Point Sources
- Municipal sewage treatment plants
- Industrial discharges (including thermal discharges from power plants)
- Feedlots and manure storage areas
- Leaking underground storage tanks
- Certain storm-water discharges

Nonpoint Sources
- Storm-water runoff (from agriculture, logging, construction, mining, contaminated soils, city streets, and yards)
- Atmospheric deposition (acid rain, snow and fog, toxic substances, and nutrients)
- Inflows of groundwater contaminated by leaching pesticides, fertilizers, waste storage and disposal sites, groundwater drawdown leading to contamination, sludge disposal, and failing septic tanks
- Leaking landfills or dumps
- Marine sources (ocean dumping, dredge spoils, boat hull paints, and marine sanitation devices, or "heads"
- Land use decisions (loss of wetlands, removal of vegetative cover, increased paved surfaces)
- Abandoned mine drainage
- Pet droppings

Source: *A Citizen's Guide to Clean Water*, Izaak Walton League, 1990.

lands in the floodplain, provided the restrictions do not constitute the taking of property without compensation. Some courts have upheld floodplain regulations while others have struck them down, but the overall direction of judicial decision has been in favor of floodplain regulations that are reasonable, nondiscriminatory, and in conformance with state and local enabling statutes. Contact your state conservation department to determine your state's regulations regarding channel alteration and wetland, river, and floodplain protection.

Federal Law

A number of federal laws support preservation rather than channelization. The objective of the Federal Water Pollution Control Act Amendments of 1972, also known as Public Law (92-500) (further amended by the Clean Water Act of 1977), is to restore and maintain the chemical, physical, and biological integrity of waters in the United States. This law has several key sections.

Section 208 of the act requires preparation of areawide wastewater management plans across the nation. These plans must address both point and nonpoint source pollution. *Point* sources refer to pollution from outfalls such as sewage treatment outlets. Nonpoint refers to runoff from streets, agriculture, construction, and other sources of contamination that do not come from a specific outlet. These account for 65 percent of surface water pollution. Currently, point sources of pollution are managed by the National Pollution Discharge Elimination System (NPDES). Under this system, the Environmental Protection Agency issues permits that regulate runoff according to adopted plans and standards.

In 1987, the Clean Water Act was amended to further strengthen regulation of nonpoint sources. Under section 319 of the act, Congress required all states to identify waters that require nonpoint source pollution control and develop management plans to reduce that pollution. It also gave the EPA more muscle in enforcing standards. Communities with populations of more than 100,000 and many industries are required by 1992 to develop storm-water management plans that address nonpoint runoff.

The implications of this amendment could be far reaching in the area of wetland and stream corridor protection, because protection of wetlands and vegetated buffer zones along streams has been shown to be among the most cost-effective ways to reduce nonpoint pollution. While the enforcement of this provision may vary, greenway planners should recognize its potential in protecting stream corridors and become familiar with its provisions. A good place to begin is your local or regional EPA office. Each state also has a designated agency that manages the state's nonpoint-source pollution plan. This agency may provide technical guidance and funding.

Section 404 of the Clean Water Act is another major tool for greenway planners. Section 404 requires that a permit be acquired from the U. S. Army Corps of Engineers before filling or dredging any waters of the United States, including wetlands. The permit process calls for multiagency review and, if the public demands, public hearings.

The beauty of Section 404 is that it gives greenway advocates or any concerned citizen a voice in a project that may alter a stream or wetland. Debate is ongoing about the meaning of its definitions, including "waters of the United States," "dredge or fill," and "wetland." Any greenway development such as a trail or bridge that involves working or placing fill in a stream or wetland may require a 404 permit.

The basic philosophy of "no net loss" rests on three tenets. First, avoid destruction of wetland if at all feasible. Second, minimize destruction if any is necessary. Third, require replacement and mitigation of any damage done. The concept received national stature after a National Wetlands Policy Forum was convened in 1988 by the Conservation Foundation. The EPA took many of the forum's recommendations to heart and issued a Wetlands Action Plan in 1989. The EPA also signed a Memorandum of Agreement with the U. S. Army Corps of Engineers, which strives to integrate the concept of no net loss into the Section 404 permitting process by strengthening enforcement and requiring mitigation for lost wetlands.

State Programs

A number of states have passed legislation and created programs to protect wetlands and stream corridors. Thirty-four states have river conservation programs; several have shore land zoning for river and lake frontage or use a variety of wetland and floodplain laws to protect sensitive river areas. For example, Oregon's "Statewide Planning Goal 5" program calls for cities and counties to "conserve open space and protect natural and scenic resources." The City of Portland Planning Bureau took this to heart when it developed an overlay zone program to protect the Johnson Creek Corridor, which it considered an important "natural and scenic resource." In the case of Johnson Creek, the overlay

A state rivers program is a formal, state structured comprehensive set of river laws, buttressed by incentives or assessments, capable of providing high-grade protection and management for included rivers. Although thirty-two states across the country have river laws, their effectiveness varies. The best state rivers programs have staff, bona fide systems of protected rivers and streams, assessment capability, the authority to protect land, emphasis on public participation, coordination of protective tools and agencies involved, and prohibitions on certain types of development. Contact American Rivers, Inc. for more information about state river programs.

zone protects vegetation and other habitat qualities on properties fronting Johnson Creek.

Minnesota passed the Wetland Conservation Act of 1991, which protects all types of wetlands, from "prairie potholes" to streamside marshes. The program includes strict enforcement and replacement requirements and funds the purchase of wetland easements and restorations.

In California, the Urban Stream Restoration Program of the Department of Water Resources assists local communities in reducing damage from floods and stream bank instability while striving to restore environmental as well as aesthetic values. Among other activities, the program has produced a pamphlet and awards grants for local demonstration projects.

Many states have laws requiring minimum buffers of varying width along the edge of wetlands and other sensitive habitat (Massachusetts and California require one hundred feet). This zone may be increased, depending on specific site circumstances and sensitivity criteria. Ohio has a program, administered through the Ohio Environmental Protection Agency, for evaluating the aquatic health of streams. Under the program, violators of water quality standards can be required to clean up pollution sources when a stream evaluation shows degradation of the adopted stream habitat values.

Missouri has a promising new program called Stream Team to build preservation consciousness as well as forge networks and alliances among conservationists, landowners, farmers, public officials, and other interests. The program puts out a stream inventory manual and an inventory form. These documents help guide local interest in developing voluntary action plans for stream corridors. The system also provides a way to report problems to agency officials so that appropriate action can be taken.

Check with your state officials for laws and regulations in your state. Some measures have teeth, some have funds, some have both. Most likely, the programs are an aid and a starting point, not a complete solution. Effective action will depend primarily on local will and commitment of local resources.

Local Programs

Communities are developing new and creative ways to protect natural corridor resources that go beyond traditional zoning techniques. Here are some approaches:

- Tampa, Florida, and Sioux Falls, South Dakota, have explored Waterfront and Greenway Overlay Zones. In Tampa, builders must provide a twenty-three-foot setback for waterfront improvements and riverwalk systems. Sioux Falls requires a twenty-five-foot setback. Planners in Sioux Falls have now recommended widening that setback and adding incentives for quality riverfront architecture. A number of other communities also use a twenty-five-foot setback from the top of a stream bank where building is not permitted. Note that in many cases, twenty-five feet is not an adequate buffer width, but these policies are a starting point.

- Oklahoma City requires a fifty-foot riverfront easement.

- Durango, Colorado, has created a special Animas River district. Through both regulation and incentive, developers there have been encouraged to provide setbacks and trail easements.

- Communities along the Upper Delaware River in New York and Pennsylvania have amended their zoning codes to protect the scenic quality of that river corridor. Provisions include minimum lot size and restriction of buildings on steep slopes and hilltops. These precedents would all have potential application to the creation of corridor protection zones.

The Planned Unit Development (PUD) is a time-tested concept with an important role in corridor protection. In many cases, PUD will permit "clustering" so that, on a given piece of land, development can be concentrated, allowing the remaining land to be left in its natural state. PUD zoning offers flexibility and a mix of uses. Greenway planners should review local PUD codes for applicability to corridor protection with respect to development sites along water resources.

Local communities can also develop water quality policies and guidelines that address runoff from the entire watershed. One way to do this is to develop stream and water quality preservation guidelines and include them in the local public works department planning process for any public flood management projects or permits issued to private developers.

Another step is to make the public aware of how runoff ultimately ends up in the streams. In some places, such as the Chesapeake Bay region, citizens and officials apply a stencil on the street next to storm sewers, reminding the public that what goes down the drain ends up in the Bay.

Maintenance of Riparian Greenways

Ongoing maintenance is an essential part of a successful drainage management project. Even the best plan can quickly be laid waste by poor maintenance practices. Greenway planners should work with drainage officials in preparing a maintenance program. Many areas of mutual interest exist, including the joint use of a bike path to carry out routine debris removal and any remedial work.

Kinder and Gentler Stream Treatment

When a long buried segment of Berkeley, California's Strawberry Creek was exhumed, landscape architect Douglas Wolfe and environmental activist David Brower convinced officials to restore the creek as part of a modestly funded four-acre park project. Initially officials resisted, but with the help of strong citizen support, the stream was restored and became a major feature of the park. Woven willow and other native

The Oconee River Greenway, which passes through Athens, Georgia, is a thirty-five-mile greenway linking and preserving open space along the north and middle forks of the Oconee River and tributaries. A one-hundred-year floodplain ordinance, scenic preservation district overlay, and regulated strip covering one mile on each bank protect the riverway.

Save Our Streams (SOS), the water quality arm of the Izaak Walton League, developed a simple, scientific way to trap, identify, and record stream life, which can be used as indicators of water quality. Macroinvertebrates, certain types of aquatic organisms that live in streams, are sampled regularly to track the stream's health. The SOS biological testing method can help citizens identify and address stream problems.

Guidelines for Maintaining and Enhancing Riparian Functions in a Greenway

1. Make greenway corridors continuous along each side of a river if possible.

2. Include in the greenway the river's floodplain, riparian forest, associated wetlands, intermittent tributaries, gullies, swales, and upland areas if possible.

3. If possible, undertake a comprehensive study of the site's sediment and nutrient flow to establish how much is entering the riparian zone and how much it will need to filter.

4. Base the greenway width on site conditions. Riparian greenways that neighbor intensive land use such as clear-cutting, monoculture, or shopping malls will need to be wide enough to absorb excess nutrients, contaminants, and toxins. Consider also soils, existing vegetation, and slope, the advice of local professionals, and local buffer studies.

5. Maintain a band of natural vegetation along the stream bank to protect the water temperature moderation function. Avoid mowing stream-side vegetation, as this practice will decrease the vegetation's filtering effectiveness and lessen wildlife habitat value.

6. Supplement the natural sediment trapping function of the greenway with retention basins or vegetated berms where necessary.

7. Supplement, if necessary, the natural nutrient filter functions of the greenway with a tree-harvesting regime (in consultation with local forester and ecologist) to maximize nutrient uptake (actively growing plants use more nutrients).

8. Advocate use of best management practices—terraces, strip cropping, vegetated buffer strips—by private landowners in your watershed to reduce nonpoint pollution of your stream.

9. Become familiar with signs of erosion, sedimentation, and pollution in your stream. Is there muddy water after a rain? Is there a buildup of silt in the stream? Notice if the channels of the stream are getting wider and deeper. Are there fallen trees in the stream? All of these are signs of erosion. Contact trained professionals for advice about erosion control. The Izaak Walton League's Save Our Streams program can give you more detailed instructions on how to detect and combat various forms of erosion and pollution in your stream.

10. Keep people, cars, and grazing animals away from the edge of the water.

11. Build steps or a ramp between the top and bottom of a bank if you need access to the water.

12. It may be necessary, depending on the condition of upstream riparian forest buffers, to rehabilitate or revegetate upstream areas.

13. Limit fill operations and use erosion-control devices such as silt fences, hay bales, diversion ditches, filter dams, and sediment basins in developing the greenway.

14. Develop methods to prevent stream channel degradation or alteration, and attempt to restore natural processes and flows on your river greenway.

15. Limit the use of toxic chemicals in the greenway.

16. Carefully review the practice of mowing stream banks and removing vegetation. Plant trees to provide shade and food, prevent erosion, and encourage the uptake of nutrients.

17. Your group may also want to monitor the water quality of your local river or stream to determine if pollution is present and if your greenway buffers have been effective. Contact Save Our Streams for information on conducting a volunteer monitoring project.

18. Conduct stream restoration projects, stream cleanups, and bank stabilization projects or build spawning beds in creeks for fish.

19. Carefully consider any new development in the floodplain. If facilities do not need to be located in the frontage portion, find an alternate site. Minimize paved areas that prevent infiltration of rain and runoff, carrying off eroded materials into the stream. Be aware of construction regulations regarding erosion control. Use porous pavement when possible.

20. Conduct any development activities so that there is minimal disturbance to the natural topography and environment and to protect the river from pollution. Concentrate recreation facilities in areas that can take high use or that are already developed (e.g., the waterfronts of villages and towns).

Source: Adapted in part from Daniel Smith and Paul Hellmund, eds., *Ecology of Greenways* (Minneapolis: University of Minnesota Press, 1993).

species were planted to reestablish the creek's lost natural habitat and splendor. The cost of the creek restoration amounted to only 10 percent of the $650,000 park budget.

Whereas private developers used to fill wetlands to gain more build-able land—and many still do—enlightened developers now build new projects around these areas and use them as key marketing features. A commercial development by the Mentor Graphics company in Portland is an example. The choice offices now face wetlands rich in wildlife. Corporate executives proudly display telescopes, which they use to view wildlife from their office windows.

Fortunately for those interested in completing greenways along watercourses, many institutional underpinnings are now in place at the federal, state, and local level to speed their development. The Clean Water Act and Federal Water Pollution Control Act, along with state and local wetland and development regulations, have recognized rivers and riparian lands and minimized their value for development. In Maryland, thanks to the state's visionary support for riparian protection over the past fifty years, people may soon be able to hike along their favorite riverbank straight to the Chesapeake Bay.

Clearly, new values are taking hold in the disciplines that shape and alter waterways. In community after community, people are coming to see that curved is better than straight, rough is better than smooth, slow moving is better than fast, and vegetated is better than concrete covered. Rivers, wetlands, lakes, bays, and streams can be rallying points for local conservation work. In come communities, however, awareness of the value of these new "soft" techniques is only beginning. Be supportive of flood control professionals by including them in your efforts and by appreciating that sometimes the range of possible nonstructural solutions may be severely limited.

Finally, remember that the watershed is the ultimate buffer zone. A stream is merely a reflection of what happens in the watershed. We must consider the whole picture and how the overall drainage system functions.

For additional help in planning a water resource greenway, refer to the organizations listed in Appendix A, particularly American Rivers, the Izaak Walton League of America, Inc., and the National Park Service Rivers and Trails Conservation Assistance Program, or these additional contacts:

The U. S. Environmental Protection Agency
401 M Street, S.W.
Washington, DC 20460
202-382-2090

The U. S. Fish and Wildlife Service
Contact your regional office or the Department of the Interior
Washington, DC 20240
202-343-5634

The Mecklenburg County Greenway, in North Carolina, is a planned network of floodplains along twenty creeks in the greater Charlotte area, designed to provide open space, recreation, habitat protection, and especially flood damage abatement. (Flood damage alone averages $1.4 million every year.) Priorities for greenway acquisition (via subdivision dedication, piggyback utility easements, or purchase) are based on population density, linkage, growth rate, aesthetics, development type, accessibility, and distribution of existing open space.

9

Preserving Our Cultural Heritage

*"The unique cultural and natural resources of the Valley are as important to our
national heritage as battlefields or homes of presidents. Yet, located as they are
amid a living community, many of these resources cannot, and should not,
be managed or cared for in isolation from the Valley communities of which
they are a part."*
—Richard T. Moore, Chairman, Blackstone River Valley National
Heritage Corridor Commission

Greenways provide us with the ability to explore the outdoor environment and learn more about the unique landscapes in our communities.
This is especially true when it comes to learning about our cultural heritage. Americans are fascinated with their past and eager to learn more
about the people and events that shaped existing landscapes. Few environments offer more interest to the average greenway user than a restored historic mill site along a stream or river, an abandoned railroad
emerging from a second growth forest, or an archaeological dig in progress.

The National Park Service defines cultural resources as the "sites,
structures, districts, and objects significantly associated with or representative of earlier people, cultures, and human activities and events."
Often we forget that America's cultural heritage dates back thousands
of years and is revealed in part as we examine the origins of travel
ways, settlement patterns, and land use of earlier cultures and societies.

River valleys, canals, roadways, and rail lines are significant components of our cultural heritage, as they were the early routes of settlement in North America. Transportation routes often evolved from
Indian trails and served as networks for travel, commerce, and enterprise within the New World. Today, many of these linear landscapes
contain vestiges of early events and early settlement patterns. Because
of population growth, loss of open space, and the continuing suburban
sprawl, many of these resources are threatened, and Americans are
looking for ways to preserve them. Greenways are an emerging method
of protecting these resources.

An idea akin to greenways is the concept of "heritage corridors."
Heritage corridors are linear landscapes that possess a distinctive collection of cultural resources. Heritage corridors often have an explicit economic focus, encouraging tourism, the adaptive reuse of old buildings,
recreation, and environmental enhancement. The techniques used to establish, design, and implement greenways are equally useful for establishing heritage corridors.

In this chapter we briefly describe a variety of methods for protecting
cultural resources as part of an overall greenway development strategy.

National and Federal Contacts for Cultural Resource Protection

National Park Service
U. S. Department of the Interior
Post Office Box 37127
Washington, DC 20013-7127
Archaeological Assistance Division
(202) 343-4101

Historic American Buildings Survey
(202) 343-9625

Historic American Engineering Record (202)
343-9625

Interagency Resources Division
(202) 343-9500

National Register of Historic Places (202) 343-9536

National Historic Landmarks

Preservation Assistance Division (202) 343-8174

Tax credit information (202) 343-9573

Certified Local Government Program
(202) 343-9505

National Conference of State Historic Preservation
Officers
444 North Capitol Street, NW, Suite 332
Washington, DC 20001
(202) 624-5465

National Alliance of Preservation Commissions
444 North Capitol Street, NW, Suite 332
Washington, DC 20001
(301) 663-6149

National Alliance of Statewide Preservation
Organizations
c/o Historic Massachusetts, Inc.
45 School St.
Boston, MA 02108
(617) 350-7032

Advisory Council on Historic Preservation
1100 Pennsylvania Avenue, NW
Washington, DC 20004
(202) 272-0533

Cultural Council of American Indians, Alaska Natives and Native Hawaiians (Keepers of the
Treasures)
c/o Shoshone-Bannock Tribal Museum
Post Office Box 306
Fort Hall, Idaho 83203

National Institute for Conservation of Cultural
Property
3299 K Street, NW, Suite 403
Washington, DC 20007
(202) 625-1495

National Trust for Historic Preservation
1785 Massachusetts Avenue, NW
Washington, DC 20036
(202) 673-4000

A first step in obtaining information on the protection and preservation of cultural artifacts, historic buildings, and significant landscapes is to contact your state historic preservation office or the nearest regional office of the National Trust for Historic Preservation or U.S. National Park Service.

Deciding What to Protect

Most of the continental United States has been settled, developed, altered, and redeveloped. In some cases, it is difficult to know through casual observation if the landscape that you see today bears any resemblance to the one that our ancestors viewed fifty, two hundred, or a thousand years earlier and more importantly to determine its

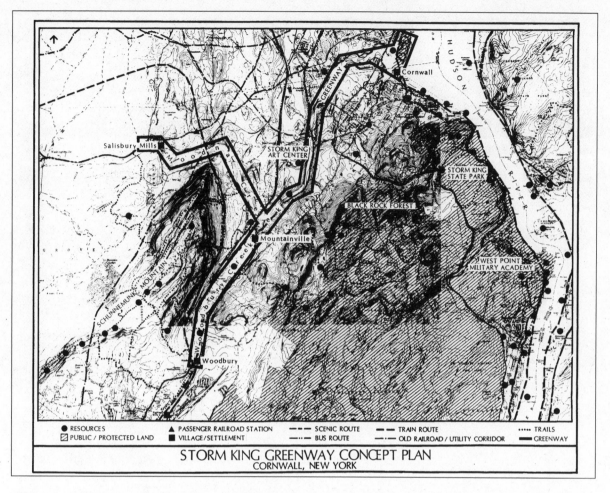

Figure 9-1 Storm King Greenway concept plan. Linking art with the environment, tourism with landscape protection, and existing towns with other open-space corridors are a few of the opportunities and challenges inherent in the Storm King Greenway in Cornwall, New York. The Conservation Fund's concept plan identifies fourteen miles of greenway corridor along Moodna and Woodbury creek tributaries in a remarkable historic portion of the Hudson River Valley. Trails from the greenway will connect settled areas to large public and privately protected landholdings, museums, historic sites, the Appalachian Trail, and to the Storm King Arts Center. (D. Horne and Co.)

significance to the historic development of your community (see Figure 9-1).

As a general rule, cultural and historic interpretation of a local landscape should begin with a careful examination of the natural features and resources of that landscape. Natural resources were often the determinants of past settlement and development patterns. In conducting a thorough investigation of natural resources, you will often find evidence of prior human use and activity.

We suggest that when conducting a landscape evaluation you investigate historic land-use patterns. The best way to begin is to look for local and regional histories in libraries, schools, or the state historic preservation office. Old family photographs, aerial photos of the landscape, and real-estate maps may also be available. Your library may have books on the history of your community, historic photos, family genealogies, or

The Schuylkill River Greenway Association coordinates Pennsylvania's Heritage Park Program feasibility study. The envisioned program will showcase places along the river greenway that have played a role in the state's industrial heritage. Interpretive centers will focus on historic and cultural relationships in the area. The park's sponsors believe the program will enhance economic development and tourism.

The Lock Port Heritage Greenway in Clinton County, Pennsylvania, connects historic, archaeological, industrial, artistic, and natural sites as a tourist attraction for this depressed area and will, when complete, connect historic sites along the West Branch of the Susquehannah. The greenway will link the town center with the Pennsylvania canal, logging era sites, an early nineteenth century iron manufacturing site, a state park, Susquehanna canoe route, Piper Aviation Museum, and Indian sites.

official government archives. Your local newspaper may have back issues describing important events and may be able to substantiate the relevance of artifacts found in the landscape. Often the best sources of information on local history are lifelong residents, particularly the elderly in your community.

Historians and preservationists distinguish between historic and architectural significance. Historic significance is associated with events and figures of the past that have shaped local, state, or national history. Architectural significance is related to the evolution of building style and structure. For example, it is unlikely that the Memphis, Tennessee, motel, where Martin Luther King was killed, was deemed to have architectural merit when it was converted to a museum, but it is undoubtedly historic; Mount Vernon, home and final resting place of George Washington, is both architecturally and historically significant; a skyscraper in New York City might be architecturally but not necessarily historically significant. Even modest vernacular buildings may be arbitrarily significant because of their rarity or condition and may be significant because they are an authentic product of a certain place, time, and people. It is important to understand these distinctions as you evaluate the greenway landscape; all too frequently, what seems ordinary and familiar is ignored in favor of what is visually splendid—the Southern mansion, for example, whereas the slave cabin moldering nearby may be the last remaining example of its type. Further study of pleasing expanses of farmland may reveal that the field patterns and arrangements of old farm buildings are characteristic of a unique ethnic influence of European settlers, perhaps Swiss, Swedish, English, or German.

Two other important cultural resource assessment tools are ethnography and archaeology. Ethnography describes the life and traditions, such as fishing, agriculture, hunting, festivals, and religious celebrations, of peoples or regions. Native Americans, Irish-Americans, African-Americans, Amish, and Hispanics can all be analyzed as ethnic groups. Ethnographic studies depend heavily on participant observation, interviews, oral histories and documentation, and memoirs. These methods can explain specific artifacts or patterns found in a landscape—sweet potato banks (for winter storage) in eastern North Carolina, for example, are just mysterious mounds of earth until you know what they are. They can also identify specific cultural traditions, either to assist their practitioners in perpetuating them or to interpret them for visitors through festivals or ongoing exhibits.

Archaeology is the scientific study of the material remains of human cultures to derive knowledge about past times and to supplement documentary evidence. The work of an archaeologist is extremely important in accurately interpreting history. Archaeological surveys should be completed by qualified historians and technicians trained and educated as archaeologists. Often, excavation is not recommended.

To decide which landscape elements are worthy of preservation, it is helpful to determine the level of protection you want for each. For example, if you plan to nominate the subject landscape, building, or structure to the National Register of Historic Places, a detailed evaluation will be required. Early on, you should consult with a professional who is skilled and qualified in cultural resource protection.

The cultural assessment of your greenway should include the following.

Historic Significance

Historic significance defines the events and figures of the past that have shaped local, state, or national history. To evaluate historic significance, you should ask such questions as: What is the social, religious, and ethnic significance of the landscape? Were settlement patterns or social structure important to the development of the community or larger society? The life of an individual, sociopolitical events, and military engagement can be influential beyond a single community.

The National Park Service defines a historic landscape as "a geographical area that historically has been used by people, or shaped or modified by human activity, occupancy, or intervention, and that possesses a significant concentration, linkage, or continuity of areas of land use, vegetation, buildings and structures, roads, waterways, and natural features." The National Park Service's Bulletin 30, *Guidelines for Evaluating and Documenting Rural Historic Landscapes*, is the best place to start in evaluating greenway areas for historic significance because of its explicit recognition of the need to evaluate the landscape as a whole. Another useful reference is National Park Service Bulletin 24, *Guidelines for Local Surveys: A Basis for Preservation Planning*. Further guidance for historic resource surveys is available from your state historic preservation office. The state office can also tell you whether survey information already exists for part or all of the area in which the greenway is located, whether a local program exists to conduct the survey, follow up with local (as opposed to state and federal) protection, and tell you what protection of any kind may already be in place.

The historic aspects of the Bethabara Trail Greenway, in Winston-Salem, North Carolina, enhance its appeal to local visitors. The Moravian settlement of Bethabara was the birthplace of the modern city of Winston-Salem and the first community developed within the 100,000-acre Wachovia tract of land. Although the land was not ideally suited for development, the Moravian social structure founded a successful society. Today, an ongoing archaeological restoration of the original Moravian village is the centerpiece of the greenway, a six-mile corridor that literally traces the growth and development of the city. For the city of Winston-Salem, the historic artifacts, buildings, and landscape of the small Moravian village were the impetus for the greenway.

Architectural or Engineering Significance

Architectural or engineering significance pertains to the evolution of building style structure and the unique application of engineering principles. Questions to consider in this area are: What is the local, state, or national significance of man-made structures or buildings found within

The C&O Canal towpath offers recreational opportunities on land and water. The historic buildings of Fletcher's Boathouse, along with many "lock-keeper's" houses, are maintained as part of an interpretive cultural heritage program. (Lisa Gutierrez)

the landscape? Are the buildings unique to your community, or were they commonplace throughout the United States?

Perhaps the best way to answer these questions is to ask your state historic preservation office to walk the property with you or to conduct an inventory of the structures within the landscape. The National Historic Landmarks Program identifies and designates properties of national significance. The Historic American Buildings Survey and Historic American Engineering Record provide drawings, photographs, and written histories of designated sites, structures, and objects. All these organizations are sources of information that might be useful.

Architectural and engineering significance can lead to cultural resource protection. Take, for example, the Delaware and Lehigh Canal National Heritage Corridor, which extends 150 miles from Wilkes-Barre to Bristol, Pennsylvania. This unique collection of historic railways and canals, industrial towns, and one-of-a-kind buildings includes the nation's longest and most intact watered towpath canal. In the 1930s, the Delaware Canal, a sixty-mile-long section of the corridor, was acquired by the Commonwealth of Pennsylvania for permanent protection and future use as a linear park. In 1942, a philanthropist provided funds to local communities for the acquisition and preservation of the Lehigh Canal. During the past fifty years, public and private interests have joined to protect, restore, and revitalize the unique communities, ethnic cultures, and architecturally significant structures found along the canal. In 1988 Congress declared the entire canal system a National Heritage Corridor and asked the Secretary of the Interior to appoint a twenty-one-member commission to oversee coordinated comprehensive planning and development. The greenway concept has been at the heart of restoration efforts; one of the most popular goals for the corridor is a recreational trail system.

Natural Significance

Natural significance describes the natural features that shaped human habitation and influence along the corridor. Questions to ask are: What is ecologically, geologically, or hydrologically unique about the landscape? Is the study area an accurate and essentially unspoiled example of natural history? Was the site altered to facilitate human activity and development? Which natural features dominate the landscape and make the area unique?

Today most states have a natural heritage inventory that identifies rare and threatened or unique natural resources of the landscape. These inventories can provide a starting point for understanding important landscape features. Also, some federal agencies have developed natural resource inventories of local rivers, native forest stands, unique geologic formations, soils, and other elements. One of your best sources of information is likely to be your local planning office.

Economic Significance

Economic significance addresses the value of protecting the corridor in terms of increased local tax revenues, tourism, and economic development. Questions to address include: Would the corridor offer economic advantages if protected, restored, and made accessible to the public? What is the potential impact of preservation and interpretation on the tax base, tourism, commercial, industrial, or residential development, infrastructure improvements, and environmental protection?

Defining economic impacts is relatively easy. Much information is readily available at local tax offices, planning agencies, and real-estate offices. Several important individuals and agencies within your community should be involved in the economic evaluation of the greenway corridor, including the local chamber of commerce, economic development office, and a realtor with experience in evaluating historic sites.

For many years, the Blackstone River shaped human development and prosperity in the Blackstone River Valley. The river, located in both Massachusetts and Rhode Island, falls 438 vertical feet in its forty-six-mile length. New England settlers recognized its potential to generate power—and the Blackstone River Valley became the birthplace of the American Industrial Revolution. This unique river valley, encompassing

The City of Lowell used its industrial riverfront and canal heritage as the cornerstone for economic redevelopment of its urban core. In 1975, the city, in partnership with the state, convinced Congress to create the Lowell Historic Canal District Commission, which developed a plan for redeveloping the city's industrial waterfront. In 1978, the Lowell National Historical Park was established.

more than 250,000 acres, has seen settlement, industrialization, and environmental degradation. Yet, the river remains the cohesive element that links together communities, influences social and economic change, and with the designation of the river as a National Heritage Corridor, improves the quality of life for half a million residents. The Blackstone River Valley National Heritage Corridor Plan emphasized the revitalization of cultural and historic resources in the valley.

Preservation Programs and Techniques

In DuPage County, Illinois, the 31st Street Greenway, also called the Salt Creek Greenway, was established when Oak Bridge Village trustees passed a resolution declaring 31st Street a "historic greenway corridor," hoping to stop county widening of the street. Thirty-first Street connects forest preserves, the Brookfield Zoo, Wolf Road Prairie Preserve, a country club, and estates and boasts Frank Lloyd Wright houses, Victorian mansions, pioneer cabins, and Native American remains. The greenway has been promoted as a scenic route to encourage preservation of the roadway, its associated structures, and open spaces.

Once you have identified and defined a cultural resource worthy of protection, you must select the best way to protect it. Serious consideration of cultural resource protection begins with a fundamental understanding of land ownership. This is because most important cultural resources in the United States are privately owned. You will want to know if the current owners are protecting or degrading the resource.

All methods of protection should include guidelines and standards for rehabilitation, construction, restoration, preservation, alteration, and reuse of properties, structures, and buildings within your corridor. Protection methods should be based on the following principles for historic preservation and protection: (a) it is better to preserve and restore than destroy and reconstruct; (b) rehabilitation should be compatible with the existing historic fabric and style of surrounding buildings and landscapes; (c) new construction should use materials, techniques, and designs that respect the character and value of the existing buildings, landscapes, and setting; and (d) not all historic sites should be fully accessible to the public.

During the past fifty years, cultural resource preservation has grown in importance in the United States. As a result, several programs have been developed to help preserve historic resources. The best-known programs are described in the following paragraphs.

The National Historic Preservation Act of 1966

The federal government has played an important role in preserving historic places since passage of the Antiquities Act of 1906. This law offered protection to prehistoric and historic sites located on federal properties. In 1935, Congress enacted the Historic Sites Act, establishing a national policy to preserve historic buildings and sites for "public use and inspiration." This Act gave the Secretary of the Interior the power to survey, document, evaluate, acquire, and preserve archaeological and historic sites throughout the country. In 1966, Congress enacted the National Historic Preservation Act, which expanded the federal role in preservation. The Act authorized the establishment of a National Register of Historic Places and provided matching grants to states, local governments, and nonprofit preservation organizations. It also created the Advisory Council on Historic Preservation, which advises the President and Congress on preservation issues related to federal and nonfederal properties. The Act has given rise to federal preservation activities within many other federal agencies and has spurred consideration of historic preservation in government planning at all levels.

National Register of Historic Places

The National Register of Historic Places is one of the programs established by the National Historic Preservation Act and is administered by the National Park Service. The register lists properties in both public and private ownership and evaluates sites, buildings, structures, and objects that are historically and culturally significant in American history. When a property becomes listed in the Register, it comes under federal protection standards, including:

- the property receives official recognition of its significance;

- the property is eligible for federal assistance, both technical and financial;

- the property is eligible for federal tax benefits, including tax incentives for rehabilitation;

- the property must be considered in any federal undertakings, action, grant, or assisted program.

The Secretary of the Interior is responsible for establishing standards for all national preservation programs. The Secretary is also empowered to advise federal agencies on the preservation of historic properties, especially those that may possess potential for inclusion within the National Register of Historic Places.

Most nominations to the register are made by states and localities, through state historic preservation offices, although federal agencies are also capable of nominating properties to the register. Generally, properties must be at least fifty years old to be eligible for listing. Younger buildings have been listed when they are regarded by the National Park Service as exceptionally significant. Currently, the National Register contains approximately 48,000 listings that include more than 670,000 cultural resources of varying kinds.

Thousands of people gather each year for the Labor and Ethnic Festival at the Stater Mill Historic Site in Pawtucket, Rhode Island. Daily, National Park Service staff interpret mill ruins to canoeists and day trippers at sites along the river. The site is one point of interest along the Blackstone River Valley National Heritage Corridor.

National Heritage Areas and Corridors

Another method of protecting and conserving linear corridors is the heritage corridor concept. This concept involves developing an overall plan for the protection of all resources within the corridor's boundaries and the enhancement of recreational and economic opportunities, including greenways and trails. A relatively new concept, the federal role in establishing heritage corridors is still evolving.

Currently, the National Park Service provides technical assistance and some financial aid to a limited number of significant cultural areas that have been designated by Congress as Heritage Corridors. The first National Heritage Corridor was the Illinois and Michigan (I&M) Canal, which links forty-two communities, many historic structures, wildlife areas, and archaeological sites. Other congressionally designated corridors include the Blackstone River Valley National Heritage Corridor and the Delaware and Lehigh Navigation Canal National Heritage Corridor. For more guidance on the heritage corridor route, contact the National Park Service.

State Historic Preservation Office

Each state has a historic preservation officer who is appointed by the governor to carry out the state's responsibilities under the National Historic Preservation Act. His or her responsibilities include conducting cultural resource surveys, preparing statewide preservation plans, nominating properties to the National Register of Historic Places, reviewing federal projects for effects on historic properties, administering a range of assistance programs, including state and/or federal grants-in-aid programs (money), providing public information, offering education and training programs, and furnishing technical assistance to counties, cities, and towns in developing local preservation programs. According the National Trust for Historic Preservation, state-level inventories have recorded approximately four million historically significant properties. One of your first steps in investigating your cultural resource should be to contact your state historic preservation officer.

Historic Preservation Districts and Commissions

Approximately 1200 communities have preservation ordinances that designate and regulate properties of historic significance. Preservation ordinances usually control rehabilitation, restoration, and new construction of building exteriors, structures, and landscaping of designated buildings or districts within defined boundaries and frequently delay or prohibit demolition of designated historic properties. Along with these ordinances, many communities have established historic districts to define groupings of significant cultural areas or sites and historically important buildings. These districts are managed by locally established preservation or historic district commissions, which are usually served by the staff of the local government's planning office. Local protection tools might include historic easements, which protect historically significant properties, or facade easements, which restrict changes made to the exterior of a significant structure.

Preservation or historic district commissions in counties, cities, and towns serve as key links in the national preservation partnership. Along with carrying out responsibilities under local preservation ordinances, they may work to revitalize whole neighborhoods or downtown areas through local "Main Street" programs and raise public awareness about history through community education activities and events.

Historic districts adjacent to portions of a greenway might be expanded easily to incorporate the greenway, thereby conferring additional significance to the greenway and perhaps obtaining for it some aspect of regulation on properties that might affect the scenic quality of the greenway. For example, local guidelines might extend controls to the backs of buildings facing into an important trail or canal towpath.

Developing an Interpretive Plan for Your Cultural Landscape

Once you have protected the cultural greenway or individual cultural resource and determined that one or more of the project sites is capable of accommodating public use, you may want to develop an interpretive plan. An interpretive plan will help explain the significance of the resource to others. The accurate and active interpretation of the landscape features, structures, and historic resources will greatly improve public acceptance of preservation strategies. Tools include displays, multimedia presentations, self-guided tours, historic reenactment, and storytelling. Interpretation can create economic opportunities for businesses in your community through tourism and increased usage of the site.

The Blackstone River Valley National Heritage Corridor Plan describes thirteen interpretive themes: industrial development, industrial decline, transportation, technology, labor and management, ethnicity and immigration, religion, early settlement, community development, social reform, commerce, agriculture, and Native Americans. This gives the visitor a choice of topics to explore, displayed in various formats to appeal to individual preferences (audiovisual, hands-on experiences, displays, etc.).

As the National Trust for Historic Preservation so eloquently states, "Preservation is not just a nice idea. It is a needed answer to many problems the [United States] faces in providing housing, saving energy, protecting our environment, creating jobs, and producing more stimulating surroundings." Cultural resources enrich the outdoor experience. Their preservation and interpretation can help community residents understand the relationship of humans to the natural world. Greenways can be used by preservationists and environmentalists to protect and preserve a diverse range of culturally significant landscapes. Many of the examples cited here began as simple, local concepts that later attracted widespread support. We hope this chapter sparks enthusiasm and generates ideas for protecting the cultural resources in your community.

For additional information about cultural resources in your greenway, contact the National Trust for Historic Preservation (address in Appendix A).

Additional contacts:

National Park Service
P.O. Box 37127
Washington, DC 20013-7121
202-343-9500
Responsible for National Register of Historic Places, National Register of Historic Landmarks.

The Centennial Trail, so-called, because it honors the one hundredth anniversary of the Metropolitan Water Reclamation District (MWRD), will create a trail connection between Chicago and the state A&M Canal trail on twenty-six miles of leased MWRD land along the banks of the Des Plaines River and the Sanitary and Ship Canal. The corridor combines natural areas and wildlife protection with industrial and transportation uses. Will County is planning to develop a Heritage Park along the trail, which will combine interpreted education themes based on old U.S. Steel blast-furnace technology.

The New Santa Fe Trail Project will link the city of Santa Fe to its past and a wide range of recreational opportunities. The trail will introduce people to prehistory, the Spanish exploration, the War of 1846, the Civil War, the railroading era, and the unique history of the trail itself. Forty miles of pathways in the study area provide recreational and environmental education opportunities.

National Conference of State Historic Preservation Offices
444 North Capitol Street, N.W. Suite 332
Hall of State Building
Washington DC 20001-1512
202-624-5465
Contact to identify the historic preservation officer in your state.

National Alliance of Statewide Preservation Organizations
c/o Historic Massachusetts, Inc.
45 School Street
Boston, MA 02108
617-723-3383
Contact for information about state preservation organizations.

National Alliance of Preservation Commissions
Suite 332, Hall of States
444 North Capitol Street, N.W.
Washington, DC 20001
202-624-5465
Can provide information about historic preservation tools and methods.

10

The Greenway Design and Implementation Process

"Through a sense of connection with a system greater than himself man achieves aesthetic satisfaction, and the more nearly universal the system, the deeper the satisfaction."
—Edmund N. Bacon, *The Design of Cities*

When your master plan for the greenway has been completed, your next step will be to prepare documents that will guide development of the greenway (see Figure 10-1).

Before we examine greenway design, the issue of accessibility deserves attention. In 1991, Congress enacted the Americans with Disabilities Act, sweeping legislation that treats accessibility as a civil right of all Americans and not just a structural component of the local building code.

Universal Design

In developing your greenway facility, you should incorporate the principles and construction practices of universal design, a concept that concludes that a majority of the population will have some form of temporary or permanent disability at some point during their lives and that all facilities should be designed free of barriers and obstructions. In order to make greenways accessible to all users, the greenway designer should be aware of several types of impaired users:

1. Temporarily impaired but able-bodied, which includes a majority of the population at some time during their lives; for example, a pregnant woman or a person carrying an armload of groceries.

2. Visually impaired, ranging from someone temporarily blinded by glare or a strong light to those with a permanent medically and legally declared loss of vision.

3. Mobility impaired, which includes the elderly and individuals confined to wheelchairs.

4. Hearing impaired, which includes individuals who have lost their ability to hear and who must rely on visual information as their primary means of communication.

5. Manually impaired, for example, an elderly person who does not possess the strength and stamina of youth.

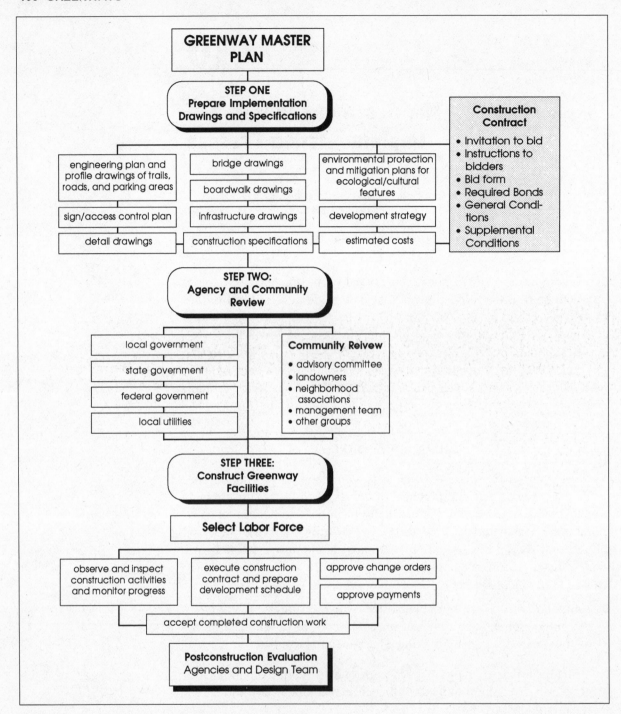

Figure 10-1 The greenway design process.

6. Learning impaired, which includes a broad range of people who may be illiterate or have an orientation problem or difficulty navigating the natural or built environment.

As you evaluate your greenway design, be sure to keep the needs of all abilities in mind and strive for solutions that provide access for most if not all users (see Figure 10-2).

Physical Needs of Persons with Disabilities

	Mobility Impaired	Visually Impaired	Manually Impaired	Agility/ Stamina Impaired	Learning Impaired
Site Organization	Continuous site access network	Consistent tactile information. Tactile maps and signs.		Proximity of facilites	Clarity of site organization
Information	Accessibility symbols. Level of accessibility information	Raised character signs, pictographs. Verbal information			Pictographs and clear information systems, visual orientation
Vehicle Parking Area	Reserved Space Size Access to paths Surface type	Readibility of signs		Distance to facilities	
Pathways/ Trails	5% longitudinal and 2% cross slopes. Width of trail. Surface type Ramp railings	Path edges delineated with tactile warning strips. Curbs		Rest areas and seating	Clarity of orientation
Fishing	Level surface type curbs, rails, shelves, shade & shelter	Curbs Casting aids Casting space	Special fishing equipment	Seating Shade Shelter	
Boating	Access to boats Safety of access	Safety at water's edge	Access to boats Operation of boats		
Restrooms	Accessible to all persons	Accessible to all persons	Fixture controls	Proximity to other facilities	
Camping and Picnic Areas	Adjacent parking Type of surface materials Convenience of utilities	Tactile warning strips around grills		Distance to restrooms and water	

Figure 10-2 Physical needs of persons with disabilities.

Several good sources of information exist on accessibility and the concept of universal design. For applicable legislation and design criteria, order the 1991 *Americans with Disabilities Act* (available from your congressional representative); the *Uniform Federal Accessibility Standards*, developed by the General Services Administration, Department of Defense, Department of Housing and Urban Development, and the U.S. Postal Service; and *Minimum Guidelines and Requirements for Accessible Design*, prepared in 1981 by the Architectural Barriers Compliance

Disabled individuals can access and enjoy the trail. (Lisa Gutierrez)

Board, Washington, D.C. These documents will provide you with the minimum acceptable design standards for surface, structure, and facility development. Whole Access, a nonprofit organization based in Redwood City, California, promotes the participation of people of varying abilities in all forms of outdoor recreation and can share vital information on the design and development of accessible trails.

Preparing Implementation Documents

In implementing the final master plan, you should first prepare working drawings and construction documents that describe materials, style, form, and specifications for all proposed facilities. These documents are essential communication tools. They convey important information about the physical development of the greenway to contractors or volunteers who will assist you in the construction of the greenway. Additionally, you may need (or the law may require you) to prepare documents for certain kinds of facilities (for example, bridges, drainage structures, and electrical fixtures) by qualified professionals. These documents generally include construction drawings, technical specifications, construction contracts, and cost estimates. Combined, these documents will serve to establish an orderly procedure, realistic schedule, and approximate costs for implementing your greenway.

Construction drawings are architectural and engineering plans and detailed drawings. They illustrate the type of construction work that you propose to undertake and what the property will look like after all greenway construction has been completed. The ground plane view is prepared as if you were looking straight down at your project from a

"Contractors can be the best volunteers. If you attempt a project or portion of a project totally as a community contribution by contractors, they will get involved. They must perceive that no one is being paid. Everyone is donating what they do."
—Tim Merrimen, Pueblo Nature Center, Pueblo, Colorado

height of several hundred feet. It is often accompanied by a view of certain greenway facilities in cross section, or longitudinal section, which illustrate how the facility will be developed through the existing landform. For example, if you propose a trail ten feet wide and a thousand feet long, drawings would illustrate the location of the trail in relation to existing features of the property. If the trail has curves, the plane view portion of the drawing illustrates and describes the length and radius of the curve. If the trail is to be built over hilly terrain, the profile portion of the drawing illustrates the longitudinal cross section of the trail.

Because these drawings will serve as a primary guide for the development of your greenway, we recommend that you have them prepared by a team of professionals, including, for example, a registered landscape architect, engineer, architect, and land surveyor.

Construction specifications describe the materials you will need and procedures you will follow to develop and install greenway facilities. For example, if you have decided to use a geotextile fabric in the greenway trail, the drawings and plans illustrate where you propose to install the fabric. The construction specifications describe the type of material you propose to use (including the manufacturer) and how the fabric should be installed (see Figure 10-3).

If you are using contractual labor to develop your greenway, you must provide construction specifications in addition to drawings and plans. If you plan on using volunteer labor, or in-house government or private workers, we recommend that you provide these laborers with a set of technical specifications before construction begins. Up-front communication will prevent difficulties during implementation.

Construction contracts are the legal basis for employing contract labor. If you plan to use contract labor, you will want to work with an attorney to draft a thorough set of contract documents. These generally include public bid forms, general conditions of the contract, supplemental conditions of the contract specific to your project, and performance, bid, and payment bonds. Make sure that all contract documents have been properly executed by your contractor and the contracting agent before the labor force begins work on your greenway.

Preconstruction cost estimates give the dollar value of constructing each element of your project. A good estimate will describe each element on the basis of its component parts, which always include the cost of raw materials and labor involved. For example, the estimated cost of an asphalt trail would be based on its component parts, which include geotextile fabric, aggregate stone subbase, and asphalt surface. To obtain the unit price for the asphalt, you would estimate the cost of the quantity of plant-mixed asphalt to be purchased, delivery to the site, and installation by the labor force. The same would hold true for the other component parts. If you have difficulty preparing a construction cost estimate for your project, contact a local design professional, staff from the local planning, engineering, parks, or public works departments, or a construction estimator. The best way to verify costs is to call suppliers and contractors directly. We also recommend that you add an

The National Guard in each state receives funding to help with community projects by providing laborers or heavy equipment. The Maryland National Guard helped the state's Greenway Program within the Department of Natural Resources build trails and construct judging stands for the World Championship White-Water Races on the Savage River Greenway. For information, contact the National Guard representative in your state.

Section 600

AGGREGATE BASE COURSE

1.0 REFERENCE: Reference Section 1010: Aggregate for Non-Bituminous Flexible Type Bases of the NCDOT Standard Specifications for Roads and Structures.

2.0 SCOPE: The work covered by this section consists of the construction of a base composed of an approved aggregate material hauled to the site, placed as shown on the drawings, compacted, and shaped conform to the lines, grades, depths and typical sections on the drawings or as directed by the Landscape Architect.

3.0 MATERIALS: The aggregate base course shall consist of crushed stone or crushed gravel. The material shall conform to the Requirements of Aggregate Base Course, as designated by the North Carolina Department of Transportation, Standards and Specifications for Roads and Structures, Sections 1010-1 and 3.

4.0 HAULING AND PLACING MATERIALS: The aggregated material shall be placed on the geotextile fabric on the subgrade to the specified depth and in such a manner as to prevent segregation. Where the required compacted thickness of base is 8 inches or less, the base material may be spread and compacted in one layer. Where the compacted thickness is more than 8 inches, the base material shall be spread and compacted in two or more approximately equal layers each about 8 inches thick. The minimum compacted thickness of any one layer shall be compacted, tested and approved before placing succeeding layers of base material or pavement.

No material shall be placed on frozen subgrade or base. Hauling equipment shall not be operated on subgrade or a previous completed layer of base material soft enough to rut or weave beneath the equipment. The maximum speed of trucks traveling over any part of the subgrade or base shall be 5 miles per hour.

The Contractor shall utilize methods of handling, hauling, and placing material that will minimize segregation and contamination. If segregation occurs, the Landscape Architect may require that changes be made in the Contractor's methods to minimize segregation, and may also require mixing on the road, which may be necessary to correct any segregated material. No additional compensation will be allowed for the work of road mixing as may be required.

Aggregate that is contaminated with foreign materials to the extent the base course will not adequately serve its intended use shall be removed and replaced by the Contractor at no additional cost to the Owner regardless of prior acceptance.

Construction Specifications   600 · 1   Aggregate Base Course

Figure 10-3 Example of construction specifications.

8 to 10 percent contingency fee to account for unforeseen expenses (see Figure 10-4).

Developing the Greenway

Who should construct your greenway facility? This depends on several factors, including who owns or has jurisdiction over greenway lands, the type of facility being proposed, your ability to choose the labor force, the ability of the labor force to complete prescribed work within the allocated time, and the cost of development based on different labor options.

Pilot Greenway Project
Construction Cost Estimate

Project Item:	"Turn Key" Project Costs:	Materials Only Costs:
Trail and Surfacing Materials		
Asphalt Trail	$84,000	$32,000
Boardwalks	$255,450	$35,000
Construction Materials		
Bridges	$80,000	$36,000
Erosion Control	$9,300	$4,000
Misc.	$3,600	$500
Signage		
Signs	$3,850	$1,450
Bollards	$6,900	$900
Crosswalks	$400	N/A
Landscaping & Site Furnishings		
Seeding	$3,100	$150
Total Greenway/Bikeway:	$446,600	$110,000
Additional/Optional Items:		
Trail and Surfacing Materials		
Sidewalks	$13,500	$5,550
Gravel Spur Trail	$1,450	$900
Boardwalks	$1,200	$300
Construction Materials		
New Curb & Gutter	$12,300	$5,300
Misc.	$2,250	$400
Landscaping & Site Furnishings		
Plant Materials	$2,200	$750
Site Furnishings	$8,000	$3,600
Total Additional/Optional Items:	$40,900	$16,800
5% Contingency Fee:	$24,375	$6,340
Grand Total:	**$511,875**	**$133,140**

Figure 10-4 Example of a preconstruction cost estimate.

Using Government Workers

Communities should consider using existing government employees and labor forces to construct a greenway facility. Government labor may have more time to be thorough and can provide a level of expertise comparable to that of experienced contractors. Like many private contractors, however, the labor force may not have experience in greenway development. Government laborors may also be committed to other duties and responsibilities, which prevent them from completing work in a timely manner.

Hiring a Contractor

Contract labor generally provides the highest degree of construction expertise and efficiency. When you use contract labor, the work program is spelled out in advance, by contract, and performance is a condition of the job. Contract labor will be more expensive than government or volunteer labor, however, and you will usually end up paying for any changes made in the design or schedule.

Using Volunteer Labor

Greenway projects all across the United States have been built by volunteer labor. Although volunteers are enthusiastic and willing to roll up their sleeves to get the job done, they often lack technical expertise. If you plan to use volunteers to implement specific elements of your greenway project, be grateful but prepared. Supply them with a good set of drawings and specifications, double or triple the amount of time needed to complete the work, and offer frequent assistance and supervision. Depending on the complexity of the project, it may be necessary to have someone on site at all times who knows every aspect of the plan and has experience managing volunteer labor.

Construction Administration

The Yakima Greenway protects and enhances the Yakima River corridor, running ten miles from Shelah Gap to Union Gap. The Yakima River Greenway Foundation has developed four river access parks, lakes with fishing piers designed especially for the disabled, two large parks, and a 4.6-mile paved pathway for joggers, bikers, and walkers. Civic groups, businesses, individuals, and governments have contributed to the greenway's development.

In order to ensure that greenway facilities are properly developed, you will need to inspect and formally accept work completed by a contractor, government staff, or volunteers. For government-funded projects, most municipal, county, and state agencies will supply their own certified inspectors. It is also possible to hire an independent inspector, such as a local landscape architect or engineer. For simple greenway projects such as bare earth trails, log footbridges, and benches and signs, an individual who has a basic understanding of construction can adequately perform these duties. More complex projects involving hard-surfaced trails, buildings, boardwalks, and bridges will require the assistance of a certified professional. Construction administration usually includes preparation of a schedule, observation of construction, inspection of completed work, and final approval of the greenway project.

Preparing an Implementation Schedule

Before construction, you should prepare an implementation schedule for all stages of construction. This should describe the labor force and establish milestones for the completion of component parts the greenway project. Schedules can be as simple as a hand-drawn diagram or as sophisticated as a computer-generated timeline chart. It matters little which method is used, as long as a realistic and clear schedule is put together and distributed to all parties involved in implementing the greenway.

Contractor installs subbase material for a concrete multiuse trail. (Robert Searns)

Observation and Inspection

As the greenway facility is being developed, you or your representative should periodically observe the activities. Projects usually change as they progress from plan implementation. At this stage you can work closely with contract labor, in-house staff, or volunteers and make adjustments or changes to the original plan.

You should keep a record of your visits to the site, file regular progress reports, and maintain a log of your observations. This will help to keep track of decisions that were made on site, enable you to accurately chart development progress, and serve as a communication link between the labor force and others.

It is a good idea to request a contractor to control erosion and weeds during construction. Check with the state agriculture department for its list of noxious weeds. There may already be state or local laws on the books to support erosion and weed control.

Inspecting Completed Construction

You or your representative will need to conduct a formal inspection to verify that work has been completed in accordance with drawings and technical specifications. This is a fact-finding review and as such should be conducted in a professional and thorough manner. Usually this will involve a meeting or a series of meetings with an individual representing the labor force. The laborers should accompany you during inspection. They will be able to answer questions regarding the quality of workmanship and interpret drawings and specifications.

You will need to use your original or revised drawings (or both) and specifications to conduct the inspection. Allow plenty of time to inspect all detailed aspects of the work. For example, if you specified a certain post-and-beam construction technique for a boardwalk, you may need to get underneath the boardwalk to ensure that this was used. If the labor force is capable of phasing the work, inspections should be conducted after each phase is completed.

After the inspection you will need to decide whether the work complies with drawings and specifications. If you have hired contract labor and the work does not comply with drawings and specifications, you can withhold payment until the work meets the standards of the contract. If you are working with in-house labor or volunteers, your inspection and acceptance of completed work will allow them to move on to other project elements.

Accepting the Completed Greenway Project

When all parts of the greenway project have been completed, you should conduct a formal and thorough technical review of the entire project in the same professional manner as earlier inspections. From this review, you should generate a *punch list* (items in bulleted form) of work that remains. Provide this list to the labor force as a statement of work that must be completed before final approval.

Formal approval means that you are satisfied that the project meets the standards and recommendations of design drawings and technical specifications, that all work is 100 percent complete, that the contractor, in-house staff, or volunteer labor force has fulfilled its obligations, and that maintenance and liability are now going to be turned over to you, an appropriate agency, or some other entity.

11

Greenway Trail Design

"They should form a framework of parks and forests connected by a series of
paths and trails for general outdoor living."
—Benton MacKaye (1929)

The most common feature of many greenways is a trail; the access trails
provide is a powerful tool to spur people to action. Trails can be on land
or water, serving a wide variety of purposes, such as passive and active
recreation, alternative transportation, and infrastructure maintenance.
There are many types of trails, and many more types of trail users. To
plan and design a successful greenway trail, you need to address the
following key issues:

1. the types of users

2. the type of trail: land or water based, single- or multiple-user oriented

3. how the trail will fit into the existing natural landscape

4. the type and width of the trail tread

5. the type of tread surface

6. the safety of the trail user

The Greenway Trail User

You must first decide which user groups you will accommodate in your
greenway. You should base your decision on an evaluation of the needs
and desires of your community. If you do not design a trail with specific
users in mind, you may well wind up with a trail that promotes conflict
among trail groups and is dangerous to use.

There are many types of trail users: walkers, equestrians, kayakers,
snowmobilers, and so on. Trail users have traditionally been grouped
into two categories: nonmotorized and motorized. We can further divide these into six subcategories: pedestrian, nonmotorized vehicular,
nonmotorized water, pack and saddle animal users, motorized, and motorized water trail users.

Pedestrian Trail Users

Pedestrian trail users are walkers, hikers, joggers, runners, persons confined to a wheelchair, bird-watchers, nature lovers, picnickers, rock
climbers, hunters, cross-country skiers, and a variety of other users who
traverse diverse landscapes on foot in all types of weather and conditions. They move along a trail corridor at a leisurely to slow pace, using

Metropolitan areas like Washington, D.C., and suburban northern Virginia and Maryland are developing coordinated bicycle elements in their new regional transportation plans. The plans are prompted by concerns about increased traffic, air pollution, and bicycle safety. The metropolitan Washington plan calls for the linking of isolated and suburban trails with main bike routes, as well as a bicycle education program. Currently, many component bicycle routes end at jurisdictional boundaries or natural features. Many of the trails parallel all-but-forgotten waterways and are seen as a way to spark interest in stream cleanup.

One of the many back country nature trails that thread through the hills surrounding the San Francisco Bay area. (Loring Schwarz)

little or no mechanical means to increase their speed beyond zero to five miles per hour. Conflicts among members of this group are minor and few. The only user in this category who must be separated from all other user groups for safety reasons is the hunter. (See Table 11-1.)

Nonmotorized Vehicular Trail Users

Nonmotorized vehicular trail users are primarily bicyclists, but also people on rollerblades, skates, and skateboards, and others who use self-propelled, wheeled nonmotorized equipment. They move through a trail corridor at a wide range of speed; the average or most comfortable speed for most users ranges from five to twenty miles per hour. With advances in bicycle design alone during the past ten years, cyclists now represent a broad and diverse subgroup, from the mountain bicyclist

Table 11-1

International Grading System of Walking Difficulty

Level of Difficulty	Walking Time	Distance Traveled	Change in Elevation
Easy	Less than 3 hr	0–6 miles	Start to 1000 ft
Moderately strenuous	3–5 hr	6–12 miles	Start to 2000 ft
Strenuous	5–8 hr	12–15 miles	Start to 3000 ft
Very strenuous	8–10 hr	15–18 miles	Start to 4000 ft
Extremely strenuous	10–12 hr	18–25+ miles	Start to 5000 ft

Source: European Ramblers Association, 1987.

who can ride on most terrain to the ten-speed cyclist who requires a hard smooth-tread surface. (See Table 11-2.)

Nonmotorized Water Trail Users

Nonmotorized water trail users include canoeists, kayakers, those in tubes or on rafts, fishermen, scuba or snorkel divers, sailboaters, pedal-power boaters, sailboarders, and wind surfers. A trail tread does not dictate movement but rather the rate of water flow, wind speed, the size and weight of the water craft, the depth to the bottom of the water course, and the physical ability of the user to direct the craft or his or her own body through the water course. Speed fluctuates dramatically

Table 11-2

Guidelines for Developing Accessible Trails

Checklist: Access to Trails	Checklist: Accessibility of Trails
☐ Accessible parking—federal compliance	☐ Trail is at least 5 ft wide
☐ Accessible passenger loading zones	☐ Trail provides adequate passing lanes
☐ Trail is accessible from parking areas	☐ Surface is stable, firm, slip resistant
☐ Trailhead and parking area are appropriately signed	☐ Running slope of trail is 1:20 to 1:12
☐ Information provided in audio/print format	☐ Trail cross slopes are 1:50
☐ All support facilities are accessible	☐ Trail contains one distinct curb edge
☐ Activity areas are provided for all people	☐ Clear head room is at least 100 inches
☐ Summary information about trail is provided at trailhead—describes trail length, width, slopes, and surfaces	☐ Rest areas provided at 200-ft intervals
	☐ Rest areas are 5 ft by 5 ft in area
	☐ International Symbols of Access used

Source: Architectural and Transportation Barriers Compliance, Washington, D.C., 1981.

Table 11-3

Horse Trail Development Specificaions

Description	Specification
Average speed	5–15 mph
Average ride	1 hr beginner; 6 hr advanced
Recommended trail length	3–5 mi beginners; 20–30 mi advanced
Longitudinal gradient	Ideal 5–10%; maximum 20% for 50 yards
Vegetation clearance (2-horse width)	8 ft minimum width; 12 ft minimum height

among the users within this group. The natural qualities of the water course determine the type of use (see Chapter 12).

Pack and Saddle Animal Trail Users

Pack and saddle animal trail users are composed mainly of equestrians. The tread width is generally similar to that for other land-based users, although the clearance height for horseback riders is greater. The surface of the trail tread should be soft, yet the base must be firm. Speeds fluctuate, depending on the skill of the rider and the user's familiarity with the greenway. (See Table 11-3.)

Motorized Vehicular Trail Users

Motorized vehicular trail users include snowmobilers (see Table 11-4), backcountry jeep users, and those in all-terrain vehicles and on motorbikes. Perhaps the most controversial of all trail users, motorized users are likely to conflict with others because they move much faster and are propelled by noisy engines that emit exhaust fumes. This group is one

Table 11-4

Snowmobile Trail Development Specifications

Description	Specifications
Trail tread width	8 ft min., 10 ft preferred, one-way traffic; 10 ft min., 14 ft preferred, two-way traffic
Turning radius	Flat terrain, 100 ft; hilly terrain, add 15 ft on outside curve
Longitudinal gradient	10–25% ideal
Sight distance	50 ft min.; 100 ft preferred
Bridges and underpasses	10 ft wide with 10 ft vertical

Source: International Snowmobile Association, Washington, D.C., 1990.

Motorized Recreation Code of Ethics

1. I will respect the rights of all recreationists to enjoy the beauty of the outdoors. I will respect public and private property.

2. I will park considerately, taking no more spaces than needed, without blocking other vehicles and without impeding access to trails.

3. I will keep to the right when meeting another recreationist. I will yield the right-of-way to traffic moving downhill.

4. I will slow down and use caution when approaching or overtaking another (trail user).

5. I will respect designated areas, trail use signs, and established trails.

6. When stopping, I will not block the trail.

7. I will not disturb wildlife. I will avoid areas posted for the protection of feeding wildlife.

8. I will pack out everything I packed in and will not litter.

9. I realize that my destination objective and travel speed should be determined by my equipment, ability, the terrain, the weather, and the traffic on the trail. In case of an emergency, I will volunteer assistance.

10. I will not interfere with or harass others. I recognize that people judge all trail users by my actions.

11. I will pull off the trail and stop my engine when encountering horseback riders.

(Courtesy of the Blue Ribbon Coalition, Pocatello, Idaho.)

---

of the fastest growing in the United States and, to some extent, has been unfairly prejudged. Given encouragement, armed with appropriate trail etiquette, and provided with an incentive to improve fuel efficiency, reduce noise levels, and lighten their impact on the environment, this group could become a more integral partner in the trails and greenway community. (Most traditional greenways with low-impact trails and many multiuse trails cannot accommodate motorized use.) The code of ethics for motorized trail use in the box above could serve as a model for minimizing conflicts along multiuse trails.

Motorized Water Trail Users

Motorized water trail users include those in ski boats, electric motor craft, motor boats of varying size, shape, and function, and fishing boats. This group may have an image problem similar to that of land-based motorized trail users. There is certainly potential for conflict between nonmotorized and motorized water trail users, as well as among different motorized users. Evaluation of user speed and skill as well as the characteristics of surface and subsurface water conditions is critical in accommodating this user group.

Types of Greenway Trails

With so many types of users in the United States, there are many types of trails, and elementary though it may seem, it is important to distinguish among them. Building a common vocabulary will be valuable as you define, plan, implement, and manage your greenway. Most trails

Scenic byways, such as the Blue Ridge Parkway in Virginia, or coastal Route 1 in California, protect important scenic and cultural resources and can induce economic development and tourism. Forty-three states have scenic byway programs, which often accommodate partnerships with federal agencies or local governments. Federal agencies (U.S. Forest Service, National Park Service, Bureau of Land Management) manage one-fifth of our nation's scenic byways and often offer guidebooks or visitor centers along the routes. Special features—widened shoulders or pass lanes, scenic overlooks, interpretive signs, and safe areas to pull off the road—can enhance enjoyment.

The multipurpose Shining Sea Rail Trail on Cape Cod connects Falmouth to Woods Hole and is a favorite with locals and tourists alike. (Loring Schwarz)

Indiana's Knobstone Trail, a fifty-eight-mile backcountry hiking trail, was constructed largely by volunteers—the Indianapolis Hiking Club and the Young Adult Conservation Corps. The trail passes through three state forests, which are managed for timber, hunting, and fishing, as well as the Knobstone Escarpment, one of Indiana's most scenic areas.

can be defined within four broad categories: land-based, water-based, single-user, and multiuser routes.

Land-based routes are the most common. These traverse urban, suburban, rural, and wilderness landscapes and are defined by the width and condition of the tread. Whereas some users may wander off the tread, creating alternative pathways or trails, most tend to stay on the defined route. One popular type of land-based trail is the abandoned railroad right-of-way. To date approximately five hundred rail-trails have been created in the nation, spanning more than three thousand miles.

Water-based routes are defined by the width, depth, and navigability of the waterway, as well as its route and the landscape it traverses.

Single-user routes, on land or water, have existed for many decades in the United States and include portions of the Appalachian Trail, which is primarily a walking or hiking trail, National Park and National Forest trails, and canoe or kayak trails limited by the navigability of a water course. The natural conditions of the environment, such as a seasonally inundated white-water course or a sensitive ecological landscape, may dictate whether a trail should be designed single use or multiuse.

Multiuser routes, on land or water, are the most common trails in the United States and represent the model for most future rural, suburban, and urban greenways. Conflict among users is one of the major problems. This is largely the result of an increase in demand for trail resources, increased use of existing limited trails, poor management, underdesigned facilities, lack of user etiquette, and disregard for the varying abilities of trail users.

Greenway Trail Layout

You are ready to select and define an appropriate trail layout. The following tasks are part of designing a greenway trail layout:

1. selecting a configuration

2. positioning the trail within the greenway corridor

3. determining the longitudinal and cross slopes of the corridor landscape that affect trail routing and adjusting trail location and alignment accordingly

4. defining the width of the trail tread based on the projected user groups

5. computing the design load and traffic load for your trail based on projected use

6. identifying the dominant soils along the selected route

7. accommodating drainage patterns and wetlands existing within the greenway corridor

8. delineating the vegetative clearing limits necessary to accommodate your trail and users

After you have routed and aligned your trail, you can more closely examine the detailed requirements of trail treads and the design of the tread cross section.

Selecting a Layout Configuration

It may surprise you to learn that there are several internationally accepted layout configurations for trails. As defined within the Pennsylvania Trails Program's 1980 publication Non Motorized Trails/An Introduction to Planning and Development, trails "must be more than simply the shortest distance between two points. They must have personality." To provide your trail with a unique personality, examine the six types of layout configurations provided on the following pages and select one (or more) that best suits the conditions of your greenway (see Figure 11-1).

Linear layout satisfies the shortest distance between two points and, because of the narrowness of most greenway parcels, is one of the most common layouts used for greenway trails. This pattern can be supplemented with connector spurs, linking several origins and destinations. One major disadvantage is that the user must retrace his or her steps from origin to destination and back to origin. This type is best suited to narrow greenways, where the primary emphasis is linkage, alternative transportation, or shared use with other community facilities such as utilities. It can also be an appropriate configuration if wildlife habitat would be disturbed by an interlacing network of trails or if land

Rock Creek Park, a complex urban greenway connecting historic, cultural and recreational opportunities in metropolitan Washington, D.C., is administered by the National Park Service. The park's main trails connect with many side trails so that users can plan circular routes. Hikers may use any trails, bikes are limited to paved bicycle routes, and horses must stay on equestrian trails, which are wide dirt and gravel bridle trails in the wooded northern section of the park. Hiker trails are maintained by the Potomac Appalachian Mountain Club. A 1.5-mile exercise course attracts joggers and exercise buffs.

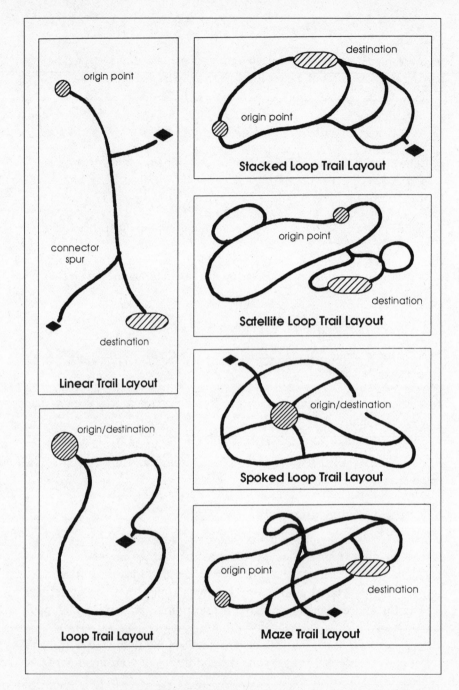

Figure 11-1 Types of trail layouts: linear trail layout, loop trail layout, stacked loop trail layout, satellite loop trail layout, spoked loop trail layout, and maze layout.

ownership dictates that trails can be routed only through selected landholdings.

Loop layout offers more versatility for a variety of greenway trail users. The origin and destination are the same. This type of layout is most effective around lakes and reservoirs, through planned community settings, or within wider greenway lands. This layout requires more land for successful implementation; trail users want to feel as though they have traveled a long distance and at the same time haven't ventured far from the trailhead. The major disadvantage can be lack of variation. The loop is best suited to recreational use, although with proper connector trails, it could serve as a transportation route.

A *stacked loop layout* consists of two or more loops stacked onto a single loop located close to the trailhead. Stacking the loops adds distance and variety to the route. This can be particularly useful if your greenway land varies in elevation and you want to provide optional levels and distances for users to explore and enjoy. A major advantage of this layout is that it provides varying lengths of trail for short-, medium-, and long-distance experiences. In a small greenway setting, this layout is best suited for recreational use for users of varying levels of ability. For a large landholding, for example, around a community of homes, alternative transportation might also be possible.

The *satellite loop layout* provides a series of looped and linear trails that radiate from a central collector loop. This provides users with a primary loop for origin-to-origin walking and offers subloops or connectors to other facilities. For the small greenway landholding, one practical application of this layout would have the main trail serving multiuse needs, while the radiating loops serve single-user groups. Additionally, different theme trails could be developed within the radiating loops. In a larger, regional landscape setting, an entire community might constitute its greenway system using this layout as the basis for development. Raleigh, North Carolina's Capital Area Greenway system is one example. The primary collector is the main trail that circles the core of the community, with radiating loops serving outlying suburban neighborhoods and adjacent rural communities. This layout can serve both recreation and transportation needs.

A *spoked loop layout* includes a series of linear trails that radiate from a central core to a main loop trail. The core could be a smaller circular trail or simply a trailhead. In a small greenway, trail users are never far from the trailhead, no matter how far they travel from the point of origin, and optional lengths and paths of travel are provided. A larger, regional greenway might use this pattern in linking together several communities. San Francisco's Bay Area Trail is one example. This system can serve as recreation or transportation or both.

The *maze layout* offers the maximum number of alternative routes through a series of interlinked looped and linear trails. It also has the greatest variety of distances and number of intersections. This layout will require a large area and the development of a sophisticated sign system so that trail users do not get lost. It is not the best layout for multiuse trails because of the numerous intersections and the complexity of the layout. The structure of the layout offers the best dispersal of users, but if the land area is small, overuse of natural resources can lead to degradation. In the larger greenway setting, origin and destination could be regional communities that are linked by a well-developed system of alternative routes, with certain routes designated exclusively for recreation or alternative transportation.

The creation of a continuous trail around San Francisco Bay focuses attention on the importance of the Bay Area's toll bridges as regional connectors. The proposed Bay Trail Alignment identifies connections across all seven of the Bay Area's toll bridges. Throughout the region, a series of trail loops provide shorter, nonrepetitive excursions for hikers and bicyclists of varying abilities.

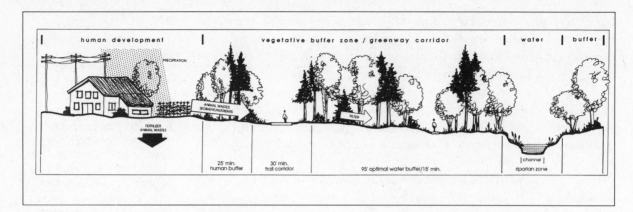

Figure 11-2 Trail location within a corridor.

Positioning Trails within the Greenway Corridor

Once you have selected a layout configuration, you should begin to refine the route by positioning the trail within the greenway. All greenway trails should be compatible with the natural landscape and its functions. This becomes a challenge when trail components or segments must provide safe access or passage through the landscape via bridges and tunnels (see Figure 11-2).

The trail route should be positioned to accommodate the following points:

1. It should blend with the natural contours of the land.

2. It should accommodate all designated users without straining the carrying capacity of the landscape. If the trail cannot accommodate all projected users, you will need to downscale development or schedule activities so that the resource isn't degraded.

3. Safe access and passage must be provided for the users. Safety includes preventing conflict among trail user groups, as well as surmounting hazardous physical conditions.

4. It should stimulate all of the human senses and heighten awareness of the environment.

5. It can be built and maintained in a cost-effective and timely manner. Remember, funding for proper initial development is more easily secured than for long-term maintenance and repair of poorly developed trails.

Trail Slopes

Another important consideration is marrying the trail to existing longitudinal and cross-sectional slopes of the natural terrain. *Longitudinal slopes* are changes in elevation that occur along the running length of the trail. Generally, all trails should flow with, not against, the natural shape of the land within the greenway corridor. Ideally, trails that

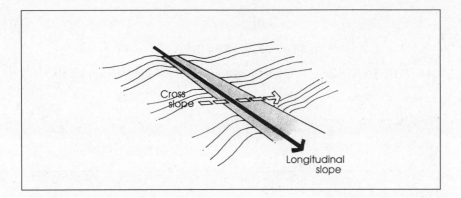

Figure 11-3 Longitudinal and cross slopes.

ascend a hill should do so gradually, at slopes that do not exceed 8 percent, in compliance with federal accessibility laws. This is possible for most landscapes if sufficient land is available; if not, you may be forced to use switchbacks, a portion of trail that reverses direction between 120 and 180 degrees in order to maintain a level grade. Remember that if the trail is accommodating cyclists, leave plenty of room for maneuvering, especially for tandem bikes and bikes with trailers. Trails next to watercourses should parallel the top of the bank of the watercourse and rise and fall with the natural landform. Alterations to the longitudinal slope of a trail are necessary at times; try to keep them to a minimum (see Figure 11-3).

Cross-sectional slopes cross the width of the trail tread, from one side to another. Once a trail is fitted to the natural landform, its cross slope will need to be modified so that the trail tread can accommodate the intended user and naturally drain water from the surface of the tread. The cross slopes for all trails, regardless of type and use, should fall between 1 and 4 percent. The most commonly used cross slope is 2 percent (see Table 11-5). Proper corridor selection and proper subgrade preparation will result in economy of surfacing materials. It is a good idea to consult a professional to determine the most appropriate slope.

Table 11-5

Trail Design Recommendations for Longitudinal and Cross Slopes

Trail User	Average Speed (mph)	Longitudinal Slopes	Cross Slope
Hiker	3–5	No restriction	4% max.
Disabled pedestrian	3–5	2% prefer, 8% max.	2% prefer
Bicyclist	8–15	3% prefer, 8 % max.	2–4%
Horseback rider	5–15	5% prefer, 10% max.	4% max.
Cross-country skier	2–8	3% prefer, 5% max.	2% prefer
Snowmobiler	15–40	10% prefer, 25% max.	2–4% max.

Table 11-6	
AASHTO Standard Tread Width for Bicycle-only Trails	
AASHTO Standards	**Recommended Minimum Width**
One-way bicycle travel, single lane	5-ft
Two-way bicycle travel, dual lanes	10-ft
Three lanes of bicycle travel	12.5-ft

Trail Tread Width

Typically, the width of a tread will depend on the amount of available land within the boundaries of the project, the type of users that will be permitted access to the trail, the potential for conflict among users, environmental sensitivity, and the cost of constructing a trail type. Individual treads can be as narrow as twenty inches for hikers in remote wilderness terrain or as wide as twenty feet for multiple users in congested urban areas.

National guidelines for trail treads have existed for years, most of them developed by individual states or national organizations. Standard widths have been developed primarily for single-user groups, not for multiple-use trails.

For example, national standards for bicycle trails were prescribed by the American Association of State Highway Transportation Officials (AASHTO) in the 1970s. Standards were updated in 1991 with commuter transportation in mind. Many communities, however, have adopted AASHTO guidelines not only for bicycle facility development but also for the development of multiuse recreational trails. Note that if greenways can be designed to uphold AASHTO standards, it will be much

Table 11-7	
Recommended Trail Tread Widths for User-Specific Trails	
Trail User Type	**Recommended Tread Width**
Bicyclist	10 ft (2-way travel)
Hiker/walker/jogger/runner	4 ft rural; 5 ft urban
Cross-country skier	8–10 ft for 2-track trail
Snowmobile	8-ft groomed surface for 1-way traffic; 10-ft goomed surface for 2-way traffic
Off-road vehicle	5-ft for 2-wheeled vehicles; 7-ft for 3- or 4-wheeled vehicles
Equestrain	4-ft tread; 8-ft cleared width
Wheelchair accessible	5-ft (1-way travel)

Courtesy of the State of Iowa Department of Natural Resources.

easier to qualify for Department of Transportation funds. (See Table 11-6.)

The state of Iowa developed a Statewide Recreational Trails Plan in 1990, which provides recommended widths for different trails based on user type and a set of sophisticated engineering principles that accommodates the travel dynamics of the user. (See Table 11-7.)

After reviewing numerous individual state plans, federal standards, and community-based plans, we have developed and include a set of *minimum* standards for greenway multiuse trail treads for rural, suburban, and urban landscapes (see Table 11-8). These do not apply to wilderness and ecologically sensitive lands. For these, see the section on "Low Impact/Low Intensity Uses."

Planners of urban and suburban recreational greenways of 8-ft diameter often regret not planning a wider trail. Heavy use by walkers and bicyclists and the introduction of rollerbladers can crowd a path and create user conflicts.

Low-Impact Trail Treads

As you plan your trail system, do not assume that all environments can be modified to accept a multiuse trail. After evaluating your greenway, you may determine that a low-impact trail is best suited to a specific landscape and whether certain uses (bicycles, horses) must be restricted. There are three factors to consider: environmental suitability of a particular use, the intensity of use, and the design and development of the trail tread. Table 11-9 provides a broad measure for use suitability.

Table 11-8 Minimum Recommended Tread Widths for Multiuse Trails (in feet)			
Tread Type	Urban	Suburban	Rural
Single-tread, multiple use			
Pedestrian/nonmotorized	12	10	10
Pedestrain/saddle and pack animal	16	12	10
Pedestrian/motorized	22	22	16
Nonmotorized/saddle and pack animal	16	16	—
Motorized/saddle and pack animal (not recommended for simultaneous use			
Motorized/nonmotorized	22	16	16
Multiple tread, multiple use (each tread)			
Pedestrian only, 2-way travel	8	8	6
Nonmotorized only, dual travel	10	10	10
Saddle and pack animal, dual travel	8	8	8
Motorized use only, dual travel	16	16	6

Table 11-9

Environmental Suitability of Use within Sensitive Environments

Ecological Sensitivity	Type of Use					
	No Access	Walking	Bicycling	Equestrian	Snowmobile	OHV
Low (upland terrace, stable-rocky soils and mature forest)	O	●	●	●	●	◐
Moderate (lowland terrace, river valley, suitable soils, successional forest)	◐	●	◐	◐	O	O
High (wetlands, primary dunes, pocosins, steep slopes, hydric soils)	●	◐	O	O	O	O

Closed circles, most suitable; half-filled circles, suitable; open circles, not suitable.

Intense trail use of any kind can damage an ecologically sensitive landscape. For example, excessive hiking along a bare-earth trail can do as much damage in one year as allowing a limited number of off-road vehicles to access the same trail for a couple of days. Anticipating the intensity of use is difficult. No hard data currently define intensive versus nonintensive use. Table 11-10 compiles available research and opinion from interviews with experts and user groups.

If you decide to provide access through a sensitive ecological landscape, you should consider several design issues determining the short- and long-term impact, including on-grade versus elevated trail treads, the impact of trail construction, and the selection of the trail surface.

To design a trail tread with minimal impact on sensitive landscape, you should first determine if a trail can occur on grade or if it should be elevated with a boardwalk. If any trail at all might encourage overuse, you might need to rethink your route.

In designing a trailhead you must consider (a) the suitability of the soil mass—if the soil is seasonally under water, you will need to install an elevated walk; (b) the fragility of the ecosystem—some landscapes

Table 11-10

Intensity of Trail Use

User Type	Low-Intensity Use	Medium-Intensity Use	High-Intensity Use
Pedestrians/walkers	2 PFM[a] or less	10–15 PFM	25 PFM
Bicyclists	50 ADBT[b] or less	250 ADBT	1000 ADBT
Equestrians	4 HTD[c] or less	20 HTD	100 HTD
Snowmobiles	100 ADT[d] or less	200 ADT	1000 ADT

[a] PFM, pedestrians per foot width or walkway/minute; source: Timesaver Standards for Landscape Architects.
[b] ADBT, average daily bicycle trip; source: Rhode Island Department of Transportation.
[c] HTD, horses per 6 foot trail/day; source: American Horse Council.
[d] ADT, average daily trips; source: International Association of Snowmobile Administrators.

are too fragile to permit on-grade human access; and (c) the type of users allowed access.

You should also determine the impact that trail construction will have on the ecosystem. Boardwalk construction can require heavy machinery to drive support piers into the ground. You may want to alter your design to allow an ecologically sound method of construction.

If you are able to install the trail tread on-grade, the selection of surface materials becomes critical. Natural surface materials blend well with the environment; you must be certain, however, that they are capable of supporting designated uses.

Other environmental impacts can be minimized through proper design. Clearing of vegetation can be reduced to protect plants and animal habitat. Human intrusion can be minimized by installing appropriate fencing between the trail and protected landscapes. Soil erosion can be mitigated by using the trail surface to control drainage and by installing open drainage ditches on both sides of the trail. Trail widths can be reduced to single-lane paths that flow in one direction. Using this design philosophy as the basis for trail layout, a minimum width for hiking trails would be two feet, for bicycles five feet, for equestrians four feet, and for snowmobiles five feet.

Design Load

The design load of a trail is its maximum carrying weight at any point along its length. To derive the design load of a greenway trail, you need to compute the weight of maintenance and emergency vehicles and compare this against the combined structural support properties of the subgrade, subbase, and surface. The minimum design load thus would be based on the static wheel load or axle loadings of an emergency vehicle, which for most communities in the United States is 2.6 tons, or 6,250 pounds, or the gross vehicle weight, which is 6.25 tons, or 12,500 pounds. The maximum speed for vehicles that equal or exceed the weight of your design load should be fifteen miles per hour. If your trail will be used frequently by vehicles that equal or exceed your design load, you should have your trail surface design evaluated by a civil engineer to determine the travel loading along the trail and whether a stronger cross section is needed.

The Impact of Native Soils

One of the most important structural factors of the greenway trail is the composition of native soils. Soils, the product of bedrock, organic matter, and drainage patterns, are the foundation of the natural landscape. Your local Soil Conservation Service can test and describe the soils within the greenway corridor, usually at no cost. Soil Conservation Service staff can evaluate soil type. Soil type is a description of the soil based on the content and composition of clay, silt, sand, or gravel; the soil wetness; its shrink or swell capacity, which is the way in which the soil expands and contracts when influenced by water and temperature; and its suitability for development. The resulting rating given to various

In Stowe, Vermont, the recreation trail route was chosen in consultation with landowners. Their greatest concern was not to lose the usefulness of their land, so the desired location was along the top of the river bank. Path location also considered aesthetics, grade, alignment, cost, view, access, and impact. The path location was finalized by the engineer, landowners, and path coordinator.

classifications of soil types is based on the soil's ability to support certain types of urban land uses.

The most conclusive method for determining soil stability is to employ a geotechnical soils testing engineer and have core samples taken from selected sites along the route. Soil coring can be done by hand but is more often completed by machines. Geotechnical testing can provide accurate information about the soil mass, including composition, load-bearing ability, permeability, and depth to bedrock. The only drawback is the cost of the service.

In determining the layout of your trail, you want to avoid soft, waterlogged, and unsuitable soils if at all possible. Because many greenways tend to be located within floodplains, this will be difficult. Where you do encounter soft soils, you will have three design and development options to consider: the use of geotextile fabrics to improve the strength of the pavement cross section for your trail, installation of a boardwalk through the soft soil area, or undercutting existing soft soils and replacing them with compacted clay soil or aggregates, or both. Although it is a common practice in roadway and highway construction, undercutting for greenway trails is expensive or may be restricted.

The Impact of Drainage on Greenway Trail Location

Proper drainage of surface and subsurface waters is an important consideration when siting and constructing the trail. Your goal is to achieve a hard and dry trail tread that drains excess water. Two types of drainage concern the trail designer: surface runoff and subsurface runoff. Surface runoff moves through rills, troughs, intermittent streams, creeks, and drainage canals into streams, rivers, and lakes. Subsurface runoff moves through soil in a horizontal and vertical fashion. The rate of subsurface flow depends on the type of soil present within the subgrade and can be defined as a measurement of permeability. A hydrologist can assist you in identifying the type of drainage in your greenway corridor. Don't cut costs by installing poor drainage systems. Correcting drainage problems is often the number one maintenance cost for many greenways.

The trail designer must address problems of on-site and off-site surface and subsurface runoff. Proper drainage can (1) prevent the erosion of the subgrade and subbase by accommodating surface water flow, (2) mitigate the effects of flooding by providing areas where floodwaters can be absorbed naturally or by structures that allow floodwaters to pass through or around the trail cross section without damaging the trail, (3) maintain or improve the water quality of adjacent or perpendicular streams and water courses, and (4) ensure that wildlife habitat is not permanently disturbed by the trail.

The environmental objective for controlling on-site drainage is to maintain preexisting rainwater exit flows, because increased water flow could speed erosion and sedimentation. Likewise, your aim for accommodating off-site drainage is to avoid permanently obstructing, or significantly altering, the environment as a result of trail development.

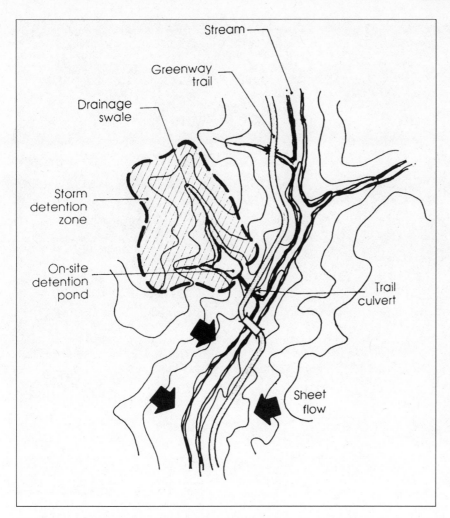

Figure 11-4 Open drainage system.

Urbanized areas, subject to new federal laws governing storm-water management, may have extensive requirements for on-site and off-site drainage control. Check with your municipal engineering office for local requirements.

Abandoned railroad corridors are one type of trail that may have drainage structures with historically established drainage release capacities. Converting railroads to trail use may alter existing storm-water management controls. You should seek the advice of a professional hydrologist or engineer to ensure that trail improvements will not cause upstream or downstream flooding or have other detrimental impacts.

Several methods can be used to mitigate surface water and subsurface water runoff. For surface water runoff there are three options: (1) an open drainage system (see Figure 11-4), which uses swales, ditches, and sheet flow, combined with on-site detention ponds to absorb excess surface water flow; (2) a closed system, which utilizes built, underground structures, such as catch basins, drain inlets, culverts, or underground piping and hardened outlet structures to contain excess surface water flow; and (3) a combination of an open and closed system, where

Greenway users relax on a boardwalk constructed over a cattail wetland on the Bicentennial Greenway in Guilford County, North Carolina. (Terri Musser)

flows are divided and directed to different systems based on the local conditions of the site. For greenways an open drainage system should be used whenever possible, since it is the most natural and cost-effective approach. Some of the drainage techniques explained in the Appalachian Mountain Club's publication *Trail Construction and Maintenance* include coweeta dips (leveling the trail periodically), bleeders (angled drainage depressions), water bars (diverting water via half-buried diagonally placed rocks or logs), and log steps in the trail.

The methods for mitigating subsurface water runoff are limited to various underground drainage techniques, which include (1) installation of perforated or porous clay tile ("field tile") or metal, plastic, or concrete underdrain piping to carry excess water from the subsurface of the trail cross section; (2) the construction of a french drain, a trench filled with permeable material such as stone or sand that collects water and routes it toward a surface drainage system; and (3) sloped and contoured underground drainage channels, where subsurface water is encouraged to flow through the trail cross section unimpeded. The technique that works best depends on local conditions. Remember that good trail layout and alignment can significantly reduce the number of drainage structures required. If you encounter difficult or large-scale drainage problems, seek advice from a professional landscape architect or environmental engineer, or work with your local Soil Conservation Service or Cooperative Extension Service representative.

Jurisdictional Wetlands

Jurisdictional wetlands are lands and waters that come under the jurisdictional control of the U. S. Army Corps of Engineers, the U. S. Fish and Wildlife Service, and the U .S. Environmental Protection Agency. Americans should be alert to the dwindling remains of wetland, their many environmental values, and how to protect them from encroachment and destruction. Three criteria are normally used to determine if a landscape is a jurisdictional wetland: the presence of (1) hydric soils, (2) surface ponds that exist for a defined period, and (3) vegetation that typically grows in lowland or wet soil conditions.

The best way to protect wetlands in your greenway is through the construction of boardwalks, observation decks, bridges, or some other form of elevated structure. Natural footpaths can also be developed. If so, trail users should be informed of the importance of keeping to the designated pathway in this fragile environment.

Some construction through jurisdictional wetlands and floodplains will require a permit from the U. S. Army Corps of Engineers, as a requirement of the Clean Water Act, Section 404. You will also need to check with state or local agencies to find out if local wetland ordinances exist. The use of impermeable surfaces and fill material in jurisdictional wetlands is usually discouraged and may be prohibited. If your trail crosses wetlands, be sure to contact your local environmental official, a professional consultant with wetlands expertise, your local Soil Conservation Service, the U. S. Army Corps of Engineers, or the U. S. Fish and Wildlife Service, or local government. Be aware that federal and state wetland guidelines and definitions may change from year to year.

The McAlpine Greenway, part of the Mecklenburg County, North Carolina, greenway system, has developed separate trails for bikeways, cross country jogging, and nature study. A nine-hundred-foot boardwalk winds through a low-lying area and enhances the natural experience. Spur trails provide access for neighborhoods along the greenway.

Vegetation Clearing for Greenway Trails

In implementing your trail, you will be concerned with two types of vegetation clearing: horizontal (clearance on either side of the trail) and vertical (clearance above the trail tread surface). Vegetative clearing should be kept to a minimum to lessen the impact on wildlife habitat and provide a natural setting. Safety and security are of prime importance in determining clearing limits.

Clearing can be wholesale or selective. Selective clearing, or thinning, involves the careful removal of specific trees, shrubs, large rocks, and obstructions to open views along the edge of the trail. In wholesale clearing, all vegetation is removed, as on the route of the trail itself. After wholesale clearing of the trail, you must "grub" the soil of remaining roots, rocks, and other loose impediments. Grubbing the soil is usually accomplished with small tractors or bulldozers. Organizations like the Appalachian Mountain Club, however, have historically relied on local

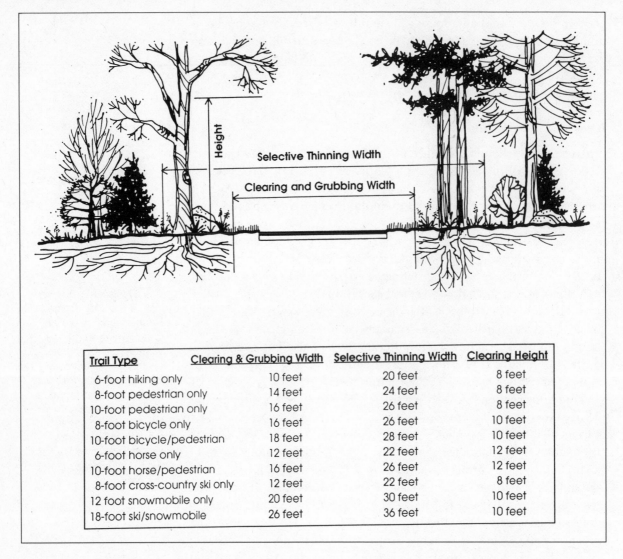

Trail Type	Clearing & Grubbing Width	Selective Thinning Width	Clearing Height
6-foot hiking only	10 feet	20 feet	8 feet
8-foot pedestrian only	14 feet	24 feet	8 feet
10-foot pedestrian only	16 feet	26 feet	8 feet
8-foot bicycle only	16 feet	26 feet	10 feet
10-foot bicycle/pedestrian	18 feet	28 feet	10 feet
6-foot horse only	12 feet	22 feet	12 feet
10-foot horse/pedestrian	16 feet	26 feet	12 feet
8-foot cross-country ski only	12 feet	22 feet	8 feet
12 foot snowmobile only	20 feet	30 feet	10 feet
18-foot ski/snowmobile	26 feet	36 feet	10 feet

Figure 11-5 Vegetative clearing.

volunteers to grub soil mass. Grubbing is not the last step in clearing. Continuous monitoring, pruning, and shaping are necessary as your trail matures (see Figure 11-5).

Trail Tread Standards

The following are six different types of treads for land-based trails (see Figures 11-6 and 11-7). The type you choose depends on the number of different user groups you intend to accommodate.

Single-Tread, Single-Use Trails

Single-tread, single-use trails can include trails within street, road, or highway rights-of-way, off-road trails and sidewalks outside of rights-of-ways, and other pedestrian ways and trails that meander through a variety of urban, suburban, rural, or wilderness landscapes.

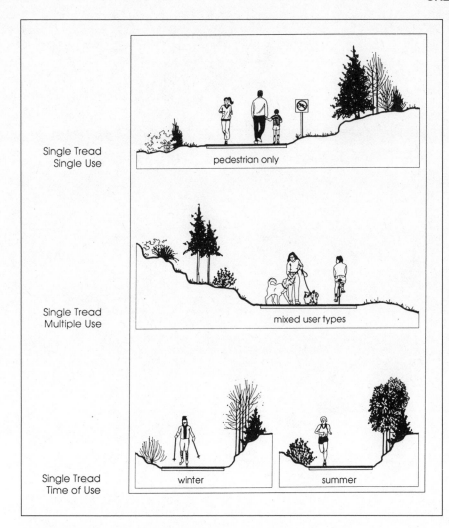

Single Tread
Single Use

pedestrian only

Single Tread
Multiple Use

mixed user types

Single Tread
Time of Use

winter

summer

About twenty years ago, John Varvaryanis noticed several large publicly owned, mostly contiguous parcels that, if connected, could provide eight miles of trail for densely suburban Westchester County, New York. Varvaryanis and other trail advocates affiliated with Appalachian Mountain Club and began a series of presentations to municipalities, which then granted permission to mark trails through public land. More challenging tasks included convincing parkway authorities to provide a 216-foot link for the trail and persuading bridle path overseers to allow hikers to use their trails. Varvaryanis, a Bronx biology teacher, almost singlehandedly groomed and blazed the trail. Work on the Westchester Greenway was inspired by the 1984 "Westchester 2000" planning study, which recommended connecting large parks when possible.

Figure 11-6 Types of trail treads: single-tread/single-use, single-tread/multiple-use, single-tread/time of use.

Single-Tread, Multiple-Use Trails

Single-tread, multiple-use trails are the most common type in the nation. These trails vary in width, from eight to more than twenty feet. Some have usage-control features, such as signs or striping to separate trail users.

Single Tread, Time of Use Trails

Single tread, time of use is a relatively new concept in the United States. Time of use permits different groups to use single-tread trails at different times of the day, week, month, or year. This concept allows all trail users to enjoy the same facility by removing potential conflict among them.

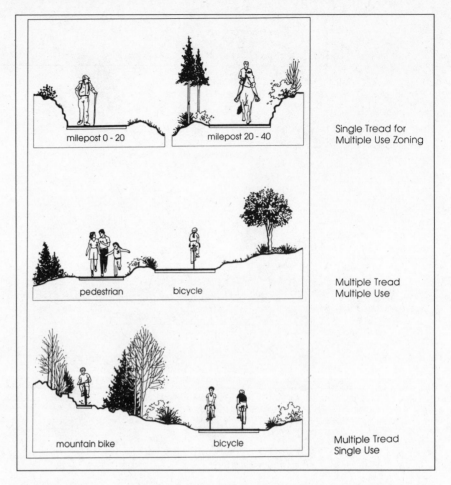

Figure 11-7 Types of trail treads: single tread/zoning for multiple use, multiple tread/multiple use, multiple tread/single use.

Single-Tread, Zoning for Multiple-Use Trails

Single-tread, zoning for multiple-use trails, also a relatively new concept in the United States, provides different segments of a trail to different users. For example, if a trail is thirty miles long, walkers could use a trail segment between mileposts zero and ten, bikers could ride between mileposts ten and twenty, and horseback riders could ride between mileposts twenty and thirty.

Multiple-Tread, Multiple-Use Trails

Multiple-tread, multiple-use trails allow for multiple use within the same right-of-way but on separate treads. This generally requires a wider right-of-way to accommodate the diversity of users. For example, a hard-surfaced trail would be developed for bicycle use, a walking path would meander along an unsurfaced earth trail, and a boardwalk could be extended into riparian areas. All of these treads could be developed in parallel along the entire corridor or a portion of it.

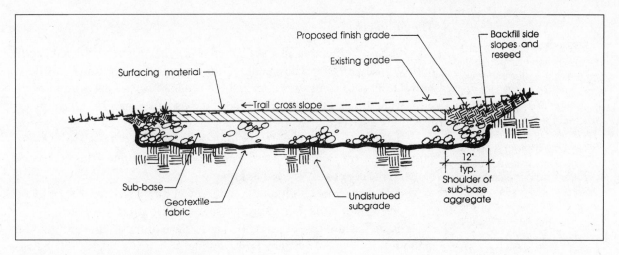

Figure 11-8 Trail tread cross section.

Multiple-Tread, Single-Use Trails

Multiple-tread, single-use trails most often accommodate different skill levels or the speeds of different users. This trail type is rare and usually developed by an organization that directly supports the single-user group, such as a walking or jogging club.

Designing the Trail Tread Cross Section

After you have determined the route and alignment of your trail tread, you will be able to design the trail tread cross section. For constructed land-based trails the cross section consists of subgrade, subbase, geotextile fabrics, and surfacing material (see Figure 11-8).

The Subgrade

The subgrade is the undisturbed earth of the corridor or, as in the case of existing railroad beds, placed and compacted fill material consisting of clay or aggregates. It is the primary foundation for the greenway trail. Because trails are built in many different landscapes, you could encounter any of several different types of subgrades. Subgrade suitability refers to the subgrade's ability to accommodate a greenway trail *without* drastic alterations or overly expensive development solutions.

A highly suitable subgrade for a greenway trail is one that contains moderate slopes, good drainage, and firm, dry soils. Because the subgrade ultimately receives all of the load or weight on the surface of the trail, it is important that the subgrade be structurally capable of supporting the trail design load. The subgrade must also be sloped, by crowning the tread (making the center of the tread higher than the outer edges) or establishing a cross slope to provide proper drainage of surface and subsurface waters.

The East Bay Bike Path is a unique transportation facility and the first major undertaking by the Rhose Island Department of Transportation to create a state-owned bicycle path in Rhode Island. Citizens will find the path a welcome transportation route, using the facility to ride to work, to shop, to attend school, or to enjoy the eight state parks along the way. The path is approximately 14.5 miles long, extending from India Point Park in Providence to Independence Park in Bristol. Constructed primarily along an inactive rail line, the path offers some of the state's most scenic views of coastline, estuaries, and woodlands. The bikeway has a ten-foot-wide asphalt paved path with grass shoulder embankments and appropriate warning signs as it intersects forty-nine streets along its route.

The Subbase

The subbase is the area of the trail cross section between the subgrade and the trail surface. The primary function of this secondary, artificial foundation is to transfer and distribute the load or weight from the surface of the trail to the subgrade. The subbase also serves vital drainage functions, preventing water from migrating up from the subgrade into the surface of the trail and allowing natural cross drainage to flow through the trail cross section. The subbase is usually constructed of stone, typically coarse graded aggregate.

The subbase can be either hand or machine placed and should be compacted with a mechanical roller that weighs at least as much as the designated design load of the trail. The surface of the subbase should be smooth and level. Any defects that remain in the subbase will be reflected in the surface of the trail.

Geotextile Fabrics

Geotextiles are woven and nonwoven fabric mats used to strengthen the subgrade, subbase, and surface of a trail, especially in areas where soft or unsuitable soils are present. Geotextiles, which have several functions, are most commonly used to separate the subgrade from the subbase and trail surface and to reinforce the trail cross section. They maintain the composition and integrity of the subbase material and prevent this material from migrating into the subgrade—one of the most common causes of cross-section and surface failure. By keeping the subbase intact, they ensure the strength and long life of the trail. Geotextiles can expedite construction schedules and reduce excavation quantities, as well as the amount of required subbase material.

The fabric is normally purchased in large rolls that contain several hundred yards of material and that can be cut by the supplier to fit a specific trail width. The material is rolled out onto the prepared surface and secured with nails or tucked into place by hand. The fabric should be extended at least one foot beyond the designated width of the trail tread. Overlap fabric ends by three feet to ensure that the geotextile fabric remains in place as you install the subbase.

The selection of a fabric, woven or nonwoven, depends completely on the type of trail project. Local conditions will determine which type and weight are best. You should consult a geotechnical engineer to assist in choosing the right product.

Surface Materials

By now you should be prepared to select a surface for your trail. The tread surface almost always will be selected on the basis of the type and intensity of trail use. In selecting a surface material you should examine those that are unique to your region and the range of materials that best depict the local character of your community. This will individualize your trail surface and the experience, distinguishing it from trails in other parts of the country. Keep in mind that indigenous surfacing material must also meet your other greenway design criteria. Surfacing material should give you a firm, even, and dry trail tread, capable of supporting the designated users. In making your selection you should also consider the availability of the surface material, its cost to purchase and install, its life expectancy, the maintenance required, and user satisfaction. Try to get an opinion from a licensed engineer about alternative opportunities for surfacing.

Materials that can be used to surface a trail include asphalt, concrete, wood, soil hardeners, gravel, limestone, crusher fines, sand, wood chips or bark, brick or masonry, cobblestone, and grass. Surface materials are categorized as either hard or soft. The primary distinction between the two is based on the ability of a material to absorb rather than repel moisture. Soft surface materials include earth, grass, hardwood bark, and wood decking. Hard surface materials include stone or rock, asphalt, brick, and concrete.

Soft surface materials are the most common trail surfaces in the United States. With the exception of wood decking, they are the least expensive type to install and the most compatible with the natural environment. A soft surface may not be the most practical, however, as most do not hold up well under intensive use and are subject to rapid deterioration. With the exception of wood decking, soft surface materials tend to be specified for low impact and low-intensity use. Soft surface materials, although less expensive to install, generally require more maintenance than hard surface materials, given equivalent subgrade and subbase preparation.

Although usually more expensive, hard surface materials are more practical for multiuse urban and suburban trails. Most hard surface materials, while not inherently compatible with the native environment, can blend well with certain landscapes. Hard surfaces require less maintenance because they better absorb the impact of repeated use.

The following materials offer both traditional and innovative solutions that have been used throughout the country. Remember that there may be local and regional variations in material type and that they may have different names (see Figures 11-9 and 11-10). Table 11-11 gives approximate installation costs for different surface materials, and Table 11-12 summarizes the advantages and disadvantages of trail surface types.

Natural surface "unprepared" tread trails are the oldest and most common type. They make use of rock, soil, water, forest litter, sand, snow, ice, pine mulch, leaf mulch, and other native materials. Preparation varies from machine-worked surfaces to those worn only by usage. Proper drainage is the key to optimal functioning of this trail surface. A well-drained subgrade and properly sloped trail will ensure its long life. Drainage can be dispersed in a sheet flow across the trail surface or collected in side ditches and routed to a crossing at a low point in the trail. Longitudinal slopes can vary greatly, up to 15 percent, though cross slopes should not exceed 4 percent. Natural surface trails require some maintenance, depending on the type and amount of use on a given segment of the trail. Most maintenance will involve repair to eroded areas

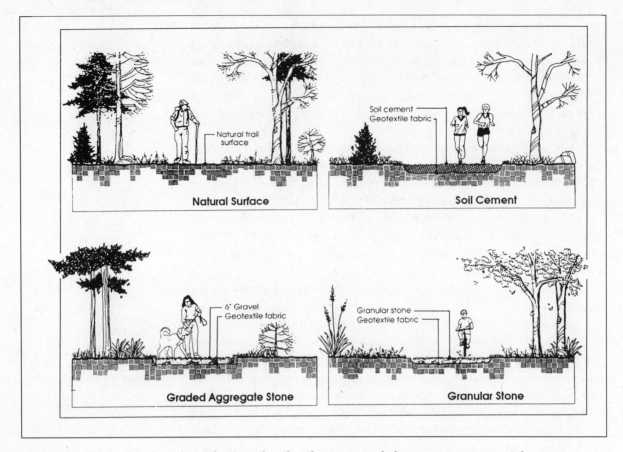

Figure 11-9 Types of surfaces for trails: natural trail, soil cement, graded aggregate stone, granular stone.

or removal of vegetation. This is the most appropriate surface for eco-logically sensitive greenways.

Soil cement is a mixture of pulverized native soil and measured amounts of portland cement. It is usually mixed at the project site and applied immediately after mixture. The mixture is then rolled and com-pacted into a dense surface by machinery. Soil cement can be placed on longitudinal slopes that do not exceed 8 percent and cross slopes not ex-ceeding 2 percent. To prevent water erosion, sheet flow can be per-mitted on longitudinal slopes of 4 percent and less; if the slope is steeper, you should crown the trail tread and direct water flow in side ditches to a low point crossing. Soil cement will support most user groups, though bicyclists and horseback riders should have only re-stricted use. Soil cement surfaces last longer if installed on top of a pro-perly prepared subgrade and subbase. Maintain them as you would a natural surface.

Graded aggregate stone is mined from natural deposits or formations. The variety of aggregate stone material suitable for trail surfacing in-cludes colored rock, pea gravel, river rock, washed stone, and coarse sand. Graded aggregate stone is a good surface for greenway trails be-cause it is locally available in most communities, easy to install, main-tain, and replenish, and accommodates the needs of a wide range of users within a single tread width. The manufacturing process for

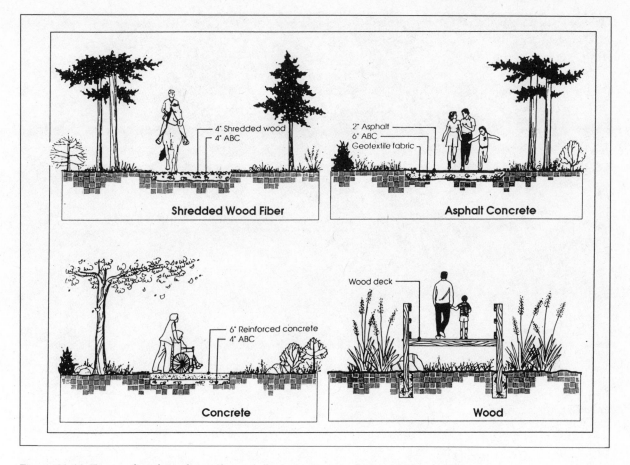

Figure 11-10 Types of surfaces for trails: asphalt, concrete, wood, shredded wood fiber.

graded aggregate washes out most finer-grained stone, resulting in a loose surface. As a result, graded aggregate is limited in application to flatter or more gently rolling slopes than granular stone because it remains a loose uncompacted surface. Thus, it is not recommended for bicycle trails or for use on wheelchair-accessible trails.

Table 11-11

Approximate Installation Costs for Different Surface Materials

Surface Material Type	Cost/sq. ft	Cost/linear ft (10 ft wide)	Cost/Mile
Bare earth	$0.50	$5.00	$25,400
Groomed snow	$0.75	$7.50	$39,600
Hardwood bark	$1.00	$10.00	$52,800
Limestone screenings	$1.25	$12.50	$66,000
Asphalt concrete	$2.00	$20.00	$105,600
Reinforced concrete	$5.00	$50.00	$264,000
Wood deck	$25.00	$250.00	$1.32 million

Includes subgrade preparation, installation of subbase with geotextile fabric, and placement of surface type.

In this greenway, a multiuse paved trail parallels an equestrian trail. (Lisa Gutierrez)

Graded aggregate stone will often need to be kept in place with wood or metal edging. Drainage is not much of a problem for this surface type; water can flow in sheets through and across the surface. The longitudinal slope for this surface should be no greater than 5 percent; the cross slope should not exceed 2 percent. As with soil cement and natural surfaces, vegetation that grows in the trail tread must be controlled.

Granular stone includes a broad range of aggregate stone, such as limestone, sandstone, crushed rock, pit gravel, chat, cinders, chert, sand, and fine gravel. This is one of the best surface types for greenway trails because it can be densely compacted, holds up well, and is compatible with the natural environment. If properly constructed, it can support bicycle and accessible trail development. Subgrade and subbase preparation is the same as for a graded aggregate surface. Drainage can sheet flow across the surface, or the trail bed can be crowned and surface water directed toward side ditches. Longitudinal slopes should not exceed 8 percent, and cross slopes should be limited to 2 percent. Maintenance of this surface should be minimal, depending on usage. Because the fine-grained stone retains moisture, vegetation will readily grow in this surface. Heavy use is the best preventive program to keep vegetation in check.

Shredded wood fiber is usually composed of mechanically shredded hardwood and softwood pulp, pine bark chips or nuggets, chipped wood pieces, or other by-products of tree trunks and limbs. This type of surface is favored by joggers and runners, equestrians, and walkers because it is soft, it blends with the natural environment, and it does not leach foreign or toxic material into the environment. It decays rapidly, however, when exposed to excesses of moisture, sun, wind, and heat. It must be installed on flat subgrades with appropriate longitudinal and cross drainage. Subgrade and subbase preparation is the same as for other surfaces, except that cross drainage must not be allowed. The trail tread should be crowned with a maximum of 2 percent side slopes. Longitudinal slopes should also be limited to less than 5 percent. Surface thickness, at the time of installation, should be no less than three inches. Maintenance requires replacement of the entire surface every two years. In areas like the Pacific Northwest, this surface may be ideal because generous supplies are available from local lumber mills.

Asphalt concrete is a hard surface material that is popular for a variety of rural, suburban, and urban greenways. It is composed of asphalt cement and graded aggregate stone. If you use a coarse-graded stone, you will have a rougher and a more porous pavement. If you use a larger proportion of asphalt cement, the surface will be smoother and less porous. Asphalt concrete is a flexible pavement, which means that it will form itself to the shapes and contours of the subbase and subgrade. Asphalt can be installed on virtually any slope. Longitudinal slopes can vary up to 20 percent; cross slopes are usually constructed not to exceed 2 percent but can exceed 4 percent. Drainage should be encouraged to sheet flow across the trail (contrary to the common claim, asphalt pavement will not "bubble up" or float away under normal surface drainage flow).

Asphalt trails require little maintenance if properly designed and installed. As with other porous pavement, they require continuous use; to prevent agressive plants from invading the surface and eventually destroying the asphalt. The asphalt trail should be coated with a special sealant, particularly where it is exposed to the sun for long periods of time. To reduce the unraveling of the pavement edges, the trail should be recompacted periodically by a mechanical roller.

Concrete surfaces are capable of withstanding the most powerful environmental forces. Most often, concrete is used for intensive urban applications. Concrete can be installed on longitudinal slopes that exceed 8 percent and cross slopes that exceed 4 percent. It comes in several raw forms, including a thick liquid that is poured from a remix truck or on-site mixing machine and a solid precast form that is available in a variety of modular units. Concrete is the only surface that can be formed vertically, horizontally, or through a range of angles and artfully tailored at the time of installation. It can also be colored, formed, or stamped into different patterns and shapes, poured into smooth curves, and finished with a variety of surface textures.

Concrete is a heavy, nonporous pavement. Of all surface types, it is the strongest and has the lowest maintenance requirement if it is

Learning from Mistakes

I saw this trail when it was just flagging on trees and assumed that some bridges and fill structures would have to be used to reduce the steep center-line profiles and cross-sectional sideslopes. Instead, the trail was constructed with a minimum of grading work, resulting in gradients *easily* in excess of 15 percent—my roadbike experienced "wheelslip" in some spots. The alignment chosen would have made sense only if some real-world consideration had been given to grading, drainage, the needs of children on single speed bikes, and disabled users. Instead, the severe trail slopes are connected by sharp curves which are washed over by sheet drainage flow. This layout could have been made user-friendly via culvert pipes and fill, which would have also provided upland storage of the significant runoff from the adjoining road corridor and other tributary flows, as well as reduced erosive velocities and the conveyance of silt into the lake.

Worse yet, during the construction of this trail, the aggregate subbase was in place for months prior to the asphalt paving, resulting in tremendous amounts of quality material being washed into the lake—a backup to the city water supply no less. When the pavement finally was placed on (what remained of) of the subbase, it was immediately covered the full width of the trail for stretches of 20 feet, 50 feet, 100 feet, etc. with eroded soil from unstable slopes, as well as aggregate from some of the adjoining, very poorly defined ditchlines. This loose material on the trail was even more treacherous given the slopes, sharp curves, and very timid clearing which resulted in twelve-inch trees within one foot of the trail. Within two months of compleion, the trail surface was repeatedly gouged by equipment used to clear the gravel and dirt from the pavement. The crew in charge of maintaining this trail was already far behind schedule on constructing several other trails, and they now have a new, eternal maintenance headache. There are people not yet born who will be clearing the trail surface.

—Greenway activist

properly installed. It holds up well against the erosive action of water, root intrusion, and subgrade deficiencies such as soft soils.

The most significant drawback to concrete is that it requires construction joints to absorb pavement cracking, which may make it bumpy for bicyclists and other users. Concrete surfaces could be lightly textured to prevent them from becoming slippery when wet. The installation of concrete trails may also severely impact the natural environment, through access of loaded concrete trucks, required formwork, and finishing work. Concrete surfaces should be lightly textured, as they can be slippery when wet.

Wood surfaces are usually composed of sawn wooden planks or lumber that forms the top layer of a bridge, boardwalk, or deck. The most commonly used woods for trail surfacing are exposure- and decay-resistant species such as pine, redwood, fir, larch, cedar, hemlock, and spruce. Almost all wood used for trails should be treated with a chemical preservative to protect it from insects.

Wood is a preferred surface type for special applications because of its strength and comparative weight, its aesthetic appeal, and its versatility. It is usually supported above the trail's existing natural grade by a superstructure. Certain trails, however, place the wood directly on top of the natural grade. Wood can be quite slippery when wet, particularly in wet areas where mossy growth can make it doubly slippery; it should be used only where other surfaces prove unsuitable.

With increasing interest in *recycled* products, a new line of surfaces is beginning to be tested for use on trails. These materials include crushed

Table 11-12
Advantages and Disadvantages of Trail Surface Materials

Surface Material	Advantages	Disadvantages
Native soil	Natural material, lowest cost, low matintenance, can be altered for future improvements	Dusty and dirty, ruts under heavy use, not an all-weather surface, limited use
Soil cement	Uses natural materials, supports more usage than native soils, smoother surface, low cost	Surface wears unevenly, not a stable all-weather surface, costly, erodes, difficult to achieve correct mix.
Graded aggregate stone (washed stone, gravel)	Hard surface supports heavy use, moderate costs, natural material, accommodates multiple use	Angular stones can be sharp, continuous maintenance required, uneven surface, erosion, ruts
Granular stone (limestone, cinders)	Soft but firm surface, natural material, moderate costs, smooth surface, accommodates multiple use	Surface can wash away, ruts, erodes, constant maintenance to keep smooth surface, replenish stone—long-term expense, not for steep slopes
Shredded wood fiber	Soft, spongy surface—good for walking, moderate cost, natural material	Decomposes under high temperature, moisture, and sunlight, requires replenishment—long-term expense
Wood (boardwalks, bridge decking)	Pliable surface—excellent for multi-use; natural material blends with native landscape, spans streams, ecologically sensitive areas, and soft soils; only surface that places trail user above surrounding grade	High installation cost, easy to damage and vandalize, expensive to maintain, deteriorates with exposure to sun, wind, and water, susceptible to fire damage. Can be slippery when wet
Asphalt concrete	Hard surface, supports most types of use, all weather, does not erode, accommodates most users simultaneously, low maintenance	High installation cost, costly to repair, not a natural surface, leaches toxic chemicals, freeze and thaw can crack surface, access of heavy construction vehicles
Concrete	Hardest surface, easy to form to site conditions, supports multiple use, lowest maintenance, resists freezing and thawing the best, can be colored, all weather	Joints result in bumpy surface, high installation cost, costly to repair, not a natural looking surface, access of construction vehicles
Recycled materials	Good use of trash, surface can vary depending on materials, good life expectancy	High purchase and installation cost, aesthetics

seashells, coal tailings, pottery fragments, broken clay pipe and brick, crushed porcelain toilets, shredded tires and other rubber by-products, plastics, paper by-products, and recycled asphalt by-products, such as pavement millings. The town of Cary, North Carolina, has built the nation's first recycled materials greenway.

If you are interested in using a recycled product, you need to carefully research how the product is made and by whom. How long has it been around? Has it been tested by a national laboratory, such as Underwriters Laboratory? Is it toxic to the environment or to humans? Will it pop bicycle tires? Can it be replaced if it proves ineffective for trail use? Unfortunately, little information exists to support the use of a wide variety of recycled products for trail surfacing. As a rule of thumb, use only those products that have been tested and for which there is documented evidence of strength and durability, and try to obtain a manufacturer's guarantee for materials, workmanship, and life expectancy.

12

Water Recreation

*"The afternoon river is golden and olive and clear, the surface netted with debris
from rising water. Ripples pattern the sandy bottom, sinking into shadowed
pools. Three feet beneath, crisp dark fronds weave in all the various filamentous,
intertwining subsurface currents."*
—Ann Zwinger, *Run, River, Run*

Water is often the aesthetic centerpiece of a greenway. Water courses
are not only picturesque scenic features, they are also major recreational
attractions. Water sports are the primary theme of many greenways.
Witness the upper Youghiogheny River, in western Maryland and Pennsylvania: thousands of rafters and kayakers ply its waters each summer.
Canoeing and kayaking have increased exponentially since the late
1970s, and many rivers offer miles of canoe "trails" for travel. By 1990
an estimated thirty-five million Americans had participated in water
rafting.

Many water sports also have a strong commercial component. More
than sixty million Americans fish each year. In most states, recreational
fishing and boating are multimillion dollar businesses. Nationwide, recreational fishing contributes approximately $28 billion annually to the
economy. Revenue comes from such sources as the sale of equipment,
provisions, lodging, guide services, and air travel to the river corridors.

Water recreation has become a boom industry for which greenways
offer a prime venue. A healthy water resource is vital to the livelihood
of the tourist industry near a water attraction. Damage to that resource
can be disastrous. When a rail tanker accident dumped weed killer into
California's Sacramento River in 1991, the damage cost millions because
a gold medal trout stream had been tainted.

Types of Water Recreation

Greenway planners need to assess the potential for various kinds of water recreation along their corridors and to address the opportunities and
impediments involved. Not all water-based greenways will allow water
recreation. Liability issues, the character of the resource, degree of access permitted, and the associated management issues will all affect the
decision to accommodate boating, fishing, or swimming. Table 12-1 de-
picts a number of currently popular water sports along with the corresponding facility needs.

Table 12-1

Greenway-Oriented Water Recreation

Recreation Type	Description of Equipment	Water & Facility Requirement
Paddle craft:		
• Flat-water canoe	Canoe seats 2–3 paddlers and has a keel for directional stability.	Slow-moving or still water, access points/canoe docks, minimum depth of 8 in. to 1 ft, rental concession.
• White-water canoe	Canoe seats 1–2 paddlers and has no keel. Canoe may have a spray cover.	Swift water with rocks, chutes, and other challenges, minimum depth of 8 in. to 1 ft.
• Down-river kayak	Long slender craft, seats 1 in a small cockpit. Built to move down river quickly.	Flat or moving water, chutes, etc. Minimum depth of 8 in. to 1 ft.
• Slalom kayak	Shorter, maneuverable craft, which seats 1. Not as efficient as a down-river kayak for traveling long distances.	Moving water with chutes and slalom gates. Higher flows (up to 750 cubic ft/second) for international competition.
• Sea kayak	1- or 2-person kayak designed for ocean use. May be formed from mold plastic or fabric on a frame. May have a rudder for steering.	Sea or lake shore use with beach or access ramp, rental concession
• Raft	Inflatable raft carries 1–12 or more people. May be propelled by paddles, oars, or motor.	Moving water, loading ramps, minimum depth 1 ft, rental concession
• Rowing shell	Long narrow single- or multiperson, propelled by oars.	Flat water, docks, storage. Minimum depth 1 ft, storage facility.
• Pedal craft	1- or 2-person craft driven by bicycle-like pedals. Craft may also have electric propulsion.	Flat water, rental concession, minimum depth 1 ft.
• Rowboat	Small 10- to 15-ft craft propelled by oars.	Flat water, rental concession, minimum depth 1 ft.
• Sportyaks and other craft	Small inflatable and noninflatable craft	Varies
Sail craft:		
• Wind surfer	Small 1- or 2-person sail craft	Flat water, minimum depth 1–2 ft, rental concession.
• Sailboat	Primarily wind-driven boat 14–30 ft long or larger.	Flat water, boat ramp, adequate room to tack and maneuver, minimum depth 3–5 ft or more.

(Table continues)

Table 12-1 (continued)

Recreation Type	Description of Equipment	Water Facility Requirement
Power craft (Use may be limited by noise restrictions, lack of adequate space, and risk of shore damage or potential damage to properties such as houseboats moored along shore from wakes):		
• Runabout	Small 16- to 30-ft craft driven by outboard or inboard engine	Flat water, room to travel and maneuver, boat ramp and/or marina, minimum depth 3–4 ft, rental concession.
• Jet ski	Self-propelled motorcycle-like craft, which carries 1 or 2 people.	Flat water, room to maneuver, rental concession, minimum depth 3–4 ft.
• Water ski (possible slalom course and jumps)	Skier pulled at higher speeds by tow boat	Flat water, room to maneuver at high speeds, minimum depth 5 ft
• Large craft	Cabin cruisers, yachts, excursion boats, etc.	Flat water and lots of room, marinas.
Immersion sports (Note: All immersion sports require good water quality, i.e., a rating by the state health department for body contact):		
• Swimming/wading	Recreational swimming	Beach or swimming hole, very slow moving or flat water, parking, lifeguard if public invited to swim.
• Inner tube	Inflated inner tube	Slow moving water, possible tube rental
• Boogie board	Small buoyant board; user may wear wet suit and swim fins.	Swift water
• Scuba diving	Special underwater breathing apparatus for prolonged submergence	Divers must be specially certified. When diving, a red flag with diagonal white stripe must be displayed on boat or on buoy.
Fishing (Note: Need suitable water quality for fishery and suitable stock of fish):		
• Fly fishing	Standing in stream and casting fly lures on surface. Special fly fishing rod used.	Trout habitat, adequate spacing of anglers, access trails.
• Casting	Using a rod and spinner reel, lures or bait are thrown out from shore and reeled in.	Sport fishing habitat, access trails.
• Dock fishing	Fishing with a rod off a dock or pier	Sport fishing habitat, dock or pier, fish cleaning station.
• Trolling and boat fishing	Fishing from a moving or standing boat	Sport fishing habitat, boat ramp, rental concession.
• Fish-cleaning station	Area to clean fish	Cleaning table and waste disposal receptacle.

Note: Depth requirements are approximate and for illustration purposes only. Specific depth criteria should be determined on a site-by-site basis. Equipment suppliers and experts in each sport should be consulted when planning.

Canoeing, Kayaking, and Rafting[1]

The Maine Island Trail, a 350-mile small-boat coastal waterway, is focused on the use of approximately eighty private and publicly owned wild islands as overnight camping stops. Private islands are open only to members of the Maine Island Trail Association (MITA), an organization that initially developed and now maintains the trail. MITA manages several islands for the state and oversees lease agreements with owners of private islands. MITA members subscribe to a low-impact use ethic and provide work-for-use to private owners and state and federal land managers. A guidebook to the trail is available to association members. Coincidentally, in the past fifteen years, a dozen sea kayaking outfitters have cropped up along the rocky Maine coast.

Paddle craft, such as canoes, kayaks, and rafts, are often the most popular form of water recreation on greenways. Their popularity can be expected to increase as lightweight, easily transportable equipment becomes available. Although a greenway may certainly include a lake or string of lakes, for the purposes of this discussion, let's assume the water course is a river or stream, that is, moving water.

Water traveling downhill in a river or stream moves with tremendous energy. Paddlers must work with this motion and energy—and know how to read a river. Greenway planners must understand how moving water behaves. To the untrained eye, water in motion can appear chaotic and threatening. Fortunately, water behavior is predictable, albeit complex. Patterns present in a rivulet running down a gutter are repeated in the Mississippi. The difference lies in the volume and power of the water.

Gravity and Friction

The first step toward understanding moving water is to examine the interplay of gravity and friction. Gravity moves water downhill and friction tries to slow it. The force of friction is strongest on the bottoms and sides of a channel, where water meets the greatest resistance. Water on the surface and in the middle of a stream encounters the least amount of friction and thus moves the fastest (see Figure 12-1).

At low speeds these different layers of flow are barely perceptible to the eye. As flows speed up, however, turbulence comes into play, and flow patterns become visible as "white water," or rapids.

Curves in the River

Where a stream channel takes a bend, another force comes into play—centrifugal force. The river surface tends to push toward the outside bank, and the water to the outside of the curve speeds up. Staying inside the curve usually permits easy navigation if the boater paddles through it correctly. The force of the water in a fast or larger stream, however, can push a boat against the outside bank, and strong flows and turbulence can even pull it under.

Hydraulics

In addition to friction and curves, rivers are filled with many other obstructions to the natural downhill motion of water—rocks, riffles, downed trees, and dams. When water hits an obstruction it must pass around, beneath, or over it. This diverting or squeezing of flow releases energy that is manifested in several ways, including suck holes, falls, surges, rollers, tail waves and bank rollers, chutes, and eddies.

---

[1]Portions of material in this section were adapted from Norman Strung, Sam Curtis, and Earl Perry, *Whitewater!* (New York: Collier Books, 1978).

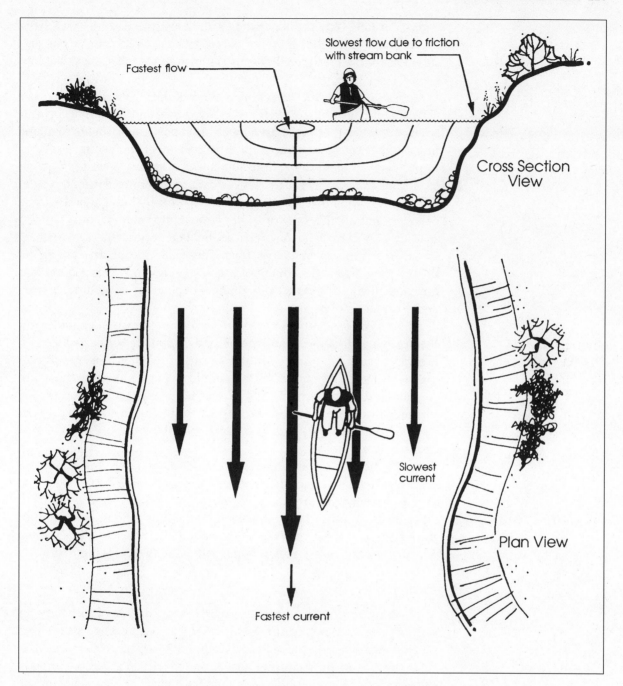

Figure 12-1 The concept of laminar flow. How friction causes varying flow speeds in a stream channel. (Adapted from Norman Strung, Sam Curtis, and Earl Perry, *Whitewater!* [New York: Collier, 1978]).

Suck Holes. A suck hole, also known as a *souse hole* or *keeper*, occurs when water rolls off the downstream side of an obstruction, such as a large rock, with enough force to create a powerful upstream flow. Often not obvious to a boater, a suck hole may appear as a large bulge in the surface with no roar, white water, or other warning present. Suck holes can trap a boat or a person indefinitely. The best way to manage suck holes is to learn to spot and avoid them.

Falls. A falls is a drop that extends all the way across the river. Falls of any height more than a foot or two must be avoided for obvious reasons. One of the most deadly forms is a man-made fall known as a low head dam or weir.

Surges, Rollers, Tail Waves, and Bank Rollers. Surges, rollers, tail waves, and bank rollers are the various waves and boils that form in strong currents. They are caused by obstructions, underwater irregularities, or other configurations in the stream channel and can take several forms, depending on the volume and speed of water. A series of gentle swells, for example, is called a *washboard* and can offer a safe, fun ride. In more extreme flows, *haystacks* or *roosters* form. These large upswells of water can trap, flip, or, worse, slam a boat into submerged rocks.

Chutes. A *chute* is a tongue of water that forms where a river or stream narrows and possibly drops. The water speeds up and, at the downstream end of the chute, releases its energy in waves. Chutes can offer a fun ride or a disastrous plunge, depending on volume, grade, and other factors.

Eddies. Eddies can be a boater's friend or nightmare, depending on their size and location. One kind of eddy, sometimes referred to as a *two-dimensional eddy,* forms around an obstruction such as a rock that protrudes above the surface in the middle of the channel. As the water rounds the obstruction, it tends to spin back upstream. In low flows, this area of reverse flow can be a welcome rest from the downstream flow. A house-sized boulder in a major river, however, might create an unmanageable situation.

Bank eddies form around projections jutting out of the bank of a stream or river. As the current rounds the projection, it creates a reverse flow just below the projection. In gentle or moderate flows, the bank eddy makes an ideal landing or launch site out of the main current of the river. The line between the main current and the bank eddy is called an *eddy fence* and may take some skill to cross without tipping.

Rating Rivers

There are several systems for ranking rivers by degree of difficulty for boaters. One system used commonly by kayakers and canoeists is based on a roman numeral scale of I to VI. Table 12-3 outlines this system.

Remember when evaluating a river that what you see at one time of the year may be totally different at another time or after a major storm. Hydraulics can change dramatically with flow volume and water level. A benign object at low flow might be a killer at high water or vice versa. Learn the moods of the river and the challenges it presents.

Water Safety

On the topic of safety, the basic assumption is that all water is dangerous. The key is to eliminate any danger that can reasonably be avoided through design, planning, management, and when appropriate, regulation. Where hazards cannot be eliminated, users must be warned

Table 12-3

International Kayakers Water Rating System

Rating No. (Class)	Description
I	Very easy. Little gradient, wide and unobstructed channel, riffles and tiny avoidable waves.
II	Easy water. Low ledges and rapids of moderate difficulty with wide passages. Regular (not breaking violently) waves to about 2 ft in height.
III	Water of medium difficulty. Lots of waves, irregular and reaching perhaps 3 ft. Clear, but small channels, beset by rock and diversified eddies. Scouting is advised, especially on the first run, although experts can probably sight-read their way through.
IV	Expert water. The rapids are long with violent and irregular waves to 5 ft. There are dangerous rocks and suck holes with a difficult but mandatory reconnaissance required for the first run. Lots of turns and drops in the river. This is serious water.
V	Almost continuous violent rapids. Rapids spattered with dangerous rocks and more dangerous holes, irregular waves over 5 ft with high flow and large gradient. Reconnaissance is mandatory but dangerous. This, even to experts, is frightening water.
VI	"Water That Has Not Been Successfully Run." It is a nightmare.

Source: Norman Strung, Sam Curtis, and Earl Perry, *Whitewater!* (New York: Collier Books, 1978).

through signs and other means. Where necessary, boat landings and portages should be provided.

Precautions. Life vests are the seat belts of water recreation. In an overwhelming majority of drowning, the failure to wear a life vest was cited as the primary or contributing factor. Life vests should always be worn.

Helmets are also strongly recommended for use by kayakers, canoeists, and anybody boating in Class III or above water conditions. The basic rules of water safety are *never boat alone* and *never boat unknown*. Everyone who enters a river must take responsibility for knowing what he or she is getting into. This includes knowing one's own ability and knowing how to identify hazards.

Strainers and Weirs: The Drowning Machines. Surprisingly, rocks and the river current are not usually deadly hazards, although hitting a well-placed rock the wrong way can bend your boat and pin you there. Of all the dangers of rivers, strainers and weirs lead the list. Strainers include fallen trees, logs, log jams, roots, and even permanently fixed bridge piers and docks in a moving river. They can trap a swimmer or boater, pinning him or her with bone-crushing force between the strainer and an object like an upset canoe or kayak. In heavily boated areas, particularly dangerous strainers should be identified and removed wherever feasible.

The most pernicious of all white-water hazards is the weir, or low-head dam. Upstream the water may be deceptively placid; the downstream side of the dam usually slopes. As the water flows down the smooth-sloping side, it dives to the bottom of the river with tremendous

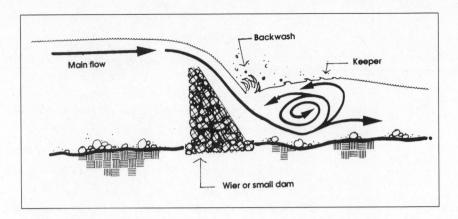

Figure 12-2 A keeper is a dangerous water hazard located downstream from a dam.

force, scouring out a hole and creating a strong, hidden suction known as a *keeper*. A keeper can trap and drown anyone who wanders too close (see Figure 12-2).

The best way to prevent keeper deaths is to avoid building dams in the first place. If a dam must be built, it should, at minimum, be designed with boater safety and access in mind. A keeper can be prevented in several ways. For example, instead of one large ten- to twelve-foot-high dam, a series of smaller ones, two to three feet high with boating notches can be built. The cost is competitive, and the drops become an exciting boating amenity rather than a death trap.

Boat chute cut through a low head dam. (Robert Searns)

The U. S. Army Corps of Engineers cooperated in building such a structure on the Platte River in Littleton, Colorado. The dam has functioned safely, while a brand new thirteen-foot-high concrete dam downstream—similar to the original design for the Littleton dam—was responsible for the deaths of several people shortly after its completion. The large killer dam was later modified to create a series of smaller drops with chutes—at an additional cost approaching $1 million.

When planning your paddle corridor, be sure to identify and map all the dams. (Boaters who pass safely through several modified dams should not be caught on one that has not yet been fixed.) Ideally, the dams should be modified with boat chutes (see Figure 12-3). This is not always financially feasible. A boat chute can cost from $25,000 to more than $1 million, depending on the size and configuration of the dam. At a minimum, warning signs well upstream should mark the dams and publicly accessible boat landings and portages should be provided. Portages should include a landing with clearly visible markings, a graded

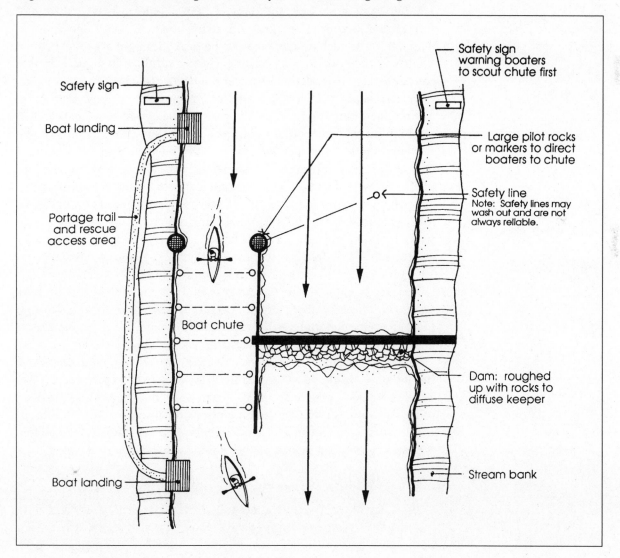

Figure 12-3 Typical design for a boat chute.

path of adequate width to carry canoes, kayaks, and rafts (ten to twelve feet wide), and a downstream put-in point.

Building a boat chute is not a job for amateurs. Hire a professional civil engineer who knows both hydraulics and boat chutes. To find engineers who specialize in this area, contact cities that have built chutes (Denver, Boulder, and South Bend, Indiana, to name a few) or the U. S. Army Corps of Engineers (the Omaha office has been involved in building several chutes).

In addition to engineering input, boating groups, police and rescue people, flood-management officials, and others who have an interest in the design should also be involved. It is important to design the chutes with a worst-case scenario in mind, that is, an unskilled family running the chute at high water in an open canoe. If they dump, they and their canoe should be safely ejected in one piece with only their pride broken.

If a boat chute cannot be built, the dam should be designed to avoid a keeper. This might be accomplished by placing large rock rubble below the dam face or shaping the dam so that a uniform hydraulic cannot form. Providing maps or signs with maps at access points showing potential hazards such as dams may be helpful but might also give boaters a false sense of security regarding river conditions and hazards that constantly change and, therefore, cannot be identified.

When Should a River Be Closed? Another safety issue that arises from time to time is whether a river should be closed to recreation during high water. This is a difficult question. Safety depends on the skill and common sense of the people who use the water. Some communities have a policy of informing users of potential hazards with signs, pamphlets, water-safety training, and canoe classes. Some communities do close rivers to paddling when the flow level is considered too high to be safe. This raises both liability and constitutional issues, because high water might be ideal for a skilled kayaker but not for a child with an inner tube. It is advisable to consult local boating groups, engineers, and law enforcement officials for guidance in setting safety policies.

Rescue is also an issue. Rescuers must be trained to work in whitewater conditions, or they, too, can become victims. Be sure to work with police and fire departments to see that they are familiar with all hazards and rescue techniques. Don't assume they know them.

The planning and design of greenway improvements should also take rescue into consideration, especially in heavily used urban rivers. Consider emergency vehicle access routes to boat chutes, rapids, dams, and other hazardous areas. Plan staging points for rescuers to throw lines or to enter the river. Consider the safety of both the rescuer and the victim. Safety signs and emergency phones should also be included.

Making Paddling Enjoyable

Canoes, kayaks, rafts, and inner tubes are some of the best and least costly ways to enjoy river greenways. Canoe "trails" offer a way to tour both urban and wilderness rivers with minimal environmental impact. In Salt Lake City, paddlers can enjoy a delightful trip on the Provo-

Jordan Parkway, which follows the Jordan River through the heart of the city. Wine lovers can rent canoes in Healdsberg, California, and paddle from winery to winery along the Russian River. Visionaries in Kane County, Illinois, have planned a canoe paddleway that runs along the Fox River, linking together the historic mill towns of Elgin, St. Charles, and Aurora.

In addition to addressing dams and other hazards, a well-planned paddleway should include the key components discussed in the following sections.

Canoe Landing and Access Points. Canoe landing and access points are public put-in and take-out points. They may include parking, adequate turning radii for cars with canoe trailers, toilets, trash facilities, drinking water if feasible, and modest picnic facilities. The size of these areas depends on a number of factors, including the local popularity of canoeing and the traffic load on the particular river. Parking for ten to twenty cars is appropriate for an average-sized facility. The launch zone can be a dirt or gravel ramp or, in urban or heavily used settings, a rock and concrete pad set in the stream. The pad might be terraced to accommodate different water levels. Floating wooden docks may be used in very slow current but can be hazardous where current can trap a canoeist or swimmer beneath the dock (see Figure 12-4).

Generally, launch points should be located on the inside of a curve in the river where the current is slower. In some instances, rock can be used to create a finger dike that forms a bank eddy in the current, making it easier to land or launch. The finger dike should be designed so it will not catch or trap boaters. For this reason, the dike should not have gaps that let the current pass through. Permits may be required from state conservation agencies, state boating safety agencies, the U. S. Army Corp of Engineers, and other entities with jurisdiction.

Camping and Lunch Stops. Some paddleway systems may be large enough for overnight trips. These larger systems should include camping facilities. They can be arranged in cooperation with existing state parks, private campgrounds, or even innkeepers along the river corridor. Camping facilities should be safe from flash flood, reasonably secure from crime, located so as not to disturb adjacent properties, and designed for minimal environmental impact. If possible, sites should be remote from parking areas to provide a greater wilderness experience. In addition to camping areas, paddleways should include lunch spots serving both commercial guides and individual canoeists. Consider paddling time from point to point when planning the spacing of put-ins, take-outs, camping, and lunch sites.

Information Systems. Information systems are a vital part of a safe, enjoyable paddleway. Elements include route maps at launch sites, brochures, and signs indicating dangerous or difficult sections, informing paddlers of water recreation hazards, and indicating the need to wear life vests and to respect private property. Street signs on bridges crossing the river are also a good idea. Signs should be placed at key entry points and well enough upstream of hazards to allow boaters to take precautions. Note that the U.S. Coast Guard has recommended

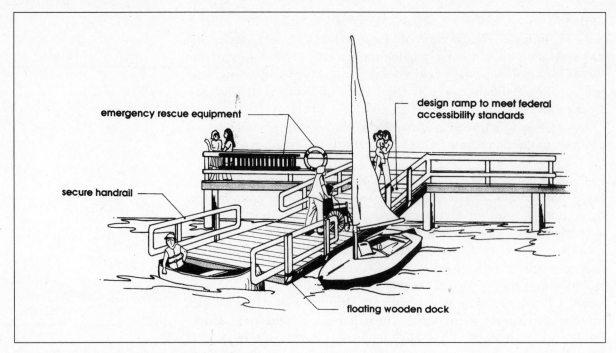

Figure 12-4 Accessible boat launch design.

standard sign marking and colors for inland waterways. Although this system is designed primarily for power boating, the scheme can be adapted for paddle craft. Contact the Coast Guard or your state's boating safety officer for further information. Also consult paddling groups for assistance in sign design and location.

Sport Paddling Facilities. A quality paddleway might include sport paddling and training facilities. Denver offers a white-water kayak slalom course in the Platte River just a few blocks from downtown. South Bend, Indiana, has created one of the nation's premier kayak facilities along a historic industrial sluiceway next to the St. Joseph River. Completed in 1984 at a cost of $4.5 million, the East Race Waterway features a two-thousand-foot run with thirteen feet of drop. The boat chute is popular with both competition kayakers and South Bend residents, who pay a dollar per ride to ply the waterway in small rafts provided by the Parks Department. The waterway, funded in part by the Indiana Department of Natural Resources, also serves as a fish passage for several species of anadromous fish returning from Lake Michigan.

Power and Sail Craft

Planning and Regulation

Some greenways include facilities for power boating. For example, Pierre, South Dakota, is developing an extensive waterfront greenway along the Missouri River that will include bike paths, nature trails, a beach, and a large nature preserve. Two of the most popular activities are power boating and water skiing. Pierre's riverfront master plan calls for boat ramps and an expanded marina. The plan also zones different areas of the water surface for different uses. Power boats have a designated area and direction of circulation when towing skiers. A no-wake zone has been established closer to shore to allow canoeing, wind surfing, and other nonmotorized activities. Some management plans also limit the motor size to control noise, which is magnified by water.

Similar systems are used elsewhere around the nation. The Colorado State Parks and Recreation Division identifies zones with buoys. There is also zoning by time period, such as limited power boating after dark, during hunting season, or when ice is present. The direction of motion for water skiing, set by state law, is posted by buoy. Several states also post a speed limit (Colorado's is forty miles per hour). Usually, signs posted at marinas, boat ramps, and park entry points post all of these rules. The increasing incidence of accidents caused by power-boaters under the influence of alcohol or drugs is being addressed by many states.

In addition to zoning and speed limits, there are rules of boater right-of-way, generally based on ability to maneuver. For example, power boats yield to sail craft, which yield to vessels engaged in fishing, which yield to vessels whose ability to maneuver is restricted.

Several organizations can provide information on regulating power craft. A pamphlet called *The Federal Requirements for Recreational Boats*, available from the U. S. Coast Guard, contains regulations and standards for coastal and inland areas. The U. S. Coast Guard, the American Red Cross, and the Power Squadron (a power boating association) can also help. The best place to start, however, is with the agency responsible for your state's boating program. Almost every state has a boating law administrator, usually in the Department of Natural Resources or State Parks agency.

Ramps and Marinas

Power boats and larger sail craft require launch ramps and marinas. Planners of launch ramps should consider such factors as fluctuation of water level, slope, depth at the end of the ramp, weight capacity, and frequency of use. Remember that sail craft often have a deep keel or centerboard, which significantly increases the depth required. Ramp planners should also consider parking and turning radii for vehicles with boat trailers. Marina planners should take into account shape, channel entrances, fueling facilities, waste disposal, and adequate turning radii for large trucks, including fuel tankers. The environmental impacts of power boat use, fueling, and maintenance must also be addressed. For information on power boating and marina planning, contact the National Marine Manufacturers Association in Chicago. Use design guide books like *Time Saver Standards for Landscape Architects*, by Charles W. Harris and Nicholas T. Dines (New York: McGraw-Hill, 1988) and engineers and marina design specialists.

Swimming and Wading

For both safety and liability reasons, public swimming areas must be well planned, designed, and managed. There are issues of safe gradient—ten to one or even gentler slopes are recommended to avoid surprise drop-offs. The current must be minimal or nonexistent. Floating buoys should define the swimming area to assure that people do not bathe in areas that may be unsafe because of current, depth, boats, or other factors. Water quality must meet state health department standards for full body contact. People also want clean sand with no sharp rocks or debris that could cut their feet. Changing facilities, toilets, and possibly food and drink concessions are often needed. An underwater ramp and access ramp across the sand should be provided for people in wheelchairs. There is also the issue of diving. Are there points where people might unknowingly dive into shallow water? Are dangerous rocks present? Any such hazards should be clearly posted. Finally, you will need to have a lifeguard if swimming is part of your greenway. Wading areas may be more informal, though you should identify likely spots and eliminate any submerged hazards.

Fishing

Fishing on greenway corridors brings with it a number of requirements. First and foremost, there must be adequate habitat. Fish, especially game species like trout, salmon, and bass, need good-quality water of the proper temperature. Excessive sediment clogs gills and interferes with reproduction. High temperatures and excessive nutrients as a result of pollution can severely reduce dissolved oxygen. Unvegetated stream banks result in adversely high water temperatures in summer and loss of water heat in winter.

Fish survive on a variety of organisms and aquatic insect larvae that live in the water or that drop off of bank vegetation. Healthy habitat, including stable vegetated banks (which help control water temperature), meanders, rough edges (rocks, logs, and tree roots along the bank), an unclogged gravel bottom, and pools and riffles will help sustain a thriving fish population.

Many fish migrate in search of food, shelter, and places to breed. A fish habitat program must address the issue of migration. Dams, for example, should be avoided where possible and fish ladders built to allow fish to move up- and downstream. In some instances, boat chutes can also serve as fish ladders.

Once a healthy habitat has been established, you may need to build up and sustain the fish supply. This includes such concerns as stocking programs, size limits, take limits, and maybe even a catch-and-release policy. Be sure water quality is acceptable before investing in improvements. Take an *ecosystem* or *watershed* approach and be sure the physical, chemical, and biological aspects of the stream are protected. The Izaak Walton League, Trout Unlimited, and state fish and wildlife agencies can all help. If a stream is regenerated, chances are that fish from other

Bridges that are historically valuable but structurally unsound for motor vehicles can be salvaged, redesigned, and even transported to your greenway to accommodate bird watchers, bicyclists, or fishermen. Platforms, stairs, or ramps can be added to provide fishing access to the water.

healthy streams will repopulate it. If you are stocking, always aim to stock fish with the same genetic makeup as those native to the stream. Be aware that restocking programs can sometimes have an impact on native populations by diluting the genetic hardiness of existing populations. Basic habitat integrity should be stressed in fishery management plans. Use forested buffer zones along streams, best management practices, and controls on overfishing, exotic species introduction, and pollution to help restore habitat. Try to avoid using wire mesh or tires in fish-habitat improvements. Fish can get torn up on wire mesh; old tires may leach oils and toxins. *After* the habitat has been restored to a more pristine condition, try some in-stream habitat enhancements. This will also speed the recovery process. Many states now have urban fisheries programs that provide funds and technical assistance to cities and towns. Wildlife officials can take a census of the fish population and assess the condition of the stream as fish habitat.

Finally, there is the question of access, both physical access and public information about it. The latter can include pamphlets, signs, and news stories telling the public the resource is there and how to get to it. Planning for physical access will depend on the types of fishing the greenway offers. Certainly, there are anglers who prefer to sit on a fishing dock and either cast or just drop a line. There are people in wheelchairs and other disabled persons who will need access. On many streams, however, the most popular form of fishing is simply to move up and down the bank or in the stream bed until a good spot is found.

The citizens of Stowe, Vermont, in an attempt to restore fish habitat, added large boulders to their river. When the snowmelt from Mount Mansfield—Vermont's tallest mountain—combined with spring rains, the river became a torrent. Water swirling around the boulders created holes on the downstream side, and the boulders eventually fell in, disappearing from sight. Locals say theirs is the river that eats boulders.

Carrying Capacity and User Conflicts

Greenway planners must take into account the carrying capacity of the stream corridor. There is also the impact of overuse on adjacent private property to consider. A carrying capacity plan is essential.

Generally, such a plan is addressed location by location. A study of comparable facilities in similar locations around the state or nation can give you an idea of probable uses and numbers of users. Public meetings and forums will also help identify local needs and interests.

A vast array of techniques and formulas exist for calculating use and capacity. Some jurisdictions gauge capacity by measuring the amount of litter and other damage to the corridor. Others use formulas for calculating canoe capacity. The Wisconsin Formula, a popular technique, works in this way:

The North Branch of the Potomac River has been under a multijurisdictional study to improve water quality, protect vital land and aquatic habitat, and promote local economic development. Participating agencies include the Maryland Department of Natural Resources, the Interstate Commission on the Potomac River Basin, and the government of West Virginia. Important headwaters along the North Branch of the Potomac River were devastated by acid mine drainage but with rehabilitative measures have the potential to become a world-class trout fishery.

River miles x 2 parties/mile = No. of parties
No. of parties x party size[1] = carrying capacity (number of people)

This formula assumes that two parties per mile is an acceptable level of use at any given time. Obviously, this will vary, depending on the

[1]Average party size is 4.7 people. Thomas G. Schafer, "Management Alternatives for the Improvement of Canoeing Opportunities and the Resolution of Problems Relating to the Recreational Use of Rivers" (Columbus: Ohio Department of Natural Resources, 1975).

The Potomac River "Ramblin' Raft Race" brings many residents of the Washington metropolitan area onto the river and its shores. (Interstate Commission on the Potomac River Basin)

type of use, the sensitivity of the resource, and other factors. Check with your state park agencies for direction and precedent in determining carrying capacity. No matter how carrying capacity is determined and reflected in the plan and design, it is important to undertake an ongoing public education program, with written pamphlets and other materials to encourage stewardship of the resource.

In-Stream Flow Management for Water Recreation

In planning water recreation, do not forget in-stream flow. Check past flow levels in your corridor by contacting the U. S. Geological Survey. It operates gauging stations along major streams and also produces published reports on drainage history. The nearest office of the U. S. Army Corps of Engineers may be able to help determine flow-level patterns and tell you of major projects that might affect flow. In the western states, it may be necessary to purchase water rights or to modify affected sections of the channel to protect aquatic habitat. If flows are low for boating, it may be possible to schedule releases from dams upstream to coincide with peak recreational boating periods (i.e., evenings and weekends). Be sure to assess the impact of timed releases first, however. A sudden water release might cause environmental damage downstream, including siltation, destruction of spawning beds, and smothering of aquatic life.

See the appendix for addresses of greenway organizations involved in water recreation. Additional contacts are:

American Canoe Association
P.O. Box 248
7217 Lockport Place
Lorton, VA 22079
703-550-7523

American Fisheries Society
5410 Grosvenor Lane, Suite 110
Bethesda, MD 20814
301-897-8616

American Whitewater Association
136 13th Street S.E.
Washington, DC 20003
202-225-6060

Bass Anglers For Clean Water, Inc.
P.O. Box 17900
Montgomery, AL 36117
205-272-9530

Colorado Water Conservation Board
1313 Sherman Street
Denver, CO 80202
303-866-3441
(Built two stair-step type dams as alternative to one large dam in cooperation with Omaha Office of U.S. Army Corps of Engineers)

Interagency Whitewater Committee
U.S. Forest Service
Hells Canyon NRA
3620-B Snake River Avenue
Lewiston, ID 83501
208-743-3648

National Association of Canoe Liveries and Outfitters
P.O. Box 1149
Murdock, FL 33938
813-743-7278

National Marine Manufacturers Association
401 North Michigan Avenue
Chicago, IL 60611
or
353 Lexington Avenue
New York, NY 10017

National Organization of River Sports (NORS)
314 North 20th Street
Colorado Springs, CO 80934
303-473-2466

Western River Guides Association
P.O. Box 1324
Moab, UT 84532
801-259-8229

13

Greenways Facilities Design

"The world is richer for those memorable places where man has planned his life and its structures in full accord with nature's forms and forces."
—John Ormsbee Simonds, *Earthscape*

This chapter provides details on design specifications, construction materials, and development strategies for a wide variety of greenway facilities. The term *facilities* is used here in its broadest sense and includes benches, bridges, water and sewer systems, signage, lane striping for shared trail use, interpretive signs, and landscaping.

Greenway Signage

Signage provides greenway users with information they need to use the facility. Greenway signs need to be carefully designed and appropriately installed. At the same time, the designer should avoid oversigning, which can clutter the environment and result in information overload. Signs must be clear, concise, and legible. Their location is critical.

Pictographs are one of the best ways to communicate information to a wide range of users. Pictographs, sometimes referred to as "symbol signs," have been standardized for international use so that, for example, the symbol for a men's restroom in Tokyo is the same as the one used in Toledo, Ohio (see Figure 13-1).

One user group often forgotten on greenway signs is the visually impaired. To accommodate this group, braille-lettered signs or brochures could be provided. Information on braille lettering can be obtained from the Uniform Federal Accessibility Standards.

Greenway signs can be divided into six categories: informational, directional, regulatory, warning, festival, and educational.

Informational signs orient users to their position within the greenway system ("You are here"), provide an overview of the facilities, programs, and activities, and describe routes to reach these facilities. These signs can also indicate the length of a trail, number of miles traveled (milepost), average time required to travel to a particular destination, and size and capacity of various greenway facilities. Additionally, signs can be used to recognize volunteers or donors who have supported the greenway.

An important consideration is a street address system for your greenway. Assigning a milepost, block number, or some other community identification system enables police, fire, and medical personnel to respond immediately to incidents on the greenway. These signs should be located at roadway and trail intersections and at key access points along the trail. They should be visible to both trail users and emergency personnel.

"Before the path existed, one always had to be in an automobile to get anywhere in the community. Now people meet on the path to walk side by side and talk. The path has given the town something to be united about, which has cut across all brackets of income, age, place of residence, and at the same time has preserved the spectacular, previously private riverbank for all to enjoy all seasons of the year."
—Stowe, Vermont, Resident

Figure 13-1 Pictographs.

Directional signs can give instructions regarding a user's bearing and route of travel. Most directional signs are in the form of graphic symbols and brief descriptions. For example, directional signage can include arrows that indicate direction of travel and give descriptive text such as "this way," or "keep to the right."

Regulatory signs describe the laws and regulations that apply within the greenway, such as permitted uses, hours of operation or accessibility, and speed limit [Figure 13-2(a)]. Regulatory signs must be uniform in terms of size, location, and information. All regulatory signs should have black lettering on white reflective background. Regulatory information should not conflict in any way with other components of the signage scheme.

In order to ensure that your regulatory signage program offers the most complete, legally defensible, and clearly legible system of communication to a wide range of user groups, you should consult the bicycle and pedestrian facility design section of the U.S. Department of Transportation's, Manual on Uniform Traffic Control Devices. This manual presents a standardized and universally used signage system, and it provides the appropriate size, applicable color range, and physical relationship for each type of greenway sign.

Pavement markings are useful in greenways that are going to be used as bikeways. Both striping and message stencils can be used to convey information. Consult the American Society of State Highway Transportation Officials' guidelines for placement, color, and size of letters. Remember that painted pavement can cause slipping and make stopping more difficult. In colder climates, snow may cover parts of important markings during winter months.

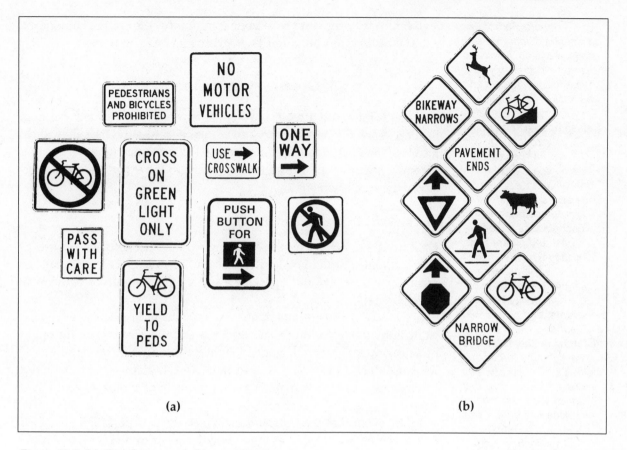

Figure 13-2 (a) Regulatory and (b) warning signs.

Warning signs are used to caution about various hazards, such as curves in the trail, slippery bridges, roadway crossings, steep downhill or uphill conditions, blind intersections, and changes in trail surface condition [Figure 13-2(b)]. All warning signs should be of uniform size and shape, located a minimum of fifty feet in advance of the hazard, and labeled with black lettering on a reflective yellow background. Once again, refer to the Manual on Uniform Traffic Control Devices.

Festival signs commemorate special events and holidays or add accent, color, and decoration. Festival signs offer limited information about a specific event. They come in many different forms, from cloth banners to flags, to specially created pole-mounted hard surface signs.

Educational or interpretive signs describe the unique qualities or significance of natural or cultural features along the greenway, such as age, habitat, and historical significance. Don't make your signs so attractive that they are a temptation to those who would steal them. Plain plywood signs replaced attractive "theft-proof" signs stolen from the Stowe Recreation Path. Although they lack the appeal of the originals, they remain in place on the greenway.

One of the benefits of greenway signage is the opportunity to develop a distinctive community symbol and identity for your greenway system. This is best accomplished through the creation of a greenway logo. A

Periodic "blazes" are used to mark many low-impact trails. Blazes should be at eye level and conspicuously placed, closer on narrow wooded trails and more widely spaced on well-worn trails. In general, a hiker shouldn't walk a hundred paces without encountering a blaze. Check with your local trails organization for advice on standard trail blaze color, size, and shape to use on your trail.

logo can convey the essence of your community—its unique landscapes, cultural history, or public spirit—to every greenway user.

Greenway Infrastructure

Greenway infrastructure includes motor vehicle access and parking, boat access, water and sanitary sewer facilities, waste removal, medical facilities, and outdoor lighting and telecommunications. Individual greenways will vary quite a bit with regard to the extent they will need any of these components.

Motor Vehicle Access and Parking

If we lived in a perfect world, everyone would be able to get to a greenway without an automobile. Realistically, however, we must plan for automobile access and parking as a component of greenway development.

Greenway designers should always evaluate and make use of any existing automobile parking adjacent or close to the greenway. This might be a nearby church or synagogue that uses parking only on certain days. Joint use may require access agreements or special-use permits and a commitment to share maintenance responsibilities for cleanup and repair.

In the event that separate automobile access and parking is required for your greenway, facilities should be designed to meet the minimum applicable local standards (municipal or county ordinances) for safe, efficient, and ecologically sound facility development. Automobile facilities should reinforce the fact that automobile access is discouraged within the greenway and discourage users from driving to and from the greenway. You can accomplish this in the following ways.

1. Place automobile access and parking lots on the outer edge of the greenway facility, away from ecologically sensitive environments and near existing highways or roads, offering the user a trail to greenway facilities.

2. Provide the minimum amount of required parking space so that users will be encouraged to share a ride or car pool to the greenway.

3. Install a mix of large (ten- by twenty-foot), compact (eight-and-a-half- by eighteen-foot), and disabled (twelve- by twenty-foot) parking spaces and install educational signage in the parking lot that promotes the use of energy-efficient automobiles.

4. Install natural surfaces as opposed to paved surfaces as a method for slowing travel within the parking lot. Disabled parking areas will require a hard surface for safety reasons.

5. Offer a convenient, safe, and accessible public transit stop and shelter close to the main or most attractive components of the greenway.

You should also incorporate transit information into greenway brochures and information materials.

6. Provide the disabled with convenient drop-off and pick-up zones near the main greenway attractions.

Greenways can offer a practical alternative to automobile transportation by providing bicycle and pedestrian routes that link community residents to schools, shops, workplaces, and other locations. Greenway designers, however, can seldom abolish or significantly change local automobile access and parking lot standards, ordinances, or requirements. Therefore, we provide the following guidelines.

Automobile access roads or driveways should be a maximum of thirty feet wide: two eleven-foot travel lanes for cars and four-foot outside shoulders for bicycle travel. The maximum speed limit for these roadways should be fifteen miles per hour. Restricting the speed limit provides greater flexibility in designing access roads at a scale that is more sensitive to the natural environment. The roadway cross section should be developed to rural standards, encouraging the installation of grassed or vegetated shoulders and natural drainage swales, rather than concrete curb and gutter. Pavement should be a natural surface or porous material concrete paver, gravel, or a porous asphalt pavement to absorb rainfall. Each community will have local standards that will have to be met in constructing other elements of the access road (see Figure 13-3).

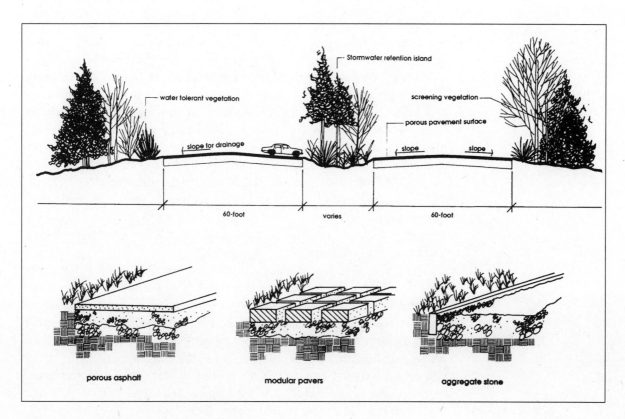

Figure 13-3 (a) Roadway and parking pavement design.

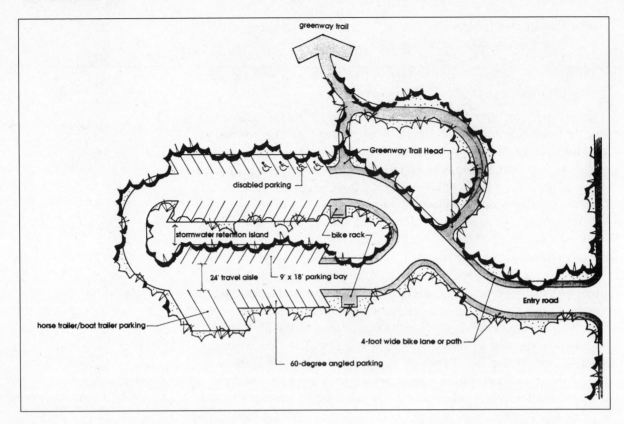

greenway trail

Greenway Trail Head

disabled parking

stormwater retention island — bike rack

24' travel aisle — 9' x 18' parking bay

Entry road

horse trailer/boat trailer parking

4-foot wide bike lane or path

60-degree angled parking

Figure 13-3 (b) Automobile parking and entry road.

Automobile parking lots should be designed and developed to meet local standards governing capacity and use [see Figure 13-3(b)]. Parking lot layouts can vary from ninety-degree right-angle parking to thirty-degree angled parking, although the most efficient layout both for drivers and land conservation is sixty-degree angled parking. In this configuration, vehicles are routed in one way and out another. Parking stalls should be no less than eight-and-a-half feet wide and no more than ten feet wide. Disabled spaces must be twelve feet wide. Aisles for vehicle pull in, back out, and travel should be twenty-four feet wide. Spaces and required turning radius should be provided for vehicles towing horse trailers, boats, or other recreational vehicles, if applicable. Where horse access is allowed, provide room for unloading outside the normal vehicle path of travel, a watering trough, and a hitching post or rail for temporary tie up.

There are no national standards for the number of parking spaces that should be provided for a greenway or how far apart parking facilities should be. Instead of trying to compute a parking lot size based on the number of potential users, it would be more helpful to understand what the community needs and the impact that a parking facility has on the ecological functions of the greenway. We recommend that an individual lot have no more than ten to twenty car spaces. If additional parking spaces are required, divide the spaces into several different sites, and once again, try to use existing facilities.

Water and Wastewater Facilities

Providing sanitary and efficient potable water and wastewater facilities can enhance a greenway. Water may also be needed for fire-fighting, irrigation of garden areas, water gardens, fountains, or water play areas. The extent to which these facilities are developed is largely a question of funding. In some cases, water and sewer systems may prohibit expensive environmental hazards. If you need them, first examine available public facilities on adjacent lands. If your greenway ties into a local park, these facilities may already be installed. As a rule of thumb, potable water and sanitary facilities should be provided on greenways that extend more than five miles from the point of origin or from a public facility that provides these services, and thereafter at five-mile intervals.

Water can come from the local public water supply system, from surface water, from on-site wells, or large cisterns. The type of system that is most appropriate depends on local resources. The most popular is the public water supply system.

Regardless of where the water comes from, before it can be used it must be purified of harmful bacteria and chemicals. Purification or treatment generally involves chlorination and fluoridation. Before supplying drinking water to a greenway, have it tested by your local health department. A water analysis will define the type and amount of treatment necessary.

Drinking water can be provided to greenway users through a variety of means, such as hand pump well heads, pressure-activated water spigots, or mechanically cooled water fountains. Water fountain manufacturers offer a wide selection of drinking fountains that can be individually designed and installed. Because of management and maintenance requirements, drinking fountains should be installed at a trailhead or in conjunction with other facilities, such as picnic areas and campsites, where access and maintenance is routine. Water should also be provided for greenway uses, such as food preparation, dish washing at campsites and fishing facilities, and rest rooms. Drinking water should also be provided for animals.

Wastewater disposal involves the treatment of water that is discharged from restroom and bath facilities. All contaminated water is classified as wastewater or graywater. Graywater does not contain human feces and originates from showers, sinks, bathtubs, washing machines, and dishwashers. Wastewater includes discharge from domestic and industrial sources and human waste.

Wastewater can be cleaned and sanitized in a variety of ways (see Table 13-1). It can be delivered to an off-site treatment facility or treated on-site in accordance with local, state, and federal laws. Off-site treatment usually involves chemical purification of industrial and domestic wastes that contain toxic substances and heavy metals. This is usually referred to as conventional treatment. On-site treatment can occur at the source by means of composting toilets or through simple sewage disposal systems, such as septic tanks with surface or subsurface leaching fields, aerobic digesters, or cesspools. On-site treatment is usually

Greenways can be exemplary models for solid waste management, illustrating the ease with which recycling programs can be operated at the community-wide level. The Town of Cary, North Carolina, has an ambitious plan to develop the nation's first greenway using recycled products and principles. Included within the development plan is the installation of a recycling center at one terminus of the greenway. It is the town's intent to have local residents use the greenway to deposit recyclables and at the same time examine the products that can be generated from them. Benches, trash containers, bollards, bridge decking and railings, signs, fencing, and trail surfaces will be manufactured from recycled plastic, rubber, aluminum, and other waste products.

limited by the capacity of the soil mass to absorb and purify the wastewater without contaminating surrounding clean water supplies.

For greenway purposes, the simplest and most effective way to treat wastewater is to divide it at the source into graywater discharge and wastewater discharge. The graywater can be recycled for use in irrigation or disposal, while wastewater can be appropriately treated using a simple and inexpensive method, such as allowing it to permeate the soil. The water is cleansed by soil bacteria before it reaches the groundwater layer. Although this scenario sounds simple, it requires the specialized services of a wastewater design professional.

New technology has produced a number of alternatives to conventional wastewater treatment. For example, a self-contained composting toilet system uses bacteria to rapidly decompose human waste. Chemical toilets, or "porta-johns," use a liquid chemical bath to break down the waste, which is subsequently pumped and transported for further conventional treatment. Another new concept is the waterless sanitary system, where solids and liquids are separated; liquids evaporate and solids decompose in a bacteria chamber.

If you anticipate the need for sophisticated sanitary wastewater facilities within the greenway, you should make every effort to connect your system to the existing local community conventional treatment system.

Storm-Water Management

Historically, the objective of storm-water management has been to remove water from roads, bridges, and urban areas and discharge it as quickly as possible into the nearest natural watercourse—a creek, stream, river, or lake. This philosophy was dramatically altered by the Environmental Protection Agency (EPA) in 1990 with the introduction of the National Pollutant Discharge Elimination System (NPDES). The EPA, recognizing that storm-water discharge is one of the nation's foremost water pollution problems and that improper storm-water management has resulted in severe flooding of downstream properties, created a new permit application process that affects many thousands of industries, as well as cities with municipal populations greater than 100,000. The NPDES program requires affected agencies and industries to develop a comprehensive plan for managing discharge.

Another goal of storm-water management is to control sedimentation. To accomplish this, many communities have implemented sedimentation and erosion control laws and programs that regulate the way land can be developed. These laws require the installation of erosion-control measures, such as silt fences, grassed swales, and sediment ponds, on land where vegetation is removed or graded. Additionally, these laws may restrict the amount of impervious surface area allowable within a specific watershed or drainage basin.

Greenway development is subject to NPDES and erosion-control guidelines administered by federal, state, and local governments. As you begin to develop your greenway facilities, you will need to be sure that you comply fully with the applicable laws. Because sediment and

Table 13-1

Wastewater/Graywater Treatment Options for Greenways

Treatment Type	Wastewater	Graywater	Approximate Costs
Centralized			
Conventional treatment	Yes	Yes	Most expensive
Direct land application	No	Yes	Moderate
Holding pond/land application	Yes	Yes	Moderate
Aquaculture	Yes	Yes	Moderate
Silvaculture	Yes	Yes	Moderate
Reuse for industrial processes	No	Yes	Moderate
Anaerobic digestion	Yes	No	Low cost
Decentralized			
Composting toilets	Yes	Yes	Low cost
Low flow toilets/devices	Yes	Yes	Low cost
Conventional package treatment	Yes	Yes	Moderate
Sand filtering	No	Yes	Low cost
Evapotranspiration	Yes	Yes	Moderate
Graywater segregation	Yes	Yes	Low cost
Waterless systems	Yes	Yes	Low cost

Consult with a local wastewater design engineer to select the most appropriate application for your greenway.
Source: The Environmental Protection Agency, 1980.

erosion control requirements vary significantly from place to place, you should contact a local soil conservation district engineer, municipal conservation engineer, or consulting landscape architect to assist with the preparation of an erosion-control plan for your greenway. The plan might include a system of diversion swales, silt fences, and sediment basins to trap eroded soil and overland runoff from entering an undisturbed creek or stream.

Solid Waste Disposal

The collection, removal, and proper disposal of solid waste, litter, and debris are the most labor-intensive components of greenway maintenance. Solid waste management involves pickup and disposal of garbage from trash receptacles, of fallen tree limbs, leaves, and litter, of mud that has been washed onto a greenway by floodwaters, and of other debris that accumulates in public places.

A designated municipal agency, like a parks or public works department, or a solid waste contractor usually removes or empties trash receptacles into garbage trucks, which take the waste to an off-site dump.

Garbage trucks usually unload their waste in certified sanitary landfills. To enter most landfills, you must be either an employee of a waste management agency or a contractor or you must obtain a permit. Waste removal should occur at regular intervals, for most greenways once a week. Volunteer groups may manage removal for smaller greenways; however, once solid waste reaches a volume and size where volunteer services become ineffective, it is advisable to seek professional assistance.

Greenway users should, of course, voluntarily dispose of trash in appropriately sized and properly located receptacles or carry trash with them if there are no receptacles. Volunteers may also be able to assist in the collection of trash and litter. For example, many local Sierra Club chapters sponsor "Stream Cleanup Days," in which members collect debris washed out of urban areas into streambeds, channels, and adjacent floodplains.

Outdoor Lighting

Whether to provide lighting on a greenway is best resolved on a case-by-case, segment-by-segment basis. Most greenways will probably not be lighted. A greenway that operates from sunrise to sunset has a clear time of use statute, which is easy to manage. It is also easy to prosecute any violators. Lighting a greenway, in effect, encourages nighttime use, and introduces safety, crime, and vandalism concerns. There is also the problem of providing enough security personnel to effectively patrol the greenway. In heavily used greenways—in urban areas and adjacent to college campuses—the need for after dark use may lead you to extend the hours of use past sunset. In this event, appropriate lighting should be installed (see Figure 13-4).

The objective of outdoor lighting is to ensure the security of greenway users and permit safe, normal activities within the corridor. Outdoor lighting should provide enough illumination to distinguish landscape features and persons using the greenway.

Lighting systems can be either utilitarian or ornamental and are designed to provide a certain level of illumination for a particular use. National lighting standards are available for highways and roads, the interior of buildings, and outdoor signs. For the purpose of greenways, the type of facility—a trail, boardwalk, boat launch, restroom, or picnic shelter—will dictate the level of illumination. The recommended level of footcandles for certain greenway facilities is listed in Table 13-2.

Several principles must be kept in mind in developing a lighting plan for your greenway:

1. Define the appropriate level of illumination required to make the greenway safe for your targeted users.

2. Develop an overall hierarchy of greenway lighting, consisting of ground plane light fixtures, overhead lighting, and specialty lighting for signs, artwork, and vegetation.

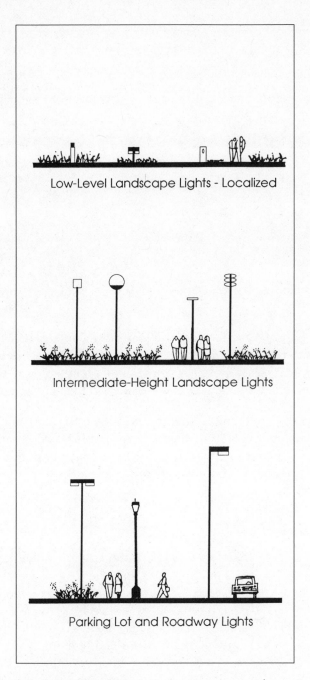

Figure 13-4 Outdoor lighting fixtures.

3. Determine the location and proper distribution of light fixtures so that you achieve the required illumination level and provide an evenly distributed light source at important areas.

4. Don't install a light fixture that might temporarily blind the greenway user and cause an accident.

5. Select a light bulb or lamp that is suitable for the greenway. Several different lamps can be used, including incandescent, fluorescent, mercury vapor, metal halide, high-pressure sodium, and low-

Table 13-2

Recommended Illumination Level for Greenway Facilities

Activity or Use	Recommended Footcandles
Bikeways	0.9
Walkways	1
Pedestrain underpasses	4
Parking lots	1
Playgrounds	5

Source: *IES Lighting Handbook*, Illuminating Engineering Society of North America, Chicago, 1981.

pressure sodium. These come in various sizes, shapes, and wattage ranges.

6. Select a fixture that will allow you to direct the light source to specific areas that require illumination, such as the trail, trail intersects, or parking lots. This is especially important if your greenway is adjacent to homes whose residents could be disturbed by night lighting.

7. Evaluate the mounting height and position of light fixtures at roadway intersections to ensure that as users enter the pedestrian crossing they are illuminated either from the front or the back in contrast to the surrounding environment in order to be easily recognizable to motorists.

Telecommunications

Providing users with access to a telephone is optional but generally a good practice. If your community feels the need to have telecommunications installed within the greenway, you should consider the following requirements. First, what type of phone system is needed? A pay phone provides users with conventional and unlimited access. On an emergency phone, the user is automatically connected to a 911 system or some other emergency response agency. Second, who will pay for installation and maintenance of the phone system? Third, is any special equipment needed for persons who have disabilities?

Fees and maintenance costs differ between pay phones and emergency phones. Most pay phones do not make enough money to support their installation and maintenance. For a typical 911 emergency telephone, an organization must pay a flat rate for service and very little for maintenance. A pay phone has a flat rate service charge and requires the caller to insert money to make a call.

Telephones should be located primarily at trailheads, both for ease of access and maintenance. If greenway users are five miles or more from a public facility, you may want to install a phone.

Phone systems can also be designed and developed to provide users with educational information about greenway special features, such as a historic site or natural area. These courtesy or information phones can be installed in conjunction with the greenway interpretative displays or as a supplemental component of other information systems within the greenway.

Finally, and perhaps most important, a telephone system can provide information to telecommunication devices for the deaf (TDD), which would offer persons with hearing or speech impairments information necessary to use and enjoy the greenway, as well as access to emergency or operational services. TDD requires specialized equipment.

Bridge Design and Development

Bridges provide greenway trail users with safe passage over streams, slopes, and roadways. They also offer trail users a unique vantage point from which to view the surrounding environment.

Several different types of bridges can be constructed for greenway trails: footbridges, constructed-in-place bridges, prefabricated bridges, low-water bridges, and suspension bridges. Regardless of the type of bridge you select, you must work with a structural engineer who can assist in its proper design and construction. You should not embark on bridge construction without sufficient education, experience, or aid; the risks and liability to you and potential greenway users are simply too high.

The information provided here is meant to serve only as a guide for the identification and selection of bridge types. Several publications listed in the References section can provide you with more detailed information.

When DuPage County officials received a $250,000 estimate to replace a burned bridge on the Illinois Prairie Path, citizen volunteers, under the direction of an engineer, rebuilt it.

Structural Considerations of Greenway Bridges

Two of the most important structural considerations in determining how a bridge is to be built are the design load and foundation.

Design load is the description of predictable forces and weights that affect the bridge over its projected life. Two types of design loads must be considered for every bridge: the dead load and the live load. The dead load refers to the total physical weight of the bridge and is calculated by figuring the weight of each component: superstructure, decking, railing, attachments, and other features of the bridge. Dead loads are distributed in a uniform manner along the entire length of each bridge component; the weight of each component is increased, however, by the combined weight of other elements it is supporting. The live load refers to the active forces and weights that it is designed to support, including the number of people that the bridge can accommodate, automobile traffic, floodwaters that might encroach and engulf the bridge, debris in floodwaters that strike the bridge, wind, soil, snow, or ice, and in some areas of the United States, earthquakes.

As a rule, bridges should be designed to support the live load that the rest of the greenway trail is expected to support. For example, if your greenway trail is designed to support a total gross vehicle weight of 12,500 pounds or 6.25 tons, then your bridge should support at least this same load. In calculating the design load for a bridge, you should project the combination of forces and weights that would place the most stress on the bridge structure. This load under stress would then become the minimum design load. The best reference on dead and live loads for bridges is the American Association of State Highway Transportation Officials' (AASHTO) Standards for Highway Bridges (see References).

Foundations support the entire dead and live load of the bridge. Even though the design loads are transferred or distributed uniformly throughout the other structural components of the bridge, all of these loads are eventually transferred vertically through the foundation into the soil. There are two typical types of bridge foundations: footings and piers. Footings spread out the design load through the soil mass and as such are constructed to be short and broad. Piers are generally tall, columnar, or rectangular posts constructed when there is a need for additional support along the length of the bridge. Piers direct the design load of the bridge to the soil, where the load is then distributed. The type of soil present within the project site will usually determine the type of footing or pier design.

Footings are usually constructed of cast-in-place concrete. They can be combined with piles, concrete, or rock columns beneath the footing. The numerous types of footing design include open abutment, wall abutment, and strutted or vertical beam abutments.

Piers are usually columns of wood, steel, or concrete constructed on suitable soils and installed where there is a need for a long, multiple-span bridge. A pier can be used as a method for reducing the size of a footing, by assuming some of the weight that a footing would normally bear.

For piers or footings that are constructed within a flowing stream or in the floodway, be sure to investigate any scouring or erosion that occurs as water flows around the foundation. This could undermine the subgrade, causing structural failure of the bridge. The simplest and least expensive method for preventing scouring or erosion is to armor the upstream and downstream base of the foundation with rip-rap rock.

Decking

Decking is the surface of a bridge. It distributes the live load to the other parts of the bridge. Decking is most often made from wood planks but can also be made from poured-in-place concrete, precast concrete, rough finished metal plates, and fill material such as stone or soil.

Wood decking is usually constructed from standard-sized wood planks, nail-laminated lumber, or glue-laminated lumber. Sawn wood planks are the most common type of wood decking used to surface bridges. Wood planks are cut in varying lengths, in widths of four, six, eight, ten, and twelve inches. A minimum thickness of two inches is recommended for most bridge applications; four-inch-thick decking provides greater strength and durability. Planks are generally laid perpendicular to the beams of the superstructure. Decking can also be laid at an angle to the superstructure. Wood decking is almost always nailed or screwed to the superstructure. Always use galvanized nails, bolts, and screws for all hardware attachments to a bridge.

The most important consideration with regard to wood decking is to ensure that the plank is laid with the bark side up so that it will not warp up over time. Wood decking also requires good drainage and ventilation so that it does not become wet and slippery. The minimum spacing between planks should be one-quarter inch, and the maximum spacing for wilderness trails should not exceed one inch. If the decking on your bridge remains wet and slippery during usage, you might try applying an epoxy and sand mix to the top or nailing down cloth strips in the travel lane along the length of the bridge. This will provide an area where walkers can obtain secure footing. One major disadvantage of wood decking is that it can be set afire by vandals or cut with hand or machine tools.

Concrete decking is another possibility. Because concrete is a workable material, you can predetermine the surface texture, drainage patterns, joints or spacing, compressive strength, length and width, and color of your bridge decking. Concrete decking adds a significant dead load weight to a typical bridge and is more expensive to install than wood decking, which is why you don't see more of this surface on greenway bridges. It is the preferred surface for several types of bridges, most importantly a low-water bridge. If frequently inundated with flowing water, the concrete may need to be scrubbed on a regular basis with a broom or chemically treated to remove algae build-up, which can form a slick sheen on the deck surface.

Bridge Railings

Bridge railings protect the greenway user from accidentally falling off the bridge and are required for most bridges. Exceptions are where the height of the bridge, measured from the top of the deck to the top of the ground surface that the bridge is spanning, is less than thirty inches, where local building codes define a minimum railing requirement for certain types of bridges, or, as in the case of a low-water bridge, where a railing is impractical because of the characteristics of the bridge crossing. Railing can be constructed from wood, metal, wire, concrete, steel cable, metal alloys, plastic, or rope. Most bridge railings for greenway trails will be constructed of wood, galvanized steel, or aluminum.

Railings have two structural components: the post and the rail. The post is the vertical support member and is usually attached to the bridge deck or superstructure. The spacing of posts can range from any desired minimum distance to a maximum distance of six feet apart, depending on the size of the post. Rails are the horizontal member and are attached either to the post or, at times, directly to the decking, as with the toe rail. Railings for most greenway bridges are generally composed of a top rail, a middle rail, and a bottom rail. AASHTO guidelines determine that the post and railing should be designed to support an outward transverse or vertical load of fifty pounds per linear foot of rail height.

There are generally three types of greenway bridge railings: pedestrian use only; pedestrian and bicycle use; and multiple uses that include motorized trail use. Pedestrian railing, or handrails, must be installed at a minimum height of three feet, six inches (top of rail) above the surface of the bridge decking. Bicycle railing must be installed at a minimum of fifty-four inches, or four feet, six inches (top of rail), above the surface of the deck. Multiple-use bridge railing, where motorized users are to be accommodated, should be a minimum of fifty-four inches high and must meet minimum strength requirements contained within AASHTO guidelines for vehicle traffic.

The maximum clear vertical opening between all railings should not exceed fifteen inches. If in lieu of three rails, vertical rails are installed, the maximum clear horizontal spacing should not exceed eight inches. If both vertical and horizontal rails are installed, the spacing requirements would apply to only one of the rail spacings and not both. You must check local or state building codes to ensure that your railings meet minimum guidelines for safety.

Approaches to Bridges

The most neglected element of bridge design is the approach. Approach railings should be constructed in the same manner as the bridge railings, except that the railing posts should be installed in the earth rather than attached to the bridge superstructure. Approach railings should extend a minimum of fifteen feet from each end of the bridge and terminate on an angle juxtaposed forty-five degrees from the edge of the trail, so that out-of-control users never hit the end of an approach rail. In addition, sight lines onto the bridge should be free of obstructions, and the approach should be wider than the normal width of the trail in order to accommodate potential congestion on and immediately before the bridge.

Methods for Reducing the Cost of Your Greenway Bridge

Bridge construction can be one of the most costly components of greenway development. To reduce cost, we recommend that you consider the following.

1. Some manufacturers may have prestressed concrete beams that did not meet minimum specifications for a proposed highway bridge, parking deck, or building. Check with the manufacturer to verify the minimum design load that these defective products are capable of supporting; make sure that the manufacturer will guarantee this specification. This same philosophy applies to wood manufacturers

Bridge railings must be high enough to prevent cyclists from accidentally flipping over the top rail. AASHTO requires a minimum fifty-four-inch top rail. (Jennifer Toole)

who make glue-laminated beams and steel manufacturers who manufacture I-beams for bridges, buildings, and structures.

2. Local bridge construction contractors or demolition contractors may have access to steel beams that were taken from old bridges, buildings, or other structures. Sometimes these contractors will sell the steel at scrap value.

3. Numerous old, steel truss bridges require replacement. Many state, county, and municipal road and highway departments must factor in the cost of demolition and removal of these structures as one component of a systemwide bridge replacement program. Contact your

local or state highway department and see what kind of deal you can strike.

4. Finally, check with your local parks department to see if it has any bridges that have become substandard because of lack of maintenance or increased usage. You might be able to purchase the major structural elements of the bridge and refurbish and reuse them for your greenway bridge.

Guidelines for Building Common Bridge Types

The Log Footbridge. The footbridge has been built all over the world for thousands of years and is the most common trail bridge found in the United States. In all that time the basic structure has remained the same. The log footbridge has three components: log beams, decking, and in some cases handrails.

The beams are long straight timber poles. A wide variety of tree species can be used for the log beams, including pine, fir, oak, poplar, and larch. The bark is usually removed from the exterior of the tree and the ends cut square and sealed to prevent rapid decay. Clear spans of between ten and forty feet can be achieved with log beams, depending on the size and length of the log, the arrangement and number of logs that span the crossing, and the type of species selected. Logs should be notched on the ends to prevent movement and provide attachment at either end of the crossing, or they can be roped or steel cabled together as one unit.

Decking for log footbridges varies, but generally consists of sawn timber planks. The timber planks can be hand or machine sawn. The decking is nailed directly onto the log beams. A toe board is also attached on top of the decking to add strength and to serve as an edge guide for trail users.

Handrails are optional, depending on the height and length of the crossing. For short spans and heights less than five feet, handrails may not be required, although some local building codes require them if the total height of the crossing exceeds thirty inches. Check your local building codes.

Constructed-in-Place Bridge. Bridges that are constructed to fit a site-specific crossing are the most common modern bridge in the United States. These are typically constructed of steel, concrete, or wood. A variety of configurations can be used, including trusses, trestles, arches, or prefabricated beams. Generally, there is no limit to the length of span that can be crossed by this type of bridge, although clear spans are restricted by subject design load and required spacing of foundations and superstructure (see Figure 13-5).

To construct this type of bridge, you must carefully complete the following steps:

1. Define the longitudinal cross section of the crossing along the center

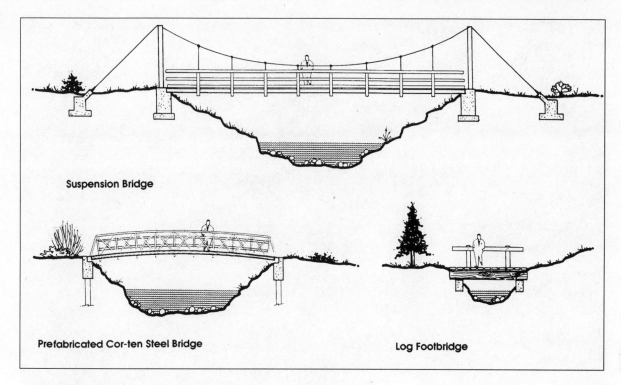

Suspension Bridge

Prefabricated Cor-ten Steel Bridge

Log Footbridge

Figure 13-5 Bridge types for use on greenways.

line of the trail, extending a distance beyond either end of the proposed bridge a minimum of twice the depth of the channel banks or fifteen feet, whichever is greater.

2. Determine the type and load-bearing capacity of the soil on both ends of the crossing where you propose to construct the footings for the bridge and/or at each point along the longitudinal section where you believe a footing, pier, or trestle will need to be constructed in order to support the design load of the bridge. Use the services of a structural or geotechnical engineer to prepare this critical information.

3. Define the two-year, ten-year, twenty-five-year, and hundred-year floodway and floodplain. These data will determine the minimum height at which your bridge decking can be constructed. Be sure to verify the proposed bridge installation with local government authorities before beginning construction.

4. Determine the upstream and downstream conditions of the stream channel. A land surveyor can provide on-site determinations of floodways and prepare required channel cross sections for engineering analysis and design.

5. For crossings that do not involve streams, you will need to work with the agency, organization, or individual to determine what is the appropriate minimum height of the bridge.

Bridge design and construction does not have to be purely utilitarian, as shown by this beautiful bridge located on The Strollway (a rail-trail) in Winston-Salem, North Carolina. (Charles Flink)

6. Determine where and how construction equipment will access the project area, and define an appropriate staging area for construction equipment, materials storage, and structure fabrication.

Once you have evaluated the conditions of the project site and crossing, you should prepare design and construction plans for the bridge. The basic bridge components that require specific design resolution include superstructure (the beams, trusses, or arches), decking, handrails, footings, piers, bridge approaches, and embankment stabilization. The documents that you prepared will need to specify all the required sizes, lengths, quantities, material description, and fabrication instructions for each component of the bridge.

Construction of the bridge should follow an orderly and systematic approach. Always start by constructing the foundations of the bridge. A typical order of construction would include: (1) bridge footings, piers, or trestles, (2) superstructure, (3) decking, (4) railing, (5) bridge approaches, and (5) embankment stabilization. If minor alterations are made to larger structural components of the bridge, as you proceed, adjustments can easily be passed along to the other components, making efficient use of time and resources.

Prefabricated Bridge. Prefabricated bridges are manufactured off site by a bridge specialist, building contractor, or agent, delivered to the site, and assembled at the specified crossing. They are usually constructed from wood, steel, high strength metal alloys, or concrete.

Prefabricated bridges have several advantages over constructed-in-place bridges: (1) the project site is generally minimally disturbed, and the size of the staging area can be reduced; (2) significant cost savings can be realized; (3) the bridge can be manufactured in advance of other construction projects, providing timely completion of the greenway facility; (4) bridge development at the project site requires a minimal amount of skill and expertise, since the prefabricated bridge is simply off-loaded from the transport vehicle and set in place at the site; (5) prefabricated bridges can often span greater distances than constructed-in-place bridges.

In order to properly construct this type bridge, you must perform the same site evaluation and obtain the same information as for constructed-in-place bridges. This information should then be conveyed to the bridge manufacturer, who will build the bridge to exact specifications. Generally, bridge manufacturers are not responsible for footings, piers, or trestles. These will have to be built in accordance with the agreed-upon design load for the bridge. Most manufacturers will supply a drawing and specifications describing how the bridge attaches to the footing or pier that you are building. This is the most important component of a prefabricated bridge; if the attachment does not match the footing design, you will be unable to install the bridge as delivered.

Prefabricated bridge manufacturers can accommodate various design load requirements, supply a variety of decking surfaces, and construct handrails of varying height and size. The span length for prefabricated bridges is limited only by such local factors as load-bearing capacity, access to the site, and type of crossing. Spans can range from twenty to more than 250 feet.

There are only a few prefabricated self-weathering (i.e., Cor-ten) steel bridge manufacturers in the United States, and they are listed in Table 13-3 for your reference.

Low-Water Bridge. As the name implies, low-water bridges are constructed to allow water to flow over the top of the bridge under certain conditions. They can be constructed in place or prefabricated from concrete, high-strength rust-resistant metal alloys such as aluminum, or, in limited applications, wood. There are several different types of low-water bridge crossings, including clear-span aluminum arches, concrete culverts or pipes encased in concrete, precast concrete superstructure and decking, and temporary wooden logs or poles. Under high water or flood conditions, the surface of the bridge is usually inundated with flowing water.

The advantage of a low-water bridge over other bridge types is the reduced length of span required for the same crossing. This situation most often occurs when you need to cross a major stream where the

Table 13-3		
Self-Weathering Steel Bridge Manufacturers		
Bridge Manufacturer	**Address**	**Phone No.**
Continental Bridge	Route 5, Box 178 Alexandria, MN 56308	800-328-2047
Steadfast Bridges (American Leisure Design)	P.O. Box 2000 Greenville, AL	800-828-8038
Hallston Supply Company	P.O. Box 41036 Sacramento, CA 95841	916-331-7211

floodway is wide and the required height of the crossing above the stream channel makes the length of an out-of-channel span bridge prohibitively expensive. A low-water bridge can cross the stream at a lower cost and, if properly designed, can be safe and accessible to all trail users.

One of the disadvantages of low-water bridges is that they collect silt from stream overwash. Another is that a low-water bridge might trap debris and clog up during high water.

Low-water bridges have different requirements than other bridge types. Because they are built within the stream channel, the evaluation of the crossing is unlike that of span bridges. The following lists the steps to construct a low-water bridge:

1. Define the length of the low-water crossing, which is usually defined as the length from the face of each stream bank.

2. Determine the composition and load-bearing capacity of the soils in the stream banks and streambed. Because these soils are frequently saturated with water or composed of deposited sand and silt, their bearing capacity is often quite low, resulting in the need for a special type of footing design.

3. Determine the force of the flowing water on the structural components of the bridge. Flowing water is the most powerful, commonly occurring, natural force on earth; you must respect and accommodate this force in the design of your bridge.

4. Define the minimum amount of clearance required to accommodate the normal flow of the stream and any objects that could be carried by the flowing water of the stream, such as fallen trees, tires, trash and debris, and junk automobiles.

5. Define appropriate access to the project site and into the stream for fabrication and construction of the low-water bridge. You should prepare a stabilization plan for those areas of the stream channel that are disturbed by bridge development.

The primary design and construction components for the low-water bridge include the bridge superstructure, which can be built as precast

An example of a low-water bridge on the Little Sugar Creek Greenway, Charlotte, North Carolina. (Charles Flink)

concrete beams, concrete culverts, or a prefabricated aluminum arch; decking; footings; and handrails, if required. Construction specifications should also define the type of materials you intend to use and the method and order of construction.

Suspension Bridge. Suspension bridges, like low-water bridges, are usually built when no other type can span the required distance of the crossing within an affordable price range. This type is more applicable in remote sites where it is virtually impossible to construct other kinds of bridges. There are two styles of suspension bridge: rope bridges, where rope cross bracing is used as the walking surface, and steel cable bridges with wood or metal superstructures and decking. It is not uncommon for these bridges to clear spans of 150 to 300 feet. Simple methods of construction can yield safe and effective clear span crossings of fifty to seventy-five feet or longer.

Suspension bridges have four structural components: a deck structure, rope or cabling, cable towers, and concrete footings at either end of the bridge. On some bridges, steel rods may serve as vertical supports, attached between the superstructure and the cable connected to each support tower. The decking superstructure can be constructed solely of wood or can have a steel beam system with a wooden deck. Flexible steel cables gracefully extend from tower to tower in a natural arc, with drop cables or steel rods running from the primary cable to the

The suspension bridge is an inexpensive and environmentally sensitive way to span large streams and rivers. This bridge is located in the Anne Springs Close Greenway in Fort Mill, South Carolina. (Charles Flink)

superstructure. The towers at the ends of the bridge are a predetermined height to support the length of the crossing and are usually constructed of large timber poles or prefabricated steel columns. The entire system is supported by concrete footings at each end of the bridge.

Wind has a significant impact on a suspension bridge and is a critical factor to evaluate at the crossing and project site. Apart from this special consideration, the same evaluation outlined for the constructed-in-place bridge applies. Table 13-4 compares various types of greenway bridges.

If your bridge crosses a stream or river, it may fall under federal jurisdiction. Therefore, you will need to secure the right to cross the stream, and, if applicable, place fill material within the stream channel or floodway, in accordance with Section 404 of the Clean Water Act.

Table 13-4

Comparison of Greenway Bridge Types

Bridge Type	Crossing Type	Maximum Span
Log footbridge	Small streams	40 ft clear span
Constructed-in-place	Small to large streams	30 ft clear span
Prefabricated wood	Streams/rivers, active Roadway intersections	60 ft clear span 200 ft with supports
Prefabricated steel	Streams/rivers, active Roadway intersections	150 ft clear span 250 ft with supports
Low-water	Streams/rivers	30 ft clear span
Suspension	Streams/rivers, active Roadway intersections	250 ft clear span 500 ft with supports

Contact the U. S. Army Corps of Engineers District office in your region and the Federal Emergency Management Agency to obtain technical specifications for securing a bridge crossing permit. These agencies can help define the vertical location of your crossing, directing you toward the selection of a proper bridge type. Also, be aware of local or state river, wetland, and floodplain protection ordinances. Once again, before you accept any structural item for your greenway bridge, you should have a certified structural engineer thoroughly examine the item.

Boardwalks

Boardwalks are most often used to provide safe and environmentally compatible trail access across ecologically sensitive landscapes. Boardwalks are almost always constructed of wood, sometimes of combined galvanized or rust-resistant steel and concrete (see Figure 13-6).

A wood boardwalk has a foundation, framing, decking, railing, and such special features as benches or overlooks. The foundation of a wood boardwalk is almost always a pier or wood post. If touching the ground or submerged in water, the post must be chemically treated, preferably with an oil-based or water-borne wood preservative such as creosote, pentachlorophenol, chromated copper arsenate, or chromated zinc chloride. Most of these wood preservatives are toxic to the natural environment and can be harmful to human health. They do, however, add the necessary longevity and structural safety. As an alternative, posts made from recycled plastics do not release harmful chemicals into the ground or water system. Check with your local recycling coordinator to obtain the names of manufacturers who can provide this new product line.

The post serves the same function as the foundation for a bridge, transferring the weight or design load from boardwalk to the soil mass. Securing the post can be accomplished either by mechanically driving the post to the depth of a stable stratum of firm soil or bedrock or by

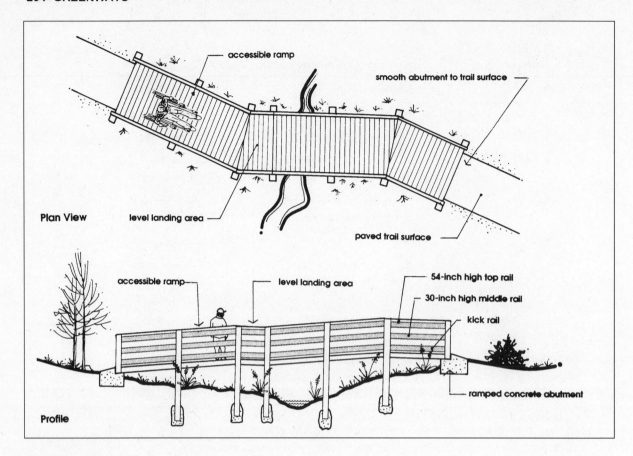

Plan View

accessible ramp

smooth abutment to trail surface

level landing area

paved trail surface

accessible ramp

level landing area

54-inch high top rail

30-inch high middle rail

kick rail

ramped concrete abutment

Profile

Figure 13-6 Accessible boardwalk.

excavating a hole and building a concrete footing around the post. The spacing and number of posts defines the ultimate design load capacity of the boardwalk.

Boardwalks can have platform framing or plank and beam framing. Platform framing involves a beam and joist system of structural support, while plank and beam framing means that only beams and wood decking are installed on top of the posts. The size, type, and spacing between beams will determine design load capacity. The most effective plank and beam construction uses the least amount of material to achieve the strongest design load capacity.

As with bridges, decking does more than serve as the surface of the boardwalk; it also plays an important structural role. Decking is usually laid flat with the bark side up; to avoid excessive and noticeable warping, most decking should be six inches wide or less. All decking for boardwalks should have a nominal thickness of at least two inches. The spacing between wood planks should be a minimum of one-quarter inch.

Boardwalk railing is not required if the height of the top surface of the decking is less than thirty inches from the surface of the ground. Railings are an optional consideration for boardwalks that meander through wetland habitat. For heights that exceed thirty inches, rails are recommended. Boardwalk railings follow the same requirements as those for bridges.

Special boardwalk features include benches, observation platforms, and partially enclosed shelters. Boardwalks can be constructed for installation directly at grade, for example, in ecologically sensitive areas where on-grade trail development would result in severe erosion of the natural soil layer. The boardwalk absorbs the foot and vehicle traffic and protects adjacent vegetation and soil structure from degradation. Boardwalks of this type are typically found in oceanside trail developments, where compaction and erosion of the sand can severely damage dune-stabilizing plant species.

Greenway Site Features

Special greenway site features offer security and safety for greenway users (e.g., fencing and vehicle barriers), provide comfort and convenience (e.g., trailhead areas, benches, trash receptacles, and shelters), offer access to the natural environment (e.g., camping facilities), and provide character and local color to the greenway (e.g., plants and outdoor art). To the extent possible, greenway features should reflect and express the environment, culture, craftsmanship, and products of the local community.

Vehicle Barriers

Keeping unauthorized motor vehicles out of greenways, particularly greenway trails, is one of the most difficult design challenges. While greenway trails may be designed to permit multiple use, including limited motorized use for some trails, facility design must discourage motorized access where it is off limits. Before committing to a vehicle barrier, consider whether you really need one or whether a symbolic barrier of some sort (e.g., loose chain or planted berm) will suffice.

Vehicle barriers provide a proven method of restricting access of unauthorized vehicles entry to the trail while allowing controlled access to emergency or maintenance vehicles. Barriers are usually installed in concrete foundations, along the property boundary between the public right-of-way or private property and the greenway. The installed height to the top of the vehicle barrier can vary, but the preferred height is thirty-six inches above the ground plane.

As a traffic control device, vehicle barriers can be designed to be lowered or removed from their foundations by authorized officials to permit access to the property. Some of the more popular barrier designs are as follows (see Figure 13-7).

1. The drop-down bollard, which contains a lock pin that can be removed to lower the bollard.

2. The hinged bollard, constructed in an L-shape to catch the front bumper of a vehicle. This bollard can be locked in place and removed as necessary.

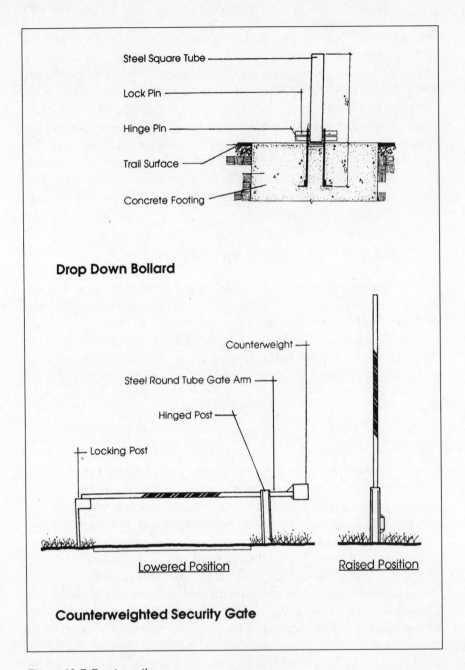

Steel Square Tube

Lock Pin

Hinge Pin

Trail Surface

Concrete Footing

Drop Down Bollard

Counterweight

Steel Round Tube Gate Arm

Hinged Post

Locking Post

Lowered Position   Raised Position

Counterweighted Security Gate

Figure 13-7 Barrier rail.

3. The removable bollard, either round or square and constructed in two parts. The lower part of the bollard is encased in a concrete foundation, and the upper part is removable, locked in position over the lower part.

4. The barrier rail with hinged or swinging gate, designed not only to restrict access but also to slow trail users as they enter the intersection of a roadway.

Vehicle barriers can be manufactured out of concrete, steel, or wood. Designs vary from simple posts, more elaborate railing, and a cable-link

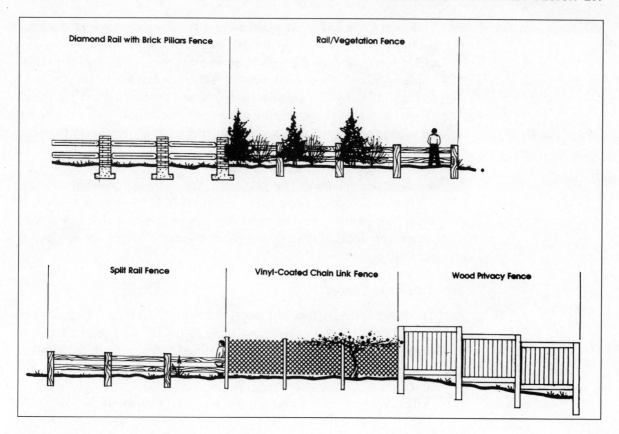

Figure 13-8 Types of fencing.

bollard system, to sophisticated and expensive concrete "Jersey barriers," which are solid precast concrete panels installed separately or
abutted one to another along a prescribed length.

Vehicle barriers should be installed so they do not conflict with trail
use. They should be placed on straightaways rather than curves, with
adequate sight distances. Be sure barriers are clearly visible, with appropriate reflective marking to avoid collisons. Per AASHTO guidelines, an open area of five feet should be provided for each direction of
travel.

Fencing

Greenway fencing serves several different functions, including separa-
tion of properties, access control, noise and wind abatement, and decoration. Fencing comes in many different forms, styles, heights, and
colors and is modular so that it can be designed to fit almost any landscape. Some types of fencing are solid walls, solid board, semitranspar-
ent panels, transparent panels, post and rail, picket, and vegetative
hedges (see Figure 13-8).

The most common reason for fencing in greenways is to separate
public and private property. Greenway fencing gives adjacent property
owners the privacy, security, and environmental conditions they desire.
Windscreens, evergreen hedges, and snow fences are three methods
used to control environmental conditions. Solid fencing can be erected

to deflect undesirable noise from the greenway. The style of the fence should be consistent with the natural surroundings. For example, a picket fence through the middle of an open range is neither a practical application, nor is it a representative feature of that sort of landscape.

Plant material is a popular and effective fencing option for greenways. Depending on their different growth habits and forms, plants can be used to separate public and private property. They make an excellent buffer along adjacent land where noise is a problem and also can be used to restrict or funnel access and direct circulation patterns. For example, thorny plants can be installed in a hedgerow to prevent unauthorized access between two adjacent tracts of land. This type of planting is often significantly less expensive than fences or walls. There are a wide variety of deciduous and evergreen plants to select for fencing or screening, listed in Table 13-5.

Trailhead Design

Trailheads (parking lots and associated facilities) are usually developed next to public rights-of-way and serve as the primary public access to the greenway. Because the trailhead shapes users' first impressions of your greenway, you should focus attention on its appearance and function.

The trailhead is the user's transition from vehicle to the greenway. The degree of transition varies, however, with each user group. For example, a horseback rider requires more distance from the parking lot to the main trail. A separate connector trail, dedicated for horse use only and approximately seven hundred feet long, enables the horse to acclimate itself to the local conditions. Horseback riders, bicyclists, and motorized users also need space in the parking lot to load and unload animals and equipment without damaging trailhead facilities or adjacent vehicles.

Trailheads also need to be secure and easily managed. A combination of fencing, lighting, and landscaping can control access and maintain adequate sight lines across the expanse of the trailhead.

A typical trailhead design includes the following:

1. maneuvering room for vehicles, pedestrians, and animals;

2. parking stalls for automobiles and (if appropriate) trucks with horse trailers or small trailers for boats, bikes, or motorcycles;

3. buildings, signs, fences, information booths or kiosks, and landscape plants;

4. connector trails to the main trail for special use;

5. security fencing and lighting, vehicle gates, and barrier systems to prevent unauthorized access to trails.

Be sure to provide convenient pedestrian access to the greenway. This will prevent short-cuts through private property. Consider installing bicycle posts or racks at key points. This will discourage riders from

Table 13-5
Plant Materials That Provide Effective Fencing and Screening

Plant Type	Attributes	Growth Habit	Climate
Evergreen			
Arborvitae	Formal shape, soft foliage	Fast, up to 15 ft	Full sun
Barberry	Weedy, thorny foliage	Medium, up to 6 ft	Partial sun
Boxwood	Formal shape, soft foliage	Slow, up to 3 ft	Partial shade
Euonymous	Loose form, glossy foliage	Medium, up to 12 ft	Partial sun
Eleagnus	Weedy, soft foliage	Fast, up to 15 ft	Full sun
Fire thorn	Weedy, thorny foliage	Fast, up to 12 ft	Full sun
Camellia	Formal, glossy foliage	Slow, up to 12 ft	Partial shade
Cotoneaster	Loose form, soft foliage	Medium, up to 12 ft	Partial sun
Cypress	Formal shape, soft foliage	Fast, up to 15 ft	Full sun
Hemlock	Loose form, soft foliage	Medium, up to 15 ft	Partial sun
Holly	Formal, spiny glossy foliage	Medium, up to 15 ft	Partial sun
Honeysuckle	Weedy, soft foliage	Fast, up to 4 ft	Full sun
Mahonia	Formal, glossy foliage	Slow, up to 3 ft	Partial shade
Oleander	Formal, soft foliage	Fast, up to 12 ft	Full sun
Osmanthus	Formal, glossy foliage	Medium, up to 15 ft	Partial sun
Pittosporum	Formal, glossy foliage	Medium, up to 12 ft	Partial sun
Privet	Weedy, soft foliage	Fast, up to 15 ft	Full sun
Laurel	Formal, glossy foliage	Fast, up to 15 ft	Full sun
Yew	Formal, soft foliage	Medium, up to 15 ft	Partial sun
Deciduous			
Buckthorn	Formal, soft foliage	Medium, up to 15 ft	Partial sun
Mock orange	Weedy, stiff thick foliage	Fast, up to 8 ft	Full sun
Forsythia	Weedy, soft foliage	Fast, up to 8 ft	Full sun
Fuchsia	Weedy, soft foliage	Medium, up to 6 ft	Partial sun
Hawthorne	Loose, thorny branching	Medium, up to 5 ft	Partial sun
Quince	Weedy, thick foliage	Fast, up to 6 ft	Full sun
Rose	Weedy, thorny branches	Fast, up to 6 ft	Partial sun

using trees, lighting fixtures, or benches to anchor their bicycles.

Benches

Greenway benches allow users to rest, congregate, or contemplate nature. Many different types of benches can be used; some are elaborately designed by architects, furniture manufacturers, or garden designers, and others are constructed from resources available to local trail clubs or parks departments.

Two key considerations are comfort and location. Greenway benches should comfortably accommodate the average adult. The preferred height of the seat is eighteen inches, and the depth of the seat should be at least fifteen inches. If a back is attached to the bench, the incline and top can vary, but the distance from the surface of the seat to the top of the backrest should equal fourteen inches, with the backrest sloping backward fifteen degrees.

Benches should be located at the primary and secondary entrances to the greenway and at regular intervals, depending on the type of greenway. On wilderness trails, benches may be provided at five-mile intervals, with room for two to four persons; on rural trails, at two-mile intervals, with accommodations for four to six persons; on suburban trails, at half-mile intervals, with space for four to six persons. On urban trails, benches may be provided as often as necessary to handle many users. Seating arrangements should vary to suit large and small groups. Seat walls or continuous vertical walls that have a finished height of eighteen inches are an option for large crowds. For multiuse or bicycle trails, benches should be set back three feet from the trail to be outside the "recovery zone" required by AASHTO for safe cycling. (The recovery zone is the strip adjacent to each side of the trail where bicyclists and other users can regain control if they wander from or are forced off the trail.)

Trash Receptacles

Trash containers are a necessary feature in all greenways. They can be attractive as well as functional.

The three basic types of trash cans are open top, semiopen or covered top, and mechanically hinged door opening. The type you select should be based on the amount of trash, overall maintenance program of the greenway, and types of users. We recommend that you use a semiopen or covered top trash receptacle when possible (see Figure 13-9).

Trash cans need to be accessible to both greenway users and maintenance personnel. At a minimum, twenty-two-gallon or thirty-two-gallon containers should be located at each entranceway and at each bench seating area. By monitoring the volume of trash, you know whether to use larger or additional receptacles. They should be set back three feet from the edge of the trail. Where you put other trash cans will depend on the location of concessions, facilities adjacent to the greenway, and areas where greenway users tend to congregate.

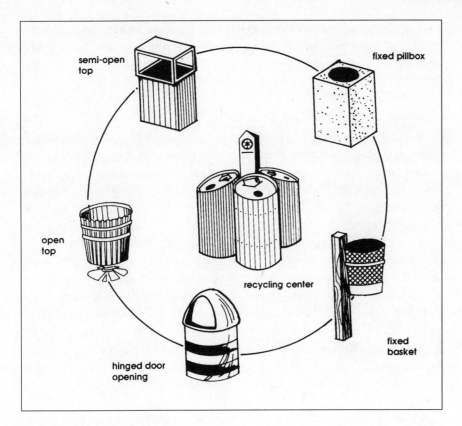

Figure 13-9 Trash receptacles.

Shelters

Shelters offer greenway users temporary cover from inclement weather and a place to congregate. They include gazebos, pavilions, and picnic shelters. Most modern shelters are designed and made by specialized manufacturers. The most cost-effective way to acquire a large shelter (sixteen feet wide by twenty-eight feet long) is to purchase it from a manufacturer. You may be able to construct smaller ones less expensively. Shelters can be multipurpose, serving, for example, as rest rooms, concession facilities, and even overnight accommodations.

Camping Facilities

Camping facilities for greenways should be designed to accommodate the user without damaging the landscape. Camping in tents or vehicles can be overnight or as long as several weeks.

Design considerations include keeping the camping facility away from developed areas and providing vehicle access and parking, washrooms and rest rooms, potable water, picnic tables, and trash disposal areas.

Tent camping areas require a level, smooth, and soft base, preferably one built above the surrounding natural grade that can drain freely, such as a six-inch sand plateau edged with landscaping ties. There should be an area where a camp fire can be safely lit and contained.

Vehicle camping requires electrical, potable water, and sanitary hookups. Sites should be designed to accommodate the largest and longest single span recreational vehicle (eleven feet wide by thirty feet long).

Plant Landscaping

Plant landscaping serves three basic functions: ecological restoration, utility, and beautification. Native vegetation is important to the health of a local environment, providing shelter and food for wildlife, emitting and absorbing essential nutrients, water, and gases within the soil and air, softening the impact of wind and rain, and retaining humidity and cooling the air. To understand how to restore native vegetation to a landscape, you should have a basic working knowledge of plant communities. Generally, there are three broad plant community groups: forest communities, open landscapes, and transitional, or edge, communities. These associations are normally further subdivided by dominant plant species and/or overstory trees. For example, there are prairie-wetland-savannah plant associations in Indiana, pine-barrens associations in New Jersey, and grassland–mixed forest associations in Virginia. All plant communities are dynamic and constantly undergo change.

In most forest communities there are overstory trees, understory trees, shrubs, and the ground layer or forest floor. Overstory trees, or canopy trees, are large deciduous and evergreen trees, with heights between thirty and one-hundred feet. Species may include oak, hickory, maple, poplar, gum, beech, sycamore, spruce, hemlock, pine, and fir. These trees are often the sign of a mature, or climax, forest. They provide shade and protection from wind and rain for other layers of the forest. The massing of these trees in forest communities creates an ecological microclimate necessary for other plant species. If you removed this layer of the forest, other layers might be replaced gradually by a totally different plant community type.

The understory is composed of medium to small trees in the forest, including sourwood, dogwood, holly, red bud, myrtle, hawthorn, magnolia, ironwood, and serviceberry. This layer of the forest, ranging in height from twelve to thirty feet, often flourishes because of the protection and benefits provided by overstory trees. Understory trees may be of greater visual interest to humans: we can more easily view the spring blooms of the dogwood, watch the cardinal pick the berries off a holly tree, and observe the change of season when the sourwood leaves turn bright red.

The shrub layer includes evergreen and deciduous species ranging in height up to twelve feet. A few of the better known species are chokeberry, privet, gooseberry, elderberry, viburnum, azalea, rhododendron, holly, blueberry, laurel, and alders. The shrub layer provides habitat and food for wildlife; it also protects and stabilizes the forest floor, enhancing the microclimate created by the overstory and understory layers. Shrubs add intricate detail to a greenway, a wide variety of colorful and pleasant-smelling spring blooms, and leaf shape, size, and texture.

The ground layer, or forest floor, is the layer where decomposing leaves mix with organic litter and debris from other layers and water to form a rich, moist habitat for succulent deciduous and evergreen plants. For upland soils these species might include ferns, honeysuckle, raspberry, strawberry, lily, sarsaparilla, sedge, orchid, sorrel, trillium, violet, moss, Virginia creeper, nettle, phlox, aster, ginger, and worts. The ground layer is habitat for a wide variety of wildlife. Most forests depend on a healthy ground layer to process and supply essential nutrients, gases, moisture, and other ecological functions to sustain the needs of other layers.

Open landscapes are those exposed to continuous sunlight, unprotected by trees or large shrubs. Open landscapes include exposed marshlands, grasslands, desert landscapes, and rocky terrain. There is far less definition to these landscapes than to forests, but this does not mean that they are not environmentally complex. Grasslands are but one example of the extreme diversity of plant species that typically can be found within an open landscape community. Plant species typical of midwest grasslands include bluestem, aster, coreposis, clover, goldenrod, sage, milkweed, thistle, and a wide variety of grasses. For open wetland or saturated soils, you may find water lily, juncus, marsh fern, and moss, alder, cattail, pondweed, bulrush, wild rice, eelgrass, reed grass, and arum. Because these landscapes lack a protective canopy, they must be able to withstand the impact of wind, sun, and rain, as well as seasonal and daily changes in temperature.

Transitional, or edge, communities occur most often where a change in moisture, soil, slope, or exposure to sunlight is present. A transition community can occur, for example, where a large tree with a broad canopy dies and falls, allowing more sunlight to reach the forest floor. Some transition communities occur gradually, over several miles. Edge landscape communities are characterized by aggressive plant species that love sunlight and wind but also moist, rich nutrients on the forest floor. Edge plants often grow wildly, with weedy, loose habits. Some plants will obtain heights of up to twelve feet. Of all three plant communities, greenway users probably find an edge community the least attractive. Ironically, it is undoubtedly the most common greenway landscape type.

Developing the Planting Plan

If greenway development includes the installation of a hard-surfaced trail, seating areas, and observation decks, the corridor may require revegetation, shaping, and beautification upon completion of construction. If, on the other hand, your corridor does not receive active trail use but has been damaged by natural forces such as floodwaters, ice, or tornados, you may simply need to replace dead or dying vegetation with new similar species.

After you have identified the plant community you are working with and enlisted the aid of an accomplished landscape architect, ecologist, or horticulturalist, you are ready to begin a planting plan for your greenway. If there is one guiding principle it is this: Make sure your landscape will look natural. A professional might use exacting measurements, plan view drawings, and cross sections or perspectives to lay out a landscape plan. Although this is useful, it is not absolutely necessary. You probably would be just as successful developing your planting plan "on site."

To begin, list some of the dominant plants found within the community. This is your "plant palate." The simpler it is, the easier it will be for you to create a successful planting plan. Be sure to select plant species that are pest free and that can withstand the environmental conditons of the location you have chosen for them (sun, wind, soils, traffic exposure). Your planting plan should address the following major design issues: the trail (if applicable) and public spaces; the function of the plants; safety and security; color and texture, spatial sequence; and installation and maintenance.

The Trail and Public Spaces

For most trails you will want to make sure that a clear ground layer exists five feet from each edge and that new trees and shrubs are planted a minimum of ten feet from each edge. This will provide better visibility around curves and a broad shoulder for multiuser safety. This also limits tree root intrusion into the subgrade and subbase of the trail. Large trees and shrubs should be installed in a manner that imitates the existing natural forest edge. Avoid planting trees in a single row. Stagger your plantings using a triangular method and plant in groups of three and five for a visually appealing result. If you want to create a more formal feel, plant trees in double rows, with every other tree staggered. Place trees and shrubs in long flowing arcs that undulate with the trail or form a curve that is independent of trail curvature. Understory trees, shrubs, and groundcover do not have to fall directly beneath overstory trees, nor do they necessarily have to follow the rows or grouping of trees already positioned. Place each successive layer in a different line or arc, again imitating the natural arrangements that are visible in the existing landscape.

The Function of the Plants

You can also use plants for functional needs. For example, to ensure that snow and ice melt from the trail, place evergreen trees and shrubs on the south side of the trail, where they are able to absorb sunlight and heat, directing that warmth back onto the trail.

There are a diverse range of functions that your planting plan might serve, including:

1. architectural: in the form of screens, walls, massings or overhead canopies

2. engineering: in the form of sound control, filtering air pollution, or erosion control

3. climate modification: in the form of temperature control, windbreaks, and shading

4. aesthetics: for framing the landscape, complementing surrounding elements, or buffering against objectionable adjacent land uses, including unsightly urban industry

5. attracting wildlife: for nesting, breeding, migration, or daily food source

6. spatial definition: for outdoor rooms, directing vision and use of the landscape

Security

Security is always a primary concern in developed greenways, and it can be dramatically enhanced by landscaping. Attention to security always begins with good visibility. Avoid placing dense and aggressive shrubs and groundcovers within the designated clear ground layer zone adjacent to trail edges, seating areas, and other public spaces. Make sure that good lines of sight are provided for approaches to bridges, tunnels, and intersections with roads or other trails. Provide breaks in your planting plan where people can escape potential trouble—don't confine a greenway user to a narrow vegetative corridor.

Color and Texture

Plants offer opportunities to add accent, texture, and color to a greenway in an aesthetically pleasing and ecologically compatible manner. The arrangement of plants by seasonal flowering or fall foliage can direct attention to special areas of the greenway. Various blooming plants can brighten up an otherwise dreary landscape. In addition, plants can create textural variety. For example, massing different shades and colors of various evergreen foliage can bring depth and character to a small outdoor space.

Be sure to mass the same color blooming plants together, as large masses of color are often more visually pleasing than individual plants. If you have a truly spectacular plant that possesses strong form and an outstanding bloom, you could surround it with a mass of other plants in order to showcase its unique qualities.

Spatial Sequence

Always consider sequencing your planting plan, especially if the plan parallels a trail. Sequencing refers to variation in plant arrangement, growth, and age.

The arrangement of plants along a linear corridor will affect the mood of the corridor. If, for example, you use only one species of tree

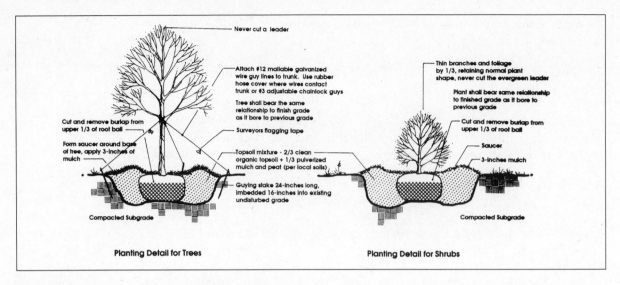

Figure 13-10 Planting details for (a) trees and (b) shrubs. Note: Planting specifications should be verified by your local nurseryman or landscape architect.

and plant it in an unyielding row ten feet away from the edge of the trail, the greenway could begin to feel monotonous. There would be little variation in height, color, shape, and texture. Altering the arrangement of plants—placing some closer to the trail edge and others farther away—provides you with an opportunity to provide a more natural setting.

Installation and Maintenance

Plant landscaping installation and maintenance are excellent projects for greenway volunteers. If this is not practical, you could use a contractor or local government labor. No matter who completes the work, always remember that a design plan is never complete until it has been successfully executed. Often changes will need to be made to the original plan, so you should be available and on site during the installation.

As you develop your planting plan, be sure to allow enough space between plants for future growth. Also keep in mind that you might lose at least 10 percent, and realistically up to 40 percent, of the plant material that has been installed. You should factor in plant loss due to natural causes or improper maintenance and balance your design so that planting will still be attractive and fulfill its function (see Figure 13-10).

Be sure that you can obtain feedback from a local government agency or organization that has volunteered to maintain your landscaping, and factor these considerations into your plan.

Greenway Art

Greenway art can reinforce the cultural, historic, or native qualities of the local environment. Greenway art not only provides a cultural amenity, it also offers a social connection between the corridor and the community by encouraging people to visit the greenway to view the latest exhibition.

You must first decide if artwork is appropriate in your greenway. If so, you should consider the following design and installation issues:

- *Artistic style.* Define the type of artwork that will be displayed. Your community may have rules and regulations governing the display of artwork. If not, contact the National Endowment for the Arts (1100 Pennsylvania Avenue, Washington, DC 20506) for guidelines that govern the display of outdoor art.

- *Location.* Determine the most appropriate place to display the greenway artwork. Generally, the best areas are highly visible, accessible, and manageable, within the boundaries of the greenway and away from adjacent private properties.

- *Safety and security.* Work with your community police and fire departments, local residential and business associations, and arts organizations to establish policies and programs for ensuring the safety of the artwork, artists, and greenway users.

- *Place responsiveness.* Be sure the art is responsive to the unique history, geography, or character of the place.

- *Management.* Develop a structure, either in cooperation with your local arts community, municipal authorities, or specially appointed volunteer organization to manage the display of greenway art. This includes methods for selecting artists and artwork, coordinating the display with interested or affected individuals or agencies, and organizing related events.

There are many ways to enhance your greenway. While we have discussed the most common features of successful greenways, we encourage you to conduct your own analysis of your greenway needs over time and develop additional facilities to make your local greenway appealing and safe for all users.

14

Greenway Safety and Liability

"The people's safety is the highest law."
—Roman maxim

Organizations and agencies that own land that is open to the public automatically assume a measure of responsibility, risk, and liability. The owner of a greenway—whether public sector, private sector, or nonprofit—must provide a safe facility for the full use and enjoyment of those who have access to it.

Public Access, Safety, and Security

Before you complete your greenway design you need to ensure that you have met at least the minimum requirements for a safe public facility. For the most part, the recommendations in this book are *minimum standards* for the design and development of greenway facilities. The standard of care you decide to meet depends on your greenway and the type of user it is designed to accommodate.

From a *legal* point of view, there are several different types of greenway users, including invitees, licensees, and trespassers. These distinctions are critical in evaluating state recreational use statutes (legislation that absolves recreation providers of liability on their lands), in evaluating insurance options, and in developing a safety program for your greenway.

1. An *invitee* is a person who has been invited to use the property by the owner for the mutual benefit of the owner and invitee. The highest standard of care is owed to an invitee. The owner of the facility must ensure that the property is safe to use during the hours of stated use and must regularly inspect the property and remove, replace, repair, or secure all hazardous features. An example of an invitee is any person who is extended an invitation from an individual or agency to use the greenway for personal or commercial interests and pursuits. Most legally permitted greenway users are considered invitees.

2. A *licensee* is a person using a property with the implied or stated consent of the owner but not for the benefit of the owner. Property owners owe a lower standard of care to licensees than to invitees. It is the owner's duty to inform or warn licensees of potentially hazardous situations and to prevent any willful harm. The owner, however, is not required to inspect the property for any potential or unknown hazards. A person who has requested permission to enter or cross a piece of property in order to launch a canoe and a Boy Scout troop that requests permission to use a private greenway are examples of licensees.

3. A *trespasser* is a person who uses property without the owner's implied or stated permission and not for the benefit of the property owner. The lowest standard of care is owed to a trespasser. If the owner knows that a trespasser is on the property, he or she has a duty not to injure the trespasser in any manner. Under certain conditions children are not regarded as trespassers and, therefore, are legally due a standard of care equivalent to that of a licensee. In many states, recreational use statutes have been written to change the status of trail users from invitees or licensees to trespassers. In effect, this reduces the liability of the landowner.

In almost every case, public facilities must be designed to higher standards than private facilities in order to accommodate those who, for whatever reason, are unable or unwilling to make use of the facility in a proper and safe manner. Design professionals call this "designing for the 1 percent." It means that, as a designer, you have to factor into your project the activities of that 1 percent. For example, if there is a chance that someone *could* fall and roll down a steep embankment, you should install a safety rail along this stretch of the trail. This 1 percent probability mainly applies to the most hazardous features of your greenway.

As a rule of thumb, you should design for the user group that has the highest safety needs. This means that a greenway trail for both bicyclists and walkers should be designed to accommodate the biker, whose safety requirements are more stringent. A boardwalk could be designed to support heavier loads than minimally required, for example, or the trail tread might be constructed wider than applicable standards suggest. By accounting for and accommodating the 1 percent, you reduce your liability.

A sound safety program for a heavily used recreational greenway includes the following:

1. A safety committee or coordinator

2. A greenway safety manual

3. User rules and regulations

4. Greenway emergency procedures

5. A safety checklist (see Figure 14-1)

6. A user response form (to solicit feedback on problem areas)

7. A system for accident reporting and analysis

8. A regular maintenance and inspection program

9. Site and facility development and review

10. A public information and management program

11. An employee training program for safety and emergency response

☐ **Vegetation clearing and management**: overhanging limbs and weedy growth obstruct views, "widow-makers" in trees, poisionous vegetation near trail, debris on trail surface.

☐ **Streams**: stream banks near trail eroding, drainage pipes clogged with debris cause stream overwash - leave standing water and mud on trail, water quality of stream is substandard.

☐ **Roadway crossings**: sight lines for motorists and greenway users obstructed, caution signs not located on trail and roadway, pavement markings for crossing inadequate

☐ **Trail tread surfaces**: hard surfaced pavement cracked and uneven, soft surface tread rutted, weedy vegetation encroaching into tread, standing water and mud in tread.

☐ **Trail bridges**: hand rails loose, bridge decking warped, loose or missing, bridge footings exposed from erosion, rotting structural timbers, approach rails missing.

☐ **Roadway underpasses/overpasses**: tread surface wet or full of litter and debris, lighting systems inoperable, light bulbs burned out, fencing inadequate to protect users.

☐ **Safety railings**: not located in areas of need, post and footings loose, handrails missing, rotting timber, corroded steel, not long enough, not high enough for all users.

☐ **Boardwalks**: rotting timber, handrails missing, bench seating vandalized, post and footings loose or sinking, decking warped, loose or missing.

☐ **Signage systems**: regulatory and warning signs missing or improperly located, information signs vandalized or missing, sign posts corroded or rotting, signs vandalized.

☐ **Lighting systems**: bulbs burned out, fixtures broken or vandalized, support pole/structure damaged, electrical wiring exposed, damaged or cut, ballast inoperable.

☐ **Drinking water systems**: water not potable, spigot clogged, spigot switch inoperable, basin drain clogged, water pressure inadequate, standing water around fountain.

☐ **Solid waste disposal**: trash receptacles overflowing, trash receptacles vandalized or damaged, litter and debris discarded throughout greenway, illegal dumping occurring.

☐ **Sanitary sewer system**: toilets clogged or inoperable, sanitary main inoperable, clean-outs damaged or inoperable, stalls and building vandalized, sinks clogged, standing water.

☐ **User conduct**: cyclists and rollerbladers riding too fast, horses using pedestrian tread, motorized users accessing trail, dogs off leashes, after dark parties, alcohol consumption.

☐ **Public parking**: pavement surface littered with broken glass and debris, parking spaces not defined, disabled spaces not provided, trailer parking not provided, entry drive has poor site lines, vegetation obscures trailhead.

Figure 14-1 Greenway safety checklist. This safety checklist describes the most common safety concerns within a typical greenway. Use this list to create a checklist for each greenway segment or for an entire system. The checklist should be used in the field, to inspect the current condition of the greenway. Check the appropriate box that defines the safety problem, and underline, circle, or highlight specific concerns. Cross check this list against maintenance reports.

12. Ongoing research and evaluation.

A good security program begins with fair, thorough policies that govern the way a greenway can be entered and used and that define the relationship that the greenway has to other adjacent land. These policies involve setting the hours of operation, who will use greenway, which local uses will be permitted or restricted, and the type of land management adopted. Policies should be published for the entire community and posted on signs at appropriate sites throughout the greenway.

The safety and security program should identify the agencies that are responsible for law enforcement, fire protection, and management in the corridor. The management agency should be a public or private body capable of responding to diverse emergencies—usually the local parks and recreation department. Law enforcement agencies include local park rangers, municipal police, county sheriffs, highway patrol, and special investigators from state and federal agencies. All management, law enforcement, and fire protection agencies should be given maps of the greenway, showing entry points, and keys to locked gates or bollards. They should be encouraged to provide the greenway owner or managing agent with a monthly safety and security report.

Education about greenway rules involves more than posting signs. A good safety and security program includes publication of maps, pamphlets, and other literature that describe policies and regulations. This information should be made available to all users through an accessible distribution system such as an information kiosk at the entrance to the greenway.

People should be instructed to use their best judgment when visiting a greenway alone; you might recommend the buddy system. Crime on greenways is rare; where it does occur it is usually directed at people who are alone and in parking lots, not on trails.

Day-to-day greenway activities require equal attention to emergency response. For example, if someone calls to report that a tree has fallen across a trail, the safety and security program should have someone designated who can remove the tree immediately. Rapid response to public concerns is essential for a truly successful greenway.

An effective safety and security program always involves the community. An Adopt-a-Greenway Program, for example, might encourage local neighborhood associations, corporations, nonprofit organizations, school groups, or individuals to adopt certain sections of the greenway and to patrol these areas to ensure that they are safe and secure. This type of program is most effectively managed by a local government entity that receives and distributes the information. These volunteer programs broaden the capabilities of the overall safety program, expanding the management team and securing the help and support of the community.

Managing Multiuser Conflicts

In heavily used multipurpose greenways, painting center lanes along a trail may be the simplest safety precaution you can take. It is a subliminal message to users that people will be traveling in both directions, whether on bike, foot, or other mode of transportation.

A well-conceived safety program that provides the user with a clear code of conduct for the greenway is the first step in avoiding conflicts (see Figure 14-2). Your community may also wish to adopt a trail user ordinance as an effective method for resolving user conflicts. The King County, Washington, Parks Department's successful "Model Path-User Ordinance" provides King County authorities with the ability to enforce specific conduct guidelines for the health, safety, and welfare of all users. One provision is the ability to assess a fine of up to $500 for bicyclists who exceed the fifteen mile per hour speed limit while on the pathway. The ordinance contains ten articles, which address:

- Where the regulations apply

- Rules for using a path

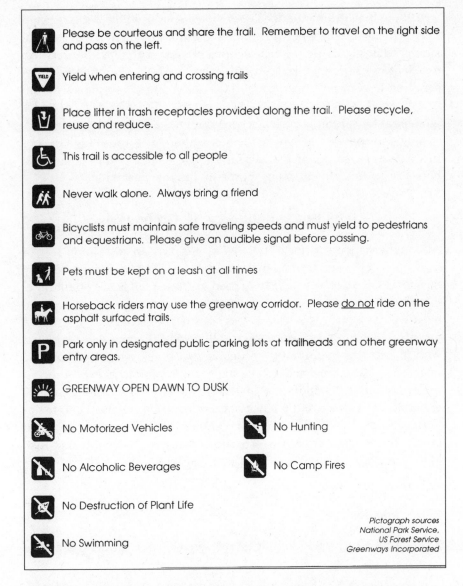

Figure 14-2 A recommended graphic and written code of conduct for greenway users. This one was developed for a single tread, multiuser greenway facility and should be modified for other greenway types. The graphic symbols should be consistent with international pictographs; written text should be brief and informative.

- Regard for other path users
- Behavior for groups on a path
- Using audible signals when passing
- Overtaking path users on the left
- Entering a crossing path
- Use of lights on path users
- Path use under the influence of alcohol
- Depositing litter on a path

Although an ordinance does not in itself resolve multiuser conflict, it does provide a framework for enforcing uniform and fair trail use regulations while clarifying the expectations placed on all types of users. An excellent brochure, published by the New England Mountain Bike Association (69 Spring Street, Cambridge, MA 02141), recognizes the inherent conflict between bikers and other trail users and provides guidelines for safe and courteous behavior on the trail.

Single-purpose trails may be the best solution in areas of high or conflicting use or environmental sensitivity. For example, trail biking and horseback riding often damage footpaths and informal trails.

Liability Associated with Greenways

Although accidents in most greenways are rare, an overriding fear of lawsuits and the rare mishap make liability a serious issue for greenway developers. Particularly in heavily used greenways, it is important to remember that bicycle accidents do happen, and drowning can occur in open water such as lakes, rivers, and streams. Regardless of how well a greenway has been designed, there will always be some risk associated with its use. It is important to recognize that public agencies or private managers may be sued and to take steps to minimize legal exposure.

As an inducement to landowners to provide recreational access to their lands, the New Jersey Open Lands Management Act requires the state to contribute to the costs of providing and maintaining recreational access to private lands. Items include installation and repair of fences and screening, parking areas, stiles, access roads, signed picnic areas, boat-launch areas, restoration of vandalized crops, and other improvements. Public meetings are used to introduce the concept to landowners, who may then file an application for financial assistance.

Several common conditions can lead to liability suits: facilities unable to handle the volume and intensity of use, poor management and maintenance, and failure to recognize a potentially hazardous situation. In an article for the Land Trust Alliance titled "Land Trust Liability and Risk Management," George Pring identifies five general areas of liability:

1. Bodily injury and death

2. Property damage

3. Personal injury, including libel, interference with business, and false arrest

4. Contract and trust violations

5. Violation of other laws, including environmental damage

Prepare your organization for potential liability suits by (1) having a well-thought-out maintenance and risk management program that reduces the likelihood of negligence; (2) acquiring an adequate liability insurance policy that covers all aspects of your greenway; (3) making sure that your organization is aware of recreational use statutes laws and recent case histories in your state or locality.

If you have created a nonprofit organization interested in owning, developing, or managing a heavily used greenway, it is strongly advised that you find a government "owner," such as a parks department, to assist you with the legal responsibilities of your project. Local governments are in a much better position than nonprofit organizations to assume the risk and liabilities associated with highly developed greenways. If yours is a small public agency and you are concerned about exposure, investigate a partnership with a larger public agency such as a county or state agency.

Recreational Use Statutes

As of this writing, forty-seven states have recreational use statutes in place. These laws are designed to limit the liability of public organizations, easements donors, landowners, and others who open their lands for public use. Some offer 100 percent protection, while others set a dollar limit on damages. A well-crafted statute can reduce liability and insurance costs while encouraging private landowners to allow recreation on their lands. In addition to recreational use statutes, many states have special conservation easement laws, recreational trail use laws, volunteer immunity laws, and good Samaritan laws, as well as individual protection through incorporation. Before you make use of your state's recreational use statutes, obtain a copy of the enabling legislation and have your organization's attorney examine it for geographic coverage and exclusions.

Inadequate recreational use statutes are routinely cited as a roadblock to drawing private landowners into the greenway vision. It is important to seek legal advice as to whether your state's recreational use statute is adequate for your liability needs. Weak statutes are often characterized by ambiguous wording or limited scope, or both. Specific problems include the following:

- Laws may require the express permission of the landowner for access to the property. This policy, which requires the owner to be a gate-keeper, discourages owners and users.

- The courts have applied recreational use statutes with a lack of consistency.

- Most statutes are out of date and do not reflect current recreation patterns. (Many statutes were written to permit hunting on privately owned agricultural or forest land.)

- Many statutes are ambiguous with respect to the definition of uses allowed on the land; the definition of the owner of the land (tenant, lesee, and manager are often excluded); the terms of use; and geographic area (urban land, for example, may not be covered).

Many statutes do not protect landowners if the public is charged a fee to use the property. This makes it difficult for conservation organizations and land trusts to defray maintenance and caretaking costs. Even donations and map sales may be cloudy issues.

In many states, an owner must wait until an injured person sues and then raise the defense of the statute, running the risk of incurring litigation expense before a determination is made by the courts. There is no way for the owner to receive a conclusive decision as to which of the statutes applies to his or her land at the time he or she is considering whether to allow access to the land.

An ideal recreational use statute

- Is well publicized so that people know about it and want to participate

- Provides tax relief in exchange for allowing public use of private land

- Allows fees to be dedicated to protection and maintenance of the resource

- Allows landowners to post warning signs without imposing liability on the landowner

- Affords owners of urban recreational land the same protection that rural landowners enjoy

- Includes all recreational uses

- Covers volunteers working on the land

- Has an "advanced registration scheme" and state indemnification so that landowners will know in advance that they cannot be sued by injured parties or awards costs of litigation to recreation providers

- Extends the definition of "owner" to include managers, lessees, conservation organizations, government entities, and others who hold an interest in the land

A subcommittee of the American Bar Association is working on draft model legislation for consideration by the states. In the meantime, contact your state Attorney General about the need for a better recreational use statute in your state.

Remember that lawsuits are very rare. Most lawsuits involve cases in which the landowner did something outrageous, charged fees for access, or failed to perform simple risk management or are in states where the courts are biased against the statute.

For more specific information about state and local liability issues that affect your greenway, contact your state attorney general's office or city attorney's office.

Risk Management Programs

Accidents can happen to anyone, anywhere, anytime. There is generally a pattern to accidents, however, and often a planning, design, or management shortcoming can be identified and remedied. Accidents in many cases are preventable through a well-planned risk management program.

Whereas each organization or agency must tailor its risk management program to meet specific needs, there are, according to Dr. Seymour Gold of the University of California, Davis, some vital components common to all, including:

- *Risk identification.* Conduct regular on-site inspections of your greenway. Make a record of your inspections of the facility, noting where potentially hazardous situations occur, what type of hazard exists, and what user group is most likely at risk.

- *Risk evaluation.* Determine the likelihood of an accident occurring at the identified hazard, as a factor of the facility's age, amount or intensity of use, or as a result of ineffective or poor design.

- *Risk treatment.* Once you have identified the problem area and determined the likelihood of an accident occurring, you have four options for correcting the problem:

1. Risk avoidance—prohibit use of the dangerous area and reroute traffic until the area or facility is repaired;

2. Risk reduction—repair the problem area immediately, increase the maintenance to the problem area, limit the intensity of use in a specific area, or post warning signs notifying users of the problem area;

3. Risk retention—obtain risk waivers from all greenway users;

4. Risk transfer—transfer property to another agency capable of effectively dealing with the problem area, or transfer the risk to the user, requiring the user to obtain necessary insurance before using the greenway.

Additionally, if an accident does occur, it is wise to immediately notify the public of the accident and take steps to secure the hazardous area. In areas where there are a high number of users, you should make every effort to notify the public of dangers associated with crowded facilities.

The Need for Insurance

While liability of landowners and managers on public and private greenways is always an issue, in reality few suits are brought against landowners. In spite of these facts, good liability insurance is a necessity in the rare event that someone is injured and to ease landowners' fear of lawsuits. Because recreational use statutes are often less than ideal, nonprofit organizations and public agencies should have liability insurance to protect themselves against unanticipated litigation.

In essence, liability insurance is a transferring of financial risk. Some large municipalities and government agencies choose to set aside a fund to pay claims rather than premiums to an insurance agency. This is known in the insurance industry as "going bare" or "self-insurance."

When it comes to insurance, three basic questions are usually asked: (1) How do you shop for insurance? (2) What type of insurance do you need? (3) How do you determine an adequate level of coverage based on the type of exposure in your greenway?

How to Shop for Insurance. To a large degree, the type of organization or agency that you represent will determine the insurance carrier that, by law, can provide insurance. For private landowners who provide greenway easements on their land, coverage might be extended

Because remediation is so costly, many land trusts and agencies won't approve gifts of land without an evaluation for possible hazardous waste contamination. This often involves a thorough inspection of the land, historical review of all land use records pertaining to the sites, and the inclusion of protective language in legal documents. Some possible problem areas include land (or neighboring lands) with illegal disposal sites, underground storage tanks, septic systems, paint shops, filling stations, industrial sites, and railroad yards.

under a local land trust's policy or the town's insurance policy. (Also, a small increase in homeowner insurance premiums might provide adequate coverage.) You should examine policies from at least three carriers. Most liability insurance policies can be evaluated on the basis of the following criteria:

1. Define the specific insurance policy coverage, terms, and conditions, including all exclusions, being offered by the carrier. Different insurance agencies will provide varying levels of coverage.

2. Determine the most recent record of the insurer regarding claims handling and defense capability—or the ability of the insurer to adequately cover a claim.

3. Establish the amount of experience and length of time the insurer has been in business in your state. Contact your local state insurance administrator, the Occupational Health and Safety Administration (in Washington, D.C.) or the A. M. Best Company of New Jersey, which rates insurance companies, in order to determine this information.

4. Define the financial strength of your insurer. During the 1980s several insurance companies made bad investments that significantly weakened their ability to offer adequate coverage.

5. Determine whether the insurer operates a quality-control and loss-prevention program. Such programs provide up-to-date communications regarding the insurance industry, review of important state and national legislation, and direct assistance to your organization in reviewing your risk management program.

6. Compare the cost of premiums among the carriers that offer the best total package.

What Type of Insurance Do You Need? There are several types of insurance coverage you may want to carry. These should be explored in detail with your organization or agency, attorney, risk manager, and insurance agent.

- *Commercial general liability* is usually set up to cover property, including buildings, structures and personal property, medical expenses, and business expenses associated with the operation and management of your greenway. If someone slips and falls on the greenway, your general liability policy will pay the claim for medical expenses associated with the injury.

- *Nonowned automobile liability* covers cars, trucks, vans, and other vehicles that you or members of your organization drive and that are not owned by the organization. This is important coverage, especially where volunteers involved with maintenance or management use their own cars to perform work.

- *Property and owned asset* insurance covers specific articles of property or assets, such as equipment, that are not covered by your general liability policy.

- *Umbrella liability* insurance is essentially an additional liability policy that increases the amount of coverage you originally purchased with your commercial general liability and may broaden your coverage to include other areas of risk. A popular and affordable plan, known as the "Green Umbrella," is available through the Land Trust Alliance. This plan has been specially prepared by the Land Trust Alliance for land trusts and other organizations that are involved in land conservation. It offers essential insurance coverage at a reduced annual premium.

- *Volunteer workers accident* insurance is a death/dismemberment/medical policy that insures volunteers who perform physical labor on the greenway. This is inexpensive insurance that serves to supplement an individual's own major medical policy and is helpful these days, as the cost of medical services continues to escalate.

- *Workers' compensation*, also known as employees' liability insurance, is usually purchased for the paid staff of an organization and is not required if your organization has no paid staff. This coverage is required by most states for all paid staff and covers medical and disability payments for employees who are injured in connection with their jobs.

- *Association liability* insurance is also called "Directors and Officers" insurance; however, it also covers the corporation, employees, and volunteers. This is a "wrongful acts" policy that covers poor business judgments, breach of contract, errors and omissions, discrimination, and interference with another business. This is quite expensive insurance and is usually only required for larger organizations that transact a good deal of business and have large staffs.

How Much Coverage Should You Purchase? Your insurance agent should be able to recommend an appropriate level of insurance, given the risk and liability your agency faces. George Pring recommends that land trusts consider purchasing policies that effectively provide for $5 million of general liability coverage. This figure is probably a realistic estimate for most organizations involved with greenway development.

Given the litigious nature of today's society, lawsuits are always a risk, but the fear of liability should not prohibit us from moving forward with greenway efforts. The key is to plan carefully, seek expert legal advice, design well, and operate with a standard of care that puts public safety first. These actions, combined with a good risk management program and adequate insurance, can make the reality of greenway liability far less intimidating.

15

Greenway Management

"A stitch in time saves nine."
—Ben Franklin

Creating a greenway is arduous but rewarding. What a thrill to see your vision take shape. Ribbon cutting ceremonies and dedications are wonderful. As new segments of the greenway materialize, however, a host of new considerations must be addressed. Who will be responsible for maintenance and operations? How will the safety and beauty of the greenway be protected in the future? How will activities be funded? Who will be liable in the event of legal action?

Like any public facility—a park, a road, a school, or a ball field—a greenway must be taken care of. Maintenance is often a subject planners and greenway champions avoid—not because of malice or neglect but because of simple oversight. Maintenance is not exciting, but it is important.

This chapter details the maintenance concerns of highly developed, publicly managed recreational greenways concerns. For low-intensity greenways, choose the elements that make sense for your situation.

Greenway Management: The Seven Key Components

Greenways are long-term investments. With proper care, they can last for many generations. A good management program requires forethought and careful planning. It is important to consider how the land, amenities, and facilities will be used, how they will age, and how they will be repaired or replaced in the future. How do you create a successful management plan? Let's look at the key components of a successful greenway management program.

1. User safety and risk management

2. Maintenance

3. Patrol and emergency procedures

4. Administration

5. Programming and events

6. Stewardship and enhancement

7. Finding money for maintenance

User Safety and Risk Management

Like almost everything in life, greenway activities involve some risk. However, it is important to minimize risks associated with greenways. Doing this involves asking two questions: Is the risk inherent? Is it obvious? An inherent risk is one that cannot be avoided when participating in a sport or activity. For example, river rafting inherently involves some risk of drowning, and bicycling involves some risk of falling. An obvious risk is one that is apparent to users. It is important to assume that avoidable hazards and risks are eliminated and unavoidable hazards are clearly marked. See Chapter 14 for additional discussion of this topic.

Maintenance

Backcountry greenways have different management concerns. Removal of trash and fallen trees, trail maintenance, camper densities at environmentally sensitive areas, forest fires, human waste, search and rescue, and whether to implement a sign-in or permit system are a few considerations. Furthermore, these sensitive areas may deteriorate with use. Trampling, soil compaction, erosion, and vegetation loss are some of the consequences of increased or inappropriate use. During certain seasons of the year it may be necessary to limit the number of hikers using certain trails.

Good greenway maintenance begins with proper planning and design, followed by quality construction. Investment in quality workmanship and materials will pay off over the life of a greenway. No matter how well conceived or built, however, greenway facilities always wear, age, and receive abuse. Thus, a good maintenance program is essential.

There are two kinds of maintenance—*routine* and *remedial*. Routine maintenance is the day-to-day regime of weed control, tree trimming, inspection, cleaning, trash collection, and other regularly scheduled activities. Routine maintenance also includes minor repairs and replacements such as fixing a broken fence post or painting a bridge. Remedial maintenance means correcting landscape problems and replacing or restoring major components that have been destroyed or damaged or have deteriorated. Examples of remedial maintenance include stabilization of a severely eroded hillside or the replacement of a pedestrian bridge lost in a flood. Ideally, remedial maintenance items should be part of a long-term capital improvements plan. The unexpected can and does occur, however, so have a contingency plan.

On a typical urban greenway that includes a river, a multiuse trail, and playgrounds, maintenance can be expected to fall into several key areas. Some of the more significant ones are discussed briefly here. Rural and nonrecreational greenways without multiuse trails will, of course, require less intensive maintenance, although some of the tasks will still apply.

Stream Channel Maintenance

Water-oriented greenways require maintenance of the channel bed, stream banks, and related structures. Activities include removal of debris and trash, litter collection, erosion control and repair, maintenance of in-stream structures, care of fish habitat, and water quality monitoring.

Stream channel maintenance helps keep the water resource in prime condition and, more importantly, improves flood control, aquatic habitat, and water quality. For this reason, opportunities for joint ventures

Bicycle-mounted "Trail Rangers" can perform many basic maintenance tasks as well as being good-will ambassadors for the greenway. (Robert Searns)

with local flood control, wildlife, and utility agencies should be considered. Be sure, however, that any maintenance vehicle access is kept to a minimum.

Multiuse Trail Maintenance

Keeping trails in good repair is important to people's safety and enjoyment. Some communities sweep their trail surfaces regularly—weekly on some heavily traveled greenways. Sweeping depends on local conditions and needs but is particularly important if, for example, there are thorny plants that could cause flat tires. Unpaved and soft-surfaced trails will need regular repair of minor washouts and other damage. Underpasses must be kept free of silt and debris. Asphalt sometimes needs patching and sealing.

In colder climates, snow and ice are a maintenance issue. Drainage structures such as culverts, ditches, and swales should be kept in good operating condition. Clean out debris from inlets and culverts. Check also for puddles and washouts caused by unchecked runoff and remedy

Youth and the environment are brought together under programs such as the California Conservation Corps (CCC). Each year the CCC employs young adults to work on conservation projects sponsored by local, state, federal government, and nonprofit organizations. This mutually beneficial program not only provides young adults with employment and the development of work skills, it also gives conservation-related organizations access to an affordable labor force. The Corps' accomplishments include construction of and rebuilding park improvements and stream rehabilitation.

them as soon as possible. Safety railings, pedestrian bridges, signs, and other structures must also be kept in good repair. This includes periodic structural inspections of bridges and other features. From time to time, the services of a structural engineer may be required to assess any deterioration or damage.

Overhead vegetation should be trimmed regularly for adequate headroom. Multiuse pedestrian and bike paths should have a minimum of eight feet, six inches clearance. For equestrian use, maintain a minimum clearance of twelve feet. Be sure also to clear away any dead trees or limbs that might fall on the trail. Ideally, a two- to five-foot-wide swath should be mowed along both sides of an urban multiuse trail to create a shoulder for joggers and horses. The mowed shoulder creates a groomed look, making the trail more inviting. This may not be appropriate on some greenways, where a more natural vegetated trail edge is preferred.

Finally, it is important to have a plan for providing detours when the trail is disrupted by various drainage, road, bridge, and utility projects. "Dead End" and "Trail Closed" signs do not score points with users. Safe, well-signed, easy-to-use detours must be a matter of interagency policy and be required of contractors who disrupt the trail.

Graffiti and Vandalism Control

Nothing does more damage to the feel of a greenway corridor than unchecked graffiti and vandalism. Clearly, the first step in addressing this issue is to use design components that are not prone to abuse. The goal is to express architectural quality with components that are both durable and attractive. Always keep in mind how a component will be replaced if broken, and where possible, avoid exotic custom-made elements if they are easily damaged.

The key to vandalism and graffiti control is quick cleanup and repair. Graffiti always invites more graffiti. Rapid cleanup dramatically reduces the likelihood that the problem will recur. Regular monitoring is a must so that action can be taken quickly.

There are several approaches to the graffiti problem, including removal by chemicals or sandblasting, special graffiti-proof surfacing, and—a favorite—the quick paint-over. For example, a concrete wall can be given a coating of a special durable concrete paint, such as Thoroseal. Maintenance crews simply paint over the graffiti. Again, speed is the key. It's amazing how quickly graffiti drops off when it is painted over within hours or days of perpetration.

Vegetation Management

Most greenways feature natural-appearing environments rather than the groomed formal turf grass you might see in a traditional city park. Where possible, minimize the size of the turf grass areas. Many greenways, however, do string together more formal parks. The illusion of a larger more attractive park can be created by landscaping and buffering focal points like trailheads and picnic areas. Another vegetation

Post rules prominently for all to see. (Lisa Gutierrez)

management tool, particularly in urban greenways, is the environmentally sustainable, low-maintenance landscape that appears natural and inviting. This kind of landscape can be developed over time using native grasses, wildflowers, selective weed removal, and in urban areas, articulated mowing. Articulated mowing means shaping a natural landscape by grooming the trail shoulders and selectively creating mowed meadows and sweeps along the corridor. Undesirable weeds are identified and removed—ideally by cutting rather than chemical application. This approach is somewhat experimental and will need to be tailored to local conditions. You should consult a landscape architect, horticulturalist, or maintenance expert.

One other important objective to keep in mind is management of the vegetative understory for user security. Maintain good lines of sight, user surveillance, and escape routes. Avoid blind thickets close to the trail where a person could hide. These areas may pose, or appear to pose, a threat to users.

Signage Systems

An information sign system is an important element in a good greenway management program. In addition to the information given in Chapter 13, here are some pointers. *Mile markers* are a good idea along a greenway trail. They let users know where they are and how far they've gone, help maintenance people locate problems, tell police and rescue personnel where an accident or incident has occurred, and index problem spots. Markers placed every quarter to one-half mile seem to satisfy these purposes. In addition, major street crossings should have clear signs. You may want to consider assigning a legal street designation to your greenway so that police and rescue crews have an address to respond to in an emergency. Many cities have grid address systems that can be applied to a greenway, for example, "go to 5100 Greenway Trail South" means a tenth of a mile south of the "5000 South" cross street.

Boating Facilities

If your greenway has boating facilities, they should be patrolled and maintained. Hazards should be well marked and signs kept in good repair. Rapids and boat chutes should be kept clear of logs and other debris. Similar considerations apply to power boating areas.

Maintenance Inventory and Schedule

A good greenway maintenance plan should include an inventory system and schedule that address both routine and remedial maintenance functions. Be sure you allow for regular reporting of maintenance needs. This can be done with a standard checklist. The checklist should itemize all maintenance functions and provide a way to report problems and their location. There should also be a way to log the resolution of each reported maintenance problem. Reporting sheets should be kept on file and periodically reviewed by maintenance supervisors. Review of maintenance logs can also identify any trends or problem areas that may point to deep rooted, less obvious function or design flaws.

The maintenance schedule should be part of the greenway master plan and revised as necessary. Key elements of the maintenance schedule should include:

1. List of specific maintenance activities

2. Frequency of each activity

3. Cost per application of each activity

4. Annual cost of each activity

5. Who will perform the activity (e.g., parks crews, flood-control agency, volunteers)

The maintenance program should also entail a public monitoring program, which allows for citizens to report maintenance problems and receive feedback. It should also provide a procedures manual for performing maintenance and give the total annual cost of the program.

The National Parks and Recreation Association provides an excellent course annually at several locations across the country. The program includes trail maintenance and other topics relevant to greenway management.

Table 15-1 presents a typical maintenance schedule for a river-oriented urban greenway that offers both land and water recreation. The list is by no means inclusive, but it does overview key costs and concerns. As a rule of thumb, annual maintenance for a full-service urban greenway corridor and adjacent parks can be expected to cost between $2,500 and $9,500 per mile. The City of Boulder, Colorado, for example, spends $45,000 per year to maintain five miles of the Boulder Creek Greenway—a state-of-the-art urban greenway. Seattle, on the other hand, spends only $2,500 per mile to maintain its bicycle trails.

Patrol and Emergency Procedures

Patrolling the Greenway

Crime is a growing concern in many urban areas, and public recreational facilities are no exception. As a result, patrol has become an element of greenway operations in some areas of the country. Patrolling a greenway serves a number of purposes: security, vandalism prevention, handling of medical emergencies, rescue, evacuation in the event of a flood or other problem, and dissemination of public information.

Patrol can be handled in several ways. In some places city police patrol greenway corridors. For others, the greenway management agency hires its own rangers. Rangers can be trained law enforcement personnel or they may be seasonal employees who merely advise and assist by traveling on foot or by bicycle with a two-way radio. Regardless of the approach, patrol should be planned for in the greenway operations budget.

Medical Treatment and Other Emergencies

Every local government should provide for medical treatment of injured or incapacitated greenway users. This involves emergency treatment and nonemergency first aid. Treatment can be provided by either full-time or part-time personnel. For this reason, all park rangers (even seasonal employees) should be certified in first aid and cardiopulmonary resuscitation (CPR). Greenway plans should also address access to telecommunications and provision of on-site medical supplies.

Emergency plans, prepared in conjunction with police, fire, and medical personnel, should define points of access, safe and effective routes for emergency vehicle travel, load limits for bridges and boardwalks, distance in minutes and miles from greenway access points to local medical facilities, and jurisdictional responsibility of police, fire, and medical agencies. Emergency plans should be illustrated and posted at entrances to the greenway system so that users will have access to essential telephone numbers and other critical information.

An important design issue is to ensure that the trails are wide enough and strong enough to support the weight of a fully loaded ambulance, generally close to 6.5 tons. As specified in Chapter 11, your trail, bridges, trailhead entrance areas, parking lots, and access roads should be designed to support this load.

The Meramec River Greenway in St. Louis cites the problem of managing parks along remote sections of the river in different jurisdictions. Agreements among agencies to trade or consolidate management responsibilities, but not ownership, of contiguous lands has been proposed to ease the burden of managing disjunct properties.

Table 15.1
Sample Greenway Maintenance Schedule

Maintenance Item	Frequency per year	Cost per year	Comments
1. River Care			
•Routine inspection	26	Varies	This can be done by volunteers with a checklist.
•Monitor water quality	As required	Varies	Testing may be provided by local health dept., water quality agency or a school biology class.
•Routine channel maintenance	2-3	$0.30 to $0.20/lf	Debris and litter removal, minor erosion control, revegetation. Cost depends on width of channel and amount of debris generated.
•Remedial channel maintenance	As required	Varies	Rock rip rap, retaining walls, grade control structure, silt removal
•Dam/boat chute maintenance	2	$ 250/ chute	Keep structures clear of debris, maintain integrity. Should be evaluated at beginning and end of each boating season. Should be checked after storms and daily by rangers to assure no obstructions are present.
•Fish habitat care & stocking	Varies	Varies	By others. May include river bank plantings.
•Insect control	As required	Varies	Identify and treat potential breeding ares.
2. Trail Maintenance			
•Inspection	26	Varies	This can be done by volunteers with a checklist.
•Sweeping (paved only)	18	$1300/mile	Applies to paved trails. Use a vacuum sweeper.
•Asphalt trail	As required	Varies	Repair, seal, replace, patch. Maintenance need for service depends on thickness and level of use. The more use, the longer the life.
•Crusher fine and non-paved trail maintenance	As required	Varies	Fill holes, remove weeds, repair, replace.
•Litter pickup	12	$500/mile	Can be supplemented by volunteers.
•Erosion control	As required	Varies	Repair erosion and silt producing areas
•Weed control	3	$400/mile	Remove noxious species from trail corridor.
•Snow/ice removal	As required	Varies	Warning: Utilize sand w/o salt in shaded spots on concrete.
•Silt removal	As required	Varies	Sweep and pickup.
•Mowing trail shoulders	3-4/yr	$250/mile	Mow a 3'-5' wide shoulder.
•Graffiti removal minor repairs	As required	$250/mile	Can be done by rangers or volunteers.
•Toilets, drinking fountains service	As required	Varies	Use chemical or composting type in attractive vandal- resistant frame.
•Police/ranger patrol	As required	$1500/mile	Ideally a bicycle mounted patrol person with radio.

(Table 15-1 continued)

Maintenance Item	Frequency per year	Cost per year	Comments
3. Parks Upland Features			
• Turf areas and plazas	As required	$2800/acre	Mow, fertilize, sweep, repair, etc.
• Natural areas	As required	$30-$90/ac.	Pick-up litter, trash.
4. Depreciation (remedial maintenance)			
• Major repair and replacement	75 year life	Varies	This covers the ultimate replacement of major components like bridges, retaining walls. Most agencies do not budget this annually. Rather, it is appropriated from the capital improvement fund as the need arises.
5. Detours and Disruptions			
• Provide detours whenever trail is blocked.	As required	Varies	Often overlooked item. Should have interagency review to assure detours are provided.
6. Emergency			
• Emergency access	As required	Varies	Design and map access points for police and emergency vehicles.
• Crime and accident Reporting	Tabulate reports	Varies	Designate corridor as a legal "street" to enable reporting by location. Place milemarkers every 1/2 mile. Mark cross streets for location identification.
• Emergency telophone	As required	Varies	Place cellular type phone to call 911 at two mile intervals.

Sources: Urban Edges, Inc. with the assisstance of: South Suburban Parks and Recreation District, Littleton, Colorado. City of Boulder Parks Department, Boulder, Colorado. Denver Urban Drainage and Flood Control District, Denver, Colorado. Denver Urban Parks Department, Denver, Colorado. Jefferson County Open Space, Golden, Colorado.

Administration

Administration concerns who inherits the greenway—that is, who will take care of it over the years? Who will maintain it, police it, determine its future use, and protect it? How exactly this role is carried out will depend on the specific greenway and the type of greenway. Let's look at some options.

Parks Agency Model

The parks agency model is the most common and conventional means of greenway administration. Under this model, the local parks and recreation agency takes possession of greenway components as they are

The Wabash River Parkway in Tippecanoe County, Iowa, combines significant natural areas and historic sites along both the Wabash River and Burnett's Creek. When finished, this trail will run from the Tippecanoe Battlefield Memorial through downtown Lafayette to Fort Quiatenon.

Along the way the trail passes though parts of ten county or city parks. In addition to hiking, the parkway provides opportunities for fishing, boating, picnicking, nature observation, and nature interpretation. Land acquisition, operation, and maintenance of the Wabash River Parkway is a cooperative venture between Tippecanoe County and the parks and recreation departments of the cities of Lafayette and West Lafayette.

developed. Maintenance is included in the department budget, and operations are carried out by department personnel. The primary advantage of this model is that it ensures administration by an established professional organization, with proper equipment, tools, and know-how. Some park agencies use in-house maintenance crews, others contract with a private landscape maintenance company. The major disadvantage of this approach is the fact that the greenway will have to compete with other parks and recreation facilities, such as ball fields, golf courses, and neighborhood parks, for limited government funding.

A second concern centers around the natural resources of the greenway. Many urban parks agencies are most familiar with formal park management; they may need to be trained to care for the natural environment in your greenway. For example, they may need to learn native vegetation management, which is quite different from turf grass care, and to manage for wildlife habitat and water quality. They may also need to learn how to care for a boat chute or other special structures if any exist along your greenway.

Examples of successful park- or agency-run greenways include the Arapahoe Greenway—run by the South Suburban Park and Recreation District in Littleton, Colorado, the American River Parkway in Sacramento, California, and the W&OD trail, administered by the Northern Virginia Regional Park Authority.

Joint Agency Operations

Two or more agencies may cooperate to care for a greenway. A common partnership is between a parks agency and a flood-control agency. Under this model, the flood-control agency cleans the channel, stabilizes the banks, cuts weeds, and repairs the trail (flood maintenance road). The parks agency cares for the landscaped uplands and other elements that are solely recreational. Successful partnerships have also been formed with water departments and utility companies.

The most obvious advantage of this approach is savings in both construction and maintenance cost. The challenge is to assure coordination and aesthetic sensitivity on the part of both participants.

Joint agency management may also come into play where a greenway crosses jurisdictional lines. A joint agency agreement might be executed to divide maintenance responsibilities. At a minimum, there should be exchange of information and, preferably, adoption of uniform standards and policies for design, maintenance, patrol, and regulation.

In metropolitan Denver, the Urban Drainage and Flood Control District shares maintenance responsibilities with local park agencies on stream greenways. In Seattle, a successful joint venture has been formed between departments to service corridors like the Burke-Gilman Trail. In the Seattle case, the engineering department maintains trails within street rights-of-way and the parks department maintains the others. As the nation seeks ways to reduce energy dependence, joint ventures with local transportation departments, regional transportation districts, and other transportation agencies should be further explored.

Creation of a Special Greenway Agency

Some communities have created special agencies to assume ownership of their greenways. Generally, this involves the creation of a special taxing district or greenway authority to generate an ongoing revenue. The major advantage of this approach is that the greenway gets specialized care. The down side is the cost, time, and effort involved in setting up a new agency. There also may be sizable political resistance to creating "another layer of government." Such an agency may also be politically isolated and thus more vulnerable to cutbacks in hard times.

The Jefferson County Open Space district in suburban Denver is one example of this approach. In the early seventies, voters in the county passed a half-cent sales tax that was dedicated to the acquisition and preservation of open space, which includes mountainsides, stream corridors, and other lands of special interest. The agency also develops parking access points, trails, and other site amenities. Funding from the tax levy pays for administration, operations, and maintenance.

Operation by a Federal or State Agency

Operation by a federal or state agency usually brings considerable experience, expertise, and financial resources to your greenway. However, it is often difficult to secure statewide or national designation. There is also the possible disadvantage of losing a degree of local control in policy-making, planning, and use.

One of the oldest and best models for this approach is the Blue Ridge Parkway, which winds four hundred miles through Virginia and North Carolina. Managed by the National Park Service, the parkway extends through numerous jurisdictions and is clearly of national interest.

Other examples include the National Capital Regional Bikeway system in and around Washington, D.C. and the Cuyahoga Valley Heritage Corridor in Ohio, both run by the National Park Service, and the Biz Johnson Trail, a forty-mile greenway funded by the U. S. Bureau of Land Management in northern California. Major greenways run by state agencies include the Willamette Greenway in Oregon, Gunpowder River State Park in Maryland, and the Provo Jordan River Parkway in Utah.

Management by a Nonprofit Group

For decades, the Appalachian Trail has been maintained by a nonprofit organization of trail enthusiasts. The Appalachian Mountain Club's "adopt-a-trail" program is probably one of the best examples of a citizens' group taking care of a greenway.

Although many low-intensity greenways are owned and managed by nonprofit organizations such as land trusts, maintenance of highly developed greenways has mixed results. One problem is the difficulty of raising funds for maintenance. Donations for land acquisition and capital improvements are often easier to secure than money for day-to-day care and upkeep.

To address this challenge, some nonprofit organizations have tried contracting with local government agencies to provide all or part of the funding for maintenance services, which the greenway nonprofit organization, in turn, provides. For example, the Denver Greenway Foundation ran a trail ranger and channel maintenance program under contract with the local parks department and drainage district for a number of years.

Regardless of the approach, it is essential that competent, qualified people carry out both administrative and day-to-day maintenance tasks, especially on heavily used urban multipurpose greenways. If volunteers carry out some or many of these functions, make sure they receive proper training or recruit skilled people.

Maintenance by Private Property Owners

Increasingly, greenways and trails are becoming a successful marketing component in new residential and commercial development. Many developers have learned that setting aside stream corridors, riverbank, or wetland is not only environmentally sound, but also good business. Home buyers are showing their desire to live near open space and trails. If the subdivision greenbelt system connects into a larger metropolitan-wide or regional greenway, all the better.

The good news is that property-owner associations often pay for upkeep. An ideal urban greenway might include a string of developments along a resource corridor, each of which maintains its reach in accordance with a set of greenway standards. Nearly every large metropolitan area has real-estate developments that feature trail and greenbelt corridors. Be aware, however, that use of subdivision greenways may be restricted to residents in the development.

Volunteers

You might consider hosting a Trails Day, similar to those sponsored by hiking or trail groups across the country. The Appalachian Mountain Club's annual Trails Day recruits volunteers to maintain and rehabilitate 1200 miles of trail on public land in the White Mountains. Instruction and tools are usually provided on site, and workers are given a choice of what to work on.

Volunteers can certainly help. They can clean up trash, plant and prune, repair trails, and serve as interpretive guides. Consider using scouts, elderly and retired people, and community service organizations. A number of school districts require students to participate in a community service project before graduating from high school.

The adopt-a-highway program used by several state highway departments to pick up litter on highways might be applied to greenways. A bicycle-mounted trail ranger patrol might be staffed by recruited volunteers. The City of Pueblo, Colorado, created a program in which volunteer rangers serve as interpretive guides, pick up trash, and provide a sense of security for users. Denver had a similar program with college students who performed that function at competitive wage rates. Figure 15-1 is a volunteer survey from the San Francisco Bay Trail Project.

Volunteers, however, are not cost-free. Nor can the consistency of workmanship or availability of volunteer labor be guaranteed. Volunteers must be recruited, trained, supervised, and outfitted with tools. This calls for an investment of resources.

The San Francisco Bay Trail Project
(Please detach this page, fold, and return.)

❑ Yes, I'd like to volunteer to help complete the Bay Trail.

Name _____

Address _____

_____
City   State   Zip

(   ) _____ (   ) _____
Daytime Phone   Evening Phone

Company/Organization (if any) with which you are associated:

_____

Sub-region in which you're interested (please prioritize: 1= most interesed, 5 = least):

___North Bay ___East Bay ___South Bay ___Marin/San Francisco ___Peninsula

Availability: ❑ Weekends ❑ Evenings ❑ Daytime

ACTIVITIES OF INTEREST

Volunteer/Citizen Input
❑ Organizing local support groups
❑ Leading bicycle rides/tours
❑ Leading hikes/nature tours
❑ Monitoring conditions of completed
   segments of Trail
❑ Attending meetings of policymakers
❑ Monitoring and advocating legislation
❑ Working at fairs expositions
❑ Working on environmental projects,
   wetland cleanups
❑ Writing letters to elected officials
❑ Typing, sorting and mailing information

Fundraising/Promotion
❑ Taking photographs
❑ Writing articles, designing brochures
❑ Speaking at public hearings, to the
   media and community groups
❑ Helping raise funds through
   ___grant writing
   ___individual campaigns
   ___product sales
   ___special events

Trail Development
❑ Surveying Trail segments
❑ Refining local routes and construction
   alternatives
❑ Providing technical assistance on
   planning, design or construction
❑ Helping develop a database inventory
   about the Trail

Bay Trail BayCycle '93
❑ Setting up the course
❑ Acting as road marshall
❑ Hosting out-of-town racers in my home
❑ Helping at "work parties" (mailing,
   information distribution, etc.)
❑ Joining the Focus Group that's planning
   and arranging the day

Figure 15-1 Bay Trail volunteer survey.

Programming and Events

"Build it and they will come." This is certainly true of any quality greenway. It will fill with people. Soon there will be inquiries about events—bike tours, boat races, and concerts. Environmental groups, historic preservation organizations, wildlife clubs, and nature centers may also plan tours and events. Planning and programming will be the first major factor in determining how the greenway will be used. If you build an amphitheater, you're going to attract concerts. If you provide a group picnic shelter, you're going to have picnickers.

In addition to programming, it is helpful to set policies for such issues as special events, vendors, concessions, and other commercial activities. All of these can benefit your greenway, but the time and place must be consistent with your plan and program. For example, a race or walk-a-thon might disrupt or inconvenience regular trail users, wildlife, commuters, or those who just came to enjoy the peace and solace of the greenway. You might start by reviewing your parks department's policies. There is no need to be overly rigid, but a little forethought in this area will pay dividends in smooth enjoyable operations later on.

Stewardship and Enhancement

The Wissahickon Greenway in Pennsylvania interprets the environmental features of the greenway to 6500 people each year. Many other groups also use the greenway for their environmental education programs.

Greenway visions usually begin with a special resource: a river, a stream, a historic rail line. That resource needs protection. If your greenway is successful, protection becomes a more pressing issue as more and more people come to visit. This brings up the subject of stewardship—the care and preservation of the greenway.

Some issues to consider include maintenance of adequate stream flow (your greenway would lose a lot of its flavor if the river dried up), protection of historic structures, addressing corridor flora and fauna, protecting views, and reviewing the design of street crossings and utility structures.

Stewardship requires both a set of design standards and stewards who will watch over the resource. These ideally include some combination of the agency staff, concerned citizens, and responsible elected officials. A good stewardship program educates all users of the greenway about the impacts of their recreational activities.

Beyond stewardship, there is the notion of enhancement. Most greenways develop slowly. In the beginning funds are scarce, and priorities must be set. Perhaps in the early years only one trail can be built. Over time, however, there are opportunities to refine and improve the greenway. A greenway is a dynamic, evolving resource. Enhancement is often the result of a series of modest steps over time in response to observed patterns of use, recreational trends, and the needs of the greenway resource itself. Typical enhancements include drinking fountains, additional landscaping, interpretive programs, additional trails, picnic areas, and outdoor art.

Finding Money for Maintenance

Now we come to the tough question. How do you fund maintenance in perpetuity? Chapter 5 talks about how to raise money for greenway development; funding maintenance creates a whole new challenge. In this time of budget deficits, tax cuts, and fiscal restraint, there is no simple answer to this question. Furthermore, you can't count on grants to provide the steady stream of cash required. In most communities, the traditional solution is an annual line item in the budget—most likely through the parks department.

Endowments

Often when a managing agent assumes fee title or receives an easement on a piece of land, it must develop a stewardship plan to monitor, manage, and enforce legal restrictions on the property. Many land trusts request endowments with each acquisition to cover their stewardship tasks. Some turn down projects unless an adequate endowment has been identified. Other creative solutions include building a maintenance endowment fund from a percentage of grants received to develop the greenway. Another way to build an endowment fund is through deferred giving. Some of the more popular sources include bequests and certain tax-saving arrangements where people donate securities to the greenway but retain rights to the earnings during their lifetime.

User Fees

Some greenways charge a trail user fee. An interesting variation on this approach has been initiated by the Iowa Natural Heritage Foundation. To raise maintenance money, the organization placed collection boxes at strategic points along the trail. Users buy trail permits on the honor system. A day permit costs $1 to $2 and a season pass costs $5 to $10. The purchaser keeps a stub to show a ranger that he has paid his way. The money, approximately $16,000 a year, is turned over to local county conservation boards, which provide maintenance services. Indications are that, in many counties, sufficient funds have been raised this way to cover full trail maintenance expenses. Permit payment envelopes are passed to the Foundation, which adds the names and addresses of users to its mailing list. While essentially an honor system, the permit system works well. Most people gladly pay because they realize that ultimately the benefit accrues to them in the form of a well-maintained trail.

Special Districts

Another idea is the creation of a special assessment district. This is a device whereby those who most directly benefit from the greenway, for example, restaurants along a river walk, pay for its upkeep. Such districts can be created under state law or through some kind of property owners' arrangement. Shopkeepers in Estes Park, Colorado, pay for the upkeep of their river greenway and other amenities in this way. Recall also the Hudson River Greenway's innovative solution presented in

A volunteer association can be a terrific asset in the management of a greenway. The benefits include committed advocacy skills, cost savings, greenway maintenance, and landowner contact. Volunteer associations are also a way to keep agencies that administer greenways on public land responsive to user needs. The Appalachian Trail Conference boasts 25,000 members as well as thirty-one affiliate hiking and outing clubs that maintain an assigned section of the Appalachian Trail in accordance with established guidelines. (The trail is a 2140-mile continuous marked greenway footpath, which extends from Maine to Georgia.) The National Park Service has formally delegated management responsibility for the trail to the Appalachian Trail Conference (ATC). ATC members also contribute to trail design and educational efforts.

To maintain a footpath or informal trail, your work plan should include the removal of blowdowns, seedlings, and encroaching vegetation from the trail; repainting trail blazes; clearing vegtation to a height of about eight feet and width of up to eight feet; examination for erosion problems (for example at shortcuts near switchbacks); and maintenance of erosion control structures such as waterbars.

The Appalachian Trail—a 2140-mile volunteer-managed greenway. (Maryland Department of Natural Resources)

Chapter 5, whereby a 0.25 percent hotel lodging tax in towns along the river helps pay for greenway development along the river.

Establishing a Greenway Management Program

Organizing the People

During greenway planning it is important to get as many agency stakeholders as possible to support the plan. Meet early on with parks staff, planning staff, drainage engineers, and the transportation officials. Try to identify areas of mutual interest and who should perform which service. Which will be the lead agency? Who will be responsible for coordinating management functions? Consult with operations and maintenance people. They offer the first-hand experience.

Design Review

You will recall that by *design review* we mean a multidisciplinary review of projects before implementation. In fact, the design review team should meet to help identify problems before any plans are put to paper. This is time well spent and can be handled in two ways. First, keep an agency review list and circulate draft plans, bid documents, design guidelines, and other materials for review and comment before implementation. Typical reviewers could include the parks department, planning department, transportation department, water, sewer, and energy utilities, the flood control agency, and police and fire personnel. The second part of design review takes place within the implementing agency. Be sure maintenance people review and comment on all projects before they go out to bid—if the work is bid.

Design review need not be a lengthy and cumbersome process. Maintain a good working relationship with each of the key reviewing agencies. The success of this process, of course, will depend on the diplomatic skills of the greenway staff and the effectiveness of support from elected officials, the mayor, or city manager.

Good maintenance is a must. Greenway planners must bring a special resourcefulness to the issue of maintenance. It is not particularly glamorous, but it is crucial, particularly since a poorly maintained stretch may give the greenway a black eye. A careful strategy must be put in place and operating resources identified before development begins. New ways must be found to promote greenway interests to those who have access to economic resources, be they concession and tourism operators, utility companies, real-estate developers, restaurateurs, or adjacent residents. This calls for creativity, diplomacy, and salesmanship on the part of greenway advocates. As the greenway movement spreads from community to community, these challenges surely can—and will—be met.

Maintenance Costs:
- *San Francisco Bay Trail: $6,000–10,000/mile/year to maintain class I, II, III bikeways or hiking trails*
- *Stowe Recreation Path (Vermont): $10,000–12,000/year to maintain 5.3 miles of trail*
- *Wissahickon Greenway (Pennsylvania): $25,000/year to maintain 10 miles of trail*
- *Iowa Heritage Trail: $31,000/year for 26 miles of abandoned railroad trail ($11,000 maintenance/$20,000 patrol/labor)*

Appendix A

Greenway Contact Organizations

American Farmland Trust
1920 N Street NW., Suite 400
Washington, DC 20036
202-659-5170

Provides technical assistance to localities implementing agricultural land preservation strategies and directly protects farms by acquisition or other means.

The American Greenways Program
The Conservation Fund
1800 North Kent Street, Suite 1120
Arlington, VA 22209
703-525-6300

Strives to establish a nationwide network of public and private open space corridors. The program serves as an umbrella organization promoting the greenways concept at the national, state, and local levels, and it provides information and technical assistance on all aspects of greenway planning and development. Administers the Dupont-American Greenways Innovative Grant Program. The Conservation Fund is a national organization committed to land and water conservation.

American Hiking Society
P.O. Box 20160
Washington, DC 20041-2160
703-385-3252

Dedicated to protecting the interests of hikers and preserving America's footpaths. Encourages volunteerism, and maintains a public information service.

American Planning Association
1776 Massachusetts Ave., NW
Washington, DC 20036
202-872-0611

and

1313 East 60th St.
Chicago, IL 60637
312-955-9100

Source of information on city and regional planning.

American Rivers
801 Pennsylvania Avenue, SE
Washington, DC 20003
202-547-6900

Devoted exclusively to preserving the nation's outstanding rivers and their landscapes. Can provide information and advice on river protection measures; administers REI Seed Grants Program through the National Rivers Coalition.

American Society of Landscape Architects (ASLA)
4401 Connecticut Avenue, NW., 5th Floor
Washington, DC 20008
202-686-ASLA

Seeks to advance knowledge, education, and skill in the art and science of landscape architecture. Accredits programs of landscape architecture at U.S. colleges and universities, offers a variety of publications.

American Trails
1400 16th Street, NW
Washington, DC 20036
202-483-5611

Promotes planning, development, and maintenance of trail systems on public and private land.

The Appalachian Mountain Club
5 Joy Street
Boston, MA 02108
617-523-0636

Sponsors research and programs in the northeast United States, including trail maintenance, outdoor education, and publication of guidebooks and maps.

Greenways Incorporated
121 Edinburgh South
Suite 107, MacGregor Park
Cary, NC 27511
919-380-0127

A for-profit planning, design, and development firm that seeks creative solutions to greenway, trail, and open-space planning.

Izaak Walton League of America
1401 Wilson Blvd., Level B
Arlington, VA 22209
703-528-1818

"Save Our Streams" program trains citizens to monitor and rehabilitate local water resources.

Land Trust Alliance
900 17th Street, NW., Suite 410
Washington, DC 20006
202-785-1410

A national organization of land trusts, which provides specialized services, publications, and training for land trusts and other land conservation organizations.

National Park Service
Rivers and Trails Conservation Assistance Program
P.O. Box 37127
Washington, DC 20013
202-343-3780

The program assists state and local governments, private groups, and landowners in protecting river corridors and establishing greenway and trail systems. Projects range from statewide river assessments to plans for a single river or urban waterfront. Can provide you with contacts in your regional NPS office.

National Recreation and Parks Association (NRPA)
2775 S. Quincy Street, Suite 300
Arlington, VA 22206
703-820-4940

Advocates parks and recreation opportunities; offers publications, conferences, training programs; and works with agencies, corporations, and citizens' groups.

National Trust for Historic Preservation
1785 Massachusetts Avenue, NW
Washington, DC 20036
202-673-4000

Provides assistance and advice on preservation of sites, objects, and buildings of historic and cultural interest.

The Nature Conservancy
1815 N. Lynn Street
Arlington, VA 22209
703-841-5300

Encourages the protection of natural diversity through acquisition and protection of land that is habitat for rare species or vanishing ecosystems. Initiates state natural heritage programs with public agency partners.

Rails-To-Trails Conservancy
1400 16th Street, NW
Washington, DC 20036
202-797-5400

Provides advice, information, and assistance to local governments and organizations that wish to convert abandoned railroad right-of-ways into public recreational trails.

Scenic America
21 Dupont Circle, NW
Washington, DC 20036
202-833-4300

Devoted to preserving America's scenic beauty. Provides information and technical assistance on ways to identify, designate, and protect scenic road corridors in both urban and rural areas.

Trout Unlimited
501 Church Street, NE
Vienna, VA 22180
703-281-1100

Dedicated to the protection of clean water and the enhancement of trout, salmon, and steelhead fishery resources.

Trust for Public Land
116 New Montgomery Street, 4th Floor
San Francisco, CA 94105
415-495-4014

Works with public agencies and citizens' groups to acquire land for open space. Offers training and assistance to local land groups.

Urban Edges
1401 Blake Street, Suite 301
Denver, CO 80202
303-623-8107

A for-profit planning, design, and development firm that seeks creative solutions to greenway, trail, and open-space planning.

The Waterfront Center
1536 44th Street
Washington, DC 20007
202-337-0356

Promotes urban waterfront enhancement and public access through conferences and consultation.

Appendix B

Federal Funding Sources

Note: Eligilbility of applicants will vary from source to source; some fund only government agencies, while nonprofit organizations or agency partners are targeted for other programs. Many of these funds are available on a matching basis only.

Source: "Financial and Technical Assistance Guide for River Trail and Conservation Projects," National Park Service. Rivers and Trails Conservation Assistance Program. June 1991. This guide lists possible sources of government and private financial and technical assistance for projects. Gives further information on types of projects, eligible applicants, funding structure, applicaton deadline, agency and contact, and special conditions.

Agricultural Conservation Program
Department of Agriculture
Agriculture Stabilization and Conservation Service

Eligible Types of Projects: Control of erosion and sedimentation, encourages voluntary compliance with federal and state requirements to solve point and non-point source pollution and improve water quality. Program is directed toward the solution of critical soil, water, energy, woodland, and pollution abatement problems on farms and ranches.

Conservation Reserve Program
Department of Agriculture
Agriculture Stabilization and Conservation Service

Eligible Types of Projects: Provides payments to farm owners or operators to place highly erodible or environmentally sensitive cropland into a ten-year contract. The participant, in return for annual payments, agrees to implement a conservation plan approved by the local conservation district for converting highly erodible cropland or environmentally sensitive land to a less intensive use; i.e., cropland must be planted with a vegetative cover, such as perennial grasses, legumes, forbs, shrubs, or trees.

Water Bank Program
Department of Agriculture
Agriculture Stabilization and Conservation Service

Eligible Types of Projects: Improvement of wetlands, conservation of surface waters, and increasing migratory waterfowl habitat in nesting, breeding, and feeding areas.

River Basin Surveys and Investigations
Department of Agriculture
Soil Conservation Service

Eligible Types of Projects: This program provides planning assistance for the development of coordinated water programs and related land resources programs. Priority is given to studies in which the degree of state or local participation is high.

Resource Conservation and Development
Department of Agriculture
Soil Conservation Service

Eligible Types of Projects: Provides assistance in rural areas to plan, develop, and carry out programs for resource conservation and development. Past projects included a stream bank stabilization project for the Bitterfoot River in Missoula County, Montana.

Watershed Protection and Flood Prevention
Department of Agriculture
Soil Conservation Service

Eligible Types of Projects: Projects may include watershed protection, flood prevention, sedimentation control, public water–based fish and wildlife, and recreation.

Public Works and Development Facilities
Department of Commerce
Economic Development Administration

Eligible Types of Projects: Grants for public facilities, including port facilities and tourism facilities.

Aquatic Plant Control
U. S. Army Corps of Engineers

Eligible Types of Projects: Control and eradication from rivers, harbors, and allied waters of obnoxious aquatic plants. The program is designed to deal primarily with weed infestations of major economic significance.

Flood Plain Management Services
U. S. Army Corps of Engineers

Eligible Types of Projects: This program can provide assistance in planning for floodplain use, developing floodplain regulations, and determining areas that should be preserved for open space. Provides advisory services and counseling and dissemination of technical information.

Planning Assistance to States
U. S. Army Corps of Engineers

Eligible Types of Projects: Preparation of comprehensive plans for the development, utilization, or conservation of water and related land-use resources of drainage basins within a state.

Small Flood Control Projects
U. S. Army Corps of Engineers

Eligible Types of Projects: Proposals designed to reduce flood damages through projects not specifically authorized by Congress.

Community Development Block Grants—Entitlement Program
Department of Housing and Urban Development
Community Planning and Development

Eligible Types of Projects: Neighborhood revitalization, economic development, and provision of improved community facilities and services. All eligible activities must benefit low- and moderate-income persons, aid in the prevention or elimination of slums and blight, or meet other community development needs having a particular urgency. Several rail-trail projects that have been awarded funding under this program include the Burke-Gilman Trail in Seattle and the Baltimore-Annapolis Trail in Maryland.

Community Development Block Grant—Small Cities Program
Department of Housing and Urban Development
Community Planning and Development

Eligible Types of Projects: Acquisition, rehabilitation, or construction of certain public works facilities, clearance, housing rehabilitation, code enforcement, relocation payments, administrative expenses, economic development, completing existing urban renewal projects, and certain public services. The city of Scottsdale, Arizona, used this program to help fund the removal (and relocation) of substandard housing from the floodplain of Indian Bend Wash before the conversion of the Wash into multiple community recreation facilities (1985).

Small Reclamation Projects
Department of Interior
Bureau of Reclamation

Eligible Types of Projects: Projects can be single-purpose or multi-purpose, including flood control, fish and wildlife, and recreation development.

Anadromous Fish Conservation
Department of the Interior
U. S. Fish and Wildlife Service

Eligible Types of Projects: Conservation, development, and enhancement of anadromous fish resources. Approval projects include planning, inventory, research supplements to natural production, fish passage and guidance facilities, and habitat improvement.

Fish and Wildlife Management Assistance
Department of the Interior
U. S. Fish and Wildlife Service

Eligible Types of Projects: Technical information, advice, and assistance on the conservation and management of fish and wildlife resources. Projects funded by this program have included studies to evaluate the impact of development on wildlife resources, the effects of environmental contaminants on wildlife and their habitat, and habitat requirements of migratory nongame wildlife.

Sport Fish Restoration
Department of the Interior
U. S. Fish and Wildlife Service

Eligible Types of Projects: Restoration and management of sport fish population for the preservation and improvement of sport fishing and related uses of these fisheries resources. Approval activities include land acquisition, development, research and coordination. This has included fish habitat improvement, lake and stream rehabilitation, and provision for public use of fishery resources.

Wildlife Restoration (Pittman-Robertson Program)
Department of the Interior
U.S. Fish and Wildlife Service

Eligible Types of Projects: Projects may include restoration or management of wildlife populations and providing for public use of these resources. Approval activities include land acquisition, development, research, and coordination.

Land and Water Conservation Fund
Department of the Interior
National Park Service

Eligible Types of Projects: Acquisition, development, or rehabilitation of neighborhood, community, or regional parks, or facilities supporting outdoor recreation activities.

Rivers, Trails, and Conservation Assistance Program
Department of the Interior
National Park Service

Eligible Types of Projects: Provides staff assistance for river, trail, and conservation projects. Selected projects have included conceptual plans for trail corridors, river corridor plans, and statewide river assessments. Projects are selected if they protect significant resources, achieve tangible results, incorporate public involvement during the planning process, and service a large number of people.

Urban Park and Recreation Recovery Program
Department of the Interior
National Park Service

Eligible Types of Projects: Rehabilitation grants for existing urban recreation sites. Projects may include rebuilding, remodeling, expanding, or developing existing outdoor or indoor recreation areas and facilities. Funds may be used to improve park landscapes, buildings, and support facilities, but are not available for routine maintenance and upkeep activities.

Senior Community Service Employment Program
Department of Labor
Employment and Training Administration

Eligible Types of Projects: This program is designed to provide, foster, and promote useful part-time work opportunities in community service activities for low income persons who are 55 years of age or older.

Nonpoint Source Implementation
Environmental Protection Agency

Eligible Types of Projects: Assistance to states in implementing EPA approved nonpoint source water pollution programs.

State Wetlands Protection Development Grant Program
Environmental Protection Agency
Eligible Types of Projects: Grant program for development of new wetlands protection programs, refinement/enhancement of existing programs, for example, broadening the scope of activities regulated, development of enforcement or monitoring. Grants can be awarded for research, investigations, experiments, training, demonstrations, surveys, and studies.

Acquisition of Flood-Damaged Structures
Federal Emergency Management Agency

Eligible Types of Projects: Structures which have been repetitively and substantially damaged by floods. Property must be located in FEMA flood-risk area and covered under National Flood Insurance Program. Community must be willing to accept title to the property and restrict its use in perpetuity to open space.

Highway Planning and Construction
(Federal-Aid Highway Program)
Federal Highway Administration

Eligible Types of Projects: Bicycle transportation, pedestrian walkways, rest areas, and fringe and corridor parking facilities as part of highway beautification projects.

Disposal of Federal Surplus Real Property
General Services Administration

Eligible Types of Projects: Surplus real property may be conveyed through sale, exchange, or donation for public uses, including public park or recreation use, and wildlife conservation.

References

Chapter 1. Envisioning Your Greenway

Recommended Reading

(Several of these are excellent for many phases of the greenway process.)

Economic Impacts of Protecting Rivers, Trails and Greenway Corridors: A Resource Book. Rivers and Trails Conservation Assistance Program, National Park Service, Washington, D.C. 1990. Outlines the many economic benefits of greenway creation, from increased property values, recreational opportunities, tourism, and quality of life, to reduced public spending on infrastructure, hazard mitigation, and pollution control.

"Greenway Fact Sheets." Scenic Hudson, Poughkeepsie, N.Y. A series of pamphlets with practical information on building and maintaining local greenways in New York. Topics include walkway design, trail construction and maintainence, volunteers, raising money, historic resources, starting your own land trust, land preservation techniques, and liability. Contact Scenic Hudson, 9 Vassar St., Poughkeepsie, NY 12601; 914-473-4440.

Grove, Noel, "Greenways: Paths to the Future." *National Geographic*, Vol. 177, No. 6, June 1990, pp. 77–99.

Howe, Linda, *Keeping Our Garden State Green: A Local Government Guide for Greenway and Open Space Planning.* New Jersey Department of Environmental Protection, Association of New Jersey Environmental Commissions, Mendham, N.J., 1989.

Illinois Railbanking Study, 1990. Illinois Department of Conservation. A series of seven reports on issues in rail-trail development. Topics include funding, landowner and community concerns, economic and tax implications, rail abandonments, public involvement, development, and greenway concerns. Conducted by the natural resources planning firm of Huffman Williams Lafen and Fletcher, Silver Spring, Maryland, 1990.

Little, Charles, *Greenways for America.* Johns Hopkins University Press, Baltimore, 1990. *The* book on the greenway movement. Case studies of diverse projects. Excellent listing of resources.

President's Commission on Americans Outdoors, *Americans Outdoors: The Legacy, The Challenge.* Report of the President's Commission with case studies. Island Press, Washington, D.C., and Covelo, California, 1987.

Additional Reading and References

Flournoy, William L., Jr., "Capital City Greenways: A Report to the City Council on the Benefits, Potential and Methodology of Establishing a Greenway System in Raleigh." Raleigh, N.C., 1972.

Flournoy, William L., Jr., "The Evolution of Environmental Consciousness and Modern Linear Open Space Systems." Photocopied paper, Raleigh, N.C., 1990.

Flournoy, William L., Jr., "Vigilantes, the Neuse, and Sure Salvation." Photocopied paper, Raleigh, N.C. 1990.

"Greenbelt Planning Kit." Pamphlet published by West Windsor Planning Department, P.O. Box 38, Princeton Junction, NJ 08550.

Greenways...A Bold Idea for Today, A Promise for Tomorrow. Program Open Space, Maryland Department of Natural Resources, Annapolis, 1990.

Lang, Laura, "From the Ground Up: Improvements in Technology Are Making It Easier to Create Accurate Base Maps for Geographic Information Systems." *Planning Magazine*, Vol. 57, No. 7 (July 1991), pp. 30–34.

Lusk, Ann, "How to Build a Path in Your Community." Photocopied paper, 1986. (Address: RD 2 Box 3780, Stowe, VT 05672)

The San Francisco Bay Area Ridge Trail Technical Coordinating Guidebook. Bay Area Trails Council, San Francisco, Calif., 1988.

Searns, Robert M., "Denver Tames the Unruly Platte: A Ten Mile River Greenway." *Landscape Architecture*, July 1980.

Shoemaker, Joe, with Leonard A. Stevens, *Returning the Platte to the People.* The Platte River Greenway Foundation, Denver, 1981 (1666 South University Blvd., Denver, CO 80210).

Chapter 2. Developing a Plan

Recommended Reading

Guse-Noritake, Judy, for George H. Siehl, *Scenic Landscape Protection.* CRS Report for Congress, Congressional Research Service, The Library of Congress, Washington, D.C., November 13, 1990. A good, brief overview of federal and state approaches to preserving open space.

Howe, Linda, *Keeping Our Garden State Green: A Local Government Guide for Greenway and Open Space Planning.* New Jersey Department of Environmental Protection, The Association of New Jersey Environmental Commissions, Mendham, N.J., 1989.

McHarg, Ian L., *Design with Nature.* The Natural History Press, Garden City, N.Y., 1969. Reprinted by John Wiley, New York, 1992.

Simonds, John Ormsbee, *Earthscape: A Manual of Environmental Planning.* McGraw-Hill, New York, 1978.

Stokes, Samuel N., A. Elizabeth Watson, Genevieve P. Keller, and Timothy J. Keller, *Saving America's Countryside: A Guide to Rural Conservation.* Johns Hopkins University Press, Baltimore, 1989. This book shows how to organize a conservation effort, inventory available resources, pass effective new laws, set up land trusts, take advantage of federal programs, and change public attitudes.

Additional Reading and References

Alexander, Christopher, *et al.*, *A Pattern Language: Towns, Buildings and Construction.* Oxford University Press, New York, 1977.

Building Greenways in the Hudson River Valley: A Guide for Action. The National Park Service and Scenic Hudson, Inc., Poughkeepsie, N.Y., December 1989.

Eugster, J. Glenn, "Steps in State and Local Greenway Conservation Planning." Prepared for the Seminar on Multi-Objective Greenways and Coordination of Wetland and Floodplain Programs. National Park Service Mid-Atlantic Regional Office, Philadelphia, 1988.

Flanagan, Ronald D., "Multi-Purpose Planning for Greenway Corridors." Paper presented at the Multi-Objective Greenways and Coordination of Wetland and Floodplain Programs Seminar, Tulsa, Oklahoma, February 1988.

Fox, Tom, and Anne McClellan, "Brooklyn/Queens Greenway: A Design Study." Technical paper, New York, July 1987.

Gibbons, C. James, "Manual of Mapping Techniques for Natural Resource Inventories." Cooperative Extension System, University of Connecticut, Storrs, Conn., 1991.

Greenspaces and Greenways. The Open Space Imperative, #1, Regional Plan Association, Inc., New York, 1987.

"Greenspace 2000: Saving What We Need to Save." Review draft, State of Rhode Island Department of Planning and Administration, Providence, May 1992.

"A Greenway for the Hudson River Valley: A New Strategy for Preserving an American Treasure." Historic Hudson Valley for the Hudson River Valley Greenway Council, Poughkeepsie, N.Y., 1989.

Knudson, Douglas M., *Outdoor Recreation*. Macmillan, New York, 1980.

Hester, Randolph T., Jr., *Neighborhood Space*. Dowden, Hutchinson & Ross, Inc., Stroudsburg, Penn., 1975.

Lynch, Kevin, *Site Planning*. The MIT Press, Cambridge, Mass., 1962.

Ontario's Niagara Parks: Planning the Next Century: A 100 Year Vision, a 20 Year Plan, and a Five-Year Action Plan. Moriyama and Teshima Planners Limited, Toronto, October 1988.

"Outdoor Recreation in a Nation of Communities: A Plan for Americans Outdoors." A Report of the Task Force on Outdoor Recreation Resources and Opportunities to the Domestic Policy Council, technical paper, Washington, D.C., July 1988.

President's Commission on Americans Outdoors, *Americans Outdoors: The Legacy, The Challenge*. Island Press, Washington, D.C., and Covelo, Calif., 1987.

The Riverfront Plan. Urban Design Assistance Team, North Carolina Chapter of the American Institute of Architects, Community Assistance Team, North Carolina Chapter of the American Society of Landscape Architects, Asheville, N.C., April 1989.

Rutledge, Albert J., *Anatomy of a Park: The Essentials of Recreation Area Planning and Design*. McGraw-Hill, New York, 1971.

Scenic Byways, Federal Highway Administration, Washington, D.C., 1988. Publication FHWA-DF-88-004.

Schumann, Marguerite, *The Living Land: An Outdoor Guide to North Carolina*. Dale Press of Chapel Hill, Chapel Hill, N.C., 1977.

Schuylkill River Design Guide, Commonwealth of Pennsylvania, Department of Environmental Resources, Philadelphia, 1984.

Spiegel, Ted, and Jeffery Simpson, *An American Treasure: The Hudson River Valley*. Sleepy Hollow Press, Sleepy Hollow Restorations, New York, 1986.

Taylor, Lisa, ed., *Urban Open Space*. The Smithsonian Institution, Washington, D.C., 1979.

Chapter 3. Partnerships: Organizing Your Greenway Effort

Recommended Reading

Building Greenways in the Hudson River Valley: A Guide of Action. Scenic Hudson, Inc., Poughkeepsie, N.Y., December 1989.

Coppock, Don, Yolanda Henderson, Reed Holderman, Jennifer Segar, and David Weinsoff, *The Non-Profit Primer: A Guidebook for Land Trusts*, 2nd ed. The California State Coastal Conservancy, Oakland, Calif., 1989 (1313 Broadway, Suite 1100, Oakland, CA 94612)

Flanigan, Joan, *The Grassroots Fund Raising Book: How to Raise Money in Your Community*. Contemporary Books, Inc., Chicago, 1983.

Greenspaces and Greenways: The Open Space Imperative #1. Regional Plan Association, Inc., New York, 1987.

Mantell, Michael A., Stephen F. Harper, and Luther Probst, *Creating Successful Communities* and *Resource Guide for Creating Successful Communities*. The Conservation Foundation, Island Press, Washington, D.C. and Covelo, Calif., 1990.

Moore, Roger L., Vicki LaFarge, and Charles Tracy, *Organizing Outdoor Volunteers*, 2nd ed. Appalachian Mountain Club, Boston, 1992.

Starting a Land Trust. The Land Trust Alliance, Washington, D.C., 1990. Provides an overview of essential steps in setup and early operation of a land trust.

Stokes, Samuel N., A. Elizabeth Watson, Genevieve P. Keller, and Timothy J. Keller, *Saving America's Countryside: A Guide to Rural Conservation*. John Hopkins University Press, Baltimore, 1989.

Additional Reading and References

Converting Rails to Trails: A Citizen's Manual for Transforming Abandoned Rail Corridors to Multipurpose Paths, Rails to Trails Conservancy, Washington, DC, 1987.

Fedelchak, Marilyn, and Byrd Wood, *Protecting America's Countryside*. National Trust for Historic Preservation, Washington, D.C., October 1988.

Hocker, Jean, "Greenways and Land Trusts—A Natural Partnership." *Exchange*, Summer 1987, pp. 6–7

Ingram, Richard, T., "Ten Basic Responsibilities of Non-Profit Boards." Photocopied pamphlet, National Center for Nonprofit Boards, 1225 19th Street, N.W., Suite 340, Washington, D.C.

Lusk, Ann, "How to Build a Path in Your Community." Resource sheet E-34. Vermont Department of Forests, Parks and Recreation, Agency of Environmental Conservation, Waterbury, Vermont, 1986.

The National Directory of Conservation Land Trusts. The Land Trust Alliance, Washington, D.C., 1991.

Schwartz, Kathleen, "A Case Study: The Charles River." *Exchange*, Vol. 4, No. 3, December 1985.

Searns, Robert M., "Denver Tames the Unruly Platte." *Landscape Architecture*, Vol. 70, No. 4 (July 1980), pp. 382–386.

Shoemaker, Joe, with Leonard Stevens, *Returning the Platte to the People*. Tumbleweed Press, Westminster, Colorado, 1981.

Trails on Electric Utility Lands: A Model of Public–Private Partnership. Edison Electric Institute, National Land Management Task Force and American Trails, Washington, D.C., 1989.

A Volunteers' Guide. Association of Bay Area Governments, San Francisco Bay Trail, Oakland, Calif., 1991. (P.O. Box 2050, Oakland, CA 94604)

Chapter 4. Building Public Support for Your Greenway

Recommended Reading

Crompton, John L., and Dennis R. Howard, *Financing, Managing and Marketing Recreation and Park Resources*. William C. Brown, Dubuque, Iowa, 1980.

Economic Impacts of Protecting Rivers, Trails and Greenway Corridors: A Resource Book, 2nd ed.. Rivers and Trails Conservation Assistance Program, National Park Service, Washington, D.C., 1991.

The Impacts of Rail-Trails: A Study of Users and Nearby Property Owners from Three Trails. National Park Service, Rivers and Trails Conservation Assistance Program, Washington, D.C., 1992.

Stokes, Samuel N., A. Elizabeth Watson, Genevieve P. Keller, and Timothy J. Keller, *Saving America's Countryside: A Guide to Rural Conservation*. Johns Hopkins University Press, Baltimore, 1989.

Additional Reading and References

Bailey, Kenneth D., *Methods of Social Research*, 2nd ed. The Free Press, New York, 1982.

Bradburn, Norman, and Seymor Sudman & Associates, *Improving Interview Method and Questionnaire Design*. Jossey-Bass, San Francisco, 1979.

Citizen Participation Handbook: For Public Officials and Other Professionals Serving the Public. Institute for Participatory Planning, University Station, Laramie, Wyoming, 1981. (Box 4068, Laramie, WY 82071)

Dillman, Don A., *Mail and Telephone Surveys: The Design Method*. John Wiley, New York, 1978.

Riverwork Book. U. S. Department of Interior, National Park Service, Mid-Atlantic Regional Office, Division of Park and Resource Planning, Philadelphia, 1988.

Lynn, Jack, "Building Community Support: Working with Reporters" and "Public Relations and Communications." *Exchange*, Winter 1990. "Druids No More: Anticipating and Responding to Criticism." *Exchange*, Summer 1991.

A Survey of Public Attitudes in the Hudson River Valley. Marist Institute for Public Opinion, Marist College, Poughkeepsie, N.Y., 1987.

Rally '91 Workbook: The Power of Partnerships, September 1991; *Rally '90 Workbook: Strength Through Diversity*, June 1990; and *Statement of Land Trust Standards and Practices*, 1992. The Land Trust Alliance, Washington, D.C. (Contact The Land Trust Alliance, 900 17th Street, N.W., Suite 410, Washington, DC 20006)

Watson, A. Elizabeth, "Visual Vitality: A Primer on Audiovisual Productions for Land Trusts." *Exchange*, Summer 1991.

Chapter 5. Funding Your Greenway

Recommended Reading

Catalogue of Federal Domestic Assistance. Superintendent of Documents, U.S. Government Printing Office, Washington, DC 20402. (202-783-3238; $20 annual cost)

Coppock, Don, Yolanda Henderson, Reed Holderman, Jennifer Segar, and David Weinsoff, *The Non-Profit Primer: A Guidebook for Land Trusts*, 2nd ed. The California State Coastal Conservancy, Oakland, Calif., 1989.

Crompton, John, and Dennis R. Howard, *Financing, Managing, and Marketing Recreation and Park Facilities*. William C. Brown Company, Dubuque, Iowa, 1980.

Diehl, Janet, and Thomas S. Barrett, *The Conservation Easement Handbook: Managing Land Conservation and Historic Preservation Easement Programs*. Land Trust Alliance and Trust for Public Land, Alexandria, Virginia, 1988.

Flanagan, Joan, *The Grass Roots Fund Raising Book: How to Raise Money in Your Community*. Contemporary Books, Inc., Chicago, 1983.

National Wildlife Federation, Conservation Directory 19—. An annually updated directory of federal, state, and local public agencies and nonprofit organizations that have programs and objectives supportive of conservation and environmental issues. (Available from The National Wildlife Federation, 1412 Sixteenth Street, N.W., Washington, DC 20036.)

Additional Reading and References

Artz, Robert M., ed., *Guide to New Approaches to Financing Parks and Recreation*. National Recreation and Park Association, Washington, D.C., 1970.

Bergan, Helen, *Where the Money Is: A Fund Raiser's Guide to the Rich*. Bioguide Press, Alexandria, Virginia, 1985.

Brenneman, Russell L., *Private Approaches to the Preservation of Open Land*. Conservation and Research Foundation, New York, 1967.

Bright, Elise, M., *Tactics for Preserving Open Space*. Institute of Urban Studies, The University of Texas at Arlington, Arlington, Texas, 1990.

Brody, Ralph, and Marcy Goodman, *Fund Raising Events, Strategies and Programs for Success*. Human Sciences Press, Inc., New York, 1988.

DeKemper, John, "Mecklenburg County Passes $10,245,000 Bond Package for Park and Recreation Facilities." Photocopied draft article, Mecklenburg County Park and Recreation Department, 700 North Tryon Street, Charlotte, NC 28202.

Fedelchak, Marilyn, and Byrd Wood, *Protecting America's Countryside*. National Trust for Historic Preservation, Washington, D.C., October 1988.

Fisher, Beth, "Economic Report for Pierre Waterfront Plan." Photocopied report, BBC, Inc., Denver, 1988.

Guse-Noritake, Judy, for George H. Siehl, *Scenic Landscape Protection*. Congressional Research Service, The Library of Congress, Washington, D.C., November 1990.

Hilman, Howard, *The Art of Winning Corporate Grants*. The Vanguard Press, New York, 1980.

Male, Rich, *Controlling Your Income: The Colorado Funding Report*. September 1991.

Margolin, Judith B., *Foundation Fundamentals: A Guide for Grant Seekers*. The Foundation Center, New York, 1991. (Provides the basics of fundraising, research and proposal writing. Call 800-424-9836 for information on this and other publications.)

White, Virginia P, *Grants: How to Find Out About Them and What to Do Next*. Plenum Press, New York, 1975.

Chapter 6. Greenway Protection and Ownership

Recommended Reading

"The Back Forty," a newsletter published by The Land Conservation Law Institute that covers current developments in legal issues commonly encountered by land conservation practitioners. (c/o The Land Trust Alliance, 900 Seventeenth Street, N.W., Suite 410, Washington, DC 20006)

Coppock, Don, Yolanda Henderson, Reed Holderman, Jennifer Segar, and David Weinsoff, *The Non-Profit Primer: A Guidebook for Land Trusts*, 2nd ed. The California State Coastal Conservancy, Oakland, Calif. (1313 Broadway, Suite 1100, Oakland, CA 94612). This is an excellent handbook on forming and operating a land trust.

Diehl, Janet, and Thomas S. Barrett, *The Conservation Easement Handbook: Managing Land Conservation and Historic Preservation Easement Programs*. The Land Trust Alliance and Trust for Plublic Land, Alexandria, Virginia, 1988.

Guse-Noritake, Judy, for George H. Siehl. *Scenic Landscape Protection*. Congressional Research Service, The Library of Congress, Washington, D.C., November 13, 1990.

Illinois Railbanking Study, 1990. Illinois Department of Conservation. A series of seven reports on issues in rail-trail development. Topics include funding, landowner and community concerns, economic and tax implications, rail abandonments, public involvement, development, and greenway concerns. Conducted by the natural resources planning firm of Huffman Williams Lafen and Fletcher, Silver Spring, Maryland, 1990.

Starting a Land Trust. The Land Trust Alliance, Washington, D.C., 1990. Provides case studies, an extensive list of resources, sample documents, and additional sources of assistance.

Standards and Practices (revised). Land Trust Alliance, Washington, D.C., 1992. This guide is essential for responsible setup and operation of a land trust. The guide addresses fifteen overarching concerns land trusts should be able to deal with competently.

Lind, Brenda, *The Conservation Easement Stewardship Guide: Designing, Monitoring, and Enforcing Easements*. The Land Trust Alliance, Washington, D.C., 1991. Step-by-step handbook to help conservation easement holders design and implement effective stewardship programs.

Mantell, Michael A., Stephen F. Harper, and Luther Probst, *Creating Successful Communities: A Guidebook to Growth Management Strategies*. The Conservation Foundation, Island Press, Covelo, Calif., 1990. A guidebook for developing workable action plans for restoring distinctiveness and liveability to communities.

Mantell, Michael A., Stephen F. Harper, and Luther Probst, *Resource Guide for Creating Successful Communities. Practical Companion Book for Creating Successful Communities*. The Conservation Foundation, Island Press, Covelo, Calif., 1990. Provides examples of legal documents used by communities as part of their planned growth management strategies.

Montagne, Charles H., *Preserving Abandoned Rights of Way for Public Use: A Legal Manual*. Rails-to-Trails Conservancy, Washington, D.C., 1989.

Tools and Strategies: Protecting the Landscape and Shaping Growth: The Open Space Imperative #3. Regional Plan Association, New York, April 1990. A user-friendly guide to land protection techniques designed to let those involved in land-use decisions understand available alternatives.

Stokes, Samuel N., A. Elizabeth Watson, Genivieve Keller, and Timothy J. Keller, *Saving America's Countryside: A Guide to Rural Conservation*. Johns Hopkins University Press, Baltimore, 1989.

Additional Reading and References

The Bay Area at a Crossroads: Choices for the Future of the San Francisco Bay Region. People for Open Space/Greenbelt Congress, San Francisco, Calif., July 1987.

"Bayshore Waterfront Access Plan." Monmouth County Planning Board, The Trust for Public Land, Monmouth County, N.J., December 1987.

The Bay Circuit: A Practical Plan for the Extension of the Metropolitan Park System and the Development of a State Parkway through a Number of Reservations in the Circuit of Massachusetts Bay. The Trustees of Reservations of Massachusetts, Boston, 1973.

Brenneman, Russell L., and Sarah M. Bates, *Land Saving Action*. Conservation Law Foundation of New England, Island Press, Washington, D.C. and Covelo, Calif., 1984.

Building Greenways in the Hudson River Valley: A Guide to Action. Scenic Hudson, Inc., with the National Park Service, Poughkeepsie, N.Y., December 1989.

Campbell, William A., *North Carolina Property Mappers*. Institute of Government, The University of North Carolina, Chapel Hill, 1988.

City of Portland, Bureau of Planning, Land Use Permits Section, Application Packet: Part C, Greenway Review Approval Criteria, The Willamette Greenway Plan. Portland, Oregon, January 1991.

Developing a Land Conservation Strategy. A Handbook for Land Trusts. Adirondack Land Trust, Elizabethtown, N.Y., 1987.

Drucker, Richard, *Dedicating and Reserving Land to Provide Beach Access to North Carolina Beaches*. Institute of Government, The University of North Carolina at Chapel Hill, Chapel Hill, September 1982.

Financing Land Acquisition and Development, National Association of Home Builders, Washington, D.C., 1989.

Flournoy, William L., Jr., "Capital City Greenway: A Report to the City Council on the Benefits, Potential and Methodology of Establishing a Greenways System in Raleigh." Raleigh, N.C., 1972.

Greenspaces and Greenways: The Open Space Imperative, #1, Regional Plan Association, Inc., New York, 1987.

"Greenways: 'Trick' or 'Treat' for Property Owners," *The Land Rights Letter*, Vol. 1, No. 10, Sharpsburg, Maryland, October 1991.

A Greenway for the Hudson River Valley: A New Strategy for Preserving an American Treasure. Historic Hudson Valley for the Hudson River Valley Greenway Council, Poughkeepsie, N.Y., 1989.

Hocker, Jean, "Greenways and Land Trusts: A Natural Partnership." *Exchange*, Vol. 6, No. 2, Summer 1987.

Howe, Linda, *Keeping Our Garden State Green: A Local Government Guide for Greenway and Open Space Planning*. New Jersey Department of Environmental Protection, The Association of New Jersey Environmental Commissions, Mendham, N.J., 1989.

A Hudson River Valley Greenway: A Report to Governor Cuomo and the New York State Legislature. Hudson River Valley Greenway Council, Albany, February 1991.

Lewis, Ralph M., *Land Buying Checklist*, 4th ed. Home Builder Press, National Association of Home Builders, Washington, D.C., 1990.

Maryland Greenways . . . A Naturally Better Idea: A Report to the Governor. Maryland Greenways Commission, Annapolis, Maryland, June 1990.

Montagne, Charles H., *Preserving Abandoned Rights of Way for Public Use: A Legal Manual*. Rails to Trails Conservancy, Washington, D.C.

"New Options for the Owner of Natural Lands." Natural Lands Trust, Philadelphia, 1981. (Contact Natural Lands Trust, 711 Widener Building, 1339 Chestnut St., Philadelphia, PA 19107)

New Tools for Land Protection: An Introductory Handbook. U. S. Department of Interior, Office of Assistant Secretary for Fish, Wildlife and Parks, Washington, D.C., 1982. (Contact the Land Trust Alliance, 900 17th Street, N.W., Suite 410, Washington, DC 20006)

Peacock, Lance, Charles Roe, Keith N. Morgan, and Jo Ann Williford, *Conservation and Historic Preservation Easements: To Preserve North Carolina's Heritage*. North Carolina Department of Natural Resources and Community Development, Raleigh, N.C.

Report to the North Carolina Greenways Advisory Panel, Ira Botvinick, City Attorney for Raleigh, North Carolina, June 1991 (interview).

Reviving the Sustainable Metropolis: Guiding Bay Area Conservation and Development into the 21st Century. Greenbelt Alliance, San Francisco, Calif., 1989.

Scenic Byways, Federal Highway Administration, Washington, D.C., 1988. Publication #FHWA - DF- 88-004. Describes federal designation and protection for scenic roads.

Sigmon, Joan, *Final Report of the Greenway Site Selection Committee: A Student Intern's Report*. University of North Carolina at Charlotte, Charlotte, N.C., June 1980.

The South Platte River: A Plan for the Future—Chatfield to Brighton. Wright Water Engineers, Inc., Urban Environments, Ltd., Denton Harper Marshall, Inc., Denver, Colorado, December 1985.

Summary, James Patrick Nollan, et ux. Appellanta versus California Coastal Commission, Argued March 30, 1987, Decided June 26, 1987 (court brief).

Tools and Strategies—Protecting the Landscape and Shaping Growth: Open Space Imperative #3. Regional Plan Association, New York, 1990.

A Workbook for Managing the Willamette Greenway in Salem. City of Salem, Planning Division, Department of Community Development, Salem, Oregon, January 1986.

Yaro, Robert D., R.G. Arendt, H.L. Dodson, and E.A. Brabec, *Dealing with Change in the Connecticut River Valley: A Design Manual for Conservation and Development*. Center for Rural Massachusetts, Amherst, Mass., 1988.

Chapter 7. Promoting the Natural Values of the Land

Recommended Reading

Adams, Lowell W., and Louise E. Dove. *Wildlife Preserves and Corridors in the Urban Environment: A Guide to Ecological Landscape Planning and Resource Conservation*. National Institute for Urban Wildlife. Columbia, Maryland, 1990. Reviews research regarding habitat reserves and corridors in urban and urbanizing areas. Also outlines some guidelines for ecological landscape planning and wildlife conservation.

Forman, Richard T.T., and M. Gudron. *Landscape Ecology*. John Wiley, New York, 1986.

Harris, L.D., *The Fragmented Forest: Island Biogeography Theory and the Preservation of Biotic Diversity*. University of Chicago Press, Chicago, 1984.

Hudson, Wendy E., ed., *Landscape Linkages and Biodiversity*. Defenders of Wildlife and Island Press, Covelo, Calif., 1991. Proceedings from 1990 North American Wildlife and Natural Resources Conference.

Labaree, Jonathan, *How Greenways Work: A Handbook on Ecology*. National Park Service and The Atlantic Center for the Environment, Ipswich, Mass., 1992.

Leedy, D.L., and L.W. Adams. *A Guide to Urban Wildlife Management*. National Institute for Urban Wildlife, Columbia, Maryland, 1984.

MacKintosh, Gay, ed. *Preserving Communities and Corridors*. Defenders of Wildlife, Washington, D.C., 1989.

The Natural Areas Journal. Source of information on natural area identification, design, planning, restoration, and management. (The Natural Areas Association, 320 S. Third St., Rockford, IL 61104; 815-964-6666)

Rodiek, Jon E., and Eric G. Bolen, eds., *Wildlife and Habitats in Managed Landscapes*. Island Press, Washington, D.C., 1991. Collection of essays that show how planning, management, and designs can be applied to an entire landscape to meet the needs of wildlife and humans.

Smith, Daniel, and Paul Hellmund, eds., *The Ecology of Greenways*. University of Minnesota Press, Minneapolis, in press (expected publication 1993).

Additional Reading and References

Barnett, John, *Boulder's Greenways, Design Guidelines*. City of Boulder, Boulder, Colorado, 1990.

Burgess, Robert L., and David M. Sharpe, *Forest Island Dynamics in Man-Dominated Landscapes*. Springer-Verlag, New York, 1981.

Callaway Gardens, Georgia, General Technical Report WO-12, U.S. Department of Agriculture, Forest Service, Washington, D.C., 410 pp.

Chadwick, Douglas H., "The Biodiversity Challenge," *Defenders*, Vol. 65, No. 3 (special insert, May/June 1990).

Duever, Linda C., "Ecological Considerations in Trail and Greenway Planning," *Proceedings of the National Trails Symposium*, Georgia, Sept., 11–14, 1988 (KBU Engineering and Applied Sciences, Inc., Gainsville, Florida, 1988).

Harris, Larry D., "Conservation Corridors, a Highway System for Wildlife" in *ENFO*, a publication of the Florida Conservation Foundation, Winter Park, Florida, 1985.

Harris, L.D., and Peter B. Gallagher, *New Initiatives for Wildlife Conservation: The Need for Movement Corridors.* Journal Series # 9668, Agricultural Experiment Station, Gainsville, Florida.

Hay, Keith, "The Role of Greenways in Conserving Biological Diversity." Photocopied paper, The Conservation Fund, Washington, D.C., 1990.

Hough, Michael, *City Form and Natural Processes: Toward a New Urban Vernacular.* Van Nostrand Reinhold Company, New York, 1984.

Howe, Linda, *Keeping Our Garden State Green: A Local Government Guide for Greenway and Open Space Planning.* New Jersey Department of Environmental Protection, Association of New Jersey Environmental Commissions, Mendham, N.J., 1989.

Johnson, A.L., "The Thin Green Line: Riparian Corridors and Endangered Species in Arizona and New Mexico," in G. Mackintosh, ed., *Preserving Communities and Corridors.* Defenders of Wildlife, Washington D.C., 1989.

McHarg, Ian, *Design with Nature.* Natural History Press, Garden City, N.Y., 1969. Reprinted by John Wiley, New York, 1992.

Moll, Gary, and Sara Ebenreck, eds., *Shading Our Cities.* Island Press, Washington, D.C. and Covelo, Calif., 1993.

Noss, Reed F., "Wildlife Corridors," J. F. Thorne, "Landscape Ecology," and Diana Balmori and Morgan Grove, "Design, Recreation and Greenways," in Daniel Smith and Paul Hellmund, eds., *The Ecology of Greenways.* University of Minnesota Press, Minneapolis, in press (expected publication 1993).

Palfrey, Raymond, and Earl Bradley, *The Buffer Area Study.* Maryland Department of Natural Resources, Annapolis, Maryland.

Proceedings from the 55th Annual North American Wildlife and Natural Resources Conference, 1990. Leading experts explore the topic of linkages as a strategy to protect endangered species and habitat.

Spirn, Anne W., *The Granite Garden.* Basic Books, New York, 1984.

Stolzenberg, William, "The Fragment Connection," in *Nature Conservancy*, July/Aug. 1991, pp. 18–25.

Sundstrom, Greg, "Living Barns Provide Protection," in *The Colorado Conservator.* Colorado State Forest Service, Ft. Collins, 1991.

Thorne, J.F., and C. S. Huang, *Toward a Landscape Ecological Ethic: Methodologies for Designers and Planners.* Landscape and Urban Planning, Amsterdam, Netherlands, September 1991.

Wegner, Daniel E., "Safe Play Among Protected Species." *Park and Recreation Magazine*, Vol. 26, No. 11, November 1991.

Whyte William, H., *The Last Landscape.* Doubleday, New York, 1968.

Wilcove, D.S., C.H. McLellan, and A.P. Dobson, "Habitat Fragmentation in the Temperate Zone," in M.E. Soule, ed., *Conservation Biology: The Science of Scarcity and Diversity.* Sinauer Association, Sunderland, Mass., 1986.

Chapter 8: Caring for Rivers, Streams, and Wetlands

Recommended Reading

A Casebook in Managing Rivers for Multiple Uses. Association of State Wetlands Managers, Association of State Floodplain Managers, National Park Service, Washington, D.C., 1992.

A Citizen's Guide to Clean Water. Izaak Walton League of America, Arlington, Virginia, 1990. A primer on causes, legislation, and actions to address water quality.

Diamant, Rolf, J. Glenn Eugster, and Christopher J. Duerksen. *A Citizen's Guide to River Conservation.* The Conservation Foundation, Washington, D.C., 1984.

Labaree, Jonathan, *How Greenways Work: A Handbook on Ecology*. National Park Service and the Atlantic Center for the Environment, Ipswich, Mass., 1992.

Riley, A.L., *Restore with Nature: Urban Stream Restoration Alternatives to Conventional Engineering*. Island Press, Washington, D.C., and Covelo, Calif., 1992.

Save Our Streambanks. Izaak Walton League of America, Arlington, Virginia, 1989. Overview of streambank stabilization methods.

Smith, Daniel, and Paul Hellmund, eds., *The Ecology of Greenways*. University of Minnesota Press, Minneapolis, in press (expected publication 1993).

Additional Reading and References

Barnett, John, *Boulder's Greenways, Design Guidelines*. City of Boulder, Boulder, Colorado, 1990.

Binford, Michael W., and Michael Bucherman, in Daniel Smith and Paul Hellmund, eds., *Ecology of Greenways*. (A 1991 draft manuscript of the National Park Service. The book will be published by the University of Minnesota Press in 1993.)

Binford, Michael W., and Michael Buchenau, "Riparian Corridors and Water Resources." Photocopied paper, Harvard University Graduate School of Design, Cambridge, Mass., 1990.

Brooks, Andrew, *Channelized River Perspectives for Environmental Management*. John Wiley and Sons Ltd., Chichester, England, 1988.

Budd, W.W., P.L. Cohen, P.R. Saunders, and F. R. Steiner, "Stream Corridor Management in the Pacific Northwest. I: Determination of Stream Corridor Widths." *Environmental Management,* Vol. 11, pp. 587–597, 1987.

Curtis, Gail, Duncan Brown, and Ester Lev, *Johnson Creek Basin Protection Plan*. Bureau of Planning, City of Portland, Portland, Oregon, 1991.

Ewel, Katherine, "Riparian Ecosystems: Conservation of Their Unique Characteristics," in *Strategies for Protection and Management of Floodplain Wetlands and Other Riparian Ecosystems: Proceedings of Symposium*, December 11–13, 1978. Callaway Gardens, Georgia. General Technical Report WO-12, U. S. Department of Agriculture, Forest Service, Washington, D.C.

The Federal Manual for Identifying and Delineating Jurisdictional Wetlands. Government Printing Office publication #024-010-00-683-8.

Floodplain Management Resource Center. Reference collection includes sources on multiobjective river corridor planning. Phone (303) 492-6818 or write Floodplains Management Resource Center, Natural Hazard Research and Applications Information Center, 1BS #6, Campus Box 482, Boulder, CO 80309.

Gore, James, A., *The Restoration of River and Streams*. Butterworth Publishers, Stoneham, Mass., 1985.

Inventory Manual. The Missouri Stream Team, Missouri Conservation Commission, Jefferson City, Missouri, 1990.

Johnson, A. L., "The Thin Green Line: Riparian Corridors and Endangered Species in Arizona and New Mexico," in G. Mackintosh, ed., *Preserving Communities and Corridors*. Defenders of Wildlife, Washington, D.C., 1989.

Kennedy, Carolyn, "Standards for Overlay Districts." *Zoning News*, The American Planning Association, Chicago, August 1991.

Lisle, T.E., "A Sorting Mechanism for a Riffle-Pool Sequence," *Geological Society of America Bulletin,* Part II, 90:1142–1157, 1979.

Lowrance, R., R. Todd, J. Fail, Jr., Ole Hendrickson, Jr., R. Leonard, and L. Asmussen, "Riparian Forests as Nutrient Filters in Agriculture Watersheds." *Bioscience,* Vol. 34, No. 6, 1983.

Luna, Leopold, M. G. Wolman, and J. P. Miller, *Fluvial Processes in Geomorphology*. W.H. Freeman, San Francisco, 1964.

1992 River Conservation Directory. National Park Service, American Rivers, Washington, D.C., 1992. Listing of river conservation efforts. Available from U.S. Government Printing Office: #024-005-01104-8.

Olson, W. Kent, *Natural Rivers and the Public Trust*. American Rivers, Washington, D.C., l988.

Palfrey, Raymond, and Earl Bradley, *The Buffer Area Study*. Coastal Resources Division, Maryland Department of Natural Resources, Annapolis, Maryland.

Phillips, J. D., "An Evaluation of Factors Determining the Effectiveness of Water Quality Buffer Zone." *Journal of Hydrology*, Vol. 107, pp. 133–145, 1989.

Powell, Kevin, "The Free Creek Movement." *Landscape Architecture*, Vol. 81, No. 1, January 1991.

Restoring the Chesapeake: A Progress Report. Office of the Governor, State of Maryland, Annapolis, Maryland, 1988.

Riley, A.L., *Urban Stream Restoration Program*. California Department of Water Resources, Sacramento, 1988.

River Network Bulletin, P.O. Box 8787, Portland, OR 97207; (503) 236-8011. River Network's mission is to conserve rivers through citizen training and acquisition and information sharing.

Salveson, David, *Wetlands, Mitigating and Regulating Development Impacts*. The Urban Land Institute, Washington, D.C., 1990.

Scheuler, T.R. "Controlling Urban Runoff: A Practical Manual for Planning and Designing Urban Best Management Practices." Washington Metropolitan Water Resources Board, Washington, D.C., 1987.

Shaeffer, John R., Kenneth Wright, Ruth Wright, and William Taggart, *Urban Storm Drainage Management*. Marcel Dekker, New York, 1982.

Strutin, Michele, "Away From the Hard Edge." *Landscape Architecture*, Vol. 81, No. 1, January 1991.

Urbonas, Ben, "Design of Channels with Wetland Bottoms." *Flood Hazard News*, Denver Urban Drainage and Flood Control District, Denver, December 1986.

Ward, James V., and Jack A. Standford, *The Ecology of Regulated Streams*. Plenum Press, New York, 1979.

Chapter 9: Preserving Our Cultural Heritage

Recommended Reading

Stokes, Samuel N., A. Elizabeth Watson, Genevieve Keller, and Timothy J. Keller, *Saving America's Countryside: A Guide to Rural Conservation*. Johns Hopkins University Press, Baltimore, 1989.

Fedelchak, Marilyn, and Byrd Wood, *Protecting America's Countryside*. National Trust for Historic Preservation, Washington, D.C., 1988.

Additional Reading and References

An Archaeological Survey for the Proposed Historic Bethabara By-Pass Corridor. Wake Forest University Archaeology Laboratories, Winston-Salem, N.C., April 1988.

Bethabara Trail Greenway Master Plan. Greenways Incorporated and the City of Winston-Salem, Winston-Salem, N.C., 1989.

Cultural Heritage and Land Management Plan for the Blackstone River Valley National Heritage Corridor. Blackstone River Valley National Heritage Corridor Commission, Providence, R.I., October 1989.

Early Raleigh Neighborhoods and Buildings. The City of Raleigh, Raleigh, North Carolina, 1983.

"Historic Preservation in Greenways." Scenic Hudson, Inc., Poughkeepsie, N.Y. (Fact sheet available from Scenic Hudson, 9 Vassar Street, Poughkeepsie, NY 12601)

"The Lowell Plan: A Partnership for Economic Development" Promotional literature provided by the City of Lowell, Lowell, Mass.

Management Policies. National Park Service, U. S. Department of the Interior, Washington, D.C., 1978.

Schuykill River Greenway Study: Executive Study. U. S. Department of the Interior, National Park Service, Washington, D.C., March 1984.

Southern, Kathleen Pepi, *Historic Preservation in Rural North Carolina: Problems and Potentials.* Ernest Wood, ed. Historic Preservation Society of North Carolina, Raleigh, 1981.

Chapter 10: The Greenway Design and Implementation Process

Recommended Reading

Alexander, Christopher, *et al., A Pattern Language: Towns, Buildings and Construction.* Oxford University Press, New York, 1977.

Evan Terry Associates PC, *Americans with Disabilities Act: Facilities Compliance Workbook.* John Wiley, New York, 1992.

Lynch, Kevin, *Site Planning.* The MIT Press, Cambridge, Mass., 1962.

Chapter 11. Greenway Trail Design

Recommended Reading

Converting Rails to Trails: A Citizens' Manual for Transforming Abandoned Rail Corridors into Multi-Purpose Public Paths. Rails-to-Trails Conservancy, Washington, D.C., 1987.

Guide for the Development of New Bicycle Facilities. American Association of State Highway and Transportation Officials, Washington, D.C., August 1991.

Harris, Charles W., and Nicholas T. Dines, *Time Saver Standards for Landscape Architecture.* McGraw-Hill, New York, 1988.

Hooper, Lennon, *NPS Trails Management Handbook.* U. S. Department of the Interior, National Park Service, Washington, D.C., 1983.

Montange, Charles, *Preserving Abandoned Railroad Rights-of-Way for Public Use: A Legal Manual.* The Rails-to-Trails Conservancy, Washington, D.C., January 1989.

Proudman, Robert D., and Ruben Rajala, *AMC Field Guide to Trail Building and Maintenance.* Appalachian Mountain Club in association with the National Park Service, National Trails Program, Boston, 1981. Trail development, reconstruction, maintenance and protection, rockworks, trail marking, stream crossing, cross country skiing, etc.

Uniform Federal Accessibility Standards. General Services Administration, Department of Defense, Department of Housing and Urban Development, U.S. Postal Service, Washington, D.C., April 1988.

Additional Reading and References

Balmori, Diana, and Morgan Grove, "Design, Recreation and Greenways," in Dan Smith and Paul Helmund, eds., *Ecology of Greenways.* University of Minnesota Press, Minneapolis, 1993. (Research for this chapter is from a draft done for the National Park Service, 1991.)

Building Greenways in the Hudson River Valley: A Guide for Action. Scenic Hudson, Inc., and National Park Service, Poughkeepsie, N.Y., December 1989.

Construction and Maintenance of Horse Trails in Arkansas State Parks. Arkansas Trails Council and U. S. Forest Service, Little Rock, Arkansas, October 1983.

Falls Lake White Water Study. Planning Department Parks and Recreation Natural Resources, Wake County, N.C., 1987.

Flournoy, William L., Jr., *Capital City Greenway.* City of Raleigh, Raleigh, N.C., 1974.

Greenway Component: City of Greenville Comprehensive Plan, Implementation Section. Greenways Incorporated, Cary, N.C., March 1991.

Hubbard, Doni, *New Trail Adventures for California Horsemen.* Hoofprints, Redwood City, Calif., 1985.

"Innovative Stream Conservation: A Case Book on Multi-Objective River Corridor Management." Technical paper, The National Park Service, Association of State Wetland Managers, and Association of State Floodplain Managers, March 1991.

Iowa Statewide Recreational Trails Plan. Barton-Aschman Associates, Inc., Madison, Wisconsin, and the Iowa Department of Transportation, Des Moines, Iowa, 1990.

Lancaster, Roger A., ed., *Recreation, Park and Open Space Standards and Guidelines.* National Recreation and Park Association, Washington, D.C., 1983.

McHarg, Ian L., *Design with Nature.* The Natural History Press, Garden City, N.Y., 1969. Reprinted by John Wiley, New York, 1992.

Mitsch, William J., and James G. Gosselink, *Wetlands.* Van Nostrand Reinhold Company, New York, 1986.

Non-Motorized Trails/An Introduction to Planning and Development. The Pennsylvania Trails Program, Division of Outdoor Recreation, Bureau of State Parks, June 1980.

The North Carolina Bicycle Facility and Program Handbook. Barton-Aschmann Associates, Inc., Minneapolis, April 1975.

North Carolina Bicycle Facility Workshop. North Carolina Department of Transportation Bicycle Program, Raleigh, 1990.

Rasmussen, Paul F., *Cross Country Ski Trails: A Guide to Their Design and Management.* Northern Illinois Planning Commission, Chicago.

"Recreation Code of Ethic." Blue Ribbon Coalition, Pocatello Idaho, 1991.

Robinette, Gary O., *Landscape Architectural Site Construction Details.* Environmental Design Press, Reston, Virginia, 1976.

Rutledge, Albert J., *Anatomy of a Park: The Essentials of Recreation Area Planning and Design.* McGraw-Hill, New York, 1971.

Schuylkill River Design Guide, Commonwealth of Pennsylvania, Department of Environmental Resources, Philadelphia, 1984.

Trail Planning and Design Guidelines: A Handbook for an Inter-Regional Trail System in the Greater Toronto Area. The Metropolitan Toronto and Region Conservation Authority, Toronto, 1991.

Trails on Electric Utility Lands: A Model of Public-Private Partnership. Edison Electric Institute, National Land Management Task Force and American Trails, Washington, D.C., 1989.

Chapter 12. Water Recreation

Recommended Reading

Harris, Charles W., and Nicholas T. Dines, *Time-Saver Standards for Landscape Architecture.* McGraw-Hill, New York, 1988. Excellent detailed guide to facility design with specific standards and dimensions.

Planning for Fishing and Waterfront Recreation. National Institute for Urban Wildlife, Columbia, Maryland, 1981.

River Conservation Directory. U. S. Department of Interior, National Park Service, Rivers and Trails Conservation Assistance Programs, Washington, D.C., 1990. (For copies contact Superintendent of Documents, U. S. Government

Printing Office, Washington, DC 20402 or call 202-783-3238. Request document #024-005-01058-1.1990.)

Strung, Norman, Sam Curtis, and Earl Perry, *Whitewater!* Collier Books, New York, 1978.

Additional Reading and References

Arighi, Scott, and Margaret Arighi, *Whitewater Touring: Techniques and Tours.* Macmillan, New York, 1974.

Chamberlain, Clinton J., *Marinas: Recommendations for Design, Construction and Management*, Vol 1, 3rd ed. National Marine Manufacturers Association, New York, 1983.

Colorado Boating Safety. Colorado Division of Parks and Outdoor Recreation, Littleton, Colorado, 1988. (Pamphlet on boating regulations from the Colorado Division of Parks and Outdoor Recreation, 13787 South Highway 85, Littleton CO 80125; 303-791-1954)

The Federal Requirements for Recreational Boats. U.S. Department of Transportation, U.S. Coast Guard, 2100 2nd Street, S.W., Washington, DC 20593. (Code #1986 COMDTINST M16760.2/85)

Report and Recommendations to the President of the United States. The President's Commission on Americans Outdoors, December 1986.

Schafer, Thomas G., *Technical Report #5. Management Alternative for the Improvement of Canoeing Opportunities and the Resolution of Problems Relating to the Recreational Use of Rivers.* Ohio Department of Natural Resources, Columbus, Ohio, 1975.

South Bend Department of Public Parks, "East Race Waterway." Pamphlet. City of South Bend, South Bend, Indiana, 1991.

Zwinger, Ann, *Run, River, Run.* Harper & Row, New York, 1975.

Chapter 13. Greenway Facilities Design

Recommended Reading

Ching, Frances D.K., *Building Construction Illustrated.* Van Nostrand Reinhold Company, 1975.

Ciacco, David J., *Site Sections and Details: A Reference Guide to Site Construction Details.* Van Nostrand Reinhold Company, New York, 1984.

Diekelmann, John, and Robert Schuster, *Natural Landscaping: Designing with Native Plant Communities.* McGraw-Hill, New York, 1982.

Handbook: Building in the Coastal Environment. Georgia Department of Natural Resources and Robert T. Segrest and Associates, June 1975.

Harris, Charles W., and Nicholas T. Dines, *Time Saver Standards for Landscape Architecture.* McGraw-Hill, New York, 1988.

U. S. Department of Transportation, *Manual on Uniform Traffic Control Devices, Bicycle Facilities.* U. S. Superintendent of Documents, Washington, D.C., 1983.

Additional Reading and References

Lancaster, Roger A., ed., *Recreation, Park and Open Space Standards and Guidelines.* National Recreation and Park Association, Washington, D.C., 1983.

McHarg, Ian L., *Design with Nature.* The Natural History, Press, Garden City, N.Y., 1969. Reprinted by John Wiley, New York, 1992.

Non Motorized Trails/An Introduction to Planning and Development. The Pennsylvania Trails Program, Division of Outdoor Recreation, Bureau of State Parks, Harrisburg, Pennsylvania, June 1980.

The North Carolina Bicycle Facility and Program Handbook, Barton-Aschmann, Inc., Minneapolis, April 1975.

Plants, People and Environmental Quality: A Study of Plants and Their Environmental Function. U. S. Department of Interior, National Park Service, in collaboration with the American Society of Landscape Archiects, Washington, D.C., 1972.

Robinette, Gary O., *Landscape Architectural Site Construction Details*. Environmental Design Press, Reston, Virginia, 1976.

Rutledge, Albert J., *Anatomy of a Park: The Essentials of Recreation Area Planning and Design*. McGraw-Hill, New York, 1971.

Standards for Highway Bridges, 12th ed. American Association of State Highway and Transportation Officials, Washington, D.C., 1977.

Chapter 14. Safety and Liability

Recommended Reading

The Impacts of Rail Trails. National Park Service Rivers, Trails, and Conservation Assistance Program, Washington, D.C., 1992.

Montange, Charles, *Preserving Abandoned Railroad Rights-of-Way for Public Use: A Legal Manual*. The Rails-to-Trails Conservancy, Washington, D.C., January 1989.

Pring, George, "Land Trust Liability and Risk Management." *Exchange*, Vol. 10, No. l (Winter 1991).

Additional Reading and References

Elleman, Tom, Charles Flink, and Bob Mosher, *Capital Area Greenway: 10 year Comprehensive Plan*. City of Raleigh, Raleigh, N.C., December 1985.

Evaluation of the Burke-Gilman Trail's Effect on Property Values and Crime. Peter Lagerway, Project Manager. Seattle Engineering Department, Seattle, May 1987.

Fowler, Timms R., "Private Landowner Liability and Urban Trail Development in Colorado: Common Concerns and Practical Solutions." Grand Junction, Colorado, February 1991.

Gold, Seymour M., "Trail Safety and Liability: The Standard of Care." Paper presented at the Statewide Recreational Trails Conference, Asilomar Conference Center, Pacific Grove, California, March 1990.

Goldstein, Linda N., Frances H. Kennedy, and Kathleen H. Telfer, "Recreation Use Statutes: Why They Don't Work," *Exchange,* Spring 1990.

Goldstein, N. Linda, Kathleen H. Telfer, and Frances H. Kennedy, "Recreational Use Statutes: Time for Reform." *Probate and Property*, July/August l989.

Guidelines for Improving Practice: Architects and Engineers Professional Liability. Office for Professional Liability Research, Victor O. Schinnerer and Company, Inc., Chevy Chase, Maryland, April 1971 through December 1986.

Hronek, Bruce B., "Reducing Trail Tort Liability." Paper delivered at the 9th National Trails Symposium, Unicoi State Park, Georgia, September 1988.

A Review of the Mecklenburg County Park and Recreation Department's Security and Maintenance of Greenways. Mecklenburg County Budget and Resource Management Department, Charlotte, N.C., February 1991.

Chapter 15. Greenway Management

Recommended Reading

Crompton, John L., and Dennis R. Howard, *Financing, Managing and Marketing Recreation & Park Resources*. William C. Brown, Dubuque, Iowa, 1980.

Proudman, Robert D., and Reuben Rajala, *AMC Field Guide to Trail Building and Maintenance*. Appalachian Mountain Club, Boston, 1981.

"Share the Trail." Izaak Walton League, Milwaukee Chapter, 3540 N. Maryland Avenue, Shorewood, WI 53211. This pamphlet contains an excellent model of how to present rules, regulations, and trail courtesy pointers to trail users.

Additional Reading and References

Adopt a Trail Handbook: A Guide to Volunteer Trail Maintenance in the Southwest. Volunteers for the Outdoors, New Mexico Natural Resources Department, 1984.

Appalachian Trail Local Management Planning Guide. Appalachian Trail Conference, Harpers Ferry, West Virginia, November 1988.

National Park Service Trails Management Handbook. National Park Service. Contact Trails Coordinator, National Park Service, P.O. Box 25287, 655 Partet Street, Denver, CO 80225.

Peterson, James A., *Risk Management for Park, Recreation and Leisure Services.* Management Learning Laboratories, Champaign, Ill., 1987. (Book can be ordered from Management Learning Laboratories, 501 S. Sixth Street, P.O. Box M, Station A, Champaign, IL 61820-8017.)

Index

G

About the Editor

Loring LaB. Schwarz is currently director of New England Greenways for the Conservation Fund, a nonprofit land protection organization based in Arlington, Virginia. For two years she served as advisor to the Maryland Greenways Commission, the nation's first state-sponsored effort to implement a statewide network of open-space corridors, cited in *Greenways for America*. She currently serves as co-chair of the Massachusetts Greenways Council and as advisor to the Connecticut Greenway Committee. Ms. Schwarz holds a B.S. in Biology from Tufts University and a Master of Forest Science from Yale University. She spent eight years with the Nature Conservancy, four as Director of State Natural Heritage Programs. Ms. Schwarz contributed substantially to the development of Chapters 1, 3, 5, 7, and 8 and provided all sidebar material as well as certain case studies, boxed material, examples, and detail throughout the text. She also served as overall project manager for the book.

About the Authors

Charles A. Flink is president of Greenways Inc., in Cary, North Carolina, and former Greenway Planner for the City of Raleigh, North Carolina. A registered landscape architect, Mr. Flink has completed master plans and site-specific development strategies for more than 300 miles of greenways in Florida, South Carolina, North Carolina, Tennessee, Kentucky, Ohio, Delaware, and Toronto, Canada. He served three terms as Chair of American Trails (1988–1990), is a gubernatorial appointee to the North Carolina Greenways Advisory Panel, and is currently an Adjunct Professor at North Carolina State University. Mr. Flink has a B.S. in Environmental Design/Landscape Architecture from North Carolina State. He has been cited for his work in *National Geographic*'s June 1990 issue on greenways and Charles E. Little's book, *Greenways for America*.

Robert M. Searns is president of Urban Edges Inc., an urban design and planning firm in Denver, Colorado. He was Project Director for Denver's Platte River Greenway and developed the award-winning Arapahoe Greenway. He also coordinated *10,000 Trees!*—a river corridor revegetation project involving more than 3,000 volunteers—helped implement a "trail ranger" program for the Denver Urban Drainage and Flood Control District, developed a nonmotorized transportation plan for Missoula, Montana, and prepared a plan for river recreation and tourism development along Illinois's Fox River. Mr. Searns has a Master of Architecture from the State University of New York and a B.A. in Economics.